T0226143

Operations Management for Healthcare

This fully updated edition of the bestselling textbook on Health Services Operations Management provides an invaluable reference for students and researchers in the fields of healthcare management; operations management and patient flow logistics. Featuring theoretical frameworks and a comprehensive set of practical case studies, this book also covers subjects such as hospital planning and supply chain management in healthcare, quality assurance and performance management. Healthcare managers work together with healthcare professionals in a multitude of challenging scenarios. Trade-offs have to be made between waiting times for customers and efficient use of scarce resources, between quality of care and quality of services, between the perspective of a single pathway and the total system, and between the perspective of a single provider and that of a network of providers working together in the chain of primary care, hospitals, nursing homes and homecare. This book guides healthcare students and professionals through a set of practical tools and resources, ranging from simple queueing models to more complicated analytical models, to help address these issues. The book can be used at an undergraduate level by introducing concepts, definitions and approaches, and at a postgraduate level through the application of approaches to operations management problems in healthcare practice. It will serve as a primary textbook for a health service operations management course module in a Master's programme in healthcare management.

Jan Vissers is affiliated to the Erasmus University Rotterdam, and the Erasmus School of Health Policy and Management where he had a chair as Professor of Health Services Operations Management between 2004 and 2016. He retired in 2016 but is still active in publishing papers and supervising students in Master Healthcare Management doing their thesis work on a topic related to operations management.

Sylvia Elkhuizen is Assistant Professor of Health Services Operations Management at the Erasmus School of Health Policy and Management, Erasmus University Rotterdam, the Netherlands.

Nathan Proudlove is an Associate Professor in the Health Management Group at Alliance Manchester Business School of the University of Manchester, UK.

Operations Management for Healthcare

Edited by Jan Vissers, Sylvia Elkhuizen
and Nathan Proudlove

Routledge
Taylor & Francis Group

LONDON AND NEW YORK

Designed cover image: @ Getty images

2nd edition published 2023
by Routledge
4 Park Square, Milton Park, Abingdon, Oxon, OX14 4RN

and by Routledge
605 Third Avenue, New York, NY 10158

Routledge is an imprint of the Taylor & Francis Group, an informa business

© 2023 selection and editorial matter, Jan Vissers, Sylvia Elkhuizen and
Nathan Proudlove; individual chapters, the contributors

First edition published by Willan 2005

British Library Cataloguing-in-Publication Data
A catalogue record for this book is available from the British Library

Library of Congress Cataloging-in-Publication Data
A catalog record has been requested for this book

ISBN: 978-0-367-89594-5 (hbk)
ISBN: 978-0-367-89595-2 (pbk)
ISBN: 978-1-003-02001-1 (ebk)

DOI: 10.4324/9781003020011

Typeset in Bembo
by Deanta Global Publishing Services, Chennai, India

Contents

PART II
Practice and improvement

Preface

Health Services Operations Management constitutes a fairly new area of research that has developed rapidly during recent years and has become an important component of studies in healthcare management.

Operations Management for Healthcare is an update and a follow-up to the book *Health Operations Management – Patient Flow Logistics in Health Care* edited by Jan Vissers and Roger Beech, and published in 2005 by Routledge, as part of a Routledge series on Health Management. The introductory chapters introduced many operations management (OM) concepts in healthcare for an audience that is interested in healthcare management, but not familiar with management science. From the feedback received from readers this content filled a need that still exists today. However, the applications were predominantly focused on hospitals. Little attention was given to OM of healthcare chains crossing the boundaries of healthcare providers.

Since then, much has happened. OM in healthcare became very popular, with much interest in the topic from healthcare managers and practitioners as well as researchers. The service features of healthcare, as opposed to the product environment of manufacturing industries, required closing the gap with Health Services Management. This resulted in better profiling the new field of research: Health Services Operations Management (HSOM). Also, the popularity of improvement approaches such as Lean Management, Six Sigma and Theory of Constraints, made it necessary to include them in a new textbook for this field of research.

The new textbook on Health Services Operations Management again has a theory part, in which terminology and concepts are introduced, but also an overview of the field of research is provided along with developments in approaches. The link is made with value-based healthcare, as this has implications for the need for OM research and quantitative approaches. Furthermore, techniques that are used in HSOM are described and illustrated. In the practical part of the book, case studies are presented to illustrate the theory and to reflect the richness of the research field. There is more attention on process chain applications crossing the borders of provider organisations and on comparative research into OM of regional networks. Some of the concepts used in this book are based on an EU project in which we had the opportunity to elaborate our ideas on a HSOM approach in combination with value-based healthcare for healthcare delivery for diabetes, stroke and hip osteoarthritis patients in regional networks in six European countries.

Throughout the book we pay special attention to two features of HSOM: studies in HSOM often make use of a quantitative model of health services and follow a design approach. A model is a formal representation of an object of study such as a hospital unit or a chain of care delivery. The model allows one to experiment with solutions and, moreover, provides evidence for the pre-dicted outcomes of performance improvement changes before implementing solutions. The design approach offers a framework for analysis of a problem and design of a solution to that problem, making use of an evidence-based methodology. The case studies are preceded by chapters in which the design approach and model support are elaborated for three important areas of OM improvement: units, process chains and networks. In this way students can develop their insight into the use of quantitative models for analysing problems and solving them.

October 2022
Jan Vissers
Sylvia Elkhuizen
Nathan Proudlove

Part I
Theory and concepts

1 Introduction

*Jan Vissers, Sylvia Elkhuizen
and Nathan Proudlove*

1.1 Defining Health Services Operations Management

The term 'operations management' (OM) refers to the planning and control of the processes that transform inputs into outputs. This definition also applies to Health Services Operations Management (HSOM). Consider the individual doctor/patient consultation. The input to the consultation process is a patient with a request for healthcare. The output of the consultation process might be that the patient is diagnosed, referred to a further service, or cured. The resources that must be managed to transform inputs into outputs are those associated with the care provided by the individual doctor: for example, their time and any diagnostic or therapeutic services that they use.

In this illustration, the role of the HSOM process is to ensure that adequate resources are in place on time to provide a service for the patient without them having to wait too long. Hence, HSOM focuses on the individual provider that produces a health service and on the tasks involved to produce this service in such a way that service standards are met, whilst also avoiding wasteful provision of excessive resources.

In the above illustration, the individual provider is a doctor. However, the 'individual' provider may be, for example, a hospital department (e.g., a radiology department), a hospital or a network of hospitals and community-based services (e.g., services for the acute care and then rehabilitation of patients who have suffered a stroke). At each different level both the scale and scope of the processes and resources to be planned and controlled increase, as does the complexity of the OM task.

Figure 1.1 presents an example of an HSOM view of an individual hospital provider, adapted from a meta-process model of a healthcare delivery system described by Roth (1993).

The central function of the care provider is to provide patient care. Hence, patient demand for care is the key input which influences the planning and control of the resources required to transform inputs into outputs. However, as Figure 1.1 illustrates, other 'inputs' influence both the types and levels of patient demand and the ways in which the hospital delivers care. These other 'inputs' include the overall level of finance available to provide care, the availability of goods from suppliers and the nature and actions of other hospitals.

DOI: 10.4324/9781003020011-2

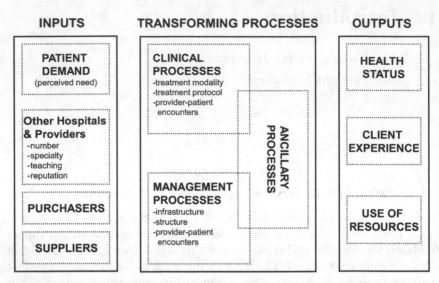

Figure 1.1 Meta-process model of a healthcare delivery system (adapted from Roth (1993)).

Figure 1.1 highlights three generic processes for transforming inputs into outputs: clinical, management and ancillary. Clinical processes are the most important as these are the primary processes in which the transformations take place. The clinical processes are supported by management processes that take care of the planning and control of resources required for the diagnosis and treatment of patients. At the operational level, individual patients are scheduled for appointments or an admission requiring outpatient clinic resources or operating theatre resources and a bed in a ward. At the tactical level, availability of resources for the coming weeks is checked and at the strategic level, checks are made on the amounts of resources required for the longer term. Therefore, management processes are needed to support the clinical processes. Finally, ancillary processes are needed to support the general functioning of the hospital. These processes include the organisation of services for cleaning hospital wards and departments and for maintaining hospital equipment.

The resources to be planned and controlled within each of these processes include staff (e.g., doctors, nurses), materials (e.g., drugs, prostheses) and equipment (e.g., X-ray machines, buildings). Inadequate planning and control of resources within any of the processes can have an impact on the others. For example, deficiencies in the management processes for ordering materials may affect the quality of care that can be delivered by the clinical processes (e.g., a shortage of equipment to support care at home may lead to delays in patient discharge from hospital). Similarly, if services for the cleaning of hospital wards are inadequate, the potential for hospital-acquired infections will be increased, as will the likelihood of subsequent ward closures.

Hence, when planning and controlling the resources that they use, an 'individual' provider must also consider the ways in which their actions might impinge upon other 'individual' providers: for example, other hospital or community-based departments. In this sense, their actions represent 'inputs' to other processes for transforming inputs into outputs.

Finally, Figure 1.1 illustrates the outputs of the OM processes that must be monitored. Health status markers (e.g., mortality rates, levels of morbidity and disability) are important metrics of the success with which clinical processes are transforming inputs into outputs, as are metrics of client experience, where the client is the patient and/or their family. In addition, the client of a process might also be a hospital doctor who requires a service from a diagnostic department, or a hospital manager who requires details of patient activity levels from doctors. Similarly, 'resource' performance output metrics are relevant to all three generic processes as they are needed to monitor the efficiency (e.g., patient lengths of stay, response times of ancillary support services, resource utilisation) and effectiveness (e.g., use of 'appropriate' or 'modern' procedures) with which resources have been used to transform inputs into outputs.

Again, there are relationships and potential conflicts between the different types of output. For example, measures to increase patient satisfaction by reducing patient waiting times might require additional investment and mean that the hospital is unable to achieve its budgetary targets. Similarly, budgetary pressures may mean that a hospital is unable to invest in all of those services that are known to be effective in improving health status: examples might include expensive treatments for rare conditions. Hence, in its attempts to ensure that there is effective and efficient organisation of the delivery of services, the role of HSOM is to achieve an 'acceptable' balance between different types of output.

Up to now we have described the traditional way to define OM in a healthcare setting with a focus on the provider's perspective on primary processes. However, the development of the value-based healthcare perspective has added another dimension to HSOM thinking. As value-based healthcare relates the value for customers to the costs of delivering services, the patient process is put in the foreground, i.e., the journey of the patient along with the services to answer the patient demand in the form of a diagnosis and treatment. So instead of a focus on individual encounters as indicated in Figure 1.1, the focus of hospital management today is on the total process of the patient, leading to output and outcomes. Therefore, when in this book we refer to a process we generally mean the total process from the perspective of the user.

Having illustrated the nature of HSOM it is now possible to offer a definition, i.e.:

> Health Services Operations Management can be defined as the analysis, design, planning, and control of all of the steps necessary to provide services for patients in such a way that their needs are met, that service standards are met, and resources are used efficiently.

1.2 Context of Health Services Operations Management

This section discusses the context of HSOM decision making: drivers for change and factors which influence decision making. The previous section demonstrated that the system of 'inputs', 'transforming processes' and 'outputs' is subject to its own internal dynamics and influences. Efforts to improve the outputs from one process might have an impact on the inputs and outputs of others. Here, we will discuss some of the key 'external' factors, and additional 'internal' factors, which influence HSOM decision making. Again, for the purposes of illustration, we will take the perspective of an individual healthcare provider, e.g., a hospital.

Probably the main external factor which affects the behaviour of individual providers is the overall healthcare system setting in which they function: for example, market and for profit, national health system or government regulated. In a for-profit setting, the emphasis for providers is on profit maximisation. As a result, providers will want to maximise the number of patients that they can treat at 'acceptable' standards of quality but at 'minimum' costs per case. The market environment, therefore, creates the incentives for providers to ensure that the processes for transforming inputs into outputs are functioning in an effective and efficient way. Providers must continually review and invest in their transforming processes as a means of maintaining their market share, attracting new patients, or reducing costs. For example, the market creates the incentives for providers to invest in new healthcare technologies in order to either attract more patients or reduce costs per case.

In a national health system or government-regulated system, providers are budgeted by the contracts annually arranged with purchasers (government-related bodies or insurance organisations). In such a system, the main incentive for providers is to ensure that budgetary targets are not exceeded. Hence, providers need to invest in mechanisms for monitoring the use of key resource areas such as the use of beds and theatres. Beyond the need to ensure that 'cost' performance targets are achieved, providers in public health services probably have lower incentives to continually review and update transforming processes or to ensure that other 'output' measures, such as client perception are 'satisfactory'.

However, this situation is changing, and in the absence of market incentives, regulation is being used as a vehicle for change. For example, in the National Health Service (NHS) of the United Kingdom (UK), National Service Frameworks have been developed for key disease areas (e.g., cancer, diabetes) or specific target groups of patients (e.g., older people with health problems). These frameworks specify the types of services that should be available for patient care: hence, they have a direct influence on clinical processes. The English NHS has also introduced performance or 'output' targets for providers: for example, maximum waiting times for an outpatient appointment or an elective procedure (Department of Health and Social Care, 2021) and use of resources (through national tariffs for reimbursement) (NHS England,

2021). Similarly, in the Netherlands (NL), the Ministry of Health and the associations of healthcare providers have agreed on the 'Treeknormen' standards for acceptable waiting times for, among others, General Practitioner practices, hospitals, mental healthcare providers and nursing homes (Nederlandse Zorgautoriteit, 2017).[1] Again, to ensure that such targets are met, providers will need to review and modify their processes for transforming inputs into outputs.

In Europe, government-regulated healthcare systems are still dominant but gradually more market incentives are being introduced. In the USA, although healthcare is shaped as a market system, the level of regulation has been increasing through developments such as ObamaCare.

Irrespective of the health system in use, all systems seem to adopt a value-based healthcare perspective (Porter and Teisberg, 2006) in which the value of a health service for the customer is key and value is defined as health per dollar or benefits for the customer versus costs (Van de Klundert, 2009). This adoption of a value-based perspective offers many challenges to healthcare providers. Firstly, value needs to be defined more precisely. What is value for the customer, how can we measure it and how can we use it to improve our delivery systems? Next, the value chain from the perspective of the customer may require collaboration with other providers. How can these developing chains of care be managed and how does this relate to the internal management of processes of the individual providers? It must be clear that in value-based health, knowledge of clinical processes and use of resources – so OM – becomes very important, and that at the same time the value perspective gives other opportunities for optimising healthcare delivery systems.

Beyond the healthcare system and the actions of governments, other external factors are affecting the context in which HSOM decisions are made. For example, most Western countries are experiencing changes in the demographic mix of their populations, in particular there is an increasing proportion of older people. Both the scale and nature of hospital resources (and those in other settings) will need to be adjusted to meet this demographic change. For example, the UK NHS is expanding its services for home-based care as an alternative to hospital care.

In addition, advances in medical technology (for example, new drugs and other forms of treatment) are either changing or expanding the options that are available for patient care. Providers will need to decide whether and how they should respond to these advances. Again, government regulation is likely to be used as a vehicle for change.

Finally, via the internet and other media outlets, patient knowledge of healthcare treatments, and so their expectations of healthcare providers, are

1 For instance: first visit hospital (80% within three weeks, maximum four weeks); ambulatory treatment (80% within four weeks, maximum six weeks); admission hospital (80% within five weeks, maximum seven weeks).

increasing. Providers are having to adjust their care processes to address this change in consumer expectations. For instance, more time in consultations might be required for implementing shared decision making.

Up until now, this discussion of the context of HSOM has focused on external factors which affect the environment in which decisions are made. In comparison to other service or manufacturing organisations, the internal environment for decision making is in itself unusual.

Often, the roles and responsibilities of those involved in decision making are either not very clearly defined or are overlapping. Healthcare management often takes the form of dual management, in which clinical professionals share management responsibilities with administrative staff and business managers. There are commonly parallel hierarchies of different staff groups. Finding out who is actually managing the system at different levels can therefore be a real issue in healthcare organisations.

In addition, healthcare management decision making often takes the form of finding consensus among the different actors involved: managers, medical professionals, nursing staff, paramedical disciplines, administrative staff. These actors often have different interests and priorities across the metrics and trade-offs of quality versus costs or effectiveness versus efficiency. As public health-care does not have the possibility of defining profit as an overall objective, it is often difficult to find the appropriate trade-off between these two perspectives of managing organisations.

Hence, there is a range of 'external' and 'internal' factors and challenges which influence HSOM decision making. This book presents a scientific body of knowledge and reflection to support the planning and control of healthcare processes.

1.3 Modelling and design cycle

Most HSOM studies make use of a quantitative model of the system under study and follow the steps of a design cycle. Therefore, we will elaborate these two topics a bit further as part of the introduction.

A model is a formal description of a system or a part of a system under study. A system is a collection of elements that are distinguished from the environment, due to a common perspective, and that have a mutual relationship. Within a system one can distinguish subsystems (grouping of elements) and aspect systems (grouping of relationships). For example, a hospital consists of several departments (subsystems). If we are studying the throughput times of radiology requests, we are only interested in the relationships between the timing of operations of the referring physician and the timing of operations of the radiology department. We can now describe how we move from the real world to a system under study and a model (see Figure 1.2).

For example, in the case of an analysis of problematically long throughput times of radiology requests in a hospital, we could demarcate the system under study from its wider context by only considering the referring physicians and

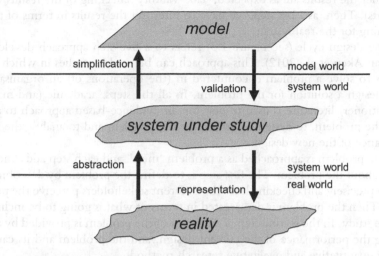

Figure 1.2 Reality – system – model.

the radiology department and by only looking at the timing of referral requests, the handling of the requests by the radiology department, the timing of radiology examinations and the timing of the reporting back to the physician. The abstraction takes place by selecting the relevant subsystems and aspect systems. Then we make a model of the system under study by simplification. A model can be a process description (according to a standardised method), an Excel spreadsheet, a mathematical formulation or a simulation model, etc. In the model we simplify the system under study to a number of relations between the elements, in this case, the difference between the timing of the referral, the timing of the appointment, the timing of the arrival of the patient for the examination, the start and end of the examination and the timing of the reporting back to the physician. This would be sufficient for the analysis of throughput times of requests. If we were also interested in the workload generated by the requests, we must include these aspects in the system description and in the model. We must check carefully whether the system under study truly can be seen as a representation of the real world. If there is much variation in the number of requests and availability of staff, this might lead to a decision to study the throughput times over several weeks.

Then, we use the model to test alternative options to reduce the throughput times, for instance by increasing radiology capacity or by introducing a walk-in system for certain types of requests in the radiology department. The model can then provide the expected performance of the system under study. Before we can do this, we first must validate the model as a true and reliable representation of the system under study. This validation can be done in a number of ways. Comparing the model results with performance data in reality, sensitivity analysis (e.g., manipulating the variables in the model one by one and checking whether the results are as expected, 'face-validity' checking of the results with experts). Then, as a last step, we have to interpret the results in terms of their meaning for the real system.

The design cycle (see Figure 1.3) refers to a five-step approach developed by Van Aken et al. (2012). This approach can be used in studies in which one wants to solve a problem encountered in (the operations of) an organisation and design a solution for the problem. In all the steps, academic (and maybe practitioner) literature is used to develop an evidence-based approach to analyse the problem, to design a solution for the problem and to analyse the performance of the new design.

The problem is approached as a problem 'mess', and each step adds knowledge about the problem. The first step is to define the problem by describing it more precisely and checking how the different stakeholders perceive the problem. Then the problem is demarcated in terms of what is going to be included in the study. In the second step, a diagnosis of the problem is provided by analysing the performance of the current design, and the problem and its causes, using quantitative and qualitative research methods.

The third step is to design a solution for the problem, by first formulating the requirements for a solution. Van Aken et al. distinguish four categories of design requirements: functional requirements (the performance targets for the new design), user requirements (the preferences of the users involved), boundary conditions (conditions which must be met unconditionally) and design restrictions (restrictions on the design formulated by the organisation). Then a few potential solutions for the problem are elaborated, based on evidence reported in the literature for the type of problem investigated, and the solution with the best expected performance is suggested for implementation, and further elaborated into a solution design.

In the full problem-solving cycle, in the fourth step the solution is implemented and in the fifth step the new design is evaluated. In case of a student project there is often no time for a full implementation and an evaluation based on actual performance of the system under study. In that case, the solution is

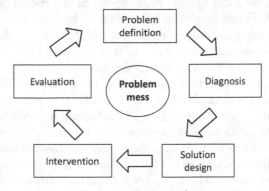

Figure 1.3 Design cycle.

often implemented in a model of the system under study and the evaluation is based on the performance of the solution in the model environment. In cases of a full implementation, an intervention takes place in the form of an implementation of the new design. As the last step the new design is evaluated on its performance in reality. If the problem is not solved satisfactorily, a new cycle can start.

As an illustration of the above approach, we can use an example of the problem of long waiting times for first access in an outpatient orthopaedic clinic. Suppose a Masters' student in healthcare management is asked by the management of the hospital to investigate the problem (how long are the waiting times actually, what are the causes, what are possible solutions?), and to develop an implementable solution for the main cause, including an underpinning of its expected performance.

For defining the problem, in the first step of the cycle, the system studied is demarcated (orthopaedics outpatient clinic/operating theatre department/ orthopaedics ward), literature on waiting times in hospitals is studied, interviews are held with the most important stakeholders and patients (for instance managers/team leaders responsible for planning of orthopaedic patients, orthopaedic surgeons/nurses, outpatient clinic staff, operating theatre management), and available information on waiting times is studied. Based on the literature on waiting times in hospitals, a cause-and-effect diagram is created with the most important possible causes (demand too high, insufficient resources, inefficient use of resources, inadequate planning and scheduling of patients, etc.). The interviews provide information on the actual size of the problem, and on the perspectives of the stakeholders on the problem and its causes. The available information on waiting times helps to check whether perceptions of stakeholders and measurements of waiting times create a coherent picture of the problem. Using for instance the 'Treeknormen' as a yardstick helps to check whether the size of the waiting times is really problematic. Suppose this initial analysis leads to a more focused problem statement that inadequate planning and scheduling of patients for orthopaedics is seen as the main cause for the long waiting times, then the further investigation can concentrate on this direction.

The next step is a further diagnosis of the problem. The student studies literature on planning and scheduling of patients in hospitals and develops an approach for the analysis of the current way of planning and scheduling patients for orthopaedics. A precise description of the current design is provided with input from stakeholders responsible for planning and scheduling, and data are gathered which are used to quantify the available resources, the use of resources and the performance of the 'production system' of orthopaedics. Interviews with patients are held to analyse the performance of the current system from the perspective of the ultimate user, and to understand what improvements can create value for customers. Suppose the diagnosis is that the throughput time for orthopaedic patients is too long, especially for hip or knee surgery, due to extra visits for pre-operative screening and inadequate planning and scheduling leading to avoidable waiting times, and that more value for customers can be created by a new design for the total patient journey for patients with hip or knee problems.

In the third step a new design for the patient journey is developed, based on requirements for the design and evidence from literature on effective solutions for waiting times. Suppose effective solutions reported in literature are to use a one-stop outpatient visit (X-ray, visit to orthopaedic surgeon, pre-operative screening), operating theatre sessions dedicated to knee and hip surgery and follow-up visits by an orthopaedic surgeon or orthopaedic nurse. Functional requirements can be based on 'Treeknormen' or specific targets for waiting and throughput times. User requirements can be based on interviews with stakeholders on the importance and expected effect of suggested solutions on waiting times (supported, for instance, by a scoring system for these dimensions). Boundary restrictions are, for instance, that the solutions should accord with the responsibilities of health professionals, and the restriction imposed on solutions by hospital management is that the solution should be cost-effective. Suppose it is decided to include all three elements in a proposed redesign of the patient journey. For this potential solution, plans are made to adapt the processes to see what is necessary to implement the new patient journey. To guide development of this solution, a focus group is created, consisting of key stakeholders and perhaps one or two patients.

In the fourth step, the new solution should be implemented but, due to the limited time available to students for thesis work, it is decided to implement the solution only in a model of the system in this timeframe. The new way of planning and scheduling is elaborated, and checks are made that all procedures for patient planning and scheduling are adapted. To allow for the calculation of the expected effects on waiting and throughput times, and use of resources, a spreadsheet model of the new patient journey is developed. This allows for what-if scenarios for each of the solution elements separately and combined. Key stakeholders, and perhaps also patients, are asked to score the redesign on effectiveness, implementability and expected performance gain. Based on the information from the model calculations and the assessment of the key stakeholders, we now have a well-developed view of the expected performance of the redesign and its benefits.

Instead of using the spreadsheet model and what-if analysis, it would also have been possible to develop a simulation model of the system. This would have offered more possibilities for analysis of the impacts of the solution but would require more time and effort. If variation (stochastics) does not play an important role in this example, a 'simple' spreadsheet model is adequate.

1.4 Outline

In this chapter we introduced a number of features of HSOM that play an important role in our book. In the remaining chapters of the theory part, we elaborate HSOM further. Chapter 2 defines and illustrates a number of concepts of HSOM, such as operations and resources, and the distinction between operations management of units, process chains and networks. Chapter 3 on models and data presents an overview of different ways of modelling OM problems in a health services context. In Chapter 4 we focus on the OM of units, within a health services provider, having to deal with the trade-off between the service level and the efficient use of resources. In Chapter 5 we focus on the OM of process chains, having to deal with the trade-offs between an ideal patient journey, outcomes and costs. Chapter 6 provides an overview of different improvement approaches that can be used in an OM study, such as Lean Management, Six Sigma and the Theory of Constraints. In Chapter 7, we provide a conceptual framework to relate operations to outcomes, and we illustrate this approach with a study on using demand segments for describing and analysing the performance of type 2 diabetes care in a regional setting.

The Practice part of the book starts with three chapters (8–10) on how to improve the OM of units, process chains and networks, making use of a design approach and model support. Then in Chapters 11–17 case studies are presented on OM approaches to improve the performance of healthcare providers in delivering services to patients, that create value and avoid waste.

1.5 Questions and exercises

What are the main differences between a national healthcare system or government-regulated system versus a market-regulated or for-profit healthcare system, and what is the impact on OM of the healthcare provider?

Given the decision-making process on managerial issues in a hospital, what will be important aims for HSOM?

Why is it important to approach an OM problem in healthcare as a 'problem mess'?

References

Department of Health and Social Care (2021). Handbook to the NHS constitution for England. https://www.gov.uk/government/publications/supplements-to-the-nhs-constitution-for-england/the-handbook-to-the-nhs-constitution-for-england.

Nederlandse Zorgautoriteit (2017). Beleidsregel TH/BR-025, Beleidsregel toezichtkader zorgplicht zorgverzekeraars Zvw. https://puc.overheid.nl/nza/doc/PUC_21832_22/1/.

NHS England (2021). National tariff payment system. https://www.england.nhs.uk/pay-syst/national-tariff/national-tariff-payment-system.

Porter ME and Teisberg E (2006). *Redefining health care, creating value based competition on results*. Harvard Business School Press, Boston, MA.

Roth AV (1993). World class health care. *Quality Management in Health*, 1, 1–9.

Van Aken J, Berends H and Van der Bij H (2012). *Problem solving in organizations: a methodological handbook for business and management students.* Cambridge University Press, Cambridge.

Van de Klundert J (2009). Value-conscious health service organisations. Inaugural lecture, Institute of Health Policy and Management, Erasmus University Rotterdam. https://www.researchgate.net/publication/241860751_Value-Conscious_Health_Service_Organisations.

Suggestions for further reading

Brandeau ML (2004). *Operations research and health care: a handbook of methods and applications.* Kluwer Academic Services, Berlin, Heidelberg, and New York.

Hopp WJ and Lovejoy WS (2014). *Hospital operations. Principles of high efficiency health care.* FT Press, Upper Saddle River, NJ.

Pidd M (2009). *Tools for thinking: modelling in management science.* 3rd ed. John Wiley & Sons, Chichester.

Powell SG and Batt RJ (2008). *Modelling for insight: a master class for business analysts.* John Wiley & Sons, Hoboken, NJ.

Roth AV and Menor LJ (2003). Insights into service operations management: a research agenda. *Production and Operations Management,* 12, 145–164.

Spraque LG (2007). Evolution of the field of operations management. *Journal of Operations Management,* 25, 219–238.

2 Health Service Operations Management concepts

Jan Vissers and Sylvia Elkhuizen

2.1 Introduction

The concept of Health Service Operations Management originates from the two parent domains of knowledge: (Health) Service Management and (Health) Operations Management. Service management is a multidisciplinary approach to designing, delivering and evaluating services for customers that add value for the customer. Service industries are nowadays responsible for a large growth in jobs and GDP. Important characteristics of services, as opposed to goods, are (Bordoloi, Fitzsimmons and Fitzsimmons, 2019):

- The customer participates in the process.
- Services are simultaneously created and consumed.
- Services are perishable and can therefore not be stored.
- Services are intangible.
- Services can vary greatly from customer to customer because of their heterogeneous nature.
- Services cannot be transferred between patients.

Operations management (OM) is an area of management concerned with designing and controlling the process of production of goods or services. As health services constitute an important service industry, Health Service Management and Health Service Operations Management have developed as more specific knowledge domains. In the definition of Health Service Operations Management (HSOM), we combine the service management approach and the OM approach. This provides us with the opportunity to make use of concepts from both areas of knowledge.

Important concepts used from the domain of Service Management are the service package, the service strategy, the service blueprint and the service modularisation. We make use of these and other methodologies often used in service management later for description, analysis and evaluation of services. We, of course, also make use of the many concepts and methodologies from OM for description and analysis of operations to deliver the services. As we proceed, we observe that there is overlap between the two approaches, and that some

DOI: 10.4324/9781003020011-3

settings make more use of one or the other approach. This illustrates that the research field of HSOM is fairly young and that insights are still developing.

2.2 Patients, clients and customers

A variety of terms is used to identify the persons who are in need of a service or are receiving a service. In general practitioner (GP), paramedic and hospital settings we tend to talk about 'patients'; in homecare/community healthcare, mental healthcare and rehabilitation we often use 'clients' or 'service users' and in services we use 'customers'. We will use these terms interchangeably.

Patients can be identified in many ways. General demographic characteristics include age, sex, marital status and home address. Relevant health-related characteristics might include weight, smoking, alcohol consumption and amount of physical exercise taken. Variables that measure health status could be blood pressure, cholesterol, glucose level, functional disabilities and personal satisfaction with their own health. Therefore, there are many ways in which clients can be grouped for designing and analysing services. This depends on the purpose of the grouping. Table 2.1 provides a number of alternative ways to group clients in health services.

Most ways of grouping clients speak for themselves. One way of grouping that needs illustration is using demand segments. A demand segment is a group of clients that have the same or similar demand characteristics for a service. This concept – from Service Management and Service Marketing – can help to organise the chain of care by forecasting the demand for a specific service. Type 2 diabetes patients, for example, do not represent a homogeneous group. As diabetes is a chronic disease, a patient can have different needs depending on their stage of the condition: in the diagnosis phase there is a need for lifestyle change;

Table 2.1 Alternative ways of grouping clients in health services

Grouping	Setting	Purpose
Clinical specialty being treated by	Hospital	Analysis of bed use, theatre use
Diagnosis	Hospital	Planning of care pathway
Treatment mode: inpatient, outpatient, day treatment/day case	Hospital	Analysis of use of resources
Urgency level	Emergency department	Determining priority of treatment
Routine/urgent/home visit **General/specific issue**	GP practice	Determining priority of seeing Planning of general versus dedicated clinics
Dependency level	Nursing home	Assessing nursing workload
Demand segment	All	Demand and care chain management
Process, product or product-process	Hospital	Focused factory

the treatment phase is based on medication and, later-on, insulin injection; and in advanced phases the emphasis is on treatment of consecutive complications. To organise services for type 2 diabetes patients, it is important to know the numbers at each phase, i.e., the size of these distinct demand segments. The last example in Table 2.1, refers to the grouping of patients according to the process, product or combination. For instance, if patients follow the same process, even though perhaps arriving on the pathway via different diagnoses, they can then be grouped for the purpose of planning the processes on the pathway. For example, hip and knee surgery patients follow the same process. If a pathway has a high volume of patients, it may be possible to purpose-design a stream-lined process with dedicated resources for them – a 'hospital-within-a-hospital' using the general OM idea of the 'focused factory' (Bredenhoff et al., 2010).

2.3 Services and operations

In this textbook on Health Services Operations Management, we use the term 'services' as well as 'operations'. There are, however, some important differences in terminology and definitions, which we elaborate in this section.

Service Management makes use of the concept of '*service package*' to describe the content of a service. The service package is defined as a bundle of services and goods with information that is provided in a particular environment (Bordoloi et al., 2019) and consists of five features:

- Explicit services: the immediate benefits of intrinsic features of the service (e.g., absence of pain after surgery).
- Implicit services: psychological benefits of extrinsic features of the service (e.g., the security of the hospital environment).
- Information: information from the service provider about the service (e.g., the health status before and after surgery).
- Facilitating goods: medical supplies used during the service, leaflets for follow-up care.
- Supporting facilities: physical resources that need to be in place for a service (e.g., hospital facilities).

All these features can be experienced by the customer and contribute to a service experience.

Services can be defined as *value-adding transactions*, in which – in principle – no physical goods are transferred from the provider to the consumer. In healthcare, services are generally delivered by healthcare professionals. The services mainly consist of human labour, and goods play a facilitating role. Examples are a consultation of a medical specialist in an outpatient clinic, and a home visit by a GP. An exception to this rule is surgical procedures involving a prosthesis, which becomes an integral part of the service.

An *operation* can be defined as a *value-adding transformation* of input to output. An example of an operation in manufacturing is, for instance, the painting of a car body on an assembly line. Though the use of 'transformation' in the definition as opposed to 'transaction' makes one think of a physical transformation, a service can also be regarded as a specific type of operation in which the customer is an input to the process and the product delivered is mainly or completely intangible.

In HSOM, we can think of a diffuse dividing line between a service and an operation. A surgical procedure, for instance, shows more operation-like features than a consultation with a healthcare professional; the surgery can lead to a transformation of the human body and also involve transfer of a physical good such as an artificial hip or cardiac pacemaker. The fact that the patient is part of the process, and the core activity is transformation using the knowledge and skills of a surgeon, makes it clear that we label surgery predominantly as a service. Therefore, operations in healthcare can generally be classified as services. In Table 2.2 we provide some definitions related to services and operations, to illustrate the differences and overlaps.

In Figure 2.1 we see an example of a user service journey and in Figure 2.2 an example of a process.

We see in Figure 2.1 a user service journey of a patient who visits a health centre, an acute hospital, a nursing home, a homecare provider and the health centre again. This might represent, for instance, a journey of a patient with a stroke: first contact via the GP, by ambulance to the hospital and diagnosis and treatment in the hospital, rehabilitation in a nursing home and final stay at home with support from homecare and the health centre. We see that within each provider, different service elements are included in the service.

In Figure 2.2 we see an OM description of the process of diagnosis and treatment in a hospital setting for a patient who is referred for hip surgery by a GP.

Table 2.2 Definitions of services and operations

Services perspective		Operations perspective	
Item	Definition	Item	Definition
Service	Value-adding transaction between provider and consumer	Operation	Value-adding transformation of inputs to output
Service element	Description of the smallest unit within a service	Activity	Description of the smallest unit within an operation
Service journey	Description of the order in which service elements are delivered to the customer for a service	(Included in definition of operation)	Description of the order in which activities are performed for an operation
User service journey	Description of the order in which services are used by the customer to answer a demand	Process or chain	Description of the set of operations that is performed in a certain order to create a product or a service

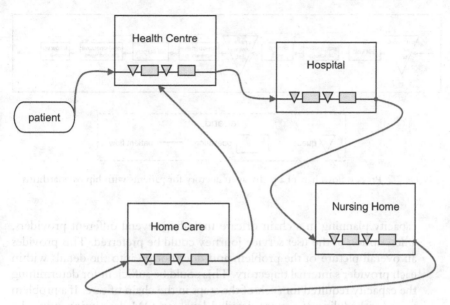

Figure 2.1 Example of user service journey.

In Figure 2.2 we see that the patient's trajectory includes different operations: a consultation in the outpatient department, an examination in the radiology department, a second visit to the orthopaedic surgeon, pre-operative screening before surgery, surgery in the operating theatre department, a stay in the inpatient ward after surgery and a follow-up visit after discharge. For each of the operations the patient interacts with different healthcare professionals and makes use of various other resources. Notice that the description is at the level of operations from the perspective of the total trajectory. Each operation could be expanded or unpacked as a sub-process, with similar symbols detailing the next level (activities). A surgery, for instance, can be seen as a very complex operation that includes many activities: arrive and receive pre-operative preparation, movement to the operating room, administration of anaesthesia, surgery, movement to a post-operative area and recovery and monitoring until taken to an inpatient or discharge ward. If the focus of a study is on the OM of the operating theatre department, then surgery can be seen as a process, including a number of operations.

If we compare the user service journey description (Figure 2.1) and the process description (Figure 2.2), we can make a number of observations:

- The two methods of description show considerable overlap. In principle, both methods could have been applied to both examples.
- The choice of which method to use depends on the problem considered and its potential solution. If, for example, the problem regards

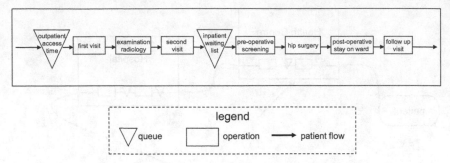

Figure 2.2 Process flowchart of a pathway/trajectory for patients with hip osteoarthritis.

capacity planning in a chain of care including several different providers, a description of the user service journey could be preferred. This provides an overall picture of the problem and does not go into the details within each provider's internal trajectory. This could be sufficient for determining the capacity required for each of the steps in the chain of care. If a problem regards scheduling at a more detailed level, an OM description might be preferred as it provides more insight into the interaction between different processes and resources.

Therefore, we can expect more use of service management descriptions in problems regarding health centres, nursing homes and homecare, and more OM descriptions in problems regarding hospitals.

If we consider the literature in health service management and HSOM in a broader sense, we can further notice that service management terminology is more used in the early stages of the product cycle (development of a new service, redesign of a service, evaluation of a service) and the OM terminology more in the later stages (running a service, improvement of performance of a service).

2.4 Operation types, resources and units

Consider the patient requiring a hip replacement as shown in Figure 2.2. Key operations involved in delivering this service for the patient include visits to the surgeon, examination procedures to diagnose the problem, surgical procedures to replace the hip and physiotherapy sessions to facilitate the rehabilitation of the patient. Each of these operations adds value and each generates an individual output. However, the cumulative effect of these individual products is a patient 'successfully' treated with a hip replacement. Hence, the first stage in the management of this health operation ('the analysis, design, planning, and control of all of the steps necessary to provide a service for patients') is to identify the key operations that are required to deliver that service.

Let us consider the operation 'hip surgery' as an input–output transformation. See Figure 2.3.

We see that the operation 'hip surgery' has as inputs the patient diagnosed with a hip problem and also some materials such as a hip prosthesis and wound dressing material. These inputs are – as facilitating goods – consumed during the operation or become part of the output. Other types of input are resources, such as the operating theatre room (with its equipment), the nurses who are monitoring the patient or are assisting the physicians during the procedure and the physicians involved in the surgery. A *resource* is an input for the operation that is used for the transformation of inputs to outputs. Also inputs for the operation are the protocols used to perform the surgical procedure according to clinical guidelines.

Note that an operation can also imply a group of activities that together constitute the operation. A surgical procedure, for instance, consists of activities by the surgeon, the anaesthetist and the supporting personnel. An *activity* in itself, again, involves different tasks. For instance, the activity 'surgical procedure' for the surgeon implies the following tasks: preparing for the procedure, starting the procedure, performing the procedure, ending the procedure and washing. From this example we can see that tasks constitute an activity, and activities constitute an operation. We regard the surgical procedure as an operation, because at this level of activity the added value (to the patient following the surgical procedure) becomes obvious. Note also that there is little

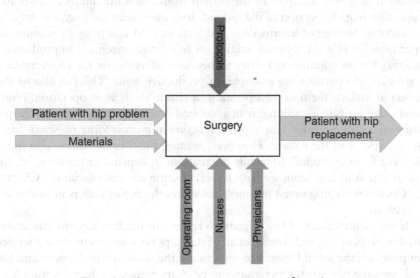

Figure 2.3 Hip surgery as input-output transformation.

or no freedom in the relative timing of tasks or activities, as they all are to contribute to the operation. Operations are, therefore, the basic elements in an OM approach.

Operations can be grouped into *operation types*. An operation type is a group of operations using the same resources, though the amounts of resources used may differ. A *resource* is an input for an operation that is used for the transformation into outputs but can be used again for another operation. This as opposed to *material inputs* that become part of the output (e.g., prosthesis), or are consumed (e.g., swabs). So, operating theatres, operating theatre personnel and operating theatre equipment are resources, but the prosthesis that is placed in a patient during an orthopaedic surgical procedure is a material input for the process that becomes part of the service.

A *unit* is a department in a health system that performs operations of the same operation type: for example, the X-ray unit, as part of the radiology department undertakes X-ray procedures. A unit also has access to the key resources (staff, capital equipment and materials) required to undertake operations of the same type.

For example, a radiology department contains the specialist staff and equipment required (resources) to carry out X-ray procedures, but the films are materials that become part of the output of the process (patient with diagnostic information). Table 2.3 gives an example overview of units, resources and operation types in different healthcare settings.

In the general OM literature, *operations* are classified under the following types: alteration, transportation, storage and inspection. In HSOM we tend to include alteration (e.g., a surgical procedure in an operating theatre), transportation (e.g., the transport of the patient from the ward and vice versa) and inspection (e.g., inspection of the wound) into one operation (e.g., the surgical procedure). Storage of intermediate products in OM compares to waiting for operations in HSOM. Not all waiting in healthcare systems is unproductive. Waiting for an administered drug to become effective, or for recovery in a ward after an operation are examples of productive waits. This can also be the reason to include them in the operation or define them as an operation. Nonproductive waits (e.g., waiting in an acute bed when medically fit for discharge, being on a waiting list for a hip replacement) are important forms of 'waste' from the viewpoint of the patient. However, waiting times in healthcare also function as a form of 'buffer', to handle fluctuations in demand or capacity. So, for effective unit management we have to accept some amount of waiting. Chapter 4, 'Operations management of units', elaborates the use of buffers in healthcare operations.

If the identification of key operations represents the first stage in 'the analysis, design, planning and control of all of the steps necessary to provide a service for patients', the second stage is to understand the ways in which operations use and consume resources. Operations can be characterised by their duration (i.e., time taken to undertake the operation) and by the workload required from

Table 2.3 Unit, resources and operation types in hospital and nursing home setting

Setting	Unit	Resources	Operation types
Hospital	Emergency department	Treatment rooms, nursing staff, physicians	First aid (minor injuries) Acute aid (major injuries) Trauma
	Outpatient department	Diagnostic and treatment rooms, administrative and nursing staff, physicians	First and follow-up visits Minor procedures
	Diagnostic and therapy departments (e.g., radiology, pathology, physiotherapy)	Diagnostic and therapy rooms, equipment, paramedical staff, physicians	Diagnostic tests Therapies
	Operating theatre department	Operating rooms, assisting operating personnel, physicians, anaesthetists	Surgical procedures
	Intensive care	Beds, equipment, nursing staff, physicians	Monitoring Acute interventions
	Wards	Beds, nursing staff, physicians	Recovery Cure and care Monitoring
Nursing home	Wards	Rooms/beds, nursing and support staff	Care activities Medication Feeding
	Therapy departments	Rooms, staff	Different therapies

the resources for the operation (e.g., number and types of staff required for the operation). A basic philosophy of OM is that these duration and workload characteristics of operations (and of processes as the constellation of operations to produce a service) determine the way operations (and processes) can be planned and controlled.

Figure 2.4 shows a distribution of the length of stay for patients admitted to general surgery wards. Such data inform decisions about the number of beds (resources) that are required to accommodate a particular volume of admissions (e.g., a schedule of planned admissions).

As can be seen, this distribution of length of stay has a peak at two days and a long tail to the right. The average length of stay is 5.4 days, while the standard deviation is large (6.5 days) due to the long tail. This is typical for many service distributions in healthcare. In Chapter 3 models are presented that can be used to fit a theoretical distribution, such as Erlang, to arrive at a good fit for these data.

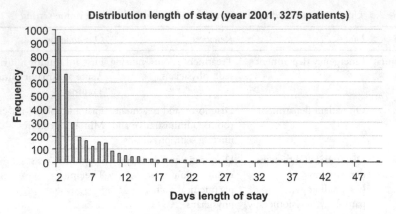

Figure 2.4 Distribution of length of stay for general surgery (n = 3275 patients).

It is important that an HSOM practitioner questions the data and asks themself whether the data shown can be used for taking decisions. For instance:

*   Is the aggregation level correct (all general surgery patients) or should the analysis be applied separately to different patient groups within general surgery?
*   Does the small peak around eight/nine days suggest there are different distributions aggregated here which would be better understood separately, for instance surgical oncology patients with longer average length of stay?
*   Are the patients with a very long length of stay to be accepted as random statistical variation or are there explanations of another kind affecting a subset of patients (e.g., some patients waiting for an empty bed in a nursing home)? This additional stay might be something to analyse separately and take different actions on.

These issues in data analysis are discussed further in Chapter 3.

The first two concerns are relevant to the earlier discussion of product definitions. Here, any decision to reclassify products would be driven by a need to identify a level of aggregation that usefully supports the HSOM task.

Figure 2.5 shows the average daily demands for nursing care for general surgery patients, expressed as Full Time Equivalent (FTE) nursing staff per day. In this illustration, the maximum length of stay of general surgery patients is seven days and they have a surgical procedure on their second day.

As can be seen, the nursing workload is less on the day of admission, rises on the day of the surgical procedure and on the day after, returns to the initial level for the following two days and is low on the days before the discharge. The operations manager needs to be aware of such fluctuation in demand when scheduling nursing resources to support ward-based operations.

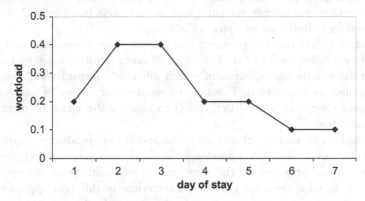

Figure 2.5 Workload for general surgery for nursing staff (expressed as FTE nurses to perform the nursing requirements on that day).

2.5 Process or chain

As indicated earlier, operations represent the building blocks which, when added together, generate the overall set of transforming the processes required to deliver a product or service for a client. Having identified these individual building blocks, and the resources that they use, an operations manager needs to identify the ways in which they should be linked to produce a particular service. This chain of operations (or overall delivery process) may include both productive activities and productive periods of waiting (e.g., waiting for a drug to become effective). A *process chain* can therefore be defined as the chain of operations that needs to be performed to produce a particular service.

Each process has a customer, whether this is an internal customer for a process that focuses on a part of a chain (for instance a specialist that orders a test from pathology), or it is an ultimate consumer of the service, i.e., a patient. Each process should also have a process owner, that is responsible for managing the process. This is, of course, a weak point in many healthcare organisations, as customer processes are often not well managed. This is due to the fact that many healthcare providers are still functionally organised based on the type of work or are in a transition to use the value-creating processes as the basis for organising the work.

Customer processes in healthcare are often only dealing with services provided by a single provider, i.e., a hospital, a general practice, a nursing home or a homecare provider. However, many patients face situations in which different providers each provide a part of the total (end-to-end) process as experienced by the patient. The process of a patient with a cerebral vascular accident (CVA, or a stroke), for example, combines ambulance services, emergency services in an emergency department, medical and nursing care at a stroke unit, recovery and therapy in a neurological ward, and then rehabilitation services at home, a nursing home or a rehabilitation centre.

To distinguish between a single provider process and process involving more providers, we refer to the latter case as a *care chain* (see Figure 2.6). If we want to refer to both, we use '*process chain*'.

It may be clear that the planning and coordination efforts of a care chain create new challenges for OM. The chain of care resembles a supply chain as used in manufacturing industries in which different companies collaborate in the manufacture of products. This opens a window for the use of supply chain techniques (Meredith and Shafer, 2002) to manage the chain of services in healthcare chains.

An analysis of existing chains may also reveal non-productive operations and periods of waiting. A knowledge of these non-productive operations helps to expose areas where the performance of health processes might be improved. In Chapter 6 we provide an overview of different approaches to analyse the performance of systems and suggest areas for improvement such as Lean Management, Theory of Constraints and Six Sigma.

In addition to having awareness of the 'links' in the chain of operations which generate healthcare processes, an OM approach requires reflection on other key characteristics of processes. This additional understanding helps the OM manager to establish appropriate control systems and it informs decisions about the allocation of resources.

Table 2.4 presents an overview of the most important *characteristics of processes* from an OM point of view. These characteristics are illustrated by considering those processes required to deliver services for different patient groups within the specialty of general surgery.

An important distinction in healthcare processes is whether access to resources can be scheduled. **Emergency** processes, such as many aspects of care for trauma patients, cannot be scheduled so the resources to undertake operations need to be readily available. This reduces flexibility in resource allocation decisions and potentially means that 'spare' capacity might need to be available. For **elective** patients, access to resources can be scheduled (and delayed) in an attempt to maximise efficiency.

Regardless of whether the chain of operations is classified as emergency or elective, along the chain judgements are required about the **level of**

Process & Chain

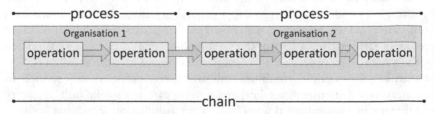

Figure 2.6 Process and chain.

Table 2.4 Characteristics of processes, illustrated for key patient groups within general surgery

Characteristics of process/chain	Patient group Trauma patients	Surgical oncology patients	Abdominal surgery patients	Vascular surgery patients
Emergency or elective	emergency	elective	elective	elective
Low, medium or high urgency	high	high	medium	low
Short, medium or long	short	long	medium	short
Complexity (++ very high, + high)				
• Diagnostics	++	+	+	
• Consultation	++	+		
• Multi-specialty	++	++		
Predictability (-- very low, - low)				
• Number of operations	--	-		-
• Durations	-			
• Routing	--			

urgency attached to its operations. The urgency of individual operations affects prioritisation decisions when different patient groups compete for the same type of resources: i.e., resource allocation decisions within units (see Chapter 4). For example, in comparison to 'vascular surgery' elective admissions, trauma patients will have a higher priority in terms of access to hospital beds and operating theatres. However, the urgency attached to operations can change and initiatives such as 'booked' admission systems and 'maximum' waiting time standards might increase the priority attached to elective patients.

The length of a process, in terms of the **number of operations** that constitute the process or chain, is another important characteristic. A short process, for instance a diagnostic consultation following a request by a GP, offers different challenges when scheduling the allocation of resources compared with a long process, involving many operations, or a chronic process, that may not have a clearly defined ending.

The *complexity* of a process also influences the ease with which it can be designed and planned. A process can be complex due to the number of diagnostic and therapeutic procedures required for patient care, or the necessity to consult another specialty for further treatment, or due to the involvement of another specialty in the treatment, or the cyclical character of parts of the process. An example of the last type is a diabetic patient who is under the care of an internal medicine consultant but needs an annual check-up with an ophthalmologist. The scheduling of the separate operations may then be simple, but to redesign such a complex process is not.

Similarly, the design and planning of a process is influenced by its **predict-ability**. We split this further into predictability of the number of operations in the process or chain, predictability of the duration of the operations and predictability of the routing of patients through the chain of operations. When there is great variation in number of operations, duration and routing, and therefore less predictability, planning these operations requires more flexibility than in the case of low variation. The predictability is one of the most important characteristics to consider when designing a process.

The **volume of patient flow** is not a characteristic of a process as such but is another important aspect to consider. Higher volume means that potentially more data are available to investigate the characteristics of the process in terms of, for example, its complexity and predictability. The patient flow volume also supports decisions about whether it makes sense to develop a dedicated service for a patient group. A short process, combined with high predictability in all aspects and a high volume, is an indicator to suggest creation of a dedicated organisation (for instance a cataract 'focused factory').

Processes might also include **decoupling points**. These are points in the process where planning characteristics change, for example from a standard-ised process to a patient-specific process. The operations before and after are decoupled by a buffer or decision point (for example a waiting list or a produc-tive period of waiting). A productive period of waiting might be a point in the process where there is a large change in the predictability of operations. For instance, until a diagnosis is reached, the nature of subsequent operations in the chain might be unpredictable. Once a diagnosis is achieved, the treatment path might become predictable.

The last aspect to be mentioned is the use of **shared resources** (those required by different patient groups or different specialties) in the process considered, or the use of a **bottleneck resource**. In the general surgery illustration, all patient groups share X-ray, ward and operating theatre resources. A process that uses many shared resources, including a bottleneck resource, is more difficult to organise than a process with no shared resources. This is because patient groups must compete for resources.

Insight into these qualitative assessments of the planning characteristics of different general surgery patient groups helps to understand why aggregate data on general surgery, such as the length of stay in Figure 2.4, are difficult to interpret and need to be broken down to patient group level to make sense for the development of appropriate forms of planning and scheduling.

2.6 Unit, chain and network perspectives

This chapter has introduced HSOM terms: products, operations, units, resources and process chains. Units carry out the same type of operation for different types of patients whereas process chains represent a series of differ-ent operations (undertaken in different units) for the same type of patient. Resources are used both within units and along chains but the requirements and incentives in terms of the planning and control of these resources differ according to whether a unit or chain perspective is adopted. This section illustrates the key differences between unit and chain logistics approaches when planning and managing resources. *Unit logistics* concentrates on the OM of a single unit. *Chain logistics* considers the OM of a single chain. *Network logistics* combines both perspectives. Each of these areas and approaches is discussed further in the remainder of the book.

Figure 2.7 illustrates these different logistical perspectives for a hospital setting. It describes a hospital as a representation of units and chains.

In the above example, general surgery has its own outpatient facilities that are not shared with, for instance, internal medicine. Diagnostic departments, such as radiology and pathology, are shared by all patient groups and specialties. Wards are shared by the different patient groups within a specialty, while the sharing of beds between specialties is limited to overflow. In addition, not all patient groups use the ward to the same extent depending on the length of stay. All surgical patient groups share the operating theatre (OT) department. Intensive care (IC) is again shared by all specialties, though the requirement for it differs greatly between patient groups.

The unit perspective is represented by the vertical groupings: outpatient department (OPD), radiology/pathology, ward, OT and IC. Managers of these units are responsible for the running of the unit, for the level of service the unit offers to physicians requiring a service on behalf of their patients, and for the efficient use of the resources available. This is regarded as a total responsibility. The unit's concern is the total flow of all patients requiring a

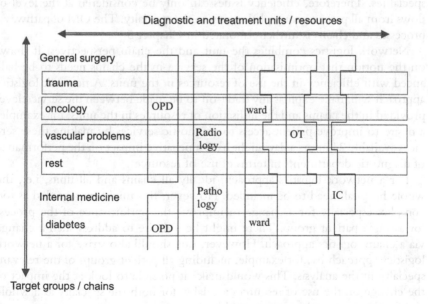

Figure 2.7 Unit, chain and network perspectives.

service from the unit, as this determines the prime objective of the unit, i.e., reaching a high but balanced use of resources without peaks and troughs in the workload during the hours of the day and days of the week. A high occupancy level or utilisation is seen as an important indicator in the 'efficiency' of the unit, whilst balanced utilisation is important not only for efficiency but also for the working environment for the personnel in the unit. Additional aims from the perspective of the unit are to produce the amount of output required with the least resources possible or to produce as much output as possible with the amounts of resources available (capacity management). The focus of unit logistics is therefore on the total flow of the patients using the unit, and on the effect of this flow on the use of resources and the workload of personnel. The OM of units is further elaborated in Chapter 4.

The chain (or pathway) perspective is represented by patient groups, i.e., trauma patients, surgical oncology patients, etc. The focus of this perspective is on the whole process of the patient, using different units on their journey through the hospital. The chain perspective strives to optimise this process according to some targets, which all relate to the time dimension. Typical targets are short access time, short throughput time and short in-process waiting times. Short throughput time can be reached by combining operations in one visit to the OPD, instead of having to come twice, or by completing the diagnostic phase in the OPD in case an admission is needed. The prime objective of the chain perspective is to maximise the service level for patients belonging to a certain patient group. As the focus is on the single patient group considered, it is difficult to look at the efficiency of the chain, in terms of use of resources. Resources are, in general, not allocated to patient groups, but to specialties. Therefore, efficiency issues can only be considered at the level of flows from all patient groups, belonging to the specialty. The OM of pathways, processes and chains is further elaborated in Chapter 5.

Network logistics combines the unit and the chain perspectives. It draws on the notion that optimisation of the service in the chains needs to be balanced with efficiency in the use of resources in the units. A network logistics approach will make explicit any trade-off to be made between the service level provided in the chains and the utilisation of resources in the units: for example, a desire to improve patient access to diagnostic services by making these services available 24 hours a day might have a negative impact on the performance of diagnostic departments in terms of use of resources.

For a network logistics approach, ideally all chains and all units, i.e., the whole hospital, need to be included. However, this might be regarded as too complex especially for a change to improve the performance of the process for a single patient group. There might be a desire to address such a change via a chain logistics approach. However, one should also strive for a network logistics approach by, for example, including all patient groups of the relevant specialty in the analysis. This would make it possible to look at the impact of the change on the use of resources available for both the specialty as a whole and for the other patient groups within it.

Table 2.5 Differences between the unit, chain and network logistics approaches

Item	Perspective Unit logistics approach	Chain logistics approach	Network logistics approach
Focus points	Resource utilisation Workload control	Service level	Trade-off between service level and resource utilisation
Strong point	Capacity management	Process management	Combination
Weak point	Not chain oriented	Risk of sub-optimisation	More effort
Suitable for	Efficiency analysis and improvement of units	Analysis, improvement and (re)design of chains	Redesign and efficiency of systems

Consider a change that aims to improve patient access to physiotherapy for stroke patients. If there is a limited supply of physiotherapy services, improvements in the process of care for stroke patients might result in a reduced level of service for other patient groups both within neurology (the specialty that treats stroke patients) and within other specialties containing patient groups which require physiotherapy. These adverse consequences would go unnoticed if only a chain logistics approach is adopted. A network logistics approach therefore helps to avoid a situation where an improvement in one process goes unnoticed at the expense of a drawback for other processes.

The OM approach implies making explicit the choices to be made from a systems perspective. This also reduces the risk of *sub-optimisation*, i.e., an improvement in one part of the system at the expense of the functioning of the system as a whole.

Table 2.5 summarises the main differences between the unit, chain and network logistics approach.

2.7 Operational, tactical and strategic levels of planning

Decisions in HSOM often concern matching supply and demand and can be made at different levels of planning. As such we can distinguish between operational, tactical and strategic levels of planning. This is inspired by Anthony (1965) who developed a hierarchical framework for management control in organisations. These different forms of planning are necessary to relate the operational performance of services delivered to clients to the objectives of the provider organisation and the requirements of different planning horizons (see Figure 2.8).

We see in Figure 2.8 a planning and control framework, showing the different levels of planning in relation to one another and to the operational performance level, illustrated for hospitals. The **operational performance** level refers to the execution of the plan: the service as actually delivered to the patient and its performance in terms of waiting times, throughput time, patient

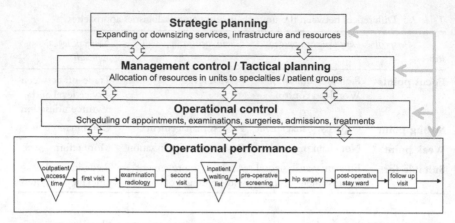

Figure 2.8 Levels of planning, adapted from Anthony (1965), illustrated for a hospital.

non-attendance, etc. To deliver good operational performance, much effort is required at the level of ***operational control*** to schedule appointments, admissions etc. At this level, requests for appointments, admissions, etc. are handled by relating them to the expected availability of resources. An essential characteristic of the operational control level of planning is that a request for a service by an individual client (patient, physician etc) is linked to specific resources: a bed for an admission, an OT slot on a theatre list (an operating room, the surgeon, the OT staff) for surgery, etc. It is short-term planning (typically days or weeks). To allow for scheduling of individual clients, clinic or OT sessions need to be organised in advance, and nurses need to be scheduled for ward shifts. This is often done a few weeks or months in advance, to ensure that scheduled staff leave is considered. ***Management control*** also labelled as ***tactical planning*** is performed by unit managers or their staff, as a back office activity, but is crucial for the smooth functioning of operational planning. It involves things like allocation of theatre sessions to specialties, and consequent expected IC and inpatient bed requirements. The ***strategic planning*** level looks at the long-term decisions to increase or decrease the resources in relation to the demand for services. These decisions are taken at the top level of hospital management, and they define the infrastructure capacity limits available for services.

The ***planning and control framework*** organises the decisions to be made for matching demand and supply at different levels. Decisions with a longer planning horizon are positioned at a higher level in the framework. Feed forward and feedback loops between the different levels make it possible to control the decisions to be made and are essential to make it a planning and control framework. Examples of elaborated hierarchical planning frameworks in healthcare can be found in Vissers et al. (2001) and Hulshof et al. (2012).

The three planning and control levels are superimposed on the operational performance level, i.e., the patient process. At the operational performance level, planned and scheduled operations are actually executed and deviations from the plan are taken care of. In the daily reality of healthcare practice many deviations can occur: the patient can be ill and not show up, the first visit of a patient can take much longer than scheduled, a surgery can run over due to complications or due to replacement of an insufficiently-experienced member of the surgical team, the stay in the recovery area after the surgery can be prolonged because there is not a bed available in the inpatient ward, etc. All of these things can happen since human beings are the main resource and the main co-producers of health services. The idea behind the use of such a planning framework is that the execution of operations is facilitated, but also guided and channelled by the decisions taken at higher levels, that most operations can be performed without loss of capacity, and that the remaining capacity is sufficient to handle all deviations from the plan. The planning framework can be used as a reference when dealing with an OM project in healthcare practice, to check whether all forms of planning are taken into account to implement a solution for an OM problem.

2.8 Operational and structural coordination

The planning framework of levels of planning (Figure 2.8, adapted from Anthony, 1965), illustrated for a hospital is also useful to provide guidance for operational and structural coordination of chains and units. The following issues need to be addressed:

* How to coordinate demand and supply?
* What variables should be controlled centrally (at the overall planning level of the chain) and what variables should be controlled locally (at the unit level)?
* What variables should be controlled in aggregates and what variables should be controlled in a detailed way?

The concepts of operational and structural coordination provide the means to balance demand for and supply of resources. *Operational coordination* refers to the acceptance of the client orders and the ordering of resources, such that these are in balance with the orders accepted. An example of operational coordination in a hospital setting is the coordination between a decision to plan a surgery for a patient and the request for a pre-operative screening to see whether the patient is fit for surgery. As the results of pre-operative screening are only valid for a limited time, it requires operational coordination at the level of an individual patient to prevent cancellation of a scheduled surgery because the results of the screening are outdated.

When these forms of operational coordination do not take place, they result in loss of capacity and delay in the process. It is important for the planning of the process chain to find out what the earliest moment is that information can become available to order resources for steps further down the chain. For instance, when can information be provided to the homecare agency about the expected discharge date of the patient to ensure that homecare is available when required and a delay in discharge is avoided?

Structural coordination refers to the setting of arrangements and conditions, including the target service level and resource utilisation level, which allow for operational coordination. Examples of structural coordination in a hospital setting are:

- The use of dedicated clinic sessions and dedicated OT sessions for specific patients (such as patients with hip osteoarthritis) to organise a separate chain process for these patients.
- The allocation of sufficient capacity to each processing point in the chain to allow for an undisturbed flow of patients through the chain.
- The reservation of capacity for large expected flows of direct service patients in diagnostic departments.
- The level of service (acceptable access time and waiting time on the waiting list) that will be provided and the trade-off with the use of resources.
- The positioning of decoupling points in the process chain, and the performance they try to accomplish.

When forms of structural coordination are not taken into account, they result in extra effort for coordination at operational level, loss of capacity and longer waiting times.

From this elaboration of the operational and structural coordination it becomes clear that the variables controlled centrally, at the level of the process chain, are:

- The amount of capacity allocated to each workstation.
- The balance between the allocations of different resources required for the chain.
- The service levels to be realised for the chain.

The variables controlled locally, at the level of the units, are:

- The resource occupancy (utilisation) level of the unit.
- The performance of the unit in terms of delivery time.

Aggregate control, at the level of the total patient flow, takes place for:

- The total amounts of resources available for each processing point in the chain.
- The reservation of capacity for direct service in diagnostic departments for the large flows of patients expected from clinics in the outpatient department.

Detailed control, at the level of the individual patient, is required for:

- A same-day second appointment for patients that can be seen directly in diagnostic departments.

- The planning of a pre-operative screening visit in relation to the date of booked surgery.
- The booking of follow-up care at home after discharge.

2.9 Questions and exercises

Describe the practice of a GP in terms of units, resources and operations.

Who is the owner of a process for a patient group in a hospital setting? Who should be the best choice for being the owner of the process and why?

In what way does working with service contracts make a difference for unit logistics?

Orthopaedics wants to redesign the process for patients who come for hip replacement. What approach would you suggest? What are the pros and cons of your approach?

There are complaints by surgeons on the long change-over times between different surgeries in the OT? What approach would you suggest? What are the pros and cons of your approach?

References

Anthony RN (1965). *Planning and control systems: a framework for analysis*. Division of Research, Graduate School of Business Administration, Harvard University, Boston, MA.

Bordoloi SK, Fitzsimmons JA and Fitzsimmons MJ (2019). *Service management: operations, strategy, information technology*. McGraw-Hill/Irwin, New York.

Bredenhoff E, Van Lent WAM and Van Harten WH (2010). Exploring types of focused factories in hospital care: a multiple case study. *BMC Health Services Research*, 10. https://doi.org/10.1186/1472-6963-10-154.

Hulshof PJH, Kortbeek N, Boucherie RJ, Hans EW and Bakker PJM (2012). Taxonomy classification of planning decisions in health care: a structured review of the state of the art in OR/MS. *Health Systems*, 1, 129–175.

Vissers JMH, Bertrand JWM and De Vries G (2001). A framework for production control in healthcare organisations. *Production Planning and Control*, 12, 591–604.

Suggestions for further reading

Lillrank P and Liukko M (2004). Standard, routine and non-routine processes in health care. *International Journal of Quality Assurance*, 17(1), 39–46.

Meredith JR and Shafer SM (2002). Operations management for MBAs. 2nd ed. John Wiley & Sons, Inc.

NHS Modernisation Agency (2002a). Improvement Leaders' Guide (series 1, guide 1). Process mapping, analysis and redesign. https://www.england.nhs.uk/improvement-hub/publication/improvement-leaders-guide-process-mapping-analysis-and-redesign-general-improvement-skills/.

NHS Modernisation Agency (2002b). Improvement Leaders' Guide (series 1, guide 2). Matching capacity and demand. https://www.scribd.com/doc/108048036/Matching -Capacity-and-Demand.

NHS Modernisation Agency (2002c). Improvement Leaders' Guide (series 1, guide 3). Measurement for improvement. https://www.england.nhs.uk/improvement-hub/ publication/improvement-leaders-guide-measurement-for-improvement-process-and -systems-thinking/.

Ploman MP (1985). Choosing a patient classification system to describe the hospital product. *Hospital and Health Services Administration*, 30, 106–117.

Plsek PE (1997). Systematic design of health care processes. *Quality in Health Care*, 1997(6), 40–48.

Rhyne DM and Jupp D (1988). Health care requirements planning: a conceptual framework. *Health Care Management Review*, 13(1), 17–27.

Roth A and Van Dierdonck R (1995). Hospital resource planning: concepts, feasibility, and framework. *Production and Operations Management*, 4(1), 2–29.

Vissers JMH (1998). Health care management modeling: a process perspective. *Health Care Management Science*, 1(2), 77–85.

3 Data and modelling

Nathan Proudlove

In this chapter, we focus on models, the activity of modelling, and consider the data we need to access and populate models. We illustrate this with several fairly simple examples. These lead to more complicated and realistic examples in later chapters.

3.1 Introduction

As was defined in Section 1.3, a model is a formal description of a system, or a part of a system, under study. We build, refine and use models to support the problem-solving cycle shown in Figure 1.3. A model itself could take the form of, for example, a set of:

- Concepts and arrows showing the relationship between them (a causal map) describing strategic options.
- Process steps and arrows showing workflow (a process or value stream map) describing how a healthcare delivery chain operates (such as Figure 2.2).
- Mathematical equations linking inputs (e.g., bed numbers and/or patient demand) to outputs (e.g., expected waiting times and/or costs) forming various types of mathematical model.
- Entities and rules expressing the logic of how entities (e.g., patients, doctors, beds) interact (various types of computer simulation).

In this book we are talking about all four, but particularly the last two. For example, a model of the cost involved in reordering consumable items might be expressed as the mathematical equation (model):

$$TC = K\frac{D}{Q} + h\frac{Q}{2}$$

Where parameters are as follows: K is the cost involved in placing and receiving an order, D is the demand in the period and h is the cost of storing an item for a period of time. More details and an accompanying spreadsheet are described in Subsection 3.5.1. We can then calculate the total cost, TC, for

DOI: 10.4324/9781003020011-4

any choice of order size Q. We could then look for an optimal (lowest *TC*) choice of Q, Q*, by trial and error, plotting a graph (see Figure 3.1), or (in some cases) through an optimisation algorithm. For this problem calculus gives a well-known solution:

$$Q^* = \sqrt{\frac{2DK}{h}}$$

So, in this example (see the graph and the spreadsheet in the online supplementary material), the lowest cost would be €273.86 per year, from ordering 183 items per order. The flatness of the curve around this optimum, shows that the cost is not very sensitive to the order volume in this region: rounder quantities would be 175 items per order at an annual cost of €274.11 or 200 items at €275.00.

The much more complicated situation of modelling patient flow along a pathway or chain, interacting with various constrained resources such as clinicians and beds, and other patients competing for those same resources, might involve representing the logic of the situation in a computer simulation, usually using specialised software with visual animations. With too many different stakeholders' objectives and possible changes to the flow structure to seek an optimum, we would usually evaluate the predicted consequences of a small number of well-thought-through changes, designs and/or scenarios. These approaches are covered in Subsection 3.5.2.

To build and use quantitative models, we of course need data, and to be able to extract from them the relationships and parameters we need to populate

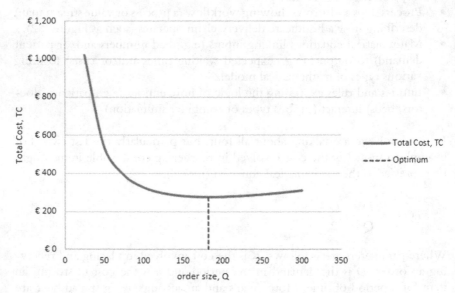

Figure 3.1 Graphical representation of inventory model.

the models. As well as technical tools (such as descriptive statistics, distribution fitting) we need to think about any shortcomings there may be in data we can extract from IT systems in healthcare, and be prepared to work with estimates and collect our own data if necessary.

Healthcare is a data-rich environment, both clinically (e.g., patient history and condition, diagnostic libraries) and managerially (e.g., patient pathway progress and state of resources). So, there can be large and complex datasets available, though there are often challenges here too. These arise from the nature of healthcare data and IT systems: fragmented, incomplete, ambiguous, manually coded, retrospective, sometimes judgemental, etc.

In this chapter, we introduce some of the core data analysis and modelling techniques used in work such as this. We only have space to give a broad overview and give some pointers to more specialised sources for readers who want to, or have to, go deeper.

There is huge potential to use modelling for a wide range of purposes to support decision making at all levels of the planning hierarchy that was illustrated in Figure 2.7, which we elaborate in Subsection 3.2.1. Much has been published (see e.g., Hulshof et al., 2012). But some notes of caution are required. The activity of modelling (everything from problem exploration through to supporting use of the results) is a skill (which we discuss in Section 3.2), often requires some expertise with handling data (Sections 3.3 and 3.4), there is a large toolkit of modelling techniques to draw on (Section 3.5) and healthcare can be a particularly complex area to model (as apparent throughout this book!) with many stakeholders, objectives, data limitations and chaotic systems (overflows, workarounds, ad hoc decisions, etc.). Though much healthcare modelling work has been published, this has generally been by academics, particularly in fields at the quantitative end of operations management and operational research, but knowledge and application on the ground, by and even with, healthcare managers are limited – which is a topic also discussed in the literature (e.g., Brailsford, 2005; Brailsford and Vissers, 2011; Brailsford et al., 2021).

There is a lot of technical depth behind all the techniques introduced in this chapter, and a lot of complex work published by specialists in particular techniques. When reading reports of healthcare modelling, a question to keep in mind is: how much operations management expertise is also in evidence: a complex model can lead to an impressive-looking publication, but have the real issues been addressed and practically useful options evaluated?! Also remember that the gaps between this and practice by healthcare managers are wide. There is plenty of valuable work that can be done by analysts combining a knowledge of operations management principles and the potential of data analysis and modelling, to support better healthcare decision making through iterative improvement cycles (as in Figure 1.3). Experts in particular data analysis or modelling techniques can be brought in as collaborators where necessary.

The purpose of this chapter is, therefore, not to teach the reader how to perform modelling and data analysis, but to illustrate how this can be done and discuss particular issues in healthcare applications. This should provide some foundation for deeper modelling cases which appear in later chapters. Familiarity with basic statistical tools is assumed, but not with mathematical modelling or specialist software.

This chapter first considers 'modelling' as an activity, then working with data, and finally some small-scale illustrative examples of modelling techniques.

3.2 Modelling

Figure 1.2 illustrated a high-level view of modelling: the activities involved in exploring the messy and complicated reality of the real world, abstracting the elements and systems relations between them of relevance, forming a simplified tangible model, checking its validity and then using it to generate insights about the real world.

Working up and down through the reality – system – model levels illustrated in Figure 1.2 many decisions have to be made, as discussed by Vissers (1998):

- Is building a model really necessary or helpful?! Would data analysis and presentation be sufficient?
- What is the purpose of the model in this context: solving a problem? illustrating behaviour? improving models currently in use? better-organising and systematising knowledge about a situation?
- What is the level of accuracy versus practical understandability and usability by managers?
- Related to this: what level of aggregation versus detail is adequate?
- Similarly: given the level of the planning hierarchy (illustrated in Figure 2.7) which we are modelling, what assumptions are necessary about processes at the levels above and below? for example, constraints imposed by higher levels and knowledge and control over lower levels.
- How much involvement can you get from stakeholders and access to the situation and data?
- What resources can you access (e.g., time and specialist software)?

The core job in modelling is moving up and down between the levels in the reality – system – model levels illustrated in Figure 1.2. Understanding the reality and deciding what to **abstract** into the middle level, which we might characterise as a conceptual model. A conceptual model can be conceptual models (a free-hand 'rich picture' drawing, capturing concepts and relationships with bullet points and arrows, various stakeholders and their points of view, etc. – see for example Crowe et al. (2017) and Pidd (2009)). Decisions have to be made about what parts of the system are important. As illustrated in Figure 1.1, there are many interacting components and stakeholders, who may have different points of view about what it is that is important. Figure 2.6 defined units, chains and networks. If we are interested in a *unit* (e.g., a department of operating theatres), can we then safely set aside dependencies on other units like intensive care recovery beds? Or if we are interested in a *chain* such as the fractured neck of femur pathway in orthopaedics, then what about the other chains that also share the same resources along our pathway (X-ray, operating theatre). On the other hand, we cannot model the whole world! So, where should we draw the boundary of our investigation.

Following Figure 1.2, we may then decide that the problem-solving task justifies *simplifying* part or parts of the conceptual model to develop one or several models. The form these models take depends on the situation modelled, the purpose and the choices and skills of the modeller(s), and these are often a useful intermediate step if we go on to quantitative modelling. As noted in Chapter 1, such quantitative models may be sets of mathematical equations from which we would seek to find optimal system settings, or a set of logical relationships described in a simulation model with which we could experiment with various parameter settings of flow designs; and we may use spreadsheets, specialist software packages or write code in a general programming language.

A model must be *validated* to give us confidence that its outputs can be trusted. This is done by checking that its internal structure has been built, and operates, as intended, and that its outputs and behaviour correspond to those of the real system, where such comparisons are possible. The final use of a model is to explain and interpret what its outputs *represent* for the stakeholders. We might also seek to 'hand over' models to healthcare managers for continued use and development.

Of course, the reality – system – model – system – reality and problem-solving cycles are rarely simple linear, one-way processes; they are processes of iterative discovery and refinement. Close involvement of stakeholders and access to the real situation are very valuable to reduce the risk of the modeller making incorrect assumptions (and becoming more interested in the model than the reality!) and the stakeholders rejecting the model or its outcomes.

Analysis of healthcare systems can be particularly challenging, at all stages, from problem definition and formulation to evaluation and use. This chapter digs a little deeper into this territory and issues requiring particular consideration in healthcare settings. First, we consider a number of uses of modelling of operations management issues in healthcare, then we go on to present a number of principles used for model building.

3.2.1 Purpose and uses of models

Expanding on the earlier definition of a model as a formal description of a system or a part of a system under study, considers a model to be:

> an external and explicit representation of part of reality as seen by the people who wish to use that model to understand, to change, to manage and to control that part of reality
>
> Pidd (2009, p. 10)

or, in the pithy shorthand of his thoughtful book, models are *tools for thinking*.

Hulshof et al. (2012) present a large review of the use of planning decisions within a taxonomy formed by the matrix of i) the levels as distinguished in Figure 2.7 (strategic, tactical, operational planning ('offline') and operational performance ('online'), and ii) across healthcare service areas (ambulatory, emergency, surgical, inpatient, homecare and residential care). Table 3.1 shows a version of this.

There are many other reviews of healthcare applications such as capacity planning (Utley and Worthington, 2012) and of specific modelling approaches applied in healthcare such as simulation (Brailsford et al., 2009; Günal and Pidd, 2010; Brailsford et al., 2021).

As a fuller example: Harper (2002) and Harper and Shahani (2002) describe a practical project for tactical-level planning such as decisions on how many beds are needed for each specialty. The project followed a typical process of conceptual modelling to gain an understanding of the system and issues, then using statistical analysis of historical data to describe demand and patient flows and lengths of stay in beds – crucially including the random variation in these. The structures of flows (routings) and parameters (e.g., mean arrival rate at different times of a day, week, year, etc.) were represented in a simulation model and parameterised from the historical data. The computer simulation model was then run many times with different internally generated random numbers to build up a picture of what could happen. These results are used to represent the trade-offs that the hospital managers face, for example between the number

Table 3.1 Planning decisions at different levels, based on Hulshof et al. (2012, Table C.4, p. 173)

Strategic	• Determining geographical coverage for a service
	• Setting intended service mix provided at a facility and target patient case mix
	• Partitioning care unit capacity
	• Setting capacity, e.g., beds, equipment and staff
	• Layout of facilities
Tactical	• Capacity allocation, e.g., bed reallocation between specialties
	• Admission control, e.g., setting a fixed or dynamic number of beds to reserve, rules to follow if wards overflow
	• Scheduling staff shifts
Operational Planning	• Scheduling elective admissions
	• Assignment of patients to beds
	• Discharge planning
	• Assigning staff to shift
Operational Performance	• Rescheduling elective admissions
	• Handling acute admissions
	• Rescheduling staff
	• Assigning nurses to patients
	• Scheduling patient transfer

and cost versus risk (e.g., bed plus ward staff resource versus the risk that the hospital becomes full).

3.2.2 Principles of model building

Pidd's *Tools for thinking* (2009) is excellent on the craft of modelling. He suggests a set of six principles.

3.2.2.1 Principle 1: model simple, think complicated

The aphorism 'all models are wrong, but some are useful' (often attributed to the statistician George Box) is a reminder both that a model is a simplification so cannot be completely 'correct' and that (anyway) the aim is help us with our thinking – for a manager to help decide what action to take next. A tendency in academic modelling work is to pursue accuracy over usefulness!

3.2.2.2 Principle 2: be parsimonious, start small and add

Following on from Principle 1 start with a simple, but working, model and iteratively add detail. Be mean – only add detail if necessary to obtain the level of detail and accuracy of 'answers' or insights we need. Then stop! Another reminder is the aphorism 'Everything should be made as simple as possible, but no simpler' (attributed to Einstein) – and the larger and more complicated your model is, the more data you will need to set it up and validate it.

3.2.2.3 Principle 3: divide and conquer, avoid mega-models

Where possible, break your model down into subcomponents, get those right (enough!) then fit them together. And don't try to model the whole world – the model will be as 'large' as the world and the world will have moved on by then! A conceptual model can be useful to help decide what aspects appear worthwhile building quantitative models of.

3.2.2.4 Principle 4: use metaphors, analogies and similarities

These can help with the creativity involved in building a model and communicating it to stakeholders. For example, a high-volume and fairly high-level model of patient flows through a treatment pathway might take the analogy of water flowing through pipes between tanks, with valves adjusting the rates of flow – and this is the analogy used in system dynamics simulation.

3.2.2.5 Principle 5: do not fall in love with data

The data are primarily dictated by the model we are building – its scope and level of detail – rather than building a model to make use of all the data we can obtain. We need to be aware, though, that data availability and issues around its accuracy (including what resources we have to collect further data ourselves or obtain estimates) may limit the ambition of our modelling. Data are also just a *sample* of what could have happened – we usually want to model the underlying *behaviour* not require our models to fit or reproduce the exact one-off outcome we saw; and, is the situation static: to what extent do we expect future behaviour to be like the past represented by our data? There is more consideration data in Section 3.3.

3.2.2.6 Principle 6: model building may feel like muddling through

Whilst a particular quantitative model will have recognised solution algorithms, an algorithm will give the same set of results each time. Each real problem is unique, so there is no template. Different modellers or different circumstances are likely to try different modelling approaches and produce different models. A modeller may try several different approaches, sometimes in parallel, to get different insights or to select which is the most appropriate. A final Einstein aphorism 'If I had an hour to solve a problem I'd spend 55 minutes thinking about the problem and five minutes thinking about solutions'.

So modelling is more craft than science, with experience mattering at least as much as technical expertise. The principles above, synthesised from experienced modellers, are intended to reduce the muddling somewhat. Powell and Batt (2008) is also good for basic modelling exercises.

3.2.3 Modelling healthcare problems

On top of all this, healthcare problems can seem particularly muddled. They are generally at least complicated.[1]

There are often several important stakeholder groups, who may have different perspectives on the purpose of a system, and so what direction 'improvement' should take (in technical terms, what the objective function should be). We might consider:

- The customers (usually patients) e.g., service quality.
- The staff e.g., workload, stress, annoyances and morale sappers (or 'niggles' (Dodds, 2018)).
- The organisation e.g., required performance, cost.

In the US, there is the Triple Aim (Berwick *et al.*, 2008):

- Improving the experience of care (quality and satisfaction).
- Improving the health of populations.
- Reducing per capita costs of healthcare.

---

1 We might use the term 'complex' to mean complicated, but we should be aware that 'complexity' and 'complex systems' has a particular meaning in systems theory.

More can be added, for example a common Quadruple Aim adds:

- Improving staff experience (quality of life and satisfaction).

Often there is an explicit trade-off, for example between waiting time for a service (or the risk of it being busy when needed) which affects the patient experience (and sometimes safety issues) versus the cost to the organisation of providing more service capacity, meaning it may spend more time idle waiting for a patient. Models can illustrate, and quantify, this for decision makers, and sometimes show how a trade-off can be shifted to a win–win (or even win–win–win) outcome, for example reducing the variation (randomness in arrivals and service durations).

We should, at least, be conscious of how an option that might make system performance 'better' from the point of view of one set of stakeholders may impact on others.

3.2.4 *Validation of models*

Validation is a crucial step before a model is used to generate results for use. This validation is the foundation for the credibility of predictions from the model.

A first step is establishing that the model represents the system under study (or conceptual map) – that it has been built as intended. This is also sometimes referred to as **verification** and is a job for the modeller. The equations or logic implemented, and the data parameters entered, must be checked carefully. The operation of the mechanisms in the model can be tested by sensitivity analysis (changing values and observing the results); testing extreme values can also be valuable.

White box (or open box) validation involves checking the content reflects the real-world features, and ideally should include stakeholders for their expertise and to foster buy-in. The content may have been captured in the conceptual map, so there can be some overlap.

When the above two are completed, **black box** (or closed box) validation consists of checking that the output of the model corresponds to real-world outputs and behaviour. For a system that is operating, we would often set the model's input to correspond with historical inputs and directly compare the outputs. With stochastic models we would compare the history with the range of model outputs generated by the randomness. Statistical methods may be useful, e.g., hypothesis tests that the underlying means are the same or comparing 95% confidence intervals or comparing histograms or percentiles. Here, it's important to remember that a fit will not be perfect – the aim is to establish whether the fit is *good enough* for the model to be plausible. Working with stakeholders on this is useful, and presenting the similarity visually is powerful in gaining trust in the model.

Another useful approach, particularly when there is not an operating system to compare with, *is face validation*. This involves showing sets of results to stakeholders and establishing whether they agree the behaviour appears realistic.

If a model is reconfigured, for example to test a redesign of a patient treatment chain, then those changes must also be validated.

For more on validation, particularly in the context of simulation, see Pidd (2009) and Robinson (2014).

3.3 Data collection

As noted in the introduction to this chapter, healthcare is often a data-rich environment, both clinically (e.g., patient history and condition, diagnostic libraries) and managerially (e.g., patient pathway progress and state of resources), but with often with any challenges as discussed in the next section.

It is important to realise that we often face a series of limitations when dealing with healthcare data.

Much data are *secondary data* – collected for purposes other than what we want to use it for, for example, length of stay data collected and processed in order to allow hospitals to construct coded data (e.g., HRG/DRG) for financial reimbursement. Thus, the level of detail and accuracy may be less than we could like. We may need to collect our own data – do we have access? How much time and resource would this require? Is it feasible? Can we use expert estimates? Or proxy metrics?

Much relies on human entry and coding decisions, so issues with quality are common. Thus, much sense in checking and cleaning can be necessary.

Data are often held in *different formats*, for example a hospital stay may be coded as many distinct episodes of care requiring combination and resolution of discrepancies if we are interested in whole stays. Data are often held across different IT systems (e.g., the emergency department, operating theatre, inpatient, diagnostics, etc. systems), which communicate with each other to varying extents. Hospitals also vary greatly (even within the same healthcare system) on the use of electronic patient records systems and transition to being paperless versus a reliance on paper notes (sometimes very voluminous). All of this means that assembling data may be very laborious and a considerable part of Health Services Operations Management (HSOM) work.

It is also important to recognise that, though data are used to develop plans, when it comes to operational performance (see Figure 2.7), the data are not used to control operations to the same extent as they are by, for example, a car factory's Enterprise Resource Planning IT. Generally healthcare operational data are a *post hoc* record of what happened *which may be irregular*, e.g., the movement of a patient to a particular ward seen in the data may not be the intended or ideal activity, instead it is a result of resource problems on that (better) route or reflecting a decision made by a clinician based on some aspect of the patient's condition not captured in the data. Another example was given with Figure 2.4 where some of the very long inpatient stays may be the result of additional waits for downstream processes to be ready rather than part of the homogeneous distribution of natural recovery times. Some demand may also be hidden by patients being turned away from the service (or choosing not to enter it) if it is full or very busy. Thus, it can be difficult to use the data alone to infer general decision rules, routing and patterns, particularly in systems with many intermingled pathways and/or operating at very high utilisation (as many acute medical systems often are).

Recent research has demonstrated the systems principle that in such high-utilisation systems, small changes in patient arrivals or exits can produce dramatic changes in performance – these have been termed 'instability wedges' (Ben-Tovim et al., 2020). Similarly, the service 'machines' in healthcare are usually people, so there are feedback effects from workload. For example, it has been empirically demonstrated that (as we might have suspected) in periods of high demand service durations can be lower (like a supermarket checkout operator working faster when there is a big queue), but if this overwork is sustained then service durations can actually go up and treatment quality and safety can decline (burnout) (Kc and Terwiesch, 2009). There can also, of course, be material differences between clinical staff on experience, skill and decision preferences.

Other issues to beware of are generic to collecting and using operational data, for example *censoring*: in Figure 2.4 are we only capturing the completed length of stays? Are we counting all patients who arrived in a time window? Or who left? Or both? Does this bias the data? How long would it take to see a change after an intervention? As in Figure 2.4 there be major *outliers* to make decisions about, and the data may hide important *subpopulations* with different behaviour.

We must also be conscious of how a particular metric is being used. In operations, we are measuring to *understand*. However, in the real system it may have other meanings and consequences. Goodhart's Law reminds us that when a measure becomes a target it ceases to be a good metric – if there are strong rewards or disbenefits from some outcomes then individuals and organisations can be incentivised to misreport or behave dysfunctionally to arrive at a desirable number; in Seddon's words, strong targets convey the message 'I want you to *cheat*!' (Seddon, 1992).

A more benign reason for caution about data is: are the definitions of what and how to measure understood and applied (uniformly) by all parties? Personal experience includes a healthcare organisation reporting worse performance than it actually had because of misunderstanding the definition of the metric it was reporting.

Picking up the earlier discussion of multiple objectives, we should remember that no single metric is likely to capture all important facets of the performance of a process, particularly if there are multiple stakeholder groups. Echoing the Triple Aim in healthcare, Simon Dodds's *Three Wins* (Dodds, 2007) is a reminder to look at a system and the impact of changes from the points of view of:

- The customers (usually patients) e.g., service quality.
- The staff e.g., workload, stress, niggles.
- The organisation e.g., required performance, cost.

Ideally, we are aiming for win-win-win solutions, or at least being conscious of whether an improvement for one group makes things worse for another group. There are nice examples of quality improvement papers taking this approach in Fillingham (2007), written by a hospital organisation chief executive.

3.4 Data analysis

As we noted when considering the modelling process, in some situations, data analysis and powerful presentation (e.g., data visualisation) may be sufficient to support problem-solving; and it's worth remembering that operational data analysis capability and expertise within healthcare organisations is often limited – often consisting of lots of stand-alone Excel sheets and paper!

However, we are focusing here on when modelling is considered worthwhile. In this context data analysis plays a role in helping us explore and understand reality and in particular capture features (parameters, probability distributions, correlations, etc.) that we will want to incorporate in our models.

Figure 2.4 shows a set of patient data from general surgery. In this section we will explore it, do some basic descriptive statistics and demonstrate fitting a theoretical probability distribution. It is beyond our scope to cover details behind the statistics or how to use Excel, but the spreadsheets online are intended to demonstrate the sorts of things than can be done with spreadsheets and how the analyses in this section were produced.

3.4.1 Exploring and describing data

Figure 2.4 shows a simple histogram of the distribution of these patients' length of stay. Data visualisation is very valuable: early in work to explore, and later to communicate findings.

Visual exploration is particularly valuable to suggest issues with a dataset before quantitative work: is it homogeneous, censored, outliers, what sort of models might fit (never do a regression without visualising first!), etc?

Then at the end of a project it often is worth investing time in a powerful visualisation of your findings. Get the most out of a 'killer graph', annotate it to bring out the messages you want to convey – you can always paste a screen snip from e.g., Excel into *PowerPoint* to layer annotation over it. Script-based software tools like *R* and *Python* (free!) allow almost unlimited customisation, animations, etc. – if you are willing to put in the time to get to grips with coding. Note, Figure 2.4 omitted patients with length of stay 1 day. These are included in the dataset, and we will consider them from here on, so we have n = 3275 datapoints.

A dataset behind Figure 2.4 is available online. The data are integer values, so it is appropriate for the histogram of Figure 2.4 to have gaps between the columns. (This is the default Excel column graph format. If the X axis represented a continuous variable, there should be no gaps, except where the frequency in an interval is zero. We can make Excel remove the gaps between columns if we want.)

It's important to think about what a variable represents, how it was measured (and sometime by whom if there could be some bias!) – in some cases we need a formal definition. Here we have Length of Stay (LoS) for a large set of inpatients. But how is the number of days measured? In the UK this is traditionally the number of midnights passed in an inpatient bed, so LoS = 1 represents from one up to two days, so we might better consider this as LoS = 1.5. We also don't see any patients who attended but did not stay overnight, so LoS = 0 (i.e., 0.5 days) may be censored.

Looking at Figure 2.4, we might notice a pronounced bump in the data around LoS = 8–9 days. In smallish datasets this could well be a feature of randomness in real data, but in a dataset this large is likely to be real. In fact, multimodal features like this suggest features to investigate in the data – perhaps cycles of behaviour (e.g., a lot of patients coming in on a Monday and leaving the following Tuesday or Wednesday) or that the data are heterogeneous (it is the aggregation of several subsets).

It is important to be able to dig into data with people involved in running the process. Here we might find that we have three types of patients in the data (PatientDataAll.xlsx), for simplicity, let's call them A, B and C.

In Figure 3.2 we now see that there is wide and fairly smooth distribution of Type As, a narrow distribution of a lot of short stay patients (Type B) and a scattering of Type C long-stay patients (staying over a week). Each might themselves consist of useful subsets. We'd describe Type As having a long right tail (technically a large positive skew).

Another often useful visualisation available in Excel is the boxplot or box-and-whiskers plot. It shows the data split into quartiles (quarters) e.g., the minimum whisker to the box is where the lowest 25% of the data is. 'Outliers' (datapoints some long distance from the rest) are separated out.

In Figure 3.3, again we can see the LoS of Types B and C are quite different, and Type A has a long upper tail – picked out by the boxplot algorithm. The median and interquartile range (IQR) are fairly robust descriptors of characteristic value and spread as they are not as affected by long tails or outliers as are the mean and standard deviation. The Excel implementation of boxplots also allows display of the mean (shown by an X). We can see that in the datasets with long upper tails, the mean is higher than the median.

We now turn to numerical descriptors (having eyeballed the data as above, so we know for example that the aggregate data ('All') might be better treated as three (or more?!) underlying subsets, and Types A and C have long upper tails so the mean and standard deviation will be inflated by these 'outliers'). It's useful to remember also that common statistical tests are based on means and standard deviations, so can be distorted ('biased') by patterns in the data, long tails, outliers, etc.

See Figure 3.4. The spreadsheet available online is useful to see Excel's functions. The functions are applied to both the 'raw' LoS data and after

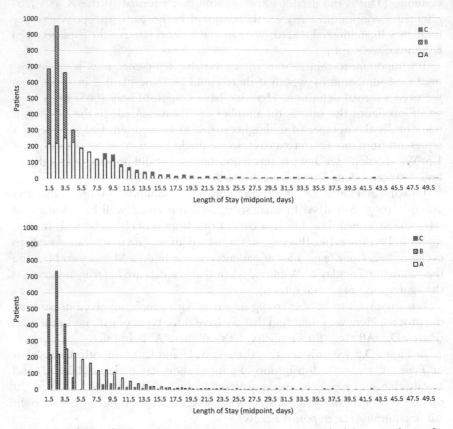

Figure 3.2 Splitting the data of Figure 2.4 by patient type (top: stacked; bottom: clustered).

adjusting (adding 0.5 days to each datapoint). You should notice the effect on the Location and Position descriptors versus the spread and shape ones.

The mean (arithmetic average) is useful in aggregate capacity planning (the mean × volume = total) but may not be representative. Much healthcare data has right (positive) skew (as these LoS examples, also costs, admission numbers, etc.). Looking, for example, at the (adjusted) Type A data, the mean LoS is 6.3 days, but the median (middle) length of stay is less (5.5 days) and the mode (most common) is much lower (3.5 days). Median or mode may be more useful when considering the 'typical' patient experience.

A useful measure of *relative* variation is the coefficient of variation (CV) = standard deviation ÷ mean. It gives us an idea about how large the 'randomness' might be, useful, for example, in considering whether (and how) to build this randomness into models. It is used directly in some queueing models as the amount of variation in arrival rates and service times.

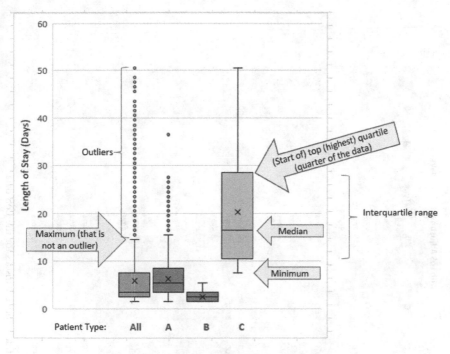

Figure 3.3 Boxplots of the LoS data.

Most of these descriptive statistics can be *estimated* from data that have already been grouped – i.e., if only a frequency table or histogram rather than the individual datapoints are available.

3.4.2 Fitting distributions

If variation is fairly large, we will need to build it into a model. For example, managing a ward (or deciding how many beds it should have) would be very different if all patients had the same LoS (CV = 0) compared with the actual situation: our data show CV > 100%, suggesting we are likely to have considerable peaks and troughs of bed occupancy, and so would need a higher number of beds to cope with the peaks. (See queueing and simulation models.) We would usually build in such variation with probability distributions, either explicitly or an assumption about what sort of distribution shape is applicable.

To illustrate this, we will consider the patient Type A data subset. We can use these 'history data' to generate an empirical distribution directly: e.g., estimating that the probability of a Type A patient having "LoS = 3" (actually 3.4 days, midpoint 3.5 days) is 254/1928 = 0.132 or 13%). A disadvantage of this is that, particularly with small datasets, the history data will inevitably contain one-off random 'bumps' and few rare (but possible) events. They are also

Numerical Descriptive Statistics					with LoS Adjustment 0.5 days			
PATIENTS:	All	A	B	C	All	A	B	C
n	3960	1928	1689	343	3960	1928	1689	343
Location:								
mean	5.42 days	5.81	2.06	19.77	5.92 days	6.31	2.56	20.27
median	3.00 days	5.00	2.00	16.00	3.50 days	5.50	2.50	16.50
mode	2.00 days	3.00	2.00	9.00	2.50 days	3.50	2.50	9.50
trimmed mean 20%	4.00 days	5.22	2.01	18.57	4.50 days	5.72	2.51	19.07
Spread:								
std dev	6.50 days	4.31	0.84	10.85	6.50 days	4.31	0.84	10.85
(std dev	6.50 days	4.31	0.84	10.83	6.50 days	4.31	0.84	10.83
variance	42.26	18.62	0.71	117.66	42.26	18.62	0.71	117.66
(variance	42.24	18.61	0.71	117.32	42.24	18.61	0.71	117.32
range	49.00 days	35.00	4.00	43.00	49.00 days	35.00	4.00	43.00
IQR	5.00 days	5.00	2.00	18.00	5.00 days	5.00	2.00	18.00
mean absolute deviation	4.24 days	3.27	0.64	9.18	4.24 days	3.27	0.64	9.18
coef of variation (CV)	1.20 120%	0.74	0.41	0.55	1.10 110%	0.68	0.33	0.54
Shape:								
skew	3.03 (right skew)	1.59	0.41	0.78	3.03 (right skew)	1.59	0.41	0.78
kurtosis	11.27	3.77	-0.41	-0.48	11.27	3.77	-0.41	-0.48
Position:								
min	1.00 days	1.00	1.00	7.00	1.50 days	1.50	1.50	7.50
max	50.00 days	36.00	5.00	50.00	50.50 days	36.50	5.50	50.50
quartile:								
1	2.00 days	3.00	1.00	10.00	2.50 days	3.50	1.50	10.50
2	3.00 days	5.00	2.00	16.00	3.50 days	5.50	2.50	16.50
3	7.00 days	8.00	3.00	28.00	7.50 days	8.50	3.50	28.50
4	50.00 days	36.00	5.00	50.00	50.50 days	36.50	5.50	50.50
percentile:								
80%	8.00 days	9.00	3.00	31.00	8.50 days	9.50	3.50	31.50

Figure 3.4 Screenshot from Excel of descriptive statistics for the LoS data.

usually cumbersome to use in models (see top-hat sampling in the simulation examples).

It would be better to use a theoretical (mathematically generated) probability distribution to model the variation, e.g., the normal distribution (AKA the Gaussian or bell-shaped curve). These are usually smooth, can generate the rare outcomes and are easier to use in models. But such a model of randomness is only useful IF it fits; fits both the situation and the data, i.e., the theoretical probability distribution/model reflects a mechanism that is plausibly generating the data and that the historical data look like could have plausibly been generated by that distribution.

The spreadsheet online demonstrates this fitting process using the Type A patients' data. The first thing is to eyeball the distribution of the data, look for any strange features, and think about what theoretical distribution shapes it represents. We should also think about the nature of the situation. Here the underlying situation is some continuous time between 0 and some possible (but very large) number (with the result having been 'bucketed' into whole-day intervals).

The earlier histograms of Figure 3.2 showed a long tail, and we notice no results below "LoS = 1" (the LoS = 1.5 midpoint interval when we adjusted the data). A patient not admitted to an inpatient ward (or not spending a night in a bed) is not in the scope of our dataset because of the way the system works, or the way data are recorded. So, in theoretical terms, we might consider the data are censored. For the sake of our modelling, let's assume we were able to find out that there were other Type A patients, who were not admitted to the inpatient ward (maybe day case patients, or some who did not spend a night). Say 87 of them. These are now added to our latest dataset as LoS = 0 (or 0.5 midpoint) patients.

The spreadsheet shows the process of fitting two alternative theoretical distributions (probability models) to the data. First the normal distribution to illustrate a very bad fit, and then an Erlang distribution, which turns out to be reasonable. The goodness-of-fit is checked visually and with a simple statistical test (chi squared). There is a limit to what is easy and sensible to do with a spreadsheet, and there are some specialist packages for distribution fitting which will test lots of other distributions and apply lots of other fit metrics, ranking fits.

As the spreadsheet shows, our uncensored dataset now has a mean LoS of 6.1 days and standard deviation 4.4 days. The spreadsheet shows the process of generating a normal distribution with these two parameters and testing the models' predictions for the expected number of patients in each LoS band against the actual number with a histogram and the chi squared goodness-of-fit test. The model is a spectacularly bad fit as both the histograms and tiny p value show!

As Figure 3.5 Fits of normal and Erlang distributions to the LoS data shows, the normal distribution is actually a very poor candidate to choose! It models a situation where the outcome is continuous (which is what we want) but one

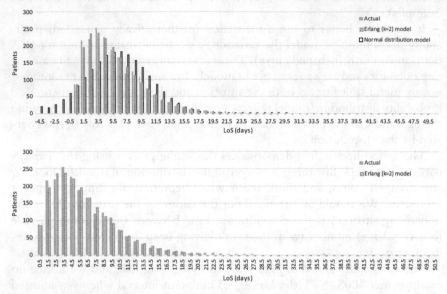

Figure 3.5 Fits of normal and Erlang distributions to the LoS data.

than lie between $-\infty$ and ∞. That it produces physically impossible results (negative days stay) is a reminder that these are *theoretical* models!

The Erlang model is much more sensible: a continuous, positive–only distribution with an upper (right) tail. The size of the tail (the skewness) is governed by the shape parameter (*k*). Setting the mean to the actual mean of 6.1 days and the shape to 2 looks a reasonable fit, visually and does not trigger the chi–squared rejection criterion of $p < 5\%$. Note that a small sample gives the test virtually no power to reject a poor fit even if it looks very poor, a very large sample gives the test so much power it can reject a fit even if it looks very good visually. Always eyeball the data. We should not expect a perfect/near-perfect fit, unless someone has (clumsily!) made up the data …

3.4.3 The potential of healthcare data

There is huge potential here, which becomes more realisable as the digital infrastructure of healthcare organisations improves, for example, through the gradual uptake of electronic health/medical records (EHR/EMR). A vision of the future for operational planning is the digital twin concept, essentially the sort of modelling tools Harper and Shahani (2002) built but running in real time and across a wider scope of the system, to help managers make real-time operational decisions about resource deployment and patient placement. They combine real-time data extraction (using e.g., EHR and the internet of things), real-time data analysis of patterns (often using advanced data science tools like machine learning) and real-time patient-flow simulation to predict the outcomes of recent and potential decisions. A small number of hospitals, mainly in the US, have such systems running which they term a Capacity Command Centre, Digital Control Centre or Mission Control. Ultimately, they are using data and modelling to make more and better predictions about patient flow, so that managers can run systems more efficiently. A vision is to have predictions reliable enough to be able to share a schedule for their hospital stay with the patients!

3.5 Types of model

In this section we outline some different types of models (or modelling techniques).

A fundamental, and very useful, model is a process map (or process flow-chart) such as that introduced in Figure 2.2. This captures a flow of objects (like patients or data) or decision logic (like admission or cancellation). Layers of information can usefully be added, such as data, metrics, known problems and potential solutions/policies to investigate. They might form a central part of the conceptual map/system under study (Figure 1.2). They can usefully be built with groups of stakeholders.

Less-structured relationships like viewpoints and chains of causal or belief logic can be captured with 'soft modelling' or 'soft operational research' problem-structuring techniques ranging from rich pictures (rather like a cartoon sketch) to highly structured logic systems such as Soft Systems Methodology (Pidd, 2009) or Current Reality Trees (Cox and Spencer, 1998).

We are mainly focusing here on 'hard' (quantitative) models. The previous section (3.4) covered some statistical models for describing variation – theoretical models like the normal probability distribution, and empirical, summarised by e.g., a histogram. Other statistical models can be built with techniques like multiple regression or machine learning algorithms such as neural networks.

Models can be labelled as **descriptive**: describing what has happened e.g., a theoretical probability distribution that fits the randomness in historical data; **predictive** e.g., how likely is it than more than 15 patients will arrive at the emergency department between 09:00 and 10:00? (and there are modelling techniques built for forecasting); and **prescriptive** to help us examine the consequences of choices and so decide what action to take. These last, prescriptive, models are our main interest in this section.

We can try to get a handle on the types of 'hard' modelling approaches by categorising them on two dimensions: their assumption about randomness/variation, and the approach to model building, as in Table 3.2.

Deterministic versus stochastic models (the vertical dimension) distinguish whether uncertainty in inputs is explicitly built into models or not. Deterministic

Table 3.2 Examples of some types of 'hard' (quantitative) models

		Model type	
		Analytical • maths *1.1 Deterministic–Analytical*	Experimental • simulation *1.2 Deterministic–Experimental*
	Deterministic • Input → Output	**Linear programming** Critical Path Project Management	**System dynamics simulation**
Assumptions about the situation	Stochastic • Input + randomness → Outputs	*2.1 Stochastic Analytical* PERT Project Management **Queueing theory** Markov processes	*2.2 Stochastic–Experimental* **Monte Carlo simulation** **Discrete event simulation**

models operate like clockwork, producing one answer. Stochastic includes inputs in the form of probability distributions and so results are in the form of expected (mean) values and a distribution of possibilities. The horizontal dimension, analytical versus experimental, distinguishes how the models are built and used. Analytical models are built with mathematical equations and solved through mathematics (e.g., optimisation). In experimental models, the logic is built and worked through iteratively to examine the consequents.

Another class of techniques is called *heuristics*: these are rules of thumb for usually producing good solutions in situations where optimisation is not possible. These situations may arise because there are too many possibilities to be evaluated (e.g., three patients could be ordered for an operation in $3 \times 2 \times 1 = 6$ ways [6!, 6 factorial], but with 10 there are 10! = 3,628,800 ways), or because our optimisation algorithm might get stuck in a local optimum (a good analogy is that it is like trying to find the highest point in a mountain range on a foggy day; from its starting point it could be set to always head in the direction of steepest ascent, but then when it reaches a highest point we can't guarantee that there isn't a higher peak at the top of another mountain out there in the fog).

There are sets of algorithms designed for situations like simple job scheduling (a basic one is to take jobs in order of shortest processing time), and also more general optimisation such as tabu search, simulated annealing and genetic algorithms. All use iterative solution-improvement. The last two use an element of randomness to perturb the current optimal candidate solutions in the hope of jumping out of a local optimum. They cannot guarantee optimality, and like a simple exhaustive search, the longer they run (and the larger the degree of random perturbation) the better the solution may be. Pidd (2009) has a very readable introduction to these algorithms. The case in Chapter 16 uses simulated annealing to schedule medical specialists.

Modelling techniques in bold in the table are introduced in this section, and the two dimensions and four categories will be explained in more detail below.

3.5.1 Analytical models

Analytical models (quadrants 1.1 and 2.1 in Table 3.2) relate input to outputs using mathematical relationships. Deterministic models do not build in any uncertainty – any uncertainty is dealt with 'manually' by constructing and running a range of scenarios. Stochastic analytical models incorporate uncertainty through probability distributions – either implicit (assumed to build the mathematical relationships) or explicitly.

With some formulations of analytical models, we might try to find optimal solutions through algorithms (e.g., calculus or the mathematics programming simplex technique) or by 'what-if?' trial and error. For some situations there may be too many possibilities to examine, for example in a scheduling problem with ten patients for surgery, there are 3,628,800 possible orders in which they can be sequenced ($10! = 10 \times 9 \times 8 \dots 1 = 3{,}628{,}800$ permutations). For such problems there may be heuristic algorithms (good rules of thumb) or other guided what-if approaches such as genetic algorithms.

3.5.1.1 Deterministic analytical models

We will introduce analytical modelling approaches through a small mathematical optimisation model.

3.5.1.1.1 ECONOMIC ORDER QUANTITY (EOQ)

As a simple introduction to models in quadrant 1.1 of Table 3.2, consider the optimisation task of deciding what quantity of a consumable to order in the following situation:

- The demand is D items per year.
- The cost of holding an item is h per year (covers things like: the cost of the space taken; the opportunity cost of capital tied up; the risk of obsolescence, damage or theft; cost of stock audit and maintenance; maintaining appropriate storage conditions and security; etc.).
- The fixed overhead cost of placing an order is K per order (covers: delivery charge; administrative and handling time; etc.).

If you place orders for quantity Q, then you would be placing D/Q orders a year with a total ordering overhead cost of KD/Q.

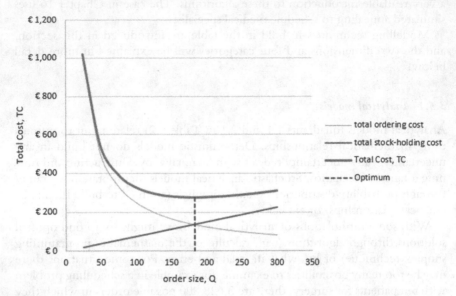

Figure 3.6 Graphical representation of inventory model and its components.

The average amount of items you would be holding would be $Q/2$, so the total annual holding cost would be $hQ/2$.

The total cost would be:

$$TC = K\frac{D}{Q} + h\frac{Q}{2}$$

The optimum order quantity, Q^*, can be determined by trial and error (what-if) or calculus.

There is an example model built in Excel with the online supplement.

Trial and error (trying different values for Q) might produce a graph such as Figure 3.6.

> We can see the trade-off between larger orders reducing the total ordering cost versus smaller orders reducing the total holding cost.

From calculus you can find the optimum quickly:

$$Q^* = \sqrt{\frac{2DK}{h}}$$

A sheet of the Inventory spreadsheet model adds a calculation of the reorder level (ROL), the stock level at which we need to reorder if we can assume what the delivery and restocking lead time is.

Elaborations of the model consider protection against uncertainty through additional safety stock – we pick this up in the stochastic models section. The model can also be used to determine the optimum batch size (e.g., for running pathology lab testing equipment), trading off the delay to build up the batch versus number processed per machine cycle. There is much more detail and many elaborations in texts such as Hopp and Spearman (2011).

3.5.1.1.2 MATHEMATICAL PROGRAMMING

A major class of techniques also in quadrant 1.1 of Table 3.2 is mathematical programming models. These are designed to optimise an objective in the subject of constraints on what solutions are allowed (feasible). We will introduce this through a small example – small enough to be solvable by Excel's inbuilt Solver function. Very much larger problems can be solved with a commercial version of Solver, or purpose-built software packages or computer code libraries. Pidd's (2009) text gives a basic introduction to linear programming and use of the inbuilt Solver, which will solve small optimisation problems.

The example is assignment of operating theatres to consultant surgeons (see the Excel file online). Suppose we have five consultants and five theatre slots, and the aim is to use as many slots as possible.

The consultants are only able (and willing) to work in particular theatres, as represented by 1s in the table in Figure 3.7 (blank cells are actually 0s, formatted to appear be blank for clarity). a_{tc} are variables, for example $a_{2,5} = 1$ indicates that the assignment of Sue to operate in Theatre B is allowed.

We need to choose how to assign who uses which theatre by putting a 1 in the corresponding cells of the table in Figure 3.8. These variables are called **decision variables** and, for this problem, should be 0 or 1 (binary variables). If $x_{2,5} = 0$ then the overall policy would include the decision *not* to assign Sue to operate in Theatre B.

Figure 3.9 shows one solution, which is *feasible* because the constraint limits are not exceeded (no consultant can be assigned to more than one theatre, and no theatre can be assigned more than one consultant).

	Allowed, a_{tc}	Theatres, t				
		A	B	C	D	E
Consultants, c Debbie			1	1		
Dick					1	1
Harry		1				
Jane			1	1	1	
Sue			1			
Tom					1	1

Figure 3.7 Screenshot from Excel showing the table of possible (allowed) assignments.

Assignment, x_{tc}	A	B	C	D	E	use	limit
Debbie						0	1
Dick						0	1
Harry						0	1
Jane						0	1
Sue						0	1
Tom						0	1
use	0	0	0	0	0		
limit	1	1	1	1	1		

Figure 3.8 Screenshot from Excel model showing the table for candidate assignments.

Assignment, x_{tc} these are the decision variables	A	B	C	D	E	use	limit
Debbie		1				1	1
Dick					1	1	1
Harry	1					1	1
Jane			1			1	1
Sue						0	1
Tom				1		1	1
use	1	1	1	1	1		
limit	1	1	1	1	1		

Figure 3.9 Screenshot from Excel showing a feasible assignment.

Excel works out the consequences of any such policy (set of assignments). Here we have set the overall metric for how good a policy is by summing up how many theatres are assigned. This is the *objective* (shaded in Figure 3.10). The value in each cell is the values in the corresponding cell of the table in Figure 3.7 and decision variable table (Figure 3.9) multiplied together e.g., $a_{2,5} \times x_{2,5}$ is $1 \times 0 = 0$.

This policy was chosen by setting up the problem in Excel's Solver, with the objective of maximising the value in the objective cell. This is set up in the accompanying spreadsheet.

An operational research analyst would usually express this analytical optimisation model as a series of mathematical equations:

Use, $a_{tc}x_{tc}$	A	B	C	D	E		use
Debbie	0	1	0	0	0		1
Dick	0	0	0	0	1		1
Harry	1	0	0	0	0		1
Jane	0	0	1	0	0		1
Sue	0	0	0	0	0		0
Tom	0	0	0	1	0		1
use	1	1	1	1	1	5	5

Figure 3.10 Screenshot from Excel showing the consequences (costs or payoffs).

Max $use = \sum_t \sum_c a_{tc} x_{tc}$ (this is the objective function, sometimes called the z function).

Subject to: (this is the list of constraints that must *all* be satisfied for a feasible solution).

$\sum_t x_{tc} \leq 1$ for all c each consultant can only be in one theatre.

$\sum_c x_{tc} \leq 1$ for all t each theatre can only have one consultant.

x_{tc} must be $(0,1)$ these are the decision variables and for this problem are binary. a_{tc} are elements of the Allowed assignments table. Instead of 0,1 they could have values representing some other aspect to maximise, for example how many patients a consultant would operate on if they were assigned that session, or some measure of preference or priority.

This mathematical programming above is an example of a binary linear pro-gramme: all variables can be only 0 or 1. We could imagine a version of this formulation where the 'able' table instead contained the expected number of patients a consultant could treat in the session, and we were trying to maximise the total number treated: an integer linear programming problem. Or that table could hold continuous variables such as the net revenue the hospital would earn: a mixed integer linear programming problem.

Problems like these then inflate very rapidly in size: many surgeons and theatres. We've also not considered the time dimension. Our problem above might represent one morning on one particular day of a particular week. A five-day week with two slots a day would have ten slots, so ten theatre-con-sultant tables. A (small) hospital with 100 consultant surgeons and 20 operating theatres looking at assignments over a four-week cycle would have 80,000 decision variables.

In addition to the above assignment problem, there are several other types that might be formulated as a type of mathematical programme including determining how much material to supply from which depots to which destinations to minimise travel distance or cost, and deciding where to locate facilities (e.g., ambulance staging posts) to minimise travel time or distance.

3.5.1.2 *Stochastic analytical models*

We now turn to mathematical programming quadrant 2.1 of Table 3.2.

3.5.1.2.1 SIMPLE STOCHASTIC INVENTORY MODEL – SAFETY STOCK

We will return to the inventory model (see spreadsheet online) to introduce stochastic analytical models with a simple example. In the previous model, we saw we could calculate the reorder level (ROL) – i.e., at what stock level to trigger a reorder. (In a lean system, there might be a reorder prompt card placed in the inventory racks this many items from the back.)

That assumes that the demand is deterministic – it goes down at a constant and known rate, reaching 0 at the same time as the reorder arrives and is ready to replenish the stock. Demand might be materially unpredictable. This ROL might be the expected (long-run mean) demand during the reorder lead time, but random peaks of demand in this period may result in us running out before the replenishment.

The usual solution is to add some extra safety margin to the previous (deterministic) ROL. This safety stock can be calculated to reduce the risk of running out to a desired level. The spreadsheet uses the assumption of a normal distribution of demand. We calculate the standard deviation of all the demand that will occur in the lead time. Then use the normal distribution to convert the risk to the corresponding z value (number of standard deviations) from the standard normal distribution (for example, common values are 10% risk corresponds to $z = 1.28$, 5% risk to 1.64). Multiplying this z value by the standard deviation in the lead time gives us the additional **safety stock** we should add to the deterministic ROL.

It is very common to use this normal distribution assumption, but we should really use history data to try to determine whether this is a reasonable fit – and if not use some other theoretical distribution or the empirical distribution (the raw history).

3.5.1.2.2 QUEUEING THEORY MODELS

A more complex example from quadrant 2.1 of Table 3.2 is modelling queueing situations. The Danish mathematician Agner Krarup Erlang pioneered queueing theory at the Copenhagen Telephone Company in the early 1900s when considering problems like how many switchboard operators would be needed to handle given volumes of calls.

As a simple example, consider a GP (family doctor) surgery with one receptionist whose job is to answer the phone when patients ring. If all calls took exactly two minutes to deal with (so he or she could deal with 30 calls an hour), and patients rang at exactly two–minute intervals (30 per hour), then the receptionist could handle all calls with no waits for patients, though they would be very busy: working at 100% utilisation. If, however, there is any variation in call lengths (some are easy, some are complex) or times of arrival (with random bunches and gaps) then queues will form. In fact, this will happen at less than 100% utilisation. This is because the receptionist cannot 'store' his/her capacity when there is no caller to bring out when callers arrive bunched close together in order to catch up. In operations management terms, we say that the capacity is 'perishable'.

We can describe the performance of the system logically, and with some basic assumptions, this description can be mathematical. The standard, basic set of assumptions are:

- Calls arrive randomly: the number of calls per hour follows a Poisson probability distribution with mean λ.
- Calls take a random amount of time to answer (talking to the patient): the average time is t_e and the variation is described by an exponential probability distribution.
- The above means that if the reception were always busy, then the number of calls per hour that could be dealt with follows a Poisson probability distribution with mean μ ($=60/t_e$).
- No caller in the queue gives up (reneges).
- There is no limit to how many calls can be held in the queue.
- The arrival and service time distributions are not changing over time.
- The system has been running long enough to reach steady state (on average the queues are not getting longer or shorter).

For illustration, Figure 3.11 shows a Poisson distribution with a mean of 25, representing the probability of any number of calls (arrival events) in an hour when the mean is 25 per hour. For service durations, the Poisson distribution models the number of calls that the receptionist could handle in an hour (the number of service events), *if* he/she were always busy. It is more natural to think about the actual duration of each call. The flip side of the Poisson distribution is the exponential distribution: the Poisson distribution models the number of events in a time interval, the exponential the time between them (so here the inter-arrival time of calls or the service durations). The means of the Poisson distribution and corresponding exponential are the reciprocal to each other. For illustration, Figure 3.11 also shows the exponential distribution modelling service (call) times taking on average two minutes (corresponding to a Poisson distribution with mean 30 per hour). The calculations are in the Excel workbook *GP Phone Queue.xlsx).*

(Poisson/exponential is often a reasonable model for random arrivals. For service time it may also be reasonable, though for human service other

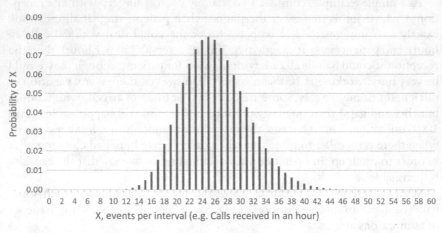

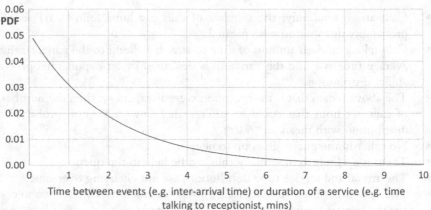

Figure 3.11 Poisson distribution with mean 25 per hour and corresponding exponential distribution with mean 2 mins.

distributions such as the Erlang or lognormal may often fit the situation better. More on this in the section on simulation.)

We then have some intermediate variables:

- The traffic intensity is called ρ and is just λ/μ.
- The utilisation of the server (here the receptionist), u, is $\lambda/(s\mu)$; s is the number of servers here = 1).

This system is called an M/M/1 queue (the M stands for Markovian, related to the assumptions of Poisson distributions).

These assumptions allow performance measures to be derived (if you are interested in the algebra behind this, see an operations research text such as Hillier and Lieberman (2020)).

For the M/M/1 queue the algebra produces this simple formula for the *average* queue length:

$$L_q = \frac{\rho^2}{1-\rho}$$

Putting some numbers:

- Say the calls are coming in are 25 per hour on average, so $\lambda = 25$ per hour.
- And it takes two minutes to answer, so $t_e = 2$ minutes, $\mu = 30$ per hour.
- And so the traffic intensity $\rho = 0.83$.
- And the utilisation (busyness) of the receptionist is 83% (he/she is talking to callers 83% of the time).
- And so the queue length $L_q = 4.17$ patients.

It's important to realise that these figures are averages (expected values): the queue length at any instant must be an integer (could be zero) and will go up and down randomly over time, and at any instant the utilisation of the receptionist must either be 100% (talking to a caller) or 0% (waiting for a call).

From one of these performance measures, we can derive others, for example we can use the well-known Little's Law in operations management $L_q = \lambda W_q$ to derive the average caller time in the queue:

$$W_q = \frac{\rho^2}{\lambda(1-\rho)}$$

Putting in our numbers gives 0.17 hours (10 minutes).

We can use the model to do what-ifs, for example what would we predict would happen if the average calls volumes increase or decrease. See Figure 3.12 and the Excel spreadsheet online.

For example, we can see that expected waiting times reach half an hour if call volumes increase to 28 per hour (a 12% demand increase), and an hour at 29 calls per hour (16% demand increase), with receptionist utilisations of 93% and 97% respectively. These could be thresholds at which we might, for example, be concerned about patients giving up and setting off for a hospital emergency department or deciding to switch practice and so they lose the headcount fee – some practices have done simple cost-benefit analysis on this.

There are many other queueing models, including multi-server models (so one can model the trade-off impacts of hiring additional receptionists) and some approximations allowing us to relax some of the assumptions. The models also allow us to quantify the great benefits from applying operations management

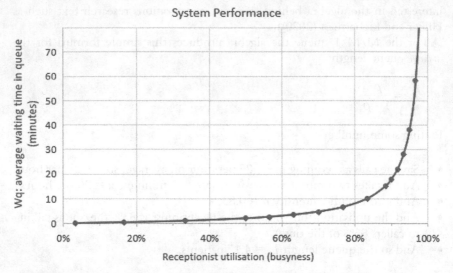

Figure 3.12 Performance of the GP phone queue as the system gets busier.

principles such as reducing variation and pooling capacity. For more models, examples and insights on queueing models and insights in healthcare management contexts, see Proudlove (2020). Chapter 11 takes queueing models a little further, drawing on that paper.

The important thing we are trying to illustrate is that, *if* the necessary assumptions fit reasonably well, analytical models enable us to produce results on some performance metrics very quickly.

We should of course check the assumptions with data from the real system – both with data on arrivals and service times and also comparing our results with real system outputs ('black box validation').

If the assumptions do *not* fit (reasonably) well, or we want to obtain some more detailed performance metrics, then we would usually turn to computer simulation modelling.

3.5.2 *Simulation models*

When a model becomes too complicated to solve analytically, we switch to simulation: describing the logic of the system to a computer programme, parameterising it with data and running it to see what happens. 'Too complicated' may happen, in particular because we have several stochastic processes in our model and/or entities in them interact (e.g., patients 'competing' through time for beds) and/or we may simply want to see the elementary logic feeding through rather than 'trusting' to a class of algorithm (for example an analytical queueing model). A major reason is because we know that the behaviour of our real system departs materially from the assumptions of an analytical model (e.g., constant mean arrival rate, with a Poisson distribution) – i.e., the simplifications necessary to build the mathematical model depart far from our reality, so we should not trust the mathematical results.

There are four main types of simulation:

- Monte Carlo (MC) simulation.
- Discrete-event simulation (DES).
- System dynamics (SD) simulation.
- Agent-based modelling and simulation (ABMS).

plus various hybrids.

Pidd's (2009) text gives an accessible introduction to the first three of these, which we recommend for going a little deeper than the following overview. The choice of approach generally depends on the characteristics of the problem, in particular the level of detail required to capture what is important.

With experimental models we are in pure 'what-if' territory and usually limited to investigating only a few policies or scenarios. Selecting these would be based on insights gained from building such detailed models, as well as drawing on principles from disciplines such as operations management and the knowledge and ideas of stakeholders.

MC simulation (quadrant 2.2 of Table 3.2) is a term now generally used to mean stochastic simulation performed using a spreadsheet. Fairly simple models are easy to build driven by using Excel's random number function (RAND()). VBA (Visual Basic for Applications script, also known as Excel macros), can make models faster and manipulate data better. Commercial add-ins are available which provide some additional functions for tasks like random sampling from probability distributions and collating results. The term 'Monte Carlo' actually means that a particular run of a simulation (trial) follows through the consequences of a particular (random) outcome from an event to the next, for example a trial might simulate one possible night out in a casino in Monte Carlo, carrying the increase or decrease in your pile of chips from roulette wheel to roulette wheel through the night. At no stage during the trial (night out) do we take an 'average outcome'. Instead, we run very many trials (possible nights out) and so capture a distribution of lots of individual possibilities. In this sense all or most stochastic simulation is 'Monte Carlo'.

As with all simulation models, the procedure is to build and validate a model (iteratively), then understand the location and cause of problematic outcomes (e.g., long patient waits) and then do 'what-if?' experiment investigations into the effects of changes to the system. The credibility of the predicted outcomes of these changes rest on validation of the initial (as-is) model.

3.5.2.1 *Operating theatre list duration – Monte Carlo simulations*

The online supplement contains a set of Monte Carlo simulations of the possible end time of an operating theatre list which consists of three operations (*theatre MC simulation*). We assume that how long each operation takes does not depend on the duration of any of the others (they are said to be independent), and we are interested in the total list duration. (More detail and examples of these types of models can be found in texts such as Pidd (2009) and Robinson (2014).)

There are three versions of this simulation in the workbook.

The first assumes each operation takes a random time according to a normal distribution (the classic 'Gaussian' bell-shaped curve). Each of the three operations has a different mean and standard deviation (spread). The *Normal Distribution* sheet is a tool to show what these look like – see top left graph in Figure 3.13. Note that theoretical statistical distributions like this are just that: *theoretical*. Some (like the normal distribution) can produce negative outcomes. In this context negative operation durations are meaningless, so are something we might consider elaborating a model to override (we've not done that here).

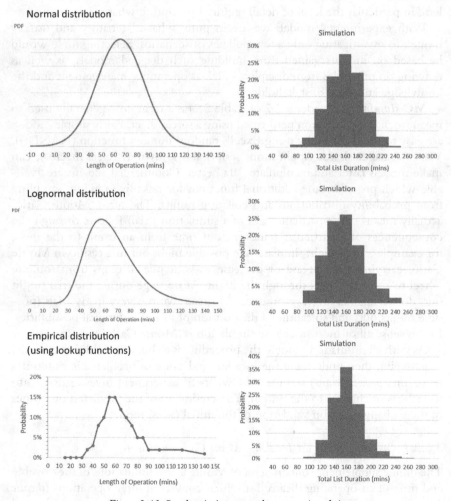

Figure 3.13 Stochastic inputs and outputs (results).

The first simulation is on the *Simulation – Normal model* sheet. At the top of the sheet, we have our input parameters. Operation A, the first on the list for the theatre session, is estimated to have a mean of 65 minutes with a standard deviation (SD) of 20 minutes (see Figure 3.14). These parameter values may come from fitting theoretical probability distributions to some historical data for this type of operation, or surgeons' estimates. We have also specified some outcome metrics we are interested in, here:

- What is the list duration which we will exceed on only 20% of occasions?
- What is the risk that the list takes more than 180 minutes?

In this particular case, with all three operations being modelled with normal distributions, we could actually persevere with an *analytical* model, since adding normal distributions produces an overall distribution which also has the same normal distribution shape. We can just add the means and variance (squares of the standard deviations) and do calculations on a normal distribution with those aggregate parameters.

The 'analytical model' part of the sheet shows this (see Figure 3.15) and uses Excel functions to calculate the results on our two performance metrics.

For demonstration, we've also set up a Monte Carlo simulation on this sheet (see Figure 3.16).

The rows headed 'Trials' are 1000 separate simulations of the operating theatre list. In each cell is a sample (a randomly chosen outcome) from a normal distribution with the parameters at the top of the sheet (e.g., for Operation

INPUTS					
Operation	A	B	C		
mean	65	60	35		mins
SD	20	20	10		mins
risk threshold				20%	
threshold duration				180	mins

Figure 3.14 Inputs to the operating theatre list duration MC model.

RESULTS				
analytical model				
results:				
Operation	A	B	C	Total List Time
mean	65	60	35	160.00 mins
SD	20	20	10	30.00 mins
Duration equating to risk threshold				185.25 mins
P(t > threshold duration)				25%

Figure 3.15 Results summary from the operating theatre list duration analytical model.

simulation model				
Operation	**A**	**B**	**C**	**Total List Time**
no. of trials				*1000*
mean	64.01	61.39	34.88	160.28 *mins*
SD	20.28	19.92	9.79	30.22 *mins*
min				55.29
max				257.46
Duration equating to risk threshold				186.24 *mins*
P(t>threshold)				27% *mins*
Trials	*press F9 to re-run the simulation*			
1	39.90	61.45	48.02	149.37 *mins*
2	72.17	29.31	37.88	139.35 *mins*
3	76.98	65.03	45.65	187.65 *mins*
4	54.78	66.58	48.48	169.84 *mins*
5	63.88	36.47	45.29	145.64 *mins*
6	65.21	57.17	36.72	159.21

Figure 3.16 Sample of results from the operating theatre list duration MC simulation model.

A mean = 65 mins, SD = 20 mins. Simulations in Excel like this are driven by Excel's RAND() function. Each time the sheet recalculates (which can be forced by the user pressing the *F9* key), this function generates a new random number between 0 and 1, with uniform probability across this range. For some theoretical probability distributions this uniform random number can then be used as an input to an Excel function that will generate an outcome from another probability distribution. (If you are interested in the statistical detail of how this works see e.g., Pidd (2004).)

The top right graph in Figure 3.13 shows a set of 1000 simulated outcomes (trials) of the list as a histogram. Each time you press *F9* the outcomes will be resampled and so the histogram will change. On the sheet above the trials are some summary statistics. Note that the means and standard deviations of the 1000 trials are not exactly the same as the input parameters (e.g., 65.0 and 25.0). This is the result of the randomness of sampling. The extent to which different sets of 1000 trials are similar helps us judge whether this number of trials is sufficient to be representative.

The other rows of Figure 3.13 shows some variation on this model. The middle row uses lognormal probability distributions to model the variation in duration of each operation. This is often a good theoretical probability model for this type of process. Outcomes are always > 0 and with a right skew: there is a small chance that the process (operation, phone call, etc.) will take very much longer than most.

The bottom row of Figure 3.13 does not use theoretical probability distributions. Instead, discrete probability values have been input for a set of possible durations. We might use this approach if we have empirical data (e.g., historical data) or estimates from surgeons which do not fit any practically useable theoretical distribution reasonably well. It is a cruder approach, with less-detailed variation than from a theoretical distribution and probably missing the possibility of rare (but maybe consequential) 'tail' events. Excel's RAND() function is used with LOOKUP functions to pick out the corresponding row from the sorted table of cumulative probabilities. See e.g., Pidd (2009) and Robinson (2014) for more examples and details.

The problem situation considered in this example is very simple. Nonetheless, compared with an analytical model, we can use a wider range of probability distributions and enquire about many types of outcome metric. Being able to build, lay out and demonstrate the logic in 'atomic' detail can be useful for validation and for explanation and demonstration to stakeholders (compared to sets of 'black-box' mathematical equations). Being able to explicitly see a large number of possible outcomes (rather than, for example, just expected [average] values or a probability for a specific outcome) may reveal patterns which give insights into the emergent behaviour of the system and suggest how it might be managed better.

The real power of simulation comes as the logic of a problem situation gets more complex. For example, there may be threshold effects (e.g., if the first two operations together take more than 120 minutes then the third is cancelled), or correlations (e.g., data may show that if a previous operation on the list has taken much more or less time than expected then the following one may usually be the same, or perhaps usually the opposite), or other events may interact (e.g., a small probability of persistent problems with equipment or staff). In Excel we can use IF statements in the logic; some software may give us the possibility to include covariances between probability distributions. Some knowledge of VBA, etc. can allow more efficient, quicker and more compact Excel models and the construction of user interfaces. There are also commercial add-ons for Excel designed to allow easier, more sophisticated and more efficient Monte Carlo simulation.

This type of simulation is often used for tasks such as financial and/or risk analysis in project management, where time can be 'sliced' into quite wide chunks (e.g., year as a unit of time). Situations like the GP phone queue require more detailed modelling of time. Although we can sample arrival times and service durations (including exponential and Poisson distributions) in Excel, this gets long-winded and messy with lots of entities (e.g., calls) flowing through a system, and introducing real-world elaborations, like different types of callers, different routings of calls through options trees, etc. makes Excel unsuitable as a tool. Instead, we turn to specialist approaches and more powerful software.

DES (quadrant 2.2 of Table 3.2) focuses on modelling the interactions of an entity (e.g., a patient) interacting with other entities and resources (e.g., beds) through simulated time. It is a common paradigm to model the flow of patients through a pathway where they may need to wait for resources to finish with other patients. Very detailed models can be built, with complicated probability distribution and logical rules determining things like arrival time, service duration, which branch or a pathway to go down etc. Entities can carry information (labels, variables, attributes) such as age, sex, severity of illness, timestamps, etc., which can be used to determine priority in queues or routing or capture information for analysis or segmentation of results. The simulation mechanics works out when the next event (e.g., patient arrival or completion of treatment) happens, so the simulation clock can jump to the time of the next event rather than having to time slice through the entire period. The discipline of building a model of successive activity (e.g., triage), queues, activity (e.g., treatment), queue, etc. maps nicely to the way we often think about flow in operations management (e.g., a process map or value stream map). It has been the most common simulation approach in HSOM.

Very simple models can be built in spreadsheets, or they can be programmed in software, but generally high-level software is used. These also provide visual interfaces to both build a model and watch it run – very useful for understanding, validation and demonstration. In the accompanying online material there are some links to examples – for example watch the video of the emergency room (ER) simulation running, and how note how the analyst uses the results to experiment with changes to the system. As we commented in the Introduction, think about how much effort may have gone into the modelling (and graphics!) relative to understanding the real system and contextually feasible options for change. What might the modeller's interests and expertise have been? Are *operations management* insights (waste, flow variation) being drawn, rather than just 'what if we had more … (doctors, beds etc)?'! Is this 'model simple, think complicated' or the reverse?!

SD simulation (quadrant 1.2 of Table 3.2) usually takes a high-level, aggregate view of stock and flow, using time-slicing. For example, the stock (number) of healthy citizens in a city or country susceptible to an infectious disease, flowing through a set of other stocks (Exposed, Infected, Recovered) – the basic SEIR model (e.g., Currie et al., 2020). The analogy is water flowing through pipes between tanks (stocks). The rate of flow (the valves) is determined by variables changing over time through user policies or feedback from elsewhere in the system, e.g., vaccination policies govern the rate of flow from unvaccinated to vaccinated, the number of infected people feeds back to determine the rate at which the exposed become infected. Again, simple models can be built in spreadsheets, but high-level specialist software is usually used – see the online materials that go with this section. A simple Excel Covid model is demonstrated in Dodds and Bradley (2020) and there are many larger models in specialist software linked in the accompanying online material.

Generally, entities are indistinguishable (cf. water molecules), so don't have attributes, and stochastic outcomes are aggregated to constant proportions going down a branch or a proportion of Infected moving to Recovered in each time slice. Some packages are starting to allow layering of identical models to represent an attribute, for example, age band or region of the country. We have placed this technique in quadrant 2.2 of Table 3.2: there are usually no stochastic elements in the model, but the interrelationships and feedbacks often produce complex emergent behaviour over the time. The consequences are worked through iteratively in a computer model in an 'experimental' manner. Some software is also starting to allow the addition of some individual discrete Monte Carlo outcomes (e.g., so a single infected person on day 1 would either result in one or two infected people on day 2 rather than the proportional outcome of e.g., 1.25 infected people).

ABMS is similar to DES, but without the 'train tracks' of a prestructured entry-to-exit pathway. The focus is entities (agents) 'bouncing' around between states and interacting. This is the paradigm used to build the detailed infectious disease models used by several governments' official teams of scientific advisers during Covid. Models are generally built using a coding language. Large models (e.g., of a population of hundreds of thousands of interacting individuals over many months of simulated time can be very computationally demanding. Goldenbogen et al. (2020) give details of the working of their Covid model. An agent's (citizen's) state is expressed by the values on each of a set of attributes (e.g., Disease = susceptible, infected, recovered, dead; Location = home, work, school, hospital, public places, morgue; Disease state = healthy, undiagnosed, diagnosed, hospitalised, in ICU, dead; etc). Demographic data was used to also set subpopulations' household, age and work profile, which govern their usual schedule of location changes. Citizens move around over time accordingly, and contacts with infected people trigger a die roll against a calculated threshold to determine whether they become infected. What-if experiments were run on different types of government interventions to reduce contacts.

ABMS and hybrid (combinations) are becoming more popular, but generally require deeper technical skills than DES or MC.

3.6 Summary and reflections

This chapter has delved into the processes involved in the transitions between the three levels: reality – system – model (Figure 1.2). The best teacher here is probably experience, but we have tried to give a flavour of the activities involved and particular issues to watch out for.

It has also opened the lid of the box labelled 'model' in Figure 1.2. There are many approaches in the modelling toolkit. This chapter has introduced the basic ideas of some common and archetypical operational research techniques, together with an introduction to the data analysis usually required to extract parameters to feed models and to test the prerequisite assumptions of the techniques and our model formulations.

All modelling approaches have their pros and cons. Table 3.3 uses the structure of Table 3.2 to summarise some of these.

But the overriding considerations should be the purpose of the modelling and the nature of the situation – i.e., what aspects of the reality are abstracted

Table 3.3 Pros and cons of types of modelling technique

	Analytical • maths	Experimental • simulation
Deterministic • Input → Output	1.1 Deterministic–Analytical ✓quick to build and solve ✓compact ✗ exacting assumptions ✗ can be hard to explain to managers	1.2 Deterministic–Experimental ✓can build models of more complex situations ✓easier to demonstrate to managers ✗time consuming and difficult to build and validate ✗ usually requires specialist software (cost and expertise)
Stochastic • Input + randomness → Outputs	2.1 Stochastic Analytical as above ✗ requires some statistical expertise	2.2 Stochastic–Experimental as left and as above

as the relevant system under study (or conceptual model) models (Figure 1.2). For example, at the tactical level of decision making (Figure 2.8), we can often work at a fairly aggregate levels, so it is not always necessary to include stochastics explicitly, so deterministic models may be sufficient. Similarly, in situations with low variation and relatively low utilisation. However, particularly at the operational level, many healthcare processes are working at high utilisation (so towards dangerously steep righthand end-of-performance curves as illustrated in the GP phone call queue example in Figure 3.12 and are subject to high variation, so the stochastics are important – so taking us into more complicated modelling techniques.

Simulation, in particular, allows us to add layers of detail and complexity, but we need to keep thinking about whether this is justified – is it taking us (usefully) closer to the important aspects of the reality, or away from it?! To paraphrase a quotation attributed to Einstein: models should be as simple as possible, but no simpler; and then, paraphrasing Pidd from the 'principles of model building' section: having modelled simple, think complicated! i.e., are we using our models to gain insight and answer questions that are sensible in the context of the reality?

An interesting cautionary tale is provided by a pair of HSOM studies of operating theatre space allocation policy. The first study (Wullink et al., 2007) used a (DES) simulation model to suggest that reserving capacity (slots) for emergency cases across the other (elective) theatre sessions is better than having a separate operating theatre dedicated to emergencies; this result was acted on and the hospital's emergency OT was closed. However, a later study (van Veen-Berkx et al., 2016) of the impact, and comparing this with other hospitals which carried on with a dedicated emergency theatre (as 'controls') found the opposite! Digging into the reasons, the later authors noted that the earlier researchers had commented on the limitations of their work, including that their model i) was (of course) an 'abbreviated version of reality' unable to incorporate all real-world constraints, and ii) the alternative policy they modelled (closing the emergency theatre) (of course) made assumptions about the subsequent behaviour of the staff in the system. In particular, van Veen-Berkx et al. (2016) found that not all the surgical departments were complying with the new policy (reserving an agreed amount of their theatre session space for emergencies).

This illustrates a couple of important points. Firstly, pooling capacity across chains for the common good can conflict with incentives within particular chains and is very important: when modelling human activity systems, we must be aware of the potential impacts on human behaviour and attempt to understand the drivers of this behaviour. Secondly, even sophisticated models make many assumptions, and so the results should be treated with caution. Empirical (real-life) evidence trumps predictions from models, so real-life testing of recommendations based on models is important to pick up aspects that may have been covered inadequately in the models. Real-life testing and iteratively refining changes are an important part of quality improvement approaches, covered in Chapter 6.

Later chapters contain some larger examples of applications of models to healthcare problems.

3.7 Questions and exercises

See online supplement.

References

Ben-Tovim D, Bogomolov T, Filar J, Hakendorf P, Qin S and Thompson C (2020). Hospital's instability wedges. *Health Systems*, 9(3), 202–211. https://doi.org/10.1080/20476965.2018.1524407.

Berwick DM, Nolan TW and Whittington J (2008). The triple aim: care, health, and cost. *Health Affairs*, 27(3), 759–769. https://doi.org/10.1377/hlthaff.27.3.759.

Brailsford S, Bayer S, Connell C, George A, Klein J and Lacey P (2021). Embedding OR modelling as decision support in health capacity planning: insights from an evaluation. *Health Systems*, 1–14. https://doi.org/10.1080/20476965.2021.1983476.

Brailsford SC (2005). Overcoming the barriers to implementation of operations research simulation models in healthcare. *Clinical & Investigative Medicine*, 28(6), 312–315.

Brailsford SC, Harper P, Patel B and Pitt M (2009). An analysis of the academic literature on simulation and modelling in health care. *Journal of Simulation*, 3(3), 130–140. https://doi.org/10.1057/jos.2009.10.

Brailsford SC and Vissers J (2011). OR in healthcare: a European perspective. *European Journal of Operational Research*, 212(2), 223–234. https://doi.org/10.1016/j.ejor.2010.10.026.

Cox JF and Spencer MS (1998). *The constraints management handbook*. The St. Lucie Press/APICS Series on Constraints Management, Boca Raton, FL.

Crowe S, Brown K, Tregay J, Wray J, Knowles R, Ridout DA, Bull C and Utley M (2017). Combining qualitative and quantitative operational research methods to inform quality improvement in pathways that span multiple settings. *BMJ Quality & Safety*, 26(8), 641–652. https://doi.org/10.1136/bmjqs-2016-005636.

Currie CSM, Fowler JW, Kotiadis K, Monks T, Onggo BS, Robertson DA and Tako AA (2020). How simulation modelling can help reduce the impact of COVID-19. *Journal of Simulation*, 1–15. https://doi.org/10.1080/17477778.2020.1751570.

Dodds S (2018). *The 4N chart – nuggets/niggles/niceifs/nonos*. The Health Foundation: The Q Community. https://q.health.org.uk/document/the-4n-chart-nuggets-niggles-niceifs-nonos.

Dodds SR (2007). *Three Wins: Service improvement using value stream design*. Chichester, UK: Kingsham Press. 978-1-84753-631-0 www.saasoft.co.uk/download/Three_Wins_Second_Edition.pdf

Dodds S and Bradley D (2020). An acute hospital demand surge planning model for the COVID-19 epidemic using stock-and-flow simulation in excel: part 1. *Journal of Improvement Science*, 68.

Fillingham D (2007). Can lean save lives? *Leadership in Health Services*, 20(4), 231–241. https://doi.org/10.1108/17511870710829346.

Goldenbogen B, Adler S, Bodeit O, Wodke J, Korman A, Bonn L, Escalera-Fanjul X, Haffner J, Karnetzki M, Krantz M, Maintz I, Mallis L, Moran Torres R, Prawitz H, Segelitz P, Seeger M, Linding R and Klipp E (2020). Geospatial precision simulations of community confined human interactions during SARS-CoV-2 transmission reveals bimodal intervention outcomes. *medRxiv*, 2020.05.03.20089235. https://doi.org/10.1101/2020.05.03.20089235.

Günal M and Pidd M (2010). Discrete event simulation for performance modelling in health care: a review of the literature. *Journal of Simulation*, 1, 42–51. https://doi.org/10.1057/jos.2009.25.

Harper PR (2002). A framework for operational modelling of hospital resources. *Health Care Management Science*, 5, 165–173. https://doi.org/10.1023/A:1019767900627.

Harper PR and Shahani AK (2002). Modelling for the planning and management of bed capacities in hospitals. *Journal of the Operational Research Society*, 53(1), 11–18. https://doi.org/10.1057/palgrave/jors/2601278.

Hillier F and Lieberman GJ (2020). *Introduction to operations research*. 11th ed. McGraw-Hill Education, New York.

Hopp WJ and Spearman ML (2011). *Factory physics*. 3rd ed. Waveland Press, Long Grove, IL.

Hulshof PJH, Kortbeek N, Boucherie RJ, Hans EW and Bakker PJM (2012). Taxonomic classification of planning decisions in health care: a structured review of the state of the art in OR/MS. *Health Systems*, 1(2), 129–175. https://doi.org/10.1057/hs.2012.18.

Kc DS and Terwiesch C (2009). Impact of workload on service time and patient safety: an econometric analysis of hospital operations. *Management Science*, 55(9), 1486–1498. https://doi.org/10.1287/mnsc.1090.1037.

Pidd M (2004). *Computer simulation in management science*. 5th ed. John Wiley & Sons, Chichester.

Pidd M (2009). *Tools for thinking: modelling in management science*. 3rd ed. John Wiley & Sons, Chichester.

Powell SG and Batt RJ (2008). *Modelling for insight: a master class for business analysts*. John Wiley & Sons, Hoboken, NJ.

Proudlove NC (2020). The 85% bed occupancy fallacy: the use, misuse and insights of queuing theory. *Health Services Management Research*, 33(3), 110–121. https://doi.org/10.1177/0951484819870936.

Robinson S (2014). *Simulation: the practice of model development and use.* 2nd ed. Palgrave Macmillan, Basingstoke, UK.

Seddon J (1992). *I want you to cheat!: the unreasonable guide to service and quality in organisations.* Vanguard Consulting Ltd., Buckingham.

Utley M and Worthington D (2012). Capacity planning. In Hall R (ed.), *Handbook of healthcare system scheduling.* Springer, New York.

van Veen-Berkx E, Elkhuizen SG, Kuijper B, Kazemier G and Collaborative DORB (2016). Dedicated operating room for emergency surgery generates more utilization, less overtime, and less cancellations. *The American Journal of Surgery,* 211(1), 122–128. https://doi.org/10.1016/j.amjsurg.2015.06.021.

Vissers JM (1998). Health care management modelling: a process perspective. *Health Care Management Science,* 1(2), 77–85. https://doi.org/10.1023/A:1019042518494.

Wullink G, Van Houdenhoven M, Hans EW, van Oostrum JM, van der Lans M and Kazemier G (2007). Closing emergency operating rooms improves efficiency. *Journal of Medical Systems,* 31(6), 543–546. https://doi.org/10.1007/s10916-007-9096-6.

4 Operations management of units

Sylvia Elkhuizen

4.1 Introduction

In this chapter, we focus on the operations management (OM) of units. A *unit* is a part of an organisation with specific resources available for the services it provides. The type of resource depends on the unit, but in general will be comprised of staff, space and equipment. Units may be large and complex, like operating theatres in a hospital, or smaller like a ward. Whereas process chains focus on a specific group of patients, units generally provide services to a wide range of patient groups. The main aim in the management of units is to be able to cope with the demand for services, having capacity available when needed in order to avoid long waiting times for patients. On the other hand, units also have to use their capacity efficiently and try to reduce costs. Getting insight into the demand for the services the unit provides, in terms of types of users as well as the arrival patterns over time, is therefore one of the first challenges of unit OM. The next challenge and the core of unit OM is balancing capacity and demand. To ensure that the right resources are available at the right time, capacity decisions must be made at different levels: strategic, tactical and operational. OM of units therefore focuses on predicting demand for services, allocating capacity to (groups of) users, controlling the use of resources and managing unit performance to meet targets. Figure 4.1 shows the connections between these topics.

In the next sections, we elaborate on each of the topics, after having first introduced some further definitions of unit OM concepts.

4.2 Units, resources and capacity

4.2.1 Units from an OM perspective

As we can see from Figure 4.1, a unit can have several workstations. They might be similar, working in parallel (e.g., different X-ray rooms in a radiology department of a hospital, having the same equipment) or in series (e.g., an operating room in an operating theatre department and a recovery room). Each workstation focuses on a specific service, and the service process usually consists of an operation preceded by a short waiting time.

DOI: 10.4324/9781003020011-5

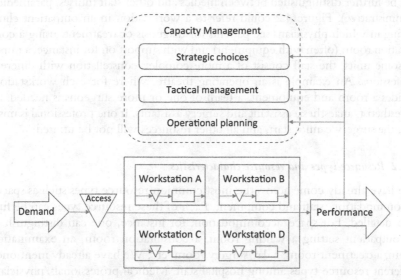

Figure 4.1 Unit operations management.

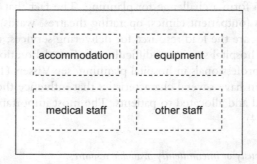

Figure 4.2 A workstation as constellation of resources.

Resources are used in a unit to provide services. Resources can be used again for a subsequent patient, in contrast to *materials* that are consumed for a specific patient. Examples of resources are a bed, an operating room or an ambulance. Also, staff (medics, nursing, paramedic, technical, administrative) can be seen as a resource. Examples of materials are dressings or medication. In this chapter we focus on resources and the way they are used in units.

In most units, resources can only be utilised when they are available in a workstation in combination with other resources. This is what we call a *constellation of resources* (see Figure 4.2).

In general, in a hospital such a constellation consists of accommodation, equipment and staff. Staff may have a one-to-one relationship with the equipment; for example, a radiology technician operating an MRI machine. In a hospital, staff can be further distinguished between medics and other staff (nurses, paramedics, administrative). Figure 4.2 could refer to a workstation in an outpatient clinic setting in which physicians see patients for diagnosis or treatment, using a consultation room (often with equipment) and with support of, for instance, a nurse. In some units, the staff consist of a more complex constellation with different professions. An example is an operating theatre, where for each workstation, besides a room and equipment, a team of one or more surgeons is needed, an anaesthetist, anaesthesia assistant and surgery assistants. If one professional is missing, the surgery cannot start, and all other resources will not be utilised.

4.2.2 Resource types and resource characteristics

We have already come across the most common resource types such as space/accommodation, staff and equipment. Each of these resource types can be further detailed. For space/accommodation, for instance, one can distinguish in an outpatient setting a waiting room, a consultation room, an examination room, a treatment room, a day surgery room, etc. We have already mentioned different resource types among hospital staff. Medical professionals/physicians represent a special category of resources in a hospital. They are not only a very important resource for offering diagnostic and treatment services in a hospital, but they also form a challenge for planning. The fact that they operate in different settings (outpatient clinics, operating theatres, wards), while in each workstation they are the lead resource for delivering services, makes the optimal planning of hospital services a difficult task. For elaboration of the special role of medical professionals in hospital planning, see Vissers (1994).

A resource can have several characteristics that influence the way resources can be scheduled and allocated to patients. The most important characteristics are (Vissers, 1994):

4.2.2.1 Continuously or intermittently available resources.

Intermittently available resources are only available for a specific amount of time, during a specific part of the day, or on specific days of the week. An example is the regular office hours of a General Practitioner where patients can have appointments between 08:00 and 16:00 on working days. *Continuously available resources* are always available, on all days and at all hours of the day. Examples are beds in a nursing ward or in an intensive care unit (ICU). Some resources are partially continuously available. An example is the operating theatre. Surgery is regularly planned during office hours, and most rooms can therefore be characterised as intermittently available. However, during the evening, night and weekends, one or a small number of rooms may be available for emergency surgery if needed.

4.2.2.2 Leading and following units and resources.

Units do not work independently but are part of a process chain or organisation. Before patients come to a unit, they may have visited other units on their pathway. Therefore, demand for the service of a unit may be dependent on earlier activities in patient journeys. In that situation, a unit or resource can be characterised as a *following unit or resource*. A following unit has to adapt its opening hours and scheduling to the planning of the preceding units. It cannot operate autonomously, and this may restrict its freedom in scheduling. On the other hand, it may be able to use information from these preceding units to support its planning decisions. An example of a following resource is an orthopaedic ward in a hospital, where the majority of admissions depends on the surgery schedule of the operating theatre.

Leading units or resources are able to make their own schedule. They are generally the starting point in patient pathways. Examples of leading units are the emergency care units, operating theatres and general practitioners. When these leading units are active, they generate demand for services from following units.

4.2.2.3 Dedicated and shared resources.

Dedicated resources are assigned to a specific patient group. An example of a dedicated resource is a diabetes nurse providing consultations for diabetes patients in a primary care centre. On the other hand, shared resources can be used by a wide range of patient groups. A CAT scan is an example of a shared resource because examination can be done for a wide range of patient groups, with very different diseases.

A further distinction can be made between time-shared units and generally shared units. Operating theatres are shared resources, but they allocate the rooms to different users on different days. These specialties may dedicate parts of their allocated capacity to specific patient groups. For example, the orthopaedic department may allocate operating room capacity to hip replacement surgery every Thursday.

A resource or unit can also become a bottleneck in a process chain when the amount of output is determined by the availability of the bottleneck resource. A *bottleneck resource* is that resource which is most scarce within a system and therefore limits the overall output of that system. In general, one tries to maximise the use of the bottleneck resource. For example, bed capacity or nursing staff capacity might be seen as the bottleneck for the overall volume of inpatient services: hence the focus on bed occupancy as a measure of efficiency. The labels bottleneck or non-bottleneck should not be confused with categorising resources as 'leading' or 'following'. For example, although access to surgical beds might be the bottleneck, operating theatre capacity is 'leading' in terms of generating output and bed capacity needs. Therefore, controlling access to leading and following resources represent a key way of ensuring that bottleneck resources are used efficiently. Bottleneck resources therefore represent constraints and are capacity-oriented terms, while 'leading' and 'following' resources refer to the resource requirements of patients and are therefore patient flow-based terms. How to determine and handle bottlenecks in a service delivery system is key in the 'Theory of Constraints' that will be discussed in Chapter 6.

4.2.3 Capacity definitions

Each resource has a capacity, which refers to the ability of a resource to generate services, measured in the number of services delivered per unit of time. When we consider the use of resources, we need to be precise about defining capacity. We can distinguish different types of capacity (Vissers, 1994):

4.2.3.1 Potential capacity.

This is the total amount of one resource type available when all these resources are used for delivering services. If we take an operating theatre department with ten operating theatres as an example, the hospital's potential operating theatre capacity is said to be ten theatres. Potentially, the operating rooms are available seven days a week and 24 hours per day.

4.2.3.2 Available and non-available capacity.

Part of the potential capacity may not be available for services if it is put out of use. This can be labelled as *non-available capacity*. The remaining capacity is, in principle, available for services and this can therefore be labelled as the *available capacity*. In the case of the operating theatre, if only one room is available for emergency surgery during the evening and night and the other nine rooms are only available between 08:00 and 17:00, the available capacity will be 9 rooms × 9 hours and 1 room × 24 hours.

4.2.3.3 Useable and non-useable capacity.

Part of the available capacity might have restrictions on its use. This can be labelled as *non-useable capacity*. In this example, restrictions in use could be that each room is not useable for one afternoon per month because of scheduled maintenance. The remaining capacity is useable for services and can therefore be labelled as *useable capacity*. The useable capacity is taken as the reference point for the calculation of utilisation figures.

4.2.3.4 Utilised and idle capacity.

Part of the useable capacity might not be used for services because there is no work available. We can call this *idle capacity*. This loss of capacity for an operating theatre department can arise when a scheduled session is cancelled by a specialist or when a session takes less time than scheduled. The part of the useable capacity that is actually used for services production, we can label as *utilised capacity*.

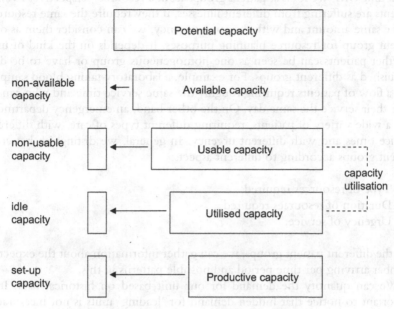

Figure 4.3 Capacity concepts for resources.

4.2.3.5 *Productive capacity and set-up capacity.*

Part of the utilised capacity may be used for non–productive purposes such as set–up activities. This will be labelled as *set-up capacity*. In the example of the operating theatre department, set–up capacity will be needed to prepare rooms and to change over from one patient to another within a session. The remaining capacity is actually used for direct patient care and is labelled as *productive capacity*. These capacity concepts are illustrated in Figure 4.3.

To define the *capacity utilisation* we focus on the utilised capacity in relation to the useable capacity, whereby the useable capacity represents the allocated capacity as indicated above. The utilisation rate of a resource is the ratio between these two capacity measures.

4.3 Demand for services

To provide the right care at the right moment, we must have insight into the demand for services from units. First of all, it is important to distinguish between 'leading' units and 'following' units. For 'following' units the demand for services is based on requests from physicians, for instance in outpatient clinics. 'Leading' units have a direct demand relationship with patients. The insight needed comprises several aspects: which patient groups do we expect, what are the characteristics of these patient groups, and how many patients do we expect per time unit?

In unit OM, we look at patient groups from a resource perspective. Even if patients are suffering from different illnesses, if they require the same resources in the same amount and with the same urgency, we can consider them as one patient group for resource planning purposes. It depends on the kind of unit whether patients can be seen as one homogeneous group or have to be distinguished as different groups. For example, a laboratory taking blood samples sees a flow of patients requiring roughly the same service time and who can all have their service the same day. On the other hand, an emergency department sees a wide variety of patients, requiring different types of care, with different service times and with different urgency. In general, we distinguish between patient groups according to different aspects:

- Type of resources required.
- Duration of resources required.
- Urgency of service.

For the different patient groups, we can gather information about the expected number arriving per time period and possible patterns in this.

We can quantify the demand for our unit based on historical data. It is important to notice that hidden demand for 'leading' units is not measurable with historical data. Hidden demand remains invisible because patients do not express their needs for care when they do not take the initiative to contact a care provider. When measuring demand based on historical data, it is important to rely on information about the moment the demand was expressed by the patient, for example, the time the telephone call with a request for an appointment was made. Historical data about services actually delivered is mostly more easily available but says more about our working patterns than about the underlying demand. For example, if we have consultation hours scheduled evenly over all weekdays, the historical service data shows almost no fluctuation. However, the real demand may have peaks and troughs or weekly patterns that remain invisible if we only use data from the consultations delivered. Moreover, the production data ignores the demand when patients express their needs but are not planned in the schedule, for example because the waiting time is so long that they decide to call another care provider. Therefore, data based on telephone calls is more reliable to get insight in demand patterns than data based on services delivered.

To forecast demand, historical data can be combined with information about expected changes in demand. Changes may result from demographic shifts in the population, new medical techniques or expected changes in the division of patient groups between care providers. Figure 4.4 gives an example of the demand for care in terms of the number of patients and duration (hours) required per week for two different patient groups. This may for, example consist, of a mix of new patients and patients with a follow-up appointment in an ambulatory care facility. In this example we assumed that patient group 1 requires 20 minutes and patient group 2 requires ten minutes of our resources.

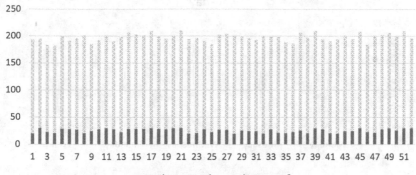

Number of patients per week

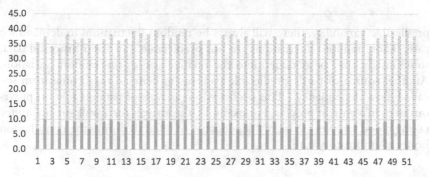

Demand in hours per week

Figure 4.4 Example of quantifying demand.

Due to the difference in time required, not only the number of patients is relevant, but also the total duration of care provided.

Beside the absolute numbers, it is also helpful to have insight into arrival patterns. Arrivals may show a continuous flow of incoming patients during opening hours, but sometimes we see specific patterns, for example regular differences on different weekdays. To derive reliable arrival patterns, we cannot rely on only one or two cycles (e.g., a couple of weeks), but need many. Figure 4.5 gives an example of weekly patterns, based on one year of data.

For some units, it may also be useful to look at arrival patterns within a day, specifically if there is a continuous flow of incoming patients with high variability, as in an emergency department.

In general, part of the variation in arrivals is predictable and underlying monthly, weekly or daily patterns may help us to forecast demand and adapt the available capacity to known fluctuations in demand. On top of the

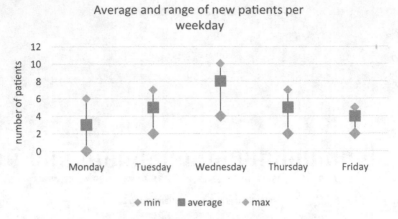

Figure 4.5 Demand patterns within a week.

predictable variability, there will always be random fluctuations in demand for care. Those random fluctuations are not predictable, but from historical data, some insight may be obtained into the relative size of this random variation. Another source of partly predictable patterns in demand may come from so-called 'flow dependency'. This occurs when arrivals of patients rely on previous steps in a patient process. For example, the arrivals for a walk-in facility for taking blood samples are highly dependable of referrals during the consultation hours of ambulatory care.

4.4 Performance management

To make informed decisions about the resources in a unit, we need to measure the performance. We can distinguish between patient-related performance measures and resource-related performance measures.

For patients, the most relevant unit performance measure is the *access time* or external waiting time. For a walk-in facility, this will be measured in minutes or hours, but when an appointment system is used, or a waiting list system, the waiting time is expressed in days or weeks.

The access time or external waiting time can be defined as the difference between the time of the request for the service and the moment the service starts to be delivered (also see Chapter 5). These waiting times can be measured in different ways: prospectively or retrospectively. For a prospective measurement, we look at specific gaps in the schedule to find the next possible appointments for a patient group. A regular measurement period is once a day or once a week. To reduce volatility in the measure from random events, it is usual to measure the time to the third next open space in the schedule (Woodcock et al., 2017). Another way to measure waiting time is retrospective, by using historical patient data. A benefit of this method is that we may have access to a lot of data, for example a year, and so get reliable results. A drawback is that we look backwards, and base decisions on history instead of focusing on the current and future situation.

Another relevant parameter is the number of *patients that are turned away* when a unit is fully occupied, and new demand arises. The wait until the next available treatment opportunity is not always clinically appropriate or may be turned down by a patient. In practice, this means that a patient may be sent (or may choose to go) to another unit or another service provider.

On the resource side, the most relevant unit performance measure is the utilisation of resources. *Utilisation* is defined as utilised capacity divided by useable capacity. The result can be presented as a fraction or percentage. Because of the possible patterns in resource use, we are not only interested in the average utilisation over the whole period of analysis, but also in the day-to-day variations of the utilisation. When presenting utilisation, it is therefore important to clarify the measurement unit.

The complex supply structure of a hospital (with its leading and following resources and its many shared resources) imposes many *resource coordination requirements* that need to be checked. Suppose we see the following average pattern of resource use by orthopaedics in a 'leading' operating theatre department over ten weeks, expressed as the number of operating theatre hours used, and the corresponding use of beds in the 'following' orthopaedic ward (see Figure 4.6).

In Figure 4.6 we see a pattern of bed resource use in the orthopaedic ward that is resulting from the pattern of orthopaedic surgery hours in the operating theatre. If variations in bed use by orthopaedics needs to be reduced, then a spreading of operating theatre hours of orthopaedics over the days of

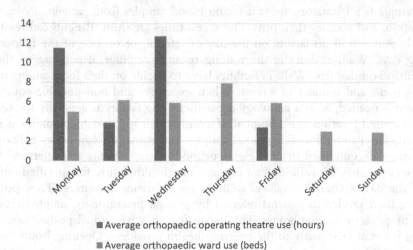

■ Average orthopaedic operating theatre use (hours)

■ Average orthopaedic ward use (beds)

Figure 4.6 Orthopaedic use of operating theatres and ward.

the week can be suggested for better performance of orthopaedics in terms of ward use.

4.5 Capacity management

Capacity management is the core of unit OM. In the next subsections, we explain capacity management decisions at three management levels: strategic, tactical and operational.

4.5.1 Strategic planning

At a strategic level, decisions are made with a horizon of one to several years. At this level, decisions have to be made to ensure the availability of the right resources in sufficient quantity. This includes defining hospital-wide service levels that need to be met, for instance waiting times. It also includes, for instance, investment decisions for equipment, hiring and training sufficient staff, and decisions to centralise or decentralise facilities as well, like the telephone lines for outpatient clinics. Another strategic decision is *how* to schedule patients in the unit.

4.5.1.1 Scheduling systems

We generally distinguish between three types of scheduling systems: walk-in systems, appointment systems and waiting list systems. Each has its merits and drawbacks and are applicable in specific types of units.

In a **walk-in system**, patients choose their own arrival time, within the opening hours of the unit. Walk-in system designs are regularly applied to services with a relatively short service duration, and a high volume of patients. An example is a laboratory assistant taking blood samples from patients. Patients walk-in and wait for their turn. The access times are short. Patients can regularly visit a walk-in facility on the day of referral, or on one of the following days. Waiting times in the waiting room may differ, depending on the demand on that day. Walk-in facilities have to decide on their location, opening hours and number of servers. When expensive and non-portable equipment is needed, as in a radiology department, the facility is generally located in a central location like a hospital. If mainly small and portable equipment is used, like material for taking blood samples, sometimes the laboratory assistant is more decentralised in the neighbourhood of the patients and referrers. A laboratory may be available in a primary care health centre for specific hours of the day. Generally, walk-in facilities are following resources. They provide their service to patients referred by general practitioners, or physicians in hospitals or nursing homes. This means that they have to adapt their opening hours at least partly to the referring health providers. Opening hours also depend on the expected demand. When demand is high, it may be necessary to have more than one server available. The system then operates as an M/M/c queuing system, where c is the number of servers (see Chapter 3). The number of servers may be constant, but it can instead be useful to be flexible with the available capacity. A facility may accommodate expected peaks in arrivals by increasing the number of servers. When peaks in demand are predictable, they can adapt the number of servers during the day or week to the forecasted demand. When there is more uncertainty, it may be necessary to have flexible extra capacity available.

In an **appointment system**, patients make an appointment before visiting the health service unit. The available capacity is divided into appointment slots. In most systems, there are different patient groups, with their own appointment slots in the schedule. An appointment system is applicable when the service time is more or less predictable for every patient group. An appointment system gives an organisation the possibility to spread the demand over the day and the week in a pattern that fits the availability of their resources. For patients there may be some waiting time between making an appointment and receiving the service, but there is less uncertainty about waiting time.

In a **waiting list system**, patients do not get a date and time for their service directly but are gathered on a list. Based on the patients on the waiting list, an optimal schedule can be created for a specific time period, for example a day or a week. In this schedule the urgency of the care needed and the length of time on the waiting list may be used to prioritise patients, but also other aspects may play a role. It may be efficient to combine a relatively long procedure with a short one to fill up the available time, even if the short one is not at the top of the waiting list. Also, the uncertainty in service duration may play a role in the schedule. In general, it is not desirable to combine procedures with a lot of uncertainty on one day. The risk of overtime then becomes too high. The advantage of using a waiting list is that there are several patients to choose from, to find an optimal fit for the schedule. There is a vast amount of literature about optimal scheduling policies. See, for instance, Abdalkareem et al., (2021), a review paper on scheduling and optimisation in healthcare.

4.5.1.2 *Resource requirements plan*

At the annual level, decisions have to be made about the volumes of services expected for units, and about the amounts of resources required for delivering these services. A common procedure to do this in a hospital setting is the annual budgeting cycle where hospital management and specialties discuss the development of services during the year and the expectations for next year. When demand for services for a specific specialty shows an upward trend over the years, it may be necessary to plan for this.

Suppose we want to determine the capacity requirements for orthopaedics. In Table 4.1 we have elaborated a calculation for next year's resource requirements.

We see from Table 4.1 that the number of patients for hip or knee replacement shows an upward trend, and that the length of stay for these patient

Table 4.1 Resource requirements plan orthopaedics

	Hip replacement			Knee replacement			Other patients			Total	
	this year	trend	next year	this year	trend	next year	this year	trend	next year	this year	next year
Number of new patients	500	10%	550	500	10%	550	800	5%	840	1800	1940
Number of follow up visits	1500	10%	1650	1500	10%	1650	2400	5%	2520	5400	5820
Number of inpatient admissions	375		413	375		413	536		563	1286	1388
Average length of stay	4	−6%	3.75	5	−5%	4.75	3		3		
Average surgery duration	1.5		1.5	2		2	1.5		1.5		
Duration first visit	15		15	15		15	15		15		
Duration follow up visit	10		10	10		10	10		10		
Number of bed days required	1500		1547	1875		1959	1608		1688	4983	5195
Target occupancy level beds	90%		90%	90%		90%	90%		90%		
Number of beds required	4.6		4.7	5.7		6.0	4.9		5.1	15.2	15.8
Number of clinic hours required	375		413	375		413	600		630	1350	1455

groups decreases. When calculating next year's resource requirements, we take into account these trends and use a 90% target occupancy level, which is high but realistic for this specialty because almost all patients concern elective admissions (see also Chapter 11).

4.5.2 *Tactical planning*

At a tactical level, decisions are made with a planning horizon of three months to one year. This concerns the exact opening hours and the resource allocation of each unit. This means that the available resources of the unit are divided between different specialties or patient groups. The resource allocation often takes one of the following forms:

* A lump sum allocation: a specialty receives the allocated resources as a total amount, and the specialty can decide later about the further detailing to individual surgeons and to patient groups.
* A detailed allocation: the allocated resources are detailed to the level of patient groups and appointment slots.

Figure 4.7 shows an example of a detailed outpatient clinic schedule and an example of a lump sum allocation in an operating theatre department.

These schedules are often on a one- or two-week basis and are used as master schedules for a number of weeks. The amount of time allocated in these schedules should correspond to the resource requirements at the annual strategic level. Often one distinguishes between schedules for the high season (when the patient volumes are higher) and the low season (for instance, holidays).

There is a vast amount of literature available on developing efficient master schedules, that not only optimise the use of a leading resource (for instance operating theatre schedule) but also takes into account the impact on the use of following resources (for instance beds in a ward). See, for instance the review papers on planning and scheduling of operating theatres by Cardoen et al. (2010) and Zhu et al. (2018), and a paper on matching demand and capacity in an outpatient clinic (Van Bussel et al., 2018).

4.5.3 *Operational planning*

Operational planning concerns the daily scheduling of specific patients. This applies specifically to units working with appointment or waiting list scheduling. This scheduling must be done within the capacity that is made available in the tactical planning. Some systems distinguish between two levels of operational planning: the scheduling of patients into a schedule or plan and the adjustments in response to actual events requiring reactive deviations from the plan on the day itself (offline and online planning, see Hulshof et al. (2012)).

Look, for example, at Figure 4.8. This example is based upon the schedule in Figure 4.7, with different treatment durations for new patients and follow-up patients.

Operating theatre room schedule

8:00 AM	Monday	Tuesday	Wednesday	Thursday	Friday
	Orthopedics	Orthopedics	Neurosurgery	Gynaecology	ENT
4:00 PM					

Outpatient clinic schedule

start	end	Monday	Tuesday	Wednesday	Thursday	Friday
8:00 AM	8:20 AM			*new patients*		
8:20 AM	8:40 AM					
8:40 AM	9:00 AM					
9:00 AM	9:20 AM					
9:20 AM	9:40 AM					
9:40 AM	10:00 AM					
10:00 AM	10:10 AM					
10:10 AM	10:20 AM					
10:20 AM	10:30 AM					
10:30 AM	10:40 AM					
10:40 AM	10:50 AM					
10:50 AM	11:00 AM					
11:00 AM	11:10 AM					
11:10 AM	11:20 AM					
11:20 AM	11:30 AM					
11:30 AM	11:40 AM					
11:40 AM	11:50 AM					
11:50 AM	12:00 PM					
12:00 PM	12:10 PM			*follow up patients*		
12:10 PM	12:20 PM					
12:20 PM	12:30 PM					
12:30 PM	12:40 PM					
12:40 PM	12:50 PM					
12:50 PM	1:00 PM					
1:00 PM	1:10 PM					
1:10 PM	1:20 PM					
1:20 PM	1:30 PM					
1:30 PM	1:40 PM					
1:40 PM	1:50 PM					
1:50 PM	2:00 PM					
2:00 PM	2:10 PM					
2:10 PM	2:20 PM					
2:20 PM	2:30 PM					
2:30 PM	2:40 PM					
2:40 PM	2:50 PM					
2:50 PM	3:00 PM					
3:00 PM	3:10 PM					
3:10 PM	3:20 PM					
3:20 PM	3:30 PM					
3:30 PM	3:40 PM					
3:40 PM	3:50 PM					
3:50 PM	4:00 PM					

Figure 4.7 Two examples of tactical resource allocation schedules: an outpatient clinic schedule and an operating theatre room schedule.

start	end	Monday	Tuesday	Wednesday	Thursday	Friday
8:00 AM	8:20 AM		patient	patient	patient	patient
8:20 AM	8:40 AM	patient	patient	patient	patient	patient
8:40 AM	9:00 AM	patient		patient		patient
9:00 AM	9:20 AM	patient		patient	patient	patient
9:20 AM	9:40 AM	patient	patient	patient	patient	
9:40 AM	10:00 AM	patient	patient	patient	patient	
10:00 AM	10:10 AM		patient	patient	patient	patient
10:10 AM	10:20 AM		patient	patient	patient	patient
10:20 AM	10:30 AM	patient	patient	patient	patient	patient
10:30 AM	10:40 AM	patient	patient	patient	patient	patient
10:40 AM	10:50 AM	patient	patient	patient	patient	patient
10:50 AM	11:00 AM	patient	patient	patient	patient	patient
11:00 AM	11:10 AM	patient	patient	patient	patient	patient
11:10 AM	11:20 AM	patient	patient	patient	patient	patient
11:20 AM	11:30 AM	patient	patient	patient	patient	patient
11:30 AM	11:40 AM	patient	patient		patient	patient
11:40 AM	11:50 AM	patient	patient	patient	patient	patient
11:50 AM	12:00 PM	patient	patient	patient	patient	
12:00 PM	12:10 PM	patient		patient	patient	patient
12:10 PM	12:20 PM	patient	patient	patient	patient	patient
12:20 PM	12:30 PM	patient	patient	patient	patient	patient
12:30 PM	12:40 PM	patient	patient	patient	patient	patient
12:40 PM	12:50 PM	patient	patient	patient	patient	patient
12:50 PM	1:00 PM	patient	patient	patient	patient	patient
1:00 PM	1:10 PM	patient	patient	patient	patient	patient
1:10 PM	1:20 PM	patient	patient	patient	patient	patient
1:20 PM	1:30 PM	patient	patient	patient	patient	patient
1:30 PM	1:40 PM	patient	patient	patient	patient	patient
1:40 PM	1:50 PM		patient	patient	patient	patient
1:50 PM	2:00 PM	patient	patient	patient	patient	patient
2:00 PM	2:10 PM	patient		patient	patient	patient
2:10 PM	2:20 PM	patient	patient	patient	patient	patient
2:20 PM	2:30 PM	patient	patient	patient	patient	patient
2:30 PM	2:40 PM	patient	patient	patient	patient	patient
2:40 PM	2:50 PM	patient	patient	patient	patient	patient
2:50 PM	3:00 PM	patient	patient	patient	patient	patient
3:00 PM	3:10 PM	patient	patient	patient	patient	patient
3:10 PM	3:20 PM	patient	patient	patient	patient	patient
3:20 PM	3:30 PM	patient	patient	patient		patient
3:30 PM	3:40 PM	patient	patient	patient	patient	patient
3:40 PM	3:50 PM	patient	patient	patient	patient	patient
3:50 PM	4:00 PM	patient	patient	patient	patient	

Figure 4.8 Example of scheduled patients and calculations of utilisation. The empty cells are idle (unused) capacity.

We see that different methods of calculation give different results for the utilisation. We can't say that one of the calculations is better than the other, both are relevant.

There is a vast amount of literature on appointment scheduling for primary care and outpatient clinics, see, for instance, the review paper by Rose et al. (2011) on advanced access outcomes, and the review paper by Cayirli (2003) on outpatient scheduling systems. For (in)patient scheduling, see for instance, the review paper by Abdalkareem et al. (2021), and for nurse scheduling the review paper by De Causmaeker et al. (2004). Fagefors et al. (2020) discuss how they can create short-term volume flexibility in healthcare to manage short-term capacity losses and demand variation.

4.6 Balancing capacity and demand

Both demand and available capacity are not constant. There will always be fluctuations in incoming patients, as already explained in Section 4.3. Also, available capacity may differ when schedules are different by day or week, but also unforeseen fluctuations may occur due to illness or breakdowns. To deal with fluctuations there must be some flexibility in scheduling. We can use buffers to provide flexibility. Buffers can be created on both sides, the demand side and the supply side (see Figure 4.9).

On the supply side, we can create a buffer by overcapacity and accepting idle time of a resource. We have already seen that the occupancy level of a ward and of an operating theatre room cannot be 100%, and that a realistic target occupancy level will be somewhere between 80% and 95%, depending on the amount of variation in resource use and the predictability of variation. In some parts of the hospital where there is more variation in operations, such as the emergency department or an ICU, we have to accept more idle time

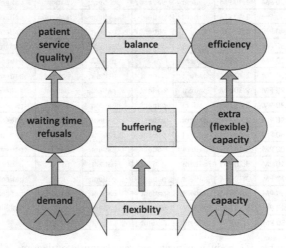

Figure 4.9 Creating flexibility by buffering.

as we need to build in a guarantee to be able to deliver services immediately in case of an emergency (see also Chapter 11). In other parts, we may try to reduce variability in order to increase capacity utilisation (Elkhuizen et al., 2007).

On the demand side, we can create a buffer of work by introducing a queue for a service and accepting waiting time for patients. This can, for instance, be an access time for the first visit to see a medical doctor, a waiting list for surgery or waiting time in the waiting room before seeing a doctor. The resulting waiting time needs, of course, be acceptable in terms of standards for service, but the waiting time serves as a protection against idle capacity.

Both forms of buffer have consequences for healthcare quality and efficiency. If we accept too much idle capacity, the efficiency of healthcare delivery can be low, resulting in extra costs of services. If we accept waiting times that are longer than acceptable from the point of view regarding standards for quality of service, we can expect complaints from patients and patient representatives, and investigations by government agencies that inspect the quality of healthcare. Therefore, we need to find the right balance between demand and supply to ensure the balance between quality of care, performance and efficiency in the use of resources.

We can improve the demand–supply match by capacity management at different levels of planning. At the strategic level it is important to define the service levels that a provider wants to keep to when delivering services, to define the amounts of resources required to realise target volumes for services at the annual level, to choose appropriate systems for allocating resources during tactical planning and scheduling of patients at the operational level. At the tactical level, it is important to develop master schedules for leading resources, within the decisions taken at strategic level on volumes of patients and resources required, and to minimise the loss of capacity for leading and following resources. If these steps at strategic and tactical level are done well, then the flexibility remaining in the system can be used optimally, to smooth the execution of operational planning. Even then, one should be aware that in healthcare practice many deviations from plans can occur, so it is important to be prepared to take the necessary steps if a clinic or operating theatre session needs to be cancelled, or patients do not show up for their appointment.

Capacity management is the main OM strategy for units, and unit OM forms the basis of OM in healthcare, because the manipulations of resources at different levels of planning is the best guarantee that strategic targets are realised, waste of resources is avoided, and services are delivered according to the service levels agreed. However, capacity management is only one side of the coin for well-developed services in healthcare, the other side being process management, i.e., the design, execution and monitoring of effective delivery processes for patients from the moment of their referral until discharge. In Chapter 5 we elaborate on process OM.

4.7 Questions and exercises

The workstation concept in Figure 4.2 combines different resources: accommodation, equipment, medical staff and other staff. Consider an operating theatre setting and discuss the characteristics of these resources in this setting.

Suppose you are going to optimise the use of these different resources. Propose a weighting function by giving each resource a weight between 1 and 10 (10 being the highest weight) that reflects their relative importance.

Suppose an X-ray department has four rooms where examinations, with an average duration of 15 minutes, can be performed that do not require preparation. Patients can be referred from clinics in the outpatient department and examined without an appointment. The workload of these rooms varies with the number of clinics held in the outpatient department and the number of patients seen in clinics. Suppose the number of (staffed) rooms available on each hour on Monday, and the number of patients arriving for an examination on each hour on Monday, is given as below.

Table 4.2 Capacity and demand for an X-Ray unit

Hour	8–9	9–10	10–11	11–12	12–13	13–14	14–15	15–16	16–7	17–18
Number of rooms available	1	3	4	4	1	2	3	4	2	1
Number of patients/ examinations	2	8	10	12	4	4	6	8	3	1

Prepare a graphical presentation of the use (in absolute numbers) of rooms by hour on Monday. What is the occupancy percentage of the rooms per hour? Visualise the occupancy per hour on a secondary axis.

What would be the maximum gain to be made by a better spreading of examinations? What would be necessary to realise this optimal use of X-ray rooms? Why is this not realistic? What would be a realistic level of improvement?

References

Abdalkareem ZA, Amir A, AlBetar MA, Ekhan P and Hammouri AI (2021). Healthcare scheduling in optimization context: a review. *Health and Technology*, 11, 445–469.

Cardoen B, Demeulemeester E and Beliën J (2010). Operating room planning and scheduling: a literature review. *European Journal of Operational Research*, 201, 921–932.

Cayirli TVE (2003). Outpatient scheduling in health care: a review of literature. *Production and Operations Management*, 12(4), 519–549.

De Causmaeker P, Van Landeghem H and Vanden Berghe G (2004). The state of the art of nurse rostering. *Journal of Scheduling*, 7, 441–499. https://doi.org/10.1023/B:JOSH.0000046076.75950.0b.

Elkhuizen SG, Van Sambeek JRC, Hans EW, Krabbendam K and Bakker PJM (2007). Applying the variety reduction principle to management of ancillary services. *Health Care Management Review*, 32(1), 37–45. https://doi.org/10.1097/00004010-200701000-00006.

Fagefors C, Lantz B and Rosén P (2020). Creating short-term volume flexibility in healthcare capacity management. *International Journal on Environmental Research and Public Health*, 17, 8514.

Hulshof PJH, Kortbeek N, Boucherie RJ, Hans EW and Bakker PJM (2012). Taxonomy classification of planning decisions in health care: a structured review of the state of the art in OR/MS. *Health Systems*, 1, 129–175.

Rose K, Ross JS and Horwitz LI (2011). Advanced access scheduling outcomes: a systematic review. *Archives of Internal Medicine*, 171(13), 1150–1159. https://doi.org/10.1001/archinternmed.2011.168.

Van Bussel EM, Van der Voort MBVR, Wessel RN and Van Merode GG (2018). Demand, capacity, and access of the outpatient clinic: a framework for analysis and improvement. *Journal of Evaluation in Clinical Practice*, 24, 1–9. https://doi.org/10.1111/jep.1292.

Vissers JMH (1994). *Flow based allocation of hospital resources*. Doctoral thesis, Eindhoven University of Technology.

Woodcock EW, Kier S and Zhao V (2017). Patient access metrics in the ambulatory enterprise. *Management in Healthcare*, 2(2), 153–164.

Zhu S, Fan W, Yang S, Pei J and Pardalos P (2018). Operating room planning and surgical case scheduling: a review of literature. *Journal of Combinatorial Optimization*, 37, 1–49.

5   Operations management of process chains

Jan Vissers

5.1 Introduction

In this chapter we focus on the operations management (OM) of 'processes and chains' or, in short 'process chains'. When we use the term 'process chain' in this book, we refer to the whole process of delivery of healthcare services by healthcare providers to patients as an answer to the patient's health complaint.

This customer process is much less visible in healthcare, compared to unit processes, and has received less attention in the development of healthcare services. The focus in healthcare is on the organisation of unit delivery processes, which are designed to deliver these services effectively and efficiently. Medical guidelines and protocols govern the service, to optimise patient safety and quality of care. Then the patient will continue the journey to a following unit where, again, a unit-based service will be provided. Each unit concentrates on the delivery of a safe and effective service, often in the form of a complex medical procedure. However, the downside of this is that the total customer process from the point of view of the user is a series of encounters with healthcare professionals in which the patient is 'pushed' from unit to unit. The customer process is not tightly organised as a whole, but consists of visits to units, one at a time and, mostly, without an overview of the whole customer process. Of course, for some medical problems, clinical pathways are developed and well coordinated, but they often only concentrate on a specific part of the care process, frequently the treatment phase, and limited to the boundaries of the hospital. Therefore, we can state that most healthcare delivery process chains were never designed from a customer point of view, but they have resulted from linking unit delivery processes. So, the customer process point of view for organising healthcare is relatively new and offers many challenges.

Figure 5.1 presents an overview of the OM of process chains in a hospital setting. The figure shows the different components of the OM of processes, with the process for patients for hip surgery in a hospital setting at the bottom. First, we need to be able to identify a process and the patients considered at the operational level when planning the process. To understand the design of the process, we further need a formal description of the process – as it is intended to be – and the timing of all the steps. Then we can apply scheduling to the process or parts of it and manage the operational process. At the level

DOI: 10.4324/9781003020011-6

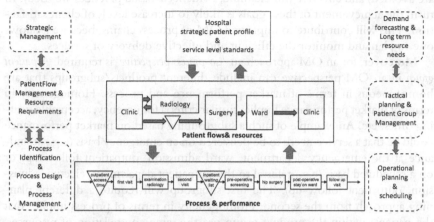

Figure 5.1 Process OM perspective (example hip surgery).

of 'patient flows and resources' we see the aggregated patient flows for hip surgery flowing between the different units that are required as a configuration of resources for hip surgery patients. At this level of planning, we can aggregate the resource requirements of the process of hip surgery patients, and we can also analyse the patterns in the flow of hip surgery patients as a group, and relate them to, for instance, a care pathway description. Having also done this for other patient groups treated by orthopaedics, we can then aggregate the different flows of orthopaedic patients to calculate the resource requirements for orthopaedics in total. Finally, at the strategic level, we can look at the forecasting of the patient flow for hip surgery patients and develop scenarios for long-term resource needs. In the remainder of this chapter, we elaborate the above-mentioned topics.

5.2 Identification of process chains in healthcare

There is no single way to classify process chains in healthcare. The existing schemes depend on the purpose (medical, economic, organisational) as the focus for classification. In this section we will explore what an OM perspective on classifying process chains implies (Subsection 5.2.1), what we can learn from alternative classification systems used in healthcare (Subsection 5.2.2), and what the difference is between a care pathway approach and an OM perspective on delivery processes in healthcare (Subsection 5.2.3).

5.2.1 An operations management perspective

Given that process chains generate a service for a client, the focus for a classification should be driven by the requirements of the client. In particular, clients want a service that is efficient (for example, unnecessary delays in treatment are avoided) and effective (for example, evidenced-based practices are used). In turn, the achievement of these goals is likely to increase levels of client satisfaction. This will contribute to improved OM of process chains, because it allows one to plan and monitor the efficient and effective delivery of services.

Moreover, for an OM approach an *'iso-process perspective'* is required. A *patient group* in an OM perspective can include different products/subgroups that are homogeneous in terms of market performance and process. Homogeneity in terms of market performance implies similar criteria for urgency, acceptable waiting times, etc. An example of such a subgrouping based on market performance could be that a service needs to be delivered on an emergency basis (e.g., attendance at the emergency department, ward admission, outpatient follow-up) or on a scheduled basis (e.g., referral to the outpatient department, elective admission, outpatient follow-up). The first subgroup will require a different planning approach from the second. Homogeneity in terms of process implies that the patients within the product group use the same constellation of resources. Patients requiring routine diabetes care (such as a one-off consultation) might be grouped with more complex patients who require more follow-up visits. This is because they are essentially using the same constellation of resources: for example, access to a clinician and a diabetes nurse. However, the overall amounts of resources used by patients within the group may vary considerably, a fact that would need to be allowed for when planning capacity requirements. This iso-process grouping makes an OM approach different from an economics approach (iso-resource grouping) and a medical approach (iso-diagnosis grouping).

Below we discuss some alternative ways of classifying healthcare products. We will focus on their suitability for analysing healthcare process chains from an OM point of view. Again, this review of alternatives will demonstrate that no single way of defining products from an OM perspective exists. Instead, we aim to offer the reader insight into alternative classification systems to judge the merits and relevance of these alternative product classifications for their application and setting.

5.2.2 Alternative classification systems

The traditional way of classifying 'individual' patient products in the acute hospital is according to their complaint or diagnosis. Iso-diagnosis groupings of patients, for instance, are based on well accepted international classification schemes such as the International Classification of Diseases (ICD). These classification systems can be very extensive: for example, the ICD-9 version counts 398 main groups and 7960 subgroups. However, such 'product' classifications are mainly used for medical purposes. The number of patient groups that they generate, and the fact that some may cover very few admissions during a planning period, means that it is difficult and usually undesirable to use them to plan and schedule care from an OM perspective.

Acute hospitals also traditionally group patients by specialty: for example, general medicine patients, orthopaedic patients, etc. However, these groupings are too aggregated from an OM perspective, as the constellation of resources used by patient types within specialties are likely to be very different. For example, patients diagnosed with asthma or stroke might both be grouped under the specialty general medicine but the care that they receive will be very different.

Hence, from an OM perspective, a product classification somewhere between these two 'traditional' approaches seems to be required. The first attempt to define hospital products from a managerial perspective can be credited to Fetter and his colleagues (Fetter, 1983). They developed the Diagnosis Related Groups (DRG) system to classify all diagnoses into groups of diagnoses that are recognisable to physicians and also homogeneous in terms of use of resources. Up until then, X-rays, lab tests, medication and surgical procedures were considered as hospital outputs; in the DRG system they are seen as intermediate outputs. Fetter developed 467 DRGs to describe a hospital's inpatient output.

Continuing lines of development have included Ambulatory Visit Groups (AVGs) for classifying ambulatory care products (Fetter et al., 1984), and a refinement of DRGs which takes into account the stage of development of the disease with the patient (Fetter and Freeman, 1986). Another line of development in the Netherlands – with many parallels to the DRG approach – is to define hospital products as combinations of diagnosis and treatment (Baas, 1996). Similarly, in the United Kingdom, and again based on the DRG approach, Healthcare Resource Groups (HRGs) have been developed.

Product groupings such as DRGs were primarily developed to support the financial reimbursement of hospitals rather than to support the planning and management of healthcare process chains. However, they have relevance to OM as there will be a direct relationship between, for example, a hospital's cost for a particular DRG and the efficiency with which resources are used within that DRG. Hence, there are parallels between the analysis of DRG costs and the efficient planning of care within process chains.

However, although specific groupings within, for example, the DRG system, may be useful for OM purposes, the overall number of groupings generated by such systems is again likely to be too large. In addition, products which use similar amounts of resources (iso-resource) will not necessarily use a similar constellation of resources (iso-process). For instance, a patient with a DRG/AVG profile involving an admission for five days, five lab tests and three outpatient visits may represent a patient admitted on an emergency basis (with five tests during admission, and three outpatient visits to a specialist), or as a patient admitted on a scheduled basis (with three preceding outpatient visits always using the same constellation of resources, i.e., the specialist, a specialised nurse and the lab). Finally, the boundaries of healthcare chains may stretch beyond, for example, DRG boundaries. For example, the care chain for a patient who has suffered a stroke will include follow-up care in the community. However, the DRG(s) to which such patients are assigned will only embrace their care within the acute hospital.

Alternatively, it might be possible to generate product groups because the care of the patients covered can be regarded as being delivered in a 'focused factory': a business unit concept. De Vries, Bertrand and Vissers (1999) specified the requirements for a 'focused factory'. These were that: there is a clear relationship between the product group and the resources required; the volume of activity is large enough to allow the allocation of dedicated resources; and that it is possible in advance to identify the level of specialisation required.

Some 'focused factory' product groups might contain the same types of patients. For example, dedicated facilities and units for patients requiring treatment for cataracts have been established. In other focused factory product groups, different types of patients might be clustered so that the volume of activity justifies the provision of dedicated resources. An example might be patients requiring day surgery. In the UK, the development of dedicated diagnostic and treatment centres will further increase the relevance of patient groups based upon the principles of a focused factory.

Finally, regardless of concerns about the volume of activity and clarity of resource requirements, client concerns about the continuity and coordination of existing services within a care chain might be the main driver for the creation of product groups. Such client concerns tend to be most evident for illnesses with a relatively long duration and/or which require contact with a range of professionals or agencies. Hence, in the UK, National Service Frameworks have been developed which map out the desirable care pathways and services required for patients receiving treatment for conditions such as diabetes and stroke. To some extent, product groupings driven by a desire to promote continuity and coordination mirror developments in clinical protocols and pathways. However, the variety of processes and agencies involved means that planning and controlling the care of patients within such multidisciplinary patient groupings is extremely complicated.

Although the above discussion has outlined a range of product classifications and groupings, it should be noted that there are some process characteristics which have a strong impact on the predictability of resource use by patients within product groups. An awareness of these characteristics is therefore helpful when developing product groups. They are that:

- Treatments for well-defined complaints with almost 100% certainty about the processes required and the outcome (e.g., a bone fracture) should be distinguished from treatments for ill-defined complaints with no routine treatment path available and no certainty about results. We call these routine and non-routine processes (see also Lillrank and Liukko, 2004).
- For routine processes it is possible to define a treatment path, often based on a clinical guideline or protocol, which defines the different operations in the process and their timing. Still the variability in resource use for these routine processes can be quite high due, for example, to practice variations, different modes of treatment, and the consequences of the interaction between doctor and patient. Nevertheless, process patterns can be recognised.

- For non-routine processes, the specialist will proceed in a step-by-step way, checking the patient's reaction to a treatment and deciding on the next step from there. There is no guarantee on the outcome, and there is no in-advance lay-out of the process the patient will follow. Naturally, the predictability of resource use is much lower here than with routine processes.

Of course, these are the extremes on a continuous spectrum; there is much variation between specialties and within a specialty. However, the variation between specialties is dominant. For a surgical specialty with many protocol patients, such as orthopaedics, the number of routine processes may be very high but for a non-surgical specialty, such as internal medicine, it may be much less.

In his book *The Logics of Healthcare*, Lillrank (2018) presents the argument that healthcare is not one industry with one logic and one set of solutions. He distinguishes seven segments in healthcare: Emergency, One Visit, Electives, Cure, Projects, Care and Prevention. Each of these segments has its own logic for finding a match between demand and supply. One Visit, for instance, refers to medical cases that are neither urgent nor severe, such as filling a dental cavity, a regular medical check-up or treating a routine infection. Services are predictable and can be selected from a menu and given a fixed price. Electives, as another example, are single procedures that are performed according to a schedule for preselected and prepared patients. This part of healthcare most strongly resembles an automobile assembly plant. Though this perspective helps to understand that the delivery of services in each of these segments is differently organised; it does not help to see the total journey of the patient who might enter the hospital via the emergency department, is admitted as an inpatient for treatment, and referred to a rehabilitation centre for follow-up treatment.

To conclude, whatever system for classifying products or product groups is chosen (diagnosis, DRG and its refinement, AVGs or diagnosis-treatment combinations, see also Ploman (1985)), some variation is likely to remain within the homogeneity of the mix of individual patients which form the product and in the range of services and resources that are used to produce the product. The reasons for a lack of homogeneity include inter-doctor variation within a product group and inter-practice variation between hospitals. For example, within the product 'treatment for arthritic hip', surgeons may differ in the proportion of patients considered eligible for surgery and/or the type of surgical procedure used. Such variations will, of themselves, affect the requirement for resources and services. In addition, variation will exist because of the fact that the eventual service delivered is always the outcome of the interaction between the patient and the doctor.

Therefore, the main characteristics of any hospital product classifications that are generated and used are that:

- There is no single way of classifying hospital products, and even the concept of a hospital product is not yet fully developed.

- Whatever classification system is used, the number of different hospital products is considerable.
- Within product groups the process variability is high, and the homogeneity is low due to inter-doctor and inter-practice variation and inter-patient variation at the level of a single specialist's practice.

The picture can also become more complicated where a patient is treated in a multidisciplinary setting. When mapping such a process, parts of the process might be identified as serial processing or parallel processing, joint treatment (team processing) or cyclical treatment/processing (see Figure 5.2).

In *serial processing* the patient is transferred from one specialty to another. For instance, a patient is admitted to internal medicine for treatment of gastro-intestinal problems. Later on, if the treatment with drugs does not have the anticipated effect, it is decided that the patient should be transferred to general surgery for a surgical intervention. In *parallel processing* the patient is processed by two specialties during the same period for clinically related problems. Often one specialty has the lead in responsibility for the treatment of the patient, and the other specialty is supportive. This happens, for instance, when during the treatment of a patient a doctor from a second specialty is asked to give an expert opinion. Another example is a patient with claudicatio intermittens, where the endocrinologist treats the diabetes, and the vascular surgeon performs the vascular procedure.

In the case of *team processing,* the patient's problem is jointly treated by two or more specialists from different specialties. This could, for instance, be

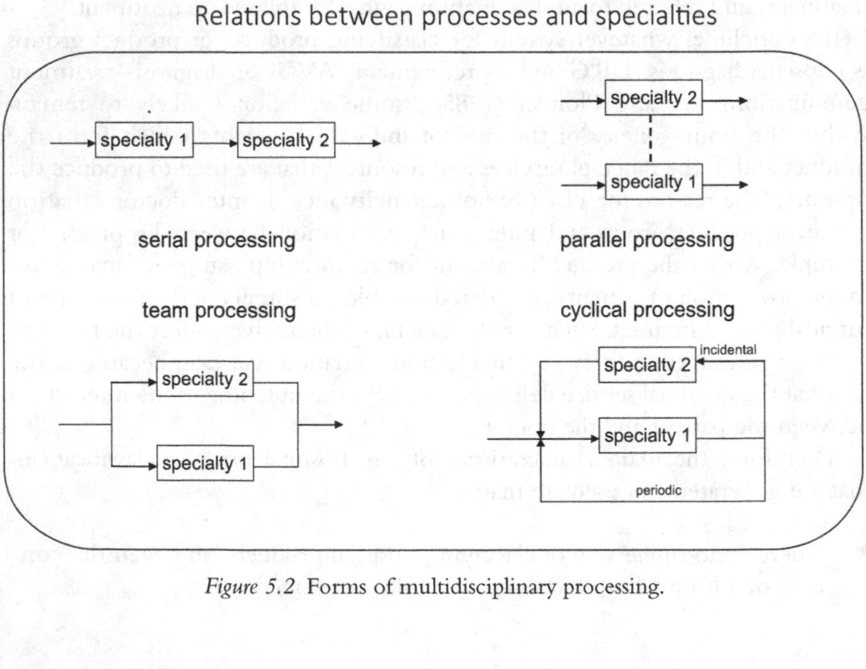

Relations between processes and specialties

Figure 5.2 Forms of multidisciplinary processing.

oncology treatment, requiring involvement of internal medicine and oncology surgery.

Cyclical processing refers to the treatment process of a patient that shows cyclic patterns. This often happens with patients with chronic conditions. A diabetes type 1 patient, for instance, might visit the clinic of a general medicine physician specialised in diabetics ten times a year but only visit an ophthalmologist for possible eyesight effects caused by diabetes once a year.

If we are looking for a suitable way to describe the OM of process chains, that can also handle these forms of multidisciplinary processing, we are bound to keep it practical and focused on care delivery in a specific setting. For such a setting, for instance patients referred to orthopaedics in a hospital, it is always possible to define a number of these iso-process patient groups that have a certain volume, similar service characteristics, and can be planned and scheduled in a similar way. The first step is to describe the process as followed by such a group of patients in a systematic way. This is further elaborated in Section 5.3. First, we illustrate in Subsection 5.2.3 the relationship between a care pathway approach and an OM approach to care processes.

5.2.3 Pathways and processes

First, we discuss the difference and overlap between these concepts. A *pathway* is an evidence-based best approach to diagnose and treat a patient for a specific medical condition. A (healthcare delivery) process is a series of operations that are required for delivering a health service to a client. A healthcare chain is a delivery process that crosses the borders of more providers. The concepts of pathway, process and chain draw from different domains of knowledge, which need further clarification.

The European Pathways Association (Vanhaecht et al., 2007) has defined a *care pathway* as follows:

> A care pathway is a complex intervention for the mutual decision making and organisation of care processes for a well-defined group of patients during a well-defined period.

Defining characteristics of care pathways include:

- an explicit statement of the goals and key elements of care based on evidence, best practice, and patients' expectations and their characteristics
- the facilitation of communication among the team members and with patients and families
- the coordination of the care process by coordinating the roles and sequencing the activities of the multidisciplinary care team, patients and their relatives
- the documentation, monitoring, and evaluation of variations and outcomes
- the identification of the appropriate resources

The aim of a care pathway is to enhance the quality of care across the continuum by improving risk-adjusted patient outcomes, promoting patient safety, increasing patient satisfaction, and optimising the use of resources.

(EPA, 2021)

The term 'pathway' has been borrowed from the planning methodologies, Critical Path Method (CPM) and Programme Evaluation and Review Technique (PERT), developed in the 1950s in manufacturing industries for planning complex processes and projects. Applications of pathway approaches to medical care started in the 1980s and, since 2000, care pathways have been introduced at a wider scale, supported by a care pathway methodology. For Europe, KU Leuven has been the main research and development centre for care pathway methodology. It developed the seven-phase model for developing a pathway for a specific group of patients in a systematic way (Vanhaecht et al., 2012).

It must be clear that in the pathways methodology, a pathway is more than a description of the process of the patient. It is also a care concept (patient-focused, evidence-based) and a tool to model the care, but also includes a process to improve the quality and efficiency of care delivery.

Looking at the definition of a care pathway makes clear that the care pathway methodology is an integrative approach to develop, manage and evaluate the delivery of care to a patient group identified by a medical condition. It combines knowledge from the healthcare professional's domain on how to deliver state-of-the-art care, knowledge from the domain of organisational behaviour on how to organise work of professionals working together for clients, knowledge from quality assurance on how to develop quality and patient safety, knowledge from OM on how to analyse and improve the process of care delivery in terms of waiting times and throughput and knowledge from financial management on how to determine the costs of care delivery.

Figure 5.3 summarises that a pathway provides a description of the process of the patient in the pathway, with an emphasis on what needs to be delivered to the patient and how it needs to be delivered to produce evidence-based outcomes and quality of care. The pathway methodology gives guidance to the development of the pathway and its improvement.

The pathway describes – in a prescriptive way – what services should be delivered and how the services should be delivered by the different healthcare professionals working together in the pathway. The pathway provides – in OM terms – the specifications of the patient process. The OM contribution to the pathway is that the process can now be described in terms of OM methodology and that the allocation of resources can be arranged in such a way that the required resources are available as specified by the pathway. The emphasis in the OM description is on the amount and timing of resources to facilitate the planning and scheduling of the process. The contribution of OM to the pathway is, furthermore, that it helps to optimise the pathway in terms of throughput time and use of resources.

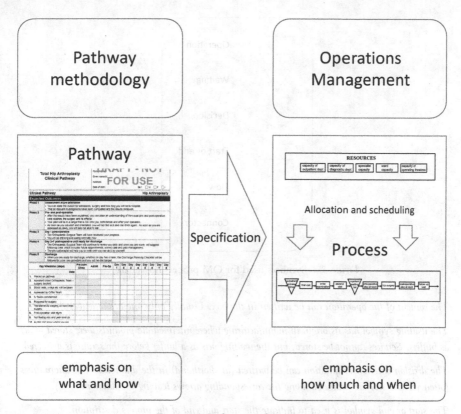

Figure 5.3 Pathway and process.

5.3 Description of process chains

For studies on OM of process chains, in Health Services Operations Management (HSOM) we distinguish different methodologies for process description. We elaborate the three most important ones in this section: process flow charting, service blueprinting, and value stream mapping.

5.3.1 Process flow charting

A process flowchart or process map is the standard way of describing a process in OM. A *process flowchart* is a graphical representation of the separate steps in a process in a sequential order. It is a generic tool that can be adapted to a wide range of purposes, and can be used to describe manufacturing processes, administrative processes and service processes. It is a commonly used tool for process analysis and is one of the basic quality tools (see also Chapter 6).

The symbols that we use in this book for process charting are shown in Figure 5.4.

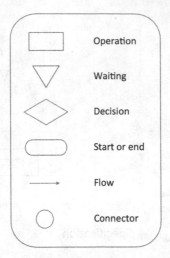

Figure 5.4 Symbols used for OM process flowchart.

The content of the operation can be written in the box. Usually only one arrow leaves the box.

The waiting symbol has its origin in manufacturing where intermediate products were stored to act as buffers. Services cannot be stored, but the waiting acts as a buffer before the service is delivered.

The decision criterion or question can be written (in shorthand) in the diamond. The alternatives (often yes and no) are indicated along the corresponding arrows leaving the diamond.

The start or end symbol is used to indicate the start and end of the process description.

The arrow is used to represent the flow of patients between steps.

The connector symbol can be used to link different parts of a flowchart.

There are several examples of process flow charts in this book (see Figures 2.2, 5.7 and 5.8). There is much freedom in drawing a flowchart. It is important, however, to provide a legend of the symbols used. More information on process flowcharts can be found via the internet, e.g., Wikipedia.

5.3.2 Service blueprinting

A *service blueprint* is a description of the process of service delivery from the perspective of possible 'customer actions'. The concept is from the knowledge domains of Service Management and Service Marketing. It was originally a technique used for service design. By creating a 'blueprint' as a first step in developing a new service, an organisation may create a coherent plan for what must be organised on different levels of the organisation to be able to deliver the expected services. In the design, possible 'failure points' are also indicated, and solutions are incorporated in the design. This is a typical approach of 'thinking before doing' from design sciences. Blueprinting starts with an investigation into all possible customer actions. From that level, the physical environment requirements are formulated, and the organisational functions are added.

There are different layers in the blueprint:

- Physical evidence: tangible elements that are associated with a step in the process and may influence the perception of the service: a room, uniforms.
- Customer actions: the steps that customers take in the service delivery process.
- Front-stage actions: the contacts with front-office employees in the process.
- Back-stage actions: the non-visible steps taken by back-office employees, including the non-physical contacts between customers and organisation.
- Support processes: activities carried out by employees who have no contact with customers, but whose actions are required for the service delivered (IT services, administration).

The line of customer interaction separates the customer actions from the service provider actions, the line of visibility separates the front-stage and back-stage actions, and the line of internal interaction separates front-office and back-office actions (see example a blueprint for a first visit to an outpatient clinic in a hospital in Figure 5.5).

Though service blueprints were originally developed for designing new services, they can also be used to check in detail where and why in a specific process things go wrong.

For more information on service blueprinting, see (Bordoloi, Fitszimmons, and Fitzsimmons, 2019).

5.3.3 *Value stream mapping*

A *value stream map* (VSM) is a lean management method to analyse the current state and to design a future state for a series of events in the manufacture of a product or in the delivery of a service. A VSM in healthcare shows the flow of patients and information and the progress through the process.

The purpose of a VSM is to identify and remove 'waste' in the value stream. Lean Management distinguishes seven types of waste (see Chapter 6): waiting, transportation, movement, overproduction, overprocessing, rework (defects) and inventory.

The VSM is created to visualise the value-adding activities and distinguish them from non-value-adding activities in a patient process. Non-value activities are seen as 'waste' and have to be reduced or eliminated. A distinction can be made between activities that don't add value for the patient but are

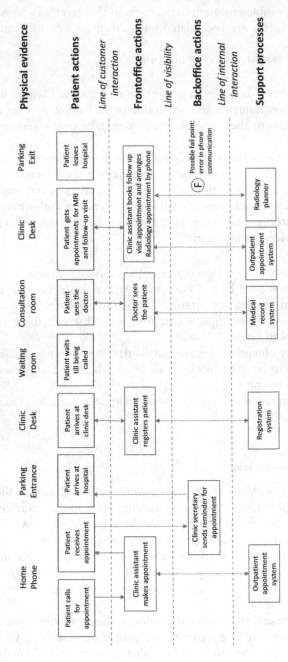

Figure 5.5 Service blueprint of first visit to outpatient clinic.

inevitable, like transportation between different physical departments, and activities that should be eliminated, like waiting time.

There is not much guidance on how a VSM should be presented. The traditional way in manufacturing is to show the progress in the production chain at the bottom and the control of the production above (see Figure 5.6 for an example).

In this example we see that the current state map indicates that the three-step production chain results in a throughput time of 14.1 days, of which 99% consists of waiting time in storage. Improved inventory control may result in considerable gain in throughput time, lower work in progress and in shorter deliver time for customers.

For service organisations the parallel can be found in reducing queues for services, resulting in shorter waiting times for patients. Therefore, we see in healthcare examples of a VSM based on a process flowchart, often created in a multidisciplinary session in which the participants draw a representation of the process of patients on a large piece of paper and use coloured pieces of paper for steps, indicating with, for example, coloured spots places where waste occurs, or value can be created. Notice that there are more possible causes of waste in a process, besides waiting time. In healthcare processes, examples are transportation, doing excess work, failure or mistakes or doing unnecessary steps in a diagnostic process. Chapter 6 elaborates further on this.

5.4 Performance of process chains

An important component of an OM approach to process chains is the definition of activities in terms of duration and timing. In this section we elaborate on this time dimension of the pathway, process or chain.

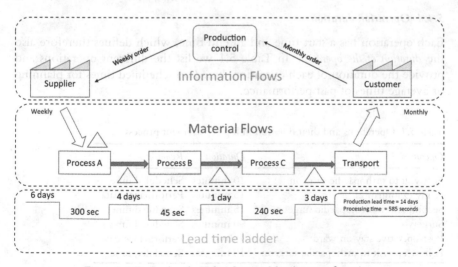

Figure 5.6 Example of a Value Stream Map in manufacturing.

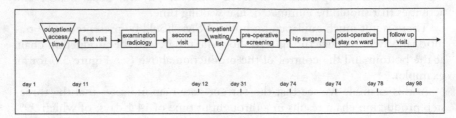

Figure 5.7 Process flowchart of a hospital trajectory for hip replacement on a time-axis (not to scale).

We return to the example of the process of a patient requiring a hip replacement from Chapter 2 and provide it with a time axis.

We see from Figure 5.7 that the process for a patient referred for a hip replacement takes on average – based on some data from actual processes – 98 days from referral to discharge. On day 11 the patient sees the orthopaedic surgeon on two occasions – on the first visit to discuss the hip problem and after the X-ray examination (on a walk-in basis at the radiology department) to discuss the treatment. Then the patient is placed on the waiting list for surgery, and an appointment is made for pre-operative screening a few weeks before the surgery date. The patient is admitted on the day of surgery. After surgery, the patient stays four days on the inpatient ward. The process of the hospital trajectory ends on day 98 after the follow-up visit, three weeks after discharge.

We now go into more detail, first on the duration of operations, then on waiting times and finally on throughput times.

5.4.1 Operation duration

Each operation has a start time and an end time, which defines therefore also the *duration of the operation*. In Table 5.1 we list the different operations and provide the duration of each operation, based on scheduled times for planning or average times of past performance.

Table 5.1 Operations and their duration in hip replacement process

Operation	Duration	Remarks
First visit to orthopaedic surgeon	10 minutes	Scheduled time
X-ray examination	15 minutes	Performance data
Second visit to orthopaedic surgeon	15 minutes	Scheduled time
Surgery	90 minutes	Scheduled time
Post-operative stay on ward	4 days	Performance data
Follow up visit to orthopaedic surgeon	10 minutes	Scheduled time

The durations are often based on slots used for scheduling appointments or on statistical data on performance, such as the length of stay or the surgery duration. For the purpose of description of the process it suffices to use standards for planning or averages from performance measurements. However, one should be aware that in reality these durations vary from patient to patient.

The durations can be defined from different perspectives, i.e., the patient, the healthcare professional or the facility. Usually, the patient perspective is used but sometimes – in more detailed analyses – a distinction is made between different definitions of duration. For surgery, for instance, the length of time that the operating room is used differs from the length of the surgery procedure.

5.4.2 Waiting time

We see different forms of waiting time in the process for patients with hip replacement. In Table 5.2 we provide an overview of these waiting times and their durations for the example hip replacement process.

The first waiting time encountered in the process is called *access time*. This is the time the patient has to wait to get access to the service delivery system, in this case ten days to see the orthopaedic surgeon for the first time. The second waiting time is the time between the first and second visits. This is actually not a waiting time but a *response time* on a walk-in request for an X-ray examination. Therefore, we can label it as a *lead time* which is necessary for the smooth flow of the process. The third waiting time is the time spent on the waiting list before the patient is admitted for the surgery. The fourth waiting time is again not a real waiting time, but the time required to recover from the surgery. So, this can also be labelled as a lead time.

In general, we can distinguish between different types of waiting time according to its cause. The most common type of waiting time is waiting in a queue before one is served. We can call this *access time* or just *waiting time*. The term access time refers to the time one has to wait before one gets access to a service. Once one has got access to a service the next time one

Table 5.2 Waiting times and lead times in the process for patients with hip replacement

Period	Description of period	Term	Duration	Remarks
1	Time between referral and first visit	Access time	10 days	Real waiting time
2	Time between first visit and second visit	Response time	60 minutes	Lead time
3	Time between second visit and day of admission	Waiting time (on waiting list)	2 months	Real waiting time
4	Time between discharge and follow up visit	Follow up time	20 days	Lead time

has to wait is called waiting time. If one wants to refer to the time in the process at the more detailed level of an operation, one often uses the label of *in-process waiting time*. This can for instance be the time in the waiting room before one sees the doctor, or the time in the waiting room before the X-ray examination.

Another type of waiting time is the **batch waiting time**. This refers to the time a patient has to wait before there are enough patients available (the batch size) to fill a clinic session or an operating theatre session.

The third type of waiting time can be labelled *'frequency of service' waiting time* and refers to the time the patient has to wait until the next session is organised. Sometimes clinic sessions are of a specific type to allow for seeing a specific category of patients, for instance a fracture clinic. If this clinic is only organised once a week, the waiting time due to the frequency of service is on average half a week.

The overall waiting time of a patient is often due to a combination of the above causes. Similarly, the above illustrates the range of issues that might need to be addressed if a reduction in patient waiting times is to be achieved.

5.4.3 Throughput time

The *throughput time* of a process is defined as the time it takes to go through all the steps of the process from beginning to end. In case of the hip replacement trajectory (see Figure 5.7), we can see that the total time for the throughput of a patient is 98 days from the moment of referral to the moment of completion (or referral back) to the general practitioner. The 98 days consist of 71 days of waiting, 7 days of processing, and 20 days of recovery time.

In a care process, a distinction is often made between the throughput time of the diagnostic phase and the throughput time of the treatment phase. In the hip replacement trajectory, the throughput time of the diagnostic phase is 11 days (10 days waiting time and 1 day processing time) and the throughput time of the treatment phase is 87 days (61 days waiting time, 6 days processing time and 20 days recovery time).

We can use the information on the hip replacement process discussed in this section to embellish the process flow chart (see Figure 5.8).

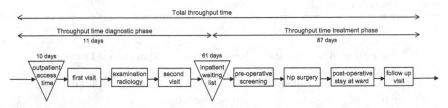

Figure 5.8 Process flowchart hip replacement trajectory with waiting times and throughput times.

5.5 Description of process chains

For a description of a process from an OM perspective, there should always be an explicit relationship with the use of resources in each step of the process. To illustrate this feature of an OM analysis of a process, we return to the example of the patient requiring a hip replacement and provide more information on each step in the process in Table 5.3.

Notice that we have only recorded the use of resources and not the use of materials such as disposables on the ward or the use of the prosthesis for the surgery. Also, the description is limited to the use of resources for the clinical process and does not include the use of ancillary processes such as housing and cleaning. Having defined each step in the clinical process, and the use of resources in each step, it is possible to look at the total use of resources by the chain (see Table 5.4).

This method of description of a care process is especially suitable for analysing a care process for resource implications.

In the above example we assumed that all patients follow each step of the process, which is often not the case in practice. Often, once the diagnosis is

Table 5.3 Description of process and resource use of the process chain for patients with hip replacement

Step	Description of the content	Duration	Resources	Resource use
1	First visit to orthopaedic surgeon	10 minutes	Specialist time	10 minutes
			Outpatient facility	15 minutes
			Clerical staff	5 minutes
2	X-ray examination	15 minutes	Radiographer	15 minutes
			Radiologist	2 minutes
			X-ray room and equipment	20 minutes
3	Second visit	15 minutes	Specialist time	15 minutes
			Outpatient facility	20 minutes
			Clerical staff	5 minutes
			Admission officer	15 minutes
4	Pre-operative screening	30 minutes	Nurse POS	20 minutes
			Anaesthetist	10 minutes
5	Surgery	90 minutes	Operating theatre	120 minutes
			Anaesthetist	10 minutes
			Anaesthetic nurse	45 minutes
			Operating assistant	120 minutes
			Specialist time	75 minutes
6	Post-operative stay at ward	4 days	Bed at ward	4 days
			Nursing staff	200 minutes
			Specialist time	10 minutes
7	Follow up visit to orthopaedic surgeon	10 minutes	Specialist time	10 minutes
			Outpatient facility	15 minutes
			Clerical staff	5 minutes

Table 5.4 Summary of resource use of the process chain for patients with hip replacement

Department	Resource	Amounts of resources used
Outpatient department	Facilities	50 minutes
	Clerical staff	15 minutes
Admission office	Admission officer	15 minutes
Radiology department	X-ray room and equipment	20 minutes
	Radiographer	15 minutes
	Radiologist	2 minutes
Pre-operative screening	Nurse POS	20 minutes
Operating Theatres	Operating theatre	120 minutes
	Anaesthetic nurse	45 minutes
	Operating assistant	120 minutes
Ward	Bed	4 days
	Nursing staff	200 minutes
Anaesthetist	Specialist time	20 minutes
Orthopaedic surgeon	Specialist time	120 minutes

clear, some patients do not need to continue the process, because they may turn out to have another problem or prefer not to be treated. Another complication might be that some investigations or tests don't need to be performed for all patients. It is fairly simple to handle these 'exemptions' from the general process by adding an extra column in the description format of Table 5.5 for the percentage of patients that follow each step.

This way of describing the care process of patients for hip replacement does more justice to the reality of healthcare practice and can be seen as a refinement of the method used in Table 5.3. It requires information on the percentage of patients that follow each step of the process. This information can be based on input from healthcare professionals who are performing the operation or based on analysis of healthcare production data.

Though we write this text from the perspective of healthcare professionals and managers, we consider a process from the point of view of the patient. Of course, the patient will not be interested in the use of resources in each step, but by emphasising the steps in the process that are adding value, we come near to the concept of the '*patient journey*'. This concept (Beleffi et al., 2021) has become increasingly popular among healthcare providers to deliver patient-centred care and organise the process around the patient. They see the patient journey concept as an example of a systems approach, to include the patient's viewpoint and experience in approaches to improve the delivery of healthcare and patient safety. Instead of focusing on individual encounters, the focus should be on the whole patient journey. McCarthy et al. (2016) define patient journey mapping as 'a description of the patient experience, including tasks within encounters, the emotional journey, the physical journey, and the various touch points'. Zomerdijk and Voss (2010) stress in their paper on service

Table 5.5 Description of flow-dependent process and resource use of the process chain for patients with hip replacement

Step	Percentage of patients	Description of the content	Duration	Resources	Resource use
1	100%	First visit to orthopaedic surgeon	10 minutes	Specialist time Outpatient facility Clerical staff	10 minutes 15 minutes 5 minutes
2	100%	X-ray examination	15 minutes	Radiographer Radiologist X-ray room and equipment	15 minutes 2 minutes 20 minutes
3	100%	Second visit	15 minutes	Specialist time Outpatient facility Clerical staff Admission officer	15 minutes 20 minutes 5 minutes 15 minutes
4	90%	Pre-operative screening	30 minutes	Nurse POS Anaesthetist	20 minutes 10 minutes
5	90%	Operation	90 minutes	Operating theatre Anaesthetist Anaesthetic nurse Operating assistant Specialist time	120 minutes 10 minutes 45 minutes 120 minutes 75 minutes
6	90%	Post-operative stay at ward	4 days	Bed at ward Nursing staff Specialist-time	4 days 200 minutes 10 minutes
7	90%	Follow up visit to orthopaedic surgeon	10 minutes	Specialist-time Outpatient facility Clerical staff	10 minutes 15 minutes 5 minutes

design for experience-centric services, the need to consider all 'touchpoints' in the customer journey, not only the interaction with frontline professionals but also the coupling with back-stage employees. It may be clear from the above that the patient journey concept covers much more than a description of the whole process of the patient. However, it provides support for our HSOM approach to describe healthcare processes as a basis that can be used to elaborate further on the influence patients and patient experiences can have on improving and redesigning healthcare services.

5.6 Planning and improvement of process chains

Now we have described the process or chain and are able to evaluate its performance, the last step to be taken in the OM approach is to consider the planning of the process chain. Of relevance here are the design principles related to the levels of planning (operational, tactical, strategic) which were introduced in Chapter 2.

5.6.1 Operational/structural coordination

The concepts of operational and structural coordination were introduced in Section 2.8 as means of balancing demand for and supply of resources. *Operational coordination* refers to the acceptance of the client orders and the ordering of resources, such that these are in balance with the orders accepted. Examples of operational coordination in the chain for treating patients with hip osteoarthritis are:

- The coordination between the first visit, X-ray examination and second visit to ensure that these take place on the same day.
- The coordination between pre-operative screening and admission to ensure that the timing of this screening does not delay the surgery.
- The coordination between the surgery and the ordering of the prosthesis that needs to be implanted during the procedure.
- The coordination between the discharge of the patient and any follow-up activities required outside the hospital such as nursing homecare or community physiotherapy.

When these forms of coordination do not take place, they result in extra visits for patients (when the 'second visit' is not taken care of on the same day), delays in the process (if the screening results are outdated at the moment of surgery, or the prosthesis is not available in time), and loss of capacity (redoing the screening, cancellation of surgery, longer length of stay). If the process chain of hip osteoarthritis patients is functioning well, it is possible to project for homecare agencies the number of patients that they can expect, which helps to avoid delay in discharge.

Structural coordination refers to the setting of arrangements and conditions which allow for operational coordination, including the target service level and resource utilisation level. Examples of structural coordination in the chain for treating patients with hip replacement are:

- Are there dedicated clinic sessions for patients with hip problems and dedicated operating theatre sessions for hip replacement surgery, or are these patients seen in general clinics and treated in operating theatre sessions with a mixed composition?
- How much capacity needs to be allocated to outpatient clinics and surgery sessions to ensure a smooth flow of patients through the chain?
- Is the radiology department consulted about sufficient capacity for direct service to patients coming from the orthopaedic clinics?
- What is an acceptable access time for the first visit of a patient with osteoarthritis, what is an acceptable waiting time on the waiting list for surgery, and what are the realistic occupancy levels of operating theatre sessions and ward beds?
- As the diagnosis and the decision to have a surgery is the decoupling point in the process, the treatment phase can be scheduled very precisely, which

primarily protects the use of expensive resources in the operating theatre department.

For a smooth flow of patients through the chain, the variables controlled at the level of the chain, are:

- The amount of capacity allocated to each workstation.
- The balance between the allocations of different resources required for the chain.
- The service levels to be achieved by the chain.

The variables controlled locally, at the level of the units, are:

- The utilisation level of the unit's resources.
- The performance of the unit in terms of waiting time.

Aggregate control, at the level of the total patient flow, takes place for:

- The total amounts of resources available for each processing point in the chain.
- The check on available capacity for the flow of patients expected from the orthopaedics clinics.

Detailed control, at the level of the individual patient, is required for:

- The appointment with the orthopaedic surgeon for the second visit on the same day.
- The booking of follow-up care at home after discharge.

5.6.2 *Push and pull*

One can distinguish different modes of planning of care processes. A common distinction is push-and-pull planning. When *push planning* is applied in a process, each step is planned separately and independently of the other steps. Each time a patient arrives for a certain step, checks are performed when capacity is available for the patient and the patient has to wait until then. Push planning is resource-oriented and protects a resource from inefficient planning. Push planning is often applied for major surgery because the resources required for surgery are very expensive and require advance planning of different resources (operating room, anaesthetist, surgeon(s), anaesthetic nurse, operating assistants). The patient is put on a waiting list and will be called when it is their turn to be treated. For minor surgery, often in day surgery, the patient is already provided with a date in advance, but this is also a form of push planning.

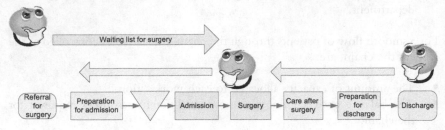

Figure 5.9 A process chain with push-and-pull planning.

Pull planning is process-oriented and a form of backward planning by defining the target date for an investigation or treatment, and by planning all the steps that need to be taken in advance before execution of the final step. Pull planning can be applied when the process is more or less standardised and more predictable. A day surgery procedure is often planned in a pull way by agreeing on the date of the procedure and then arranging the pre-operative screening visit at an appropriate time in advance of this.

In many care processes, part of the process can be organised in a pull manner and part as push (see Figure 5.9).

Figure 5.9 illustrates a process in which the surgery is planned in a push manner, while the preparation for the surgery is organised in a pull way. After the surgery the discharge is organised as pull by defining the date of discharge and by organising the preparation of the discharge (homecare or follow-up care) in advance.

5.7 Questions and exercises

Compare different approaches for classifying hospital products, i.e., International Classification of Diseases (ICD), Diagnosis Related Groups (DRGs), Healthcare Resource Groups (HRGs) and the patient grouping system (iso-process) as used in this book. What are their differences and similarities? What are their strengths and weaknesses?

What are possibilities to improve the chain for patients with hip replacements (see Figure 5.8)? What will be the impact on the throughput time? What will be the impact on the use of resources?

Suppose hip replacements are going to be organised in a standalone treatment centre. The procedures are going to be performed by a group of orthopaedic surgeons who are also working at the hospital where they perform other orthopaedic procedures. What will be the consequences for the chains of patient groups that can be distinguished in the patient flow of orthopaedics? What will be the impact on the throughput time? What will be the impact on the use of resources? What will be the impact on the need for coordination of the different chains?

References

Baas LJC (1996). Producttypering medisch specialistische ziekenhuiszorg (Dutch). *Medisch Contact*. 51, 356–358.

Beleffi E, Mosconi P and Sheridan S (2021). The patient journey. In Donaldson L, Sheridan S and Tartaglia R (eds), *Textbook of patient safety and clinical risk management*. Springer, Cham. https://doi.org/10.1007/978-3-030-59403-9_10.

Bordoloi SK, Fitzsimmons JA and Fitzsimmons MJ (2019). *Service management: operations, strategy, information technology*. McGraw-Hill/Irwin, New York.

De Vries G, Bertrand JWM and Vissers JMH (1999). Design requirements for health care production control systems. *Production Planning and Control*, 10(6), 559–569.

E-P-A European Pathway Association (2021). https://e-p-a.org.

Fetter RB (1983). The new ICD-9-CM Diagnosis related Groups Cliassification Scheme. Health Care Financing Administration Pub. no. 03167. US Government Printing Office, Washington, DC.

Fetter RB, Averill RF, Lichtenstein JL and Freeman JL (1984). Ambulatory visit groups: a framework for measuring productivity in ambulatory care. *Health Services Research*, 19(4), 415–437. PMID: 6490373; PMCID: PMC1068824.

Fetter, RB and Freeman JL (1986). Diagnosis related groups: product line management within hospitals. *Academy of management review. Academy of Management*, 11 (1), 41–54

Lillrank P (2018). *The logics of healthcare: the professional's guide to health systems science*. Taylor & Francis Group, London.

Lillrank P and Liukko M (2004). Standard, routine and non-routine processes in health care. *International Journal of Quality Assurance*, 17(1), 39–46.

McCarthy S, O'Raghallaigh P, Woodworth S, Yoke Lin L, Kenny LC and Adam F (2016). An integrated patient journey mapping tool for embedding quality in healthcare service reform. *Journal of Decision Systems*, 25(sup1), 354–368. https://doi.org/10.1080/12460125.2016.1187394.

Vanhaecht K, De Witte K and Sermeus W (2007). *The impact of clinical pathways on the organisation of care processes*. PhD dissertation, KU Leuven.

Vanhaecht K, Van Gerwen E, Deneckere S, Lodewijckx C, Janssen I, Van Zelm R and Sermeus W (2012). The 7-phase method to design, implement and evaluate care pathways. *International Journal of Person Centered Medicine*, 2(3), 341–351.

Zomerdijk LG and Voss CA (2010). Service design for experience-centric services. *Journal of Services Research*, 13(1), 67–82. https://doi.org/10.1177/1094670509351960.

Further reading

De Vries GG, Vissers JMH and De Vries G (2000). The use of patient classification systems for production control of hospitals. *Casemix*, 2(2), 65–70.

NHS Modernisation Agency (2002a). *Improvement leaders' guides* (series 1, guide 1). Process mapping, analysis and redesign.

NHS Modernisation Agency (2002b). *Improvement leaders' guides* (series 1, guide 2). Matching capacity and demand.

NHS Modernisation Agency (2002c). *Improvement leaders' guides* (series 1, guide 3). Measurement for improvement.

Ploman MP (1985). Choosing a patient classification system to describe the hospital product. *Hospital and Health Services Administration*, 30, 106–117

Plsek PE (1997). Systematic design of health care processes. *Quality in Health Care*, 6, 40–48.

Van der Bij JD and Vissers JMH (1999). Monitoring health-care processes: a framework for performance indicators. *International Journal of Health Care Quality Assurance*, 12(5), 214–221.

6 Improvement approaches

Sylvia Elkhuizen and Nathan Proudlove

6.1 Introduction

Healthcare is changing continuously. Budget restrictions, a changing population, increasing technical and medical possibilities or evolution in patient preferences may be the trigger for the re-organisation of units and processes in healthcare. Since around 1980, many concepts and approaches to improve healthcare organisations and systems have arisen. Most of them have their origin in industry (Young et al., 2004; Holweg et al., 2018). Each approach has some basic principles and ideas about the focus of improvement and steps to be taken. Most approaches also have a toolbox of methods to help in analysing and improving the system. Most of those tools are applicable widely, and toolboxes may be combined from different approaches.

In general, we can distinguish between two main change strategies: continuous improvement of existing systems or (re)design from scratch. *Redesigning* assumes a start with a 'blank sheet of paper'. In general, redesign focuses on a specific unit, part of a unit or process. Redesign is organised as a project with a specific start and a clear end. A redesign project may have several stages, and eventually a pilot implementation, but is completed after implementing the new design of the process or unit. Business Process Redesign, elaborated in Section 6.3 is such an approach. On the other hand, a *continuous improvement* approach never ends. It is a cyclical process, in which phases of generating ideas for improvements and implementing them are repeated continuously. In practice, completing implementation of a new design should be the start of continuous thought about improvement to iron out problems and adapt to changes in the dynamic world. There are several specific approaches for continuous improvement. In Sections 6.4, 6.5 and 6.6 we explain three concepts that are applied in health organisations frequently: Theory of Constraints, Lean Management and Six Sigma.

In fact, it doesn't matter which approach you adopt; all approaches will lead to improvement, if applied rigorously enough (Boaden et al., 2008). However, because the focus and organisation of approaches differ, a specific approach may fit better to the kinds of problems you want to solve and with the organisational culture. We come back to this issue at the end of this chapter when

DOI: 10.4324/9781003020011-7

we compare and discuss the different approaches, also in relation to the body of operations management (OM) knowledge.

6.2 The basics of quality improvement

Deming can be seen as the founding father of continuous quality improvement (Best, 2005) and his Plan-Do-Study-Act (PDSA) Cycle forms the underlying principle for continuous improvement approaches. In the Plan phase, ideas are generated for improvement, based on the goals and aims of the improvement initiative. Additionally, measurements and modelling help to analyse the current situation and generate ideas for improvement. Ideally, preliminary (quantitative) analyses may provide some prior confidence (perhaps even validation) of planned changes. In the Do phase, the ideas are implemented. This can be a large-scale implementation, but more frequently, small pilot implementations precede a fuller implementation during a subsequent cycle. In the Study phase, the new (pilot) situation is analysed and in the Act phase, decisions are made based on these analyses whether to implement the change idea on a larger scale, adapt it and test again, or park or abandon it and instead seek a new change idea. The idea is that there is always something to improve, so after completing a full round of the cycle, another PDSA cycle is initiated. Figure 6.1 (left side) sketches this approach. The approach is small, rapid-cycle experiment-based learning about the real-world impact of change (intended and unintended) in the complex, dynamic reality; individual cycles may 'fail', but the learning gained is valuable for future cycles (Leis, 2016). Many studies show that discipline and fidelity to the method is important to avoid poor PDSA practice and outcomes (McNicholas, 2019; Taylor, 2014). Using a roadmap as logical guidance through a Quality Improvement (QI) project, in which tools and techniques may be used at various stages, may help. Figure 6.1, right-hand side, shows the Model for Improvement (Langley et al., 1996; Provost and Murray, 2011), adopted and promoted by the Institute for Healthcare Improvement (IHI) in the US and the National Health Service (NHS) in the UK. Its three questions guide construction of a sensible plan for PDSA and consideration of the outcomes.

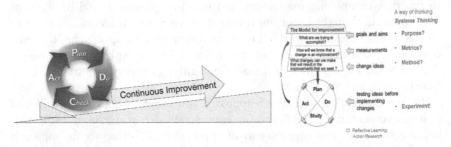

Figure 6.1 Deming's PDSA approach and IHI's Model for Improvement roadmap as guidance for QI project.

To get insight in the problem and possible solutions, seven 'basic tools' for quality improvement (or Total Quality Management, TQM) are frequently used (Bordoloi et al., 2019).

6.2.1 *Tool #1* Cause-and-effect diagram

In a cause-and-effect diagram, also called a fishbone or Ishikawa diagram, a central problem is broken down into different categories of causes, and further into underlying (root) causes. The idea is that by structuring causes in a hierarchical way, the root causes can be identified and solved, instead of finding solutions for symptoms. Moreover, by categorising the causes of a problem, the issues can be addressed in a coherent and structured way. Traditionally the categories for a cause-and-effect diagram are 'man', 'machine', 'method' and 'material'. However, if other categories fit better for a specific problem, you may choose a different set of categories. Generally, four to six categories are used. Information for creating a cause-and-effect diagram can be gathered by performing observations, interviews, focus group meetings or quantitative data analysis. This may lead to a list of issues which can be structured in a cause-and-effect diagram. Figure 6.2 gives an example of a cause-and-effect diagram for the problem 'waiting times for an MRI'.

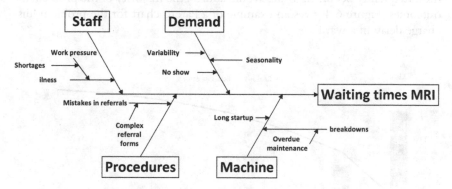

Figure 6.2 An example of a cause-and-effect diagram for long waiting times for MRI.

6.2.2 *Tool #2* Check sheet

A check sheet can be used to get insight into the frequency of issues. A check sheet can simply be a piece of paper or a whiteboard where employees record the incidence of problems, but it may also be somewhat more sophisticated in an online software tool. Figure 6.3 gives an example of a check sheet.

issue	Monday	Tuesday	Wednesday	Thursday	Friday
waiting for material	I	IIII		HH	IIII
patient not ready	III	II	II	I	II
waiting for staff	II		I		I

Figure 6.3 Example of a check sheet for reasons for waiting.

6.2.3 Tool #3 Pareto chart

A Pareto chart gives visual insight into the relative importance of a problem's causes. In a Pareto chart, the relative or absolute frequency of a list of causes is given and are sequenced in order from most to least frequently occurring. The data for a Pareto chart can be a measurement, for example supported by a check sheet. The underlying idea of a Pareto chart is that a small proportion of the causes is responsible for a large majority of occurrences of the problematic outcome. This is also known as the Pareto principle or 80/20 rule: 20% of the causes may typically account for 80% of the problems. In practice, it is not always exactly 80/20, but the underlying idea remains that a focus on the few most frequently occurring issues would address the majority of the problematic outcomes. Figure 6.4 gives an example of a Pareto chart for the problem 'discharge delay in a ward'.

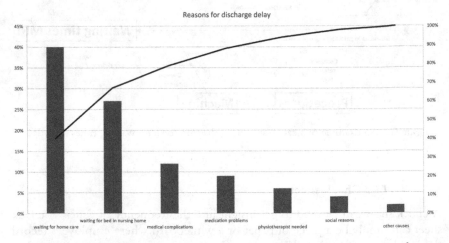

Figure 6.4 Example of a Pareto chart for reasons for discharge delay in a ward.

6.2.4 Tool #4 Scatterplot

A scatterplot visualises the relation between two variables. The main purpose is to get insight into whether there is a relation between the two variables and to get an indication of how strong this relation is. A scatterplot doesn't say anything about the *causality* of this relation. One variable may be seen as the cause of the other or just a related factor. Figure 6.5 gives a scatterplot for the relation between patient age and length of discharge delay.

To quantify the relationship between two quantitative scale variables, we can use the Pearson correlation as an indicator for linear correlation (see any statistics handbook or e.g., Wikipedia). The correlation can be positive or negative. A positive correlation means that both variables tend to increase or decrease together. With a negative correlation, one variable increases when the other is decreasing. Beside the direction, we can give an interpretation of the strength of the linear relationship, as given in Table 6.1.

The Pearson correlation in the example in Figure 6.5 is 0.62 and can be characterised as a strong positive correlation. For ordinal (e.g., high, medium, low) variables, the Pearson correlation is not applicable, and as an alternative a Spearman's rho can be applied (see any statistics handbook or e.g., Wikipedia).

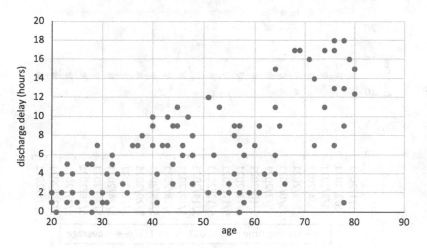

Figure 6.5 Example scatterplot for relation between age and discharge delay.

Table 6.1 Interpretation of a correlation

Absolute correlation	Indication of relation between variables
0.8–1	very strong correlation
0.6–0.8	strong correlation
0.4–0.6	moderate correlation
0.2–0.4	weak correlation
0–0.2	no relation

6.2.5 Tool #5 Control chart

A control chart, also known as Statistical Process Control (SPC) chart, visualises the behaviour of a variable over time. It highlights when a variable is no longer exhibiting random behaviour, for example a datapoint is outside the 'control limits' (upper control limit, UCL = average + 3 × standard deviation, and lower control limit, LCL = average − 3 × standard deviation), in which case it might be said to be 'out of control'.

Figure 6.6 shows a control chart for the waiting time for an X-ray in a radiology department.

We see from Figure 6.6 that the average waiting time of an X-ray in the radiology department is about 13 minutes, and that in the daily measurements of the waiting time, the waiting time was longer than the upper control limit on one day. This implies that the waiting time is out of control, and corrective measures need to be taken. See the online material for more details, software tools and exercises.

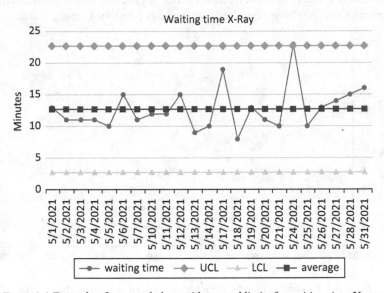

Figure 6.6 Example of a control chart with control limits for waiting time X-ray.

6.2.6 Tool #6 Flowchart

A flowchart is a type of diagram that represents a process or workflow. In Chapter 5 we have already introduced the flowchart as the standard way of describing a process in OM (Subsection 5.3.1) and provided examples of process flowcharts in healthcare.

6.2.7 Tool #7 Histogram

A histogram represents the frequency distribution of a continuous variable, in which data are grouped and represented by columns. The example in Figure 6.7 shows a distribution of waiting time for surgery, measured in days, with grouped data in classes with a width of two days. For further explanation, see also Chapter 3.

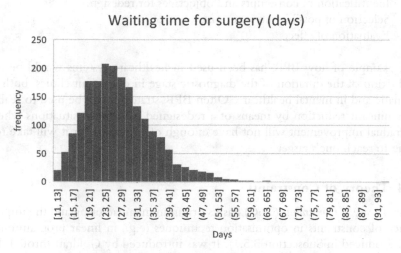

Figure 6.7 Example of a histogram of waiting time for surgery.

6.3 Business Process Redesign

Business Process Redesign (BPR), also known as Business Process Reengineering, is a management strategy to restructure business processes in a fundamental and radical way with the objective to realise a dramatic change in performance (Davenport, 1993; Hammer and Champy, 1993). The strategy starts from the premise that processes should not be redesigned from an existing situation that must be improved, but rather from a clean slate, and that a fundamentally new approach must be designed from scratch. BPR has been a well-known approach in healthcare for several decades (Locock, 2003; Elkhuizen et al., 2006; Elkhuizen, 2007). In situations where companies have got 'stuck' using existing methods or in situations that require a drastically improved performance, they will often opt for a reengineering approach. BPR allows organisations to check once again which process design best matches their objectives. In order to be able to abandon their current design and be receptive to new solutions, teams will often have a preparatory awayday including a brainstorming session and drawing up a new design. Although the basic premise of process redesign strategies is to start from scratch and design a 'perfect world', things often turn out differently in reality, and it often proves more sensible to start from process analysis. For more on this see, for instance, Jarvenpaa and Stoddard (1998). The method generally used in BPR comprises the following steps (Elkhuizen, 2007; Elkhuizen et al., 2007):

1. Process analysis.
2. Identification of constraints and objectives for redesign.
3. Selection of possible interventions.
4. Evaluation of effects.

An example of how BPR has been used in healthcare systems would be the reduction of the duration of the diagnostic stage in outpatient clinics, both in somatic and in mental healthcare. Often BPR strategies will be used to realise a significant reduction by means of a redesigned process, in situations where a gradual improvement will not have enough of an impact, or it will take too long to reach one's target.

6.4 Theory of Constraints

The *Theory of Constraints* (ToC) has its origin in manufacturing and the importance of constraints in optimisation techniques (e.g., in linear programming, as introduced in Subsection 3.5.1). It was introduced by Goldratt through his business novel 'The Goal' (Goldratt and Cox, 1986). The underlying idea of the ToC is that there is always one bottleneck (constraint) in a process chain and that this bottleneck determines the performance of the system. Easing this bottleneck will improve the output of the whole process.

Figure 6.8 shows a process with a bottleneck in the middle. In this example, ten patients per day may enter the process, but the limited capacity of process step 3 hinders the flow through the process and leads to queues and waiting times. The output of this process is constrained to five patients per day (on average if there is variation around these averages), despite the higher capacity of the other process steps. The ToC assumes that the current chain is fixed and tries to improve the flow of products or patients through it. It doesn't address poor process design (Nave, 2002). Commercially, the aim of the ToC is to increase the profit of an organisation. To achieve this, it focuses on three

Figure 6.8 A process with a bottleneck.

performance indicators: throughput of processes, inventory and operating expenses (Watson et al., 2007).

A central technique in the ToC is the Five Focusing Steps to address bottlenecks and improve process performance (Figure 6.9).

Step 1: *identify the bottleneck*. In a simple process with a fixed sequence of process steps and a continuous flow of patients, this is not so difficult. The bottleneck is the step with the lowest capacity per time unit, and in general is detectable by the increasing waiting time (and long queue) before this step in the process. In a more complex organisation, with different processes sharing different units, it may be more difficult the detect the bottleneck. However, in general, persistent and increasing waiting times for a unit may indicate a unit is a bottleneck for the chain.

Step 2: *exploit the bottleneck*. This step strives to get the most out of the bottleneck without big investments or changes. This may be done by standardising working procedures, training employees, changing working schedules, small investments in material and making sure only jobs really requiring that step pass through it. The exact possibilities depend on the unit and the current way of working. Before deciding about improvement possibilities, a quantitative or qualitative analysis of working processes, demand and resources may be required. However, the ToC doesn't provide a toolbox for such analyses. Tools described in Section 6.2 may be helpful to perform analyses in this step.

Step 3: *support the bottleneck*. Where step 2 focuses on the bottleneck itself, in step 3 the whole chain is included in trying to get more out of the bottleneck. In this step, the aim is to find possibilities in the chain to support the bottleneck and subordinate the chain to the bottleneck to get the most out of it. This may be done by moving tasks from the bottleneck to the previous or next steps in the process. Another way to support the bottleneck is to adapt the pace of the chain to the bottleneck, since there is no point in items

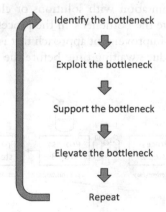

Figure 6.9 The Five Focusing Steps of the Theory of Constraints.

entering the chain faster than the bottleneck can process them. This implies two aspects: ensure that the bottleneck is always productive and prevent increasing waiting times before the bottleneck. Lost productive time at the bottleneck limits the output of the whole chain. The productivity of the bottleneck is protected by having a *small* buffer of waiting work before the bottleneck. If there is variation in work arrival rates and processing times, the buffer prevents the bottleneck being 'starved' of work. However, this buffer must be managed to prevent uncontrollable and growing waiting times. To manage the trade-off between buffer size and risk of bottleneck-resource starvation, the ToC introduced the '*drum-buffer-rope*' (DBR) method. The bottleneck step acts as the drum, determining the pace of the flow. Before the bottleneck, there is a small but critical buffer of work-in-process (goods or patients) to ensure it can always continue working. The rope pulls new work into the chain when the buffer is depleted, maintaining but also limiting the size of the buffer, and limiting chain throughput time. It prevents uncontrolled inflow of goods or patients to the process chain.

Step 4: *elevate the bottleneck*. When the previous steps are not sufficient to ease the bottleneck as much as desired, further actions are required. This means increasing the capacity of the bottleneck step, for example, investment in extra equipment and staff, or an extension of opening hours (also requiring extra staff). In general, the actions to be taken in this step must be agreed at the strategic level.

Step 5: *repeat the cycle*. When a bottleneck is eliminated, a new bottleneck may become visible. With this new bottleneck, the cycle starts over again. The idea is that by finding new bottlenecks and going through cycles to remove them, the system is continuously improved. In fact, this fifth step is not a separate activity, but mainly stresses the concept of continuous improvement by explicitly referring to the cyclical element in the approach.

Applying the ToC doesn't require major effort in educating staff in the method; it is quite easy to understand the basic principles. On the other hand, the ToC doesn't support the organisation with solutions or clear tools about how to exploit, support or elevate the bottleneck in the process. The DBR method is the only specific process-improvement approach that is advocated by the ToC. This method helps to reduce waiting time before the bottleneck and increase

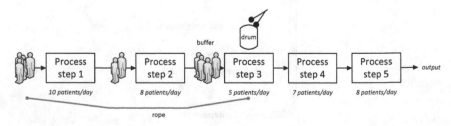

Figure 6.10 Drum-Buffer-Rope method.

the flow through the process chain but doesn't give suggestions about how to increase the capacity of the bottleneck. In healthcare, the notion of (the rope) pulling patients in might be applied to some parts of chains, e.g., the on-the-day activities in elective surgery, but is harder to conceptualise in others, e.g., the emergency department.

6.5 Lean Management

Lean Management has its origin in the Toyota Production System (TPS) in Japan. One of the main ideas of the TPS is to continuously improve the efficiency of workflow and reduce production costs, by all workers continuously spotting and eliminating problems at source and by incremental reductions in inventory towards 'just-in-time' delivery of parts and sub-assemblies to the production lines. The broadening of this concept arose when Womack et al. (1990) presented their book *The machine that changed the world* in which they describe Lean Management as a set of general principles to continuously improve processes. Lean Management is based on five principles (see Figure 6.11).

Principle 1: *define value*. The starting point for Lean Management is to define what value is from a customer's perspective. The idea is that if customers value a product or service, they are willing to pay the price set for it and the organisation makes a profit. In Porter's definition, value in healthcare is defined as 'health outcomes per dollar spent' (Porter and Teisberg, 2006). In this perspective, value is created in the full cycle of care, and organisations compete on value by increasing health outcomes and reducing costs. From a patient perspective, health outcomes are a combination of clinical outcomes, functional outcomes, and experiences (Lloyd, 2019). Clinical outcomes are the direct results of a patient care process, for example the surgical replacement of an arthritic hip. Functional outcomes are what a patient can do again after this medical procedure, for example work or play sport again. The patient experience is how the patient feels about the service (feeling safe and being treated kindly and respectfully) and how

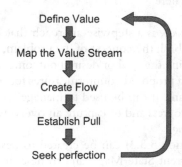

Figure 6.11 Principles of Lean Management.

long they have to wait. Costs from a patient perspective are not only out-of-pocket expenses but may also include the time and effort needed to obtain the service. Therefore, patient value can be increased by improving clinical outcomes and functional outcomes, but also by giving a patient a better experience or reducing the (waiting) time. Anything involved in the process that is not contributing to customer value (i.e., they, or service commissioners, would pay for that specific activity or aspect) is waste. The core goal of Lean Management is maximising value by reduction of waste.

Principle 2: *map the value stream*. A Value Stream Map (VSM) is created to visualise the process, distinguishing value-adding activities from non-value-adding activities (waste) in a chain. Non-value-adding activities are seen as waste, so are targets for reduction or elimination through improvement activity. A distinction can be made between activities that don't add value for the patient but are inevitable within the design constraints ('necessary waste'), like transportation between different physical departments and regulatory checks, and activities that could be eliminated (pure waste), like excessive waiting time.

Principle 3: *create flow*. Ensure that the service is delivered in an uninterrupted flow. Remove barriers that cause delay or other issues. Waiting lines (queues) and waiting times need to be avoided.

Principle 4: *establish pull*. The actual demand of patients should trigger the delivery process of services: it should be capable at working at the rate and time of demand.

Principle 5: *seek perfection*. Lean Management explicitly stimulates staff on the work floor to continuously look for possibilities to add value for customers and reduce non-value-adding activities from the process. In an organisation adopting the Lean Management approach, all staff members are given a mandate to change things in the organisation of the work if it adds to creating a leaner patient process. Such continuous improvement is also known in lean as kaizen.

There is a number of lean tools available that can be used during a lean approach to analyse a problem or to develop a solution for a problem. The most important tools are described here.

- The *A3 lean framework* is a stepwise approach that involves outlining the background to establish the context of the problem, describing the current condition, identifying the goal or desired outcome, analysing causes of the problem, providing proposed countermeasures for improvement, and creating follow-up plans. It can be used to manage an improvement project, to show current progress and to capture an overview of finished projects.
- *Value stream mapping*
  VSMs (see Subsection 5.3.3) can be created to describe the current state of a problem (Current State Map), and to describe the desired state of a solution (Future State Map).

- *Waste spotting*
  Originally, in manufacturing, seven types of waste were distinguished:
  - Transportation: waste due to unnecessary movement of products and materials or, in a healthcare organisation, patients.
  - Inventory: waste due to excess products and materials that aren't immediately required in order to perform the task.
  - Motion: waste due to unnecessary movement by staff or production machines.
  - Waiting: waste due to the time waiting for a product or resource to be ready.
  - Overproduction: waste due to making more products than customers demand.
  - Overprocessing: waste due to doing more work on a product or to a higher quality than is required by the customer.
  - Defects: waste due to product or service failure to meet customer expectations and maybe requiring work to be redone.

  More recently another other type of waste was added to the list:
  - Unused human potential: not making optimal use of the talents, skills and knowledge of people, including their workplace insights into problems and change ideas.

  Waste spotting can be undertaken in patient flow chains, information flows and/or use of resources.

  An important additional aspect of waste in service industries, especially public sector service and healthcare, is that some *demand* may also be 'waste': there may be customers entering our chain because of a previous failure ('failure demand') (Seddon, 2008), e.g., we didn't do the job well enough previously (readmission) or a non-optimal decision was made by staff. Examples are inappropriate admission to a bed, or a request for non-value-adding diagnostic, or a patient attending the emergency department when a General Practitioner (GP) appointment or advice from a pharmacist may have been adequate.

- *5 whys:* asking successive 'why?' questions to dig deeper and deeper into what really caused a problem to look for root causes (maybe up to five levels of 'why?').

- *5S method:* sort, straighten, shine, standardise, sustain. Establishing order, and systems to maintain order, in the work environment and clear out unused inventory and equipment. In healthcare this can be '6S' with the addition of working conditions that promote patient safety.

- *Rapid Improvement Event:* a standard approach to team-based problem solving in a relative short period of time. A cycle of data preparation and analysis; team process mapping, root cause analysis and generation of change ideas and 'to-be' process maps; perhaps 5/6S; then follow-up PDSAs and study of impact.

- *Standardised work* (which can include *management* standard work), and mistake proofing.

- *Visual management*: making the workflow and the state of the process visible, for example patient progress and discharge status indicators on whiteboards at a nursing station in an inpatient ward.

6.6 Six Sigma

Six Sigma is a management strategy developed by Motorola in the US, designed to reduce variability in processes. The main improvement roadmap is Define-Analyse-Measure-Improve-Control (DMAIC), and when adopted formally by an organisation this is conducted and supported by an infrastructure of training levels and facilitator roles (e.g., green belts, black belts, master black belts). One of the key characteristics of the Six Sigma approach is that it is data driven. The DMAIC project structure is:

1. Define: define which processes or products must be improved, which employees must be involved in this process, who the customer is and what needs and desires s/he has. Now map the process.
2. Measure: identify the key factors that most affect the process and determine how they will be measured.
3. Analyse: analyse the impact and inter-relations of the factors contributing to the process outcome that must be improved. There is often an emphasis on statistical analysis of data here.
4. Improve: design and implement the most effective solution, then assess the result.
5. Control: verify that the implementation was successful and ensure that the improvements will have a lasting effect, leaving the system in control at the new performance level through maintaining performance monitoring – typically by applying ongoing SPC (see Section 6.2).

6.7 Comparing and combining the approaches

Table 6.2, based on Nave (2002), compares the three major process improvement methodologies in OM and their characteristics.

The first part of Table 6.2 compares the three approaches on theory focus, steps in the approach and its focus. Lean Management (LM) theory focuses on adding value by eliminating waste for customers. The theory behind the ToC is about managing the constraints in the system. Six Sigma's theory focuses on the reduction of variation. All three have a stepwise approach to realising their goal, but the goals and steps differ. The most striking operational outcome of the LM approach is to produce smoother flow, for the ToC it is management of the key constraint and for Six Sigma that the problem of excessive variation is addressed.

There are also some differences between the three approaches regarding working from bottom-up or top-down in an organisation, focusing on unit

Table 6.2 Comparison of Lean Management, Theory of Constraints and Six Sigma

Approach	Lean Management	Theory of Constraints	Six Sigma
Theory focus	Increase value	Manage constraints	Reduce variations
Steps	1 Value	1 Identify constraint	1 Define
	2 Value stream	2 Exploit constraint	2 Measure
	3 Flow	3 Subordinate processes	3 Analyse
	4 Pull	4 Elevate constraint	4 Improve
	5 Perfection	5 Repeat cycle	5 Control
Focus in approach	Process flow	System constraints	Process variation
Other characteristics			
Top down/bottom up	Bottom up	Top down	Top down
Unit/process	Process oriented	Unit-oriented	Unit-oriented
Resources/demand	Demand oriented	Resource-oriented	Resource-oriented
Strong points	Customer perspective	Systems perspective	Data-driven
	Lean toolbox	Bottleneck	Quantitative methods
Weak points	Attention for other processes and network	Attention for quality and customer	Attention for process design
	Not all buffers are waste		

perspective versus process perspective and focusing on customer demand organisational resources. LM may often be characterised as having a bottom-up approach (from the frontline), while the ToC and Six Sigma can be labelled as top-down approaches (direction and support from above). LM has a strong process focus, while the ToC and Six Sigma use a unit perspective. LM is demand oriented, while the ToC and Six Sigma are resource-oriented.

The strong points of LM are the customer perspective, and the focus on waste and value. As weak points of LM one could say that there is not much attention on other processes that may show dependencies with the process investigated (for instance, shared resources), and the fact that buffers and waiting time are not always 'pure' waste (they can be important in protecting valuable resources from starvation). The strong points of the ToC are its system perspective and the handling of bottlenecks. As weak points one could mention the lack of attention to quality and the customer perspective. The strong point of Six Sigma is the data-driven way of handling variation in operations. As weak points one could say that there is no attention on the fact that problems could also be due to a poor design of a process, and little inherent insight into flow issues. There are some hybrid approaches, e.g., 'Lean Six Sigma' – see the online supplement.

The three strategies are similar in that each focuses on incremental improvements embedded in a culture of continuous improvement. All three strategies aim to improve existing process designs, which are further improved.

However, they do not address the question of whether these process designs should be completely reviewed, and it is not clear whether they eventually arrive at the 'best' possible solution.

The three approaches are also similar in that they all have compact and simple messages. Each is based on one or two core principles, from the broader knowledge base of OM.

All three programmes are popular among healthcare institutions. To a large extent, this is because they combine OM principles with practical change management-led approaches. For example, LM takes a bottom-up approach in which ideas proposed by employees constitute a major part and guide them through the stages of A3 thinking. Getting members of the organisation to agree on the 'next' constraint, the ToC can encourage everyone to be motivated to tackle the same issue, methodically using the five focusing steps, and achieve a high level of support for a concerted effort. Six Sigma may encourage the parties involved to actively collect data on the process themselves, thus creating support for the outcomes as they work through the DMAIC roadmap under close facilitation from a master black belt.

When these approaches are criticised, it is because there can be a tendency to regard them as isolated and self-contained complete systems of thought. They have their own terminologies, and adherents (perhaps particularly some specialist management consultants) can be convinced that their approach is the only correct one, without any reference to other approaches. ('If your only tool is a hammer, then every problem looks like a nail …').

It is challenging importing any of these approaches in a wide, deep and sustained way into an organisation, and there is much literature about this (e.g., Bordoloi et al. 2019; Netland et al., 2015). In particular, there are many critiques of attempts to use LM in the public sector, and particularly in healthcare (e.g., Radnor and Boaden, 2008; Radnor et al., 2012; Radnor and Osborne, 2013; Blackmore and Kaplan, 2017). Academic literature also contains critiques of the approaches themselves. See, for instance, Young et al. (2004) and Young and McClean (2008).

Some enthusiasts for particular approaches argue that implementation of an approach is subject to strict requirements and organisations must choose to implement only one of them, because a proper culture of improvement requires the senior managers to fully embrace the particular philosophy behind the approach. However, in healthcare systems, the approaches are generally introduced in an ad hoc and combined manner, which may result in mixtures of, say, LM and Six Sigma. One might wonder to what extent these combined strategies still share any common ground with the ideas from which both philosophies originated. More often, the tools from the different approaches are combined to improve units and processes, instead of a full implementation of the concepts.

'Purity' also has its drawbacks. A LM focus on one single process leaves little room for interdependencies with other parts of the organisation. A simplistic focus on 'waste' prevention may result in medical specialists who spend a little more time with their patients than scheduled being criticised for 'wasting time', even though the extra time they devote to their patients may actually result in better health outcomes or higher patient satisfaction rates. Redesign strategies, too, are essentially about simplification. In principle, in BPR, analysts do not care at all about existing process designs. They focus on drawing up the ideal design from scratch. Once an idea is implemented in actual practice, organisations will often encounter interdependencies with other processes, as a result of which the innovative aspects of the new approach will often suffer (Nave, 2002; Boaden, 2008).

In the end, each of the three improvement approaches have their own niches of application in which their strengths show: customer process improvement (LM), system performance (ToC) and unit performance improvement (Six Sigma). Together they provide an abundance of tools and methods to improve the performance of healthcare providers.

Taking a step back, it is worth remembering that OM academics see all approaches as being particular perspectives on and assemblies of parts of the underlying and unifying body of knowledge of OM. For example, Holweg et al. (2018) provide a useful and concise listing of the core principles of OM for designing, improving and controlling operational systems. In tune with this, Johnson et al. (2020) is a nice case study of using these principles to make material and sustained improvements to hospital performance without using labels such as 'lean', 'ToC' etc. As we pointed out in the introduction (Section 6.1), it doesn't matter too much which approach is taken, especially when there is so much potential for improvement in healthcare systems – what matters more is good leadership and commitment (Boaden et al., 2008). If starting out on improvement, there is a lot that can be done within units with a fairly straightforward approach such as the Model for Improvement and disciplined use of core tools and techniques such as process mapping, SPC and PDSA (see for example, White et al., 2021; McCullagh et al., 2021; May et al., 2021; Pridgeon and Proudlove, 2022).

6.8 Questions and exercises

How do the four phases of the PDSA cycle relate to the five stages in the DMAIC approach? What is the relation between the four phases of the PDSA cycle and the Five Focusing Steps of the Theory of Constraints?

'Flow' is one of the principles in Lean Management. Implicitly, flow also plays a role in the Theory of Constraints. Can you explain how?

See also the online material for exercises.

References

Best M and Neuhauser D (2005). W Edwards Deming: father of quality management, patient and composer. *BMJ Quality & Safety*, 14, 310–312.

Blackmore CC and Kaplan GS (2017). Lean and the perfect patient experience. *BMJ Quality & Safety*, 26(2), 85–86. https://doi.org/10.1136/bmjqs-2016-005273.

Boaden R, Harvey G, Moxham C and Proudlove NC (2008). *Quality improvement: theory and practice in healthcare*. NHS Institute for Innovation and Improvement, Coventry. www.england.nhs.uk/improvement-hub/wp-content/uploads/sites/44/2017/11/Quality-Improvement-Theory-and-Practice-in-Healthcare.pdf.

Bordoloi SK, Fitzsimmons JA and Fitzsimmons MJ (2019). *Service management: operations, strategy, information technology*. McGraw-Hill/Irwin, New York.

Davenport TH (1993). *Process innovation: reengineering work through information technology*. Harvard Business Press, Boston, MA.

Elkhuizen SG (2007). *Patient oriented logistics. Studies on organizational improvement in an academic hospital*. Doctoral thesis, University of Amsterdam.

Elkhuizen SG, Burger MP, Jonkers RE, Limburg M, Klazinga N and Bakker PJ (2007). Using business process redesign to reduce wait times at a University Hospital in the Netherlands. *Joint Commission Journal on Quality and Patient Safety*, 33(6), 332–341.

Elkhuizen SG, Limburg M, Bakker PJM and Klazinga NS (2006). Evidence-based reengineering: reengineering the evidence. *International Journal of Health Care Quality Assurance*, 196, 477–499.

Goldratt EM and Cox J (1986). *The goal: a process of ongoing improvement*. North River Press, New York.

Hammer M and Champy J (1993). *Reengineering the corporation: a manifesto for business revolution*. Scientific Research: An Academic Publisher, Harper Collins, New York. https://doi.org/10.1016/S0007-6813(05)80064-3.

Holweg M, Davies J, de Mayer A, Lawson B and Schmenner RW (2018). *Process theory: the principles of operations management*. Oxford University Press, Oxford.

Jarvenpaa SL and Stoddard DB (1998). Business process redesign: radical and evolutionary change. *Journal of Business Research*, 41, 15–27.

Johnson M, Burgess N and Sethi S (2020). Temporal pacing of outcomes for improving patient flow: design science research in a National Health Service hospital. *Journal of Operations Management*, 66(1–2), 35–53. https://doi.org/10.1002/joom.1077.

Langley GJ, Nolan KM, Nolan TW, et al. (1996). *The improvement guide: a practical approach to enhancing organizational performance*. Jossey-Bass, San Francisco, CA.

Leis JA and Shojania KG (2016). A primer on PDSA: executing plan–do–study–act cycles in practice, not just in name. *BMJ Quality & Safety*. https://doi.org/10.1136/bmjqs-2016-006245.

Lloyd RC (2019). *Quality health care: a guide to developing and using indicators*. Jones & Barlett Learning, Burlington, VT.

Locock L (2003). Healthcare redesign: meaning, origins and application. *Quality & Safety in Health Care*, 12, 53–70.

May F, Pepperall J, Davies E, Dyer S, Proudlove N and Rees MT (2021). Summarised, verified and accessible: improving clinical information management for potential haematopoietic stem cell transplantation patients. *BMJ Open Quality*, 10(4), e001605. https://doi.org/10.1136/bmjoq-2021-001605.

McCullagh J, Proudlove N, Tucker H, Davies J, Edmondson D, Lancut J, Maddison A, Weaver A, Davenport R and Green L (2021). Making every drop count: reducing wastage of a novel blood component for transfusion of trauma patients. *BMJ Open Quality*, 10(3), e001396. https://doi.org/10.1136/bmjoq-2021-001396.

McNicholas C, Lennox L, Woodcock T, Bell D and Reed JE (2019). Evolving quality improvement support strategies to improve Plan–Do–Study–Act cycle fidelity: a retrospective mixed-methods study. *BMJ Quality & Safety*, 28(5), 356–365. https://doi.org/10.1136/bmjqs-2017-007605.

Nave D (2002). How to compare six sigma, lean and the theory of constraints: a framework for choosing what's best for your organisation. *Quality Progress*, 2002, 73–78.

Netland TH, Schloetzer JD and Ferdows K (2015). Implementing corporate lean programs: the effect of management control practices. *Journal of Operations Management*, 36, 90–102. https://doi.org/10.1016/j.jom.2015.03.005.

Porter ME and Teisberg E (2006). *Redefining health care, creating value based competition on results*. Harvard Business School Press, Boston, MA.

Pridgeon M and Proudlove N (2022). "Getting going on time: reducing neurophysiology setup times in order to contribute to improving surgery start and finish times". *BMJ Open Quality* 11(3), e001808. https://doi.org/ 10.1136/bmjoq-2021-001808

Provost LP and Murray SK (2011). *The health care data guide: learning for data improvement*. Jossey-Bass, San Francisco, CA.

Radnor Z and Boaden R (2008). Editorial: lean in public services—panacea or paradox? *Public Money & Management*, 28(1), 3–7.

Radnor ZJ, Holweg M and Waring J (2012). Lean in healthcare: the unfilled promise? *Social Science & Medicine*, 74(3), 364–371. https://doi.org/10.1016/j.socscimed.2011.02.011.

Radnor ZJ and Osborne SP (2013). Lean: a failed theory for public services? *Public Management Review*, 15(2), 265–287. https://doi.org/10.1080/14719037.2012.748820.

Seddon J (2008). *Systems thinking in the public sector*. Triarchy Press, Axminster, UK.

Taylor MJ, McNicholas C, Nicolay C, Darzi A, Bell D and Reed JE (2014). Systematic review of the application of the plan–do–study–act method to improve quality in healthcare. *BMJ Quality & Safety*, 23(4), 290–298. https://doi.org/10.1136/bmjqs-2013 -001862.

Watson KJ, Blackstone JH and Gardiner SC (2007). The evolution of a management philosophy: the theory of constraints. *Journal of Operations Management*, 25(2), 387–402.

White E, Proudlove N and Kallon D (2021). Improving turnaround times for HLA-B★27 and HLA-B★57:01 gene testing: a barts health NHS trust quality improvement project. *BMJ Open Quality*, 10(3), e001538. https://doi.org/10.1136/bmjoq-2021-001538.

Womack J, Jones D and Roos D (1990). *The machine that changed the world*. Rawson Associates, New York.

Young T, Brailsford S, Connell C, Davies R, Harper P and Klein JH (2004). Using industrial processes to improve patient care. *BMJ*, 328, 162–164.

Young TP and McClean SI (2008). A critical look at lean thinking in healthcare. *Quality and Safety in Healthcare*, 17(5), 382–386. https://doi.org/10.1136/qshc.2006.020131.

7 Linking operations with outcomes

A conceptual framework for operational modelling and an illustration to diabetes type 2 care

Jan Vissers, Sylvia Elkhuizen
and Mahdi Mahdavi[1]

7.1 Introduction

We tend to relate operations management to the planning of services, resulting in better access, shorter waiting and throughput times and better utilisation of resources. We are less pronounced when it comes to the contribution of operations management to better outcomes, improved health and satisfaction over health services delivered. Therefore, we elaborate in this chapter on how we see the relationship between operations and outcomes in healthcare by elaborating a framework we developed for an EU funded project *Managed Outcomes*. The objective of this project was to demonstrate demand management and operations management to operational processes of healthcare delivery in regional networks in six countries in Europe. This offered us the opportunity to develop a framework to make the relationships between the operations of healthcare providers and the outcomes in four different healthcare delivery networks (type 2 diabetes, stroke, hip osteoarthritis, dementia) more explicit. We first introduce the framework (Section 7.2) and then elaborate it in the form of an operational model, illustrated for type 2 diabetes (Section 7.3), developed for a region in the Netherlands – as part of the Managed Outcomes project.

By way of background, diabetes is defined as a chronic loss of capability to regulate the blood glucose level (Clinical Guidelines Task Force, 2005). A common distinction is between type 1 diabetes, where the body fails to produce insulin, and type 2 diabetes (T2D), where it concerns the way in which the body uses insulin. Type 2 is the most common form of diabetes. Its progression is characterised by an insidious onset and steady deterioration of the health state over a long period of time, during which a complex of comorbid

1 This chapter is based on a paper published in *Frontiers in Public Health*: Elkhuizen SG, Vissers JMH, Mahdavi M and van de Klundert JJ (2020), 'Modeling Patient Journeys for Demand Segments in Chronic Care, With an Illustration to Type 2 Diabetes'. Front. Public Health 8:428. doi: 10.3389/fpubh.2020.00428.

DOI: 10.4324/9781003020011-8

health conditions such as problems with the heart, kidneys, vision and lower extremities may appear (Clinical Guidelines Task Force, 2005).

Treatment of T2D requires long-term, continuous and personalised care. Commonly, the larger part of health services for T2D, such as health promotion, health education, diagnosis, regular monitoring, medication, check-up, is mostly performed by primary care professionals such as GPs and nurses (Institute of Medicine, 2000). It is expected that the role of primary care professionals (as opposed to secondary care in hospitals and/or specialised physicians) will increase (Cavanagh and Bamford, 1997; Temmink et al., 2003; Shojania et al., 2006).

Due to the complexity and variety of T2D services, diabetes care typically involves multiple professionals to meet the demands of service users (Raak et al., 1999; Montenegro et al., 2011). Consequently, providers usually establish relationships with other providers to integrate the elements of an often-fragmented service process (Kodner and Spreeuwenberg, 2002). This benefits different groups of stakeholders. As well as being useful to care providers, it is also of interest to service users, informal care givers, insurers and policy makers. It may smooth the flow of service delivery by eliminating overlaps, delays, misuse and overuse caused by fragmentation of service processes. Furthermore, it may help to contain costs (Raak et al., 1999).

Together, the collection of service providers involved forms a *'health service provisioning'* network. These networks can be formed by means of explicitly defined relationships, or more implicitly as collections of providers jointly visited by (a population of) T2D patients. The public health system arising from the National Health Service in the United Kingdom (UK) is a prime example of explicitly regionally organised provider networks with structural mechanisms for integration (Ferlie et al., 2010). In the Netherlands, a change in reimbursement schemes has also encouraged a variety of regional networks to be formed (Struijs and Baan, 2011). These networks include GPs, dieticians, specialists, laboratory services, etc. In other countries however, the networks may differ on a patient-by-patient basis as they choose the service providers to service their needs.

7.2 Methods

7.2.1 Operational modelling

In Health Service Operations Management, operational models are used to describe and improve health service provisioning by networks of provider organisations. An *operational model* is a formal description of services that are performed to meet patient demands and that make use of structures to improve outcomes (Provan et al., 2011). An operational model of a provider network, therefore, describes the components of operations of a network and the relationships between those components, thereby also enabling calculations of patient flows, resource use and costs to be made.

7.2.1.1 Framework

As part of our methods, we present the *generic framework* developed for the EU FP7 Managed Outcomes project (Elkhuizen et al., 2010; Mahdavi, 2015) which provided a comparative analysis of healthcare delivery networks for T2D, ischaemic stroke, osteoarthritis patients and dementia in six EU countries (Finland, Germany, Greece, the Netherlands, Spain, UK). This generic framework, as presented in Figure 7.1, extends the well-known model of Donabedian (1966).

Donabedian's *structure-process-outcome (SPO) model* presents a seminal paradigm regarding the relationships between structure and process and patient outcomes. According to Donabedian, high-quality structures are more likely to lead to high-quality processes and, combined, they are more likely in turn to generate high-quality outcomes (Donabedian, 1966). In this model, structure refers to factors such as (but not limited to) distribution and organisation of human resources, financial resources, healthcare facilities and ease of access by patients.

The main conceptual model of the relationships between operations and outcomes as depicted in Figure 7.1 contains not three but five entities, thereby extending Donabedian's SPO model. Based on this conceptual model the basic entities of provider networks are *demand, behaviour, structure, services* and *outcomes*. The *services* replace Donabedian's processes, thus recognising contemporary understanding of the nature of the co-creating interaction patterns between provider organisations and patients. The *structure* entity refers to the resources and other static features of the regional health service provider network operations. The structure defines the available tangibles and intangibles necessary to provide the services. Following Donabedian, a prime interest is to advance understanding of the impact of operations – in the form of *services* and the underlying *structures* – on *outcomes*. The *outcomes* entity refers to the results obtained through the service provisioning, for which we will distinguish health outcomes and service outcomes.

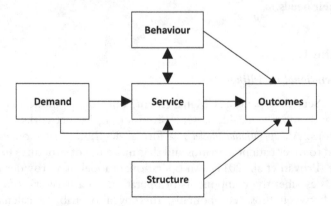

Figure 7.1 Generic health service operations framework.

The new *demand* entity forms an extension of Donabedian's original SPO model and represents the demand for health services as resulting from the health conditions of individuals in the population. Demand may, by definition, form an independent determinant of outcomes and is therefore valuable in understanding outcomes and their relationships with operations. A second extension is the explicit inclusion of the *behaviour* entity. The model takes into consideration both that health services may influence the patients' behaviour, e.g., by inducing them to increase exercising, and also that patient behaviour may affect the service provisioning. For instance, lack of therapy compliance by a patient may cause other, extra services to be required if their disease stage becomes altered as a result. By relating behaviour to services, the model captures the common understanding that health service users are active co-creators of health services, rather than simply passive recipients (Makhni, 2017). Correspondingly, the relationship between behaviour and services is thought to be bi-directional (Sampson, 2000).

7.2.1.2 Operationalisation

The generic conceptual framework is further elaborated by disaggregating the five main entities into subcomponents which can subsequently be defined to analyse the journeys of a set of patient subpopulations through a provider network (see Figure 7.1).

We now briefly discuss the level two components in Table 7.1. *Demand* describes health service users, in terms of, for example, their demographics and health conditions. The geography of demand can be described through *demand locations*, to which socioeconomic characteristics (and others) can be attributed if desired to distinguish as confounder in the subsequent analysis. The population of health service users can be partitioned into *demand segments* (or subpopulations) for which different health services are provided. The atomic units by which *services* are defined are referred to as *service elements* (e.g., an outpatient visit). The next larger unit is the '*service journey*', which is an ordered set of service elements describing the health service elements commonly used by a segment of health service users (e.g., according to an evidence-based clinical guideline). Over time, service users may transition between different demand segments and, in doing so, they will follow different sequences of service journeys. Such a health service user's specific sequence of service journeys is referred to as a '*service user journey*'.

The *structures* underlying the service provisioning are partly defined in terms of current and non-current assets, such as buildings and equipment. Each of these resources has a type (e.g., X-ray machine) and an availability (e.g., weekdays 09.00 to 16.00), a capacity (e.g., three patients per hour) and a cost (e.g., €100 per hour). The resources are assigned to service providers (e.g., based on ownership) and located at service provision points. Service providers may have resources at various service provision points, and service provision points may hold resources from various service providers. Human resources also form part

Table 7.1 Components and subcomponents of the generic health services network operational model

Component	Subcomponent	Definition
Demand	Health service user	Service user refers to the individual patient who demands health services. Service user is defined with regard to demographic characteristics, disease history and disease – specific medical conditions requiring the health services.
	Demand segment	Segments refer to mutually exclusive subsets of the population of health service users with a common demand for health services (e.g., because of sharing a same health condition).
	Demand location	Locations define areas within the geographical areas which are meaningful to distinguish because of differences in demand and or geographical, socioeconomic and political characteristics.
Service	Service element	A service element is the atomic unit of service. For each service element the resource requirements specify the type of resources (see below) required to perform the service element, as well as the expected usage of each of these types (e.g., in hours). A service element can be described in terms of an operational performance (waiting times, frequency, length of stay, transitions to another service element) and a financial performance i.e., cost. The costs of a service element are defined as the sum of the costs of the required resource usages (see below).
	Service journey	A service journey consists of a partially ordered set of service elements, which are provided to health service users from a demand segment. Operational and financial performances of a service journey are aggregated from corresponding service elements performance. The costs of a service journey are defined as the sum of the costs of the service elements involved. Transition probability refers to the distribution of health service users from the demand segment corresponding to the service journey over possible succeeding demand segments (and corresponding service journeys).
	Service user journey	User journey refers to the sequence of services that a health service user follows (defined through the sequence of service journeys). The costs of a service user journey consist of the sum of the costs of the service journeys involved.

(*Continued*)

Table 7.1 (Continued)

Component	Subcomponent	Definition
Structure	Resource	A resource is a means to provide a service. Resources are described according to their type, availability, capacity and unit cost. With regard to type, resources are distinguished into devices, facilities and human resources. Resource availability refers to the amounts of resources which is available to deliver services per time period. Resource capacity refers to the number of health service users that can be treated in a time period. Resource cost refers to the monetary cost of a resource per unit (e.g., per hour).
	Service provision point	Provision point refers to a location where resources required to provide a service are located. Access to provision point is measured by physical distance of and travel time from the demand location of the health service user to the provision point.
	Service provider	A health service provider is a person or a legal entity who/which delivers health services to patients.
Behaviour	General health related behaviour	General health behaviour refers to the lifestyle of the health service user, such as smoking, diet and physical exercise behaviour.
	Service-related behaviour	Service-related behaviour refers to behaviour which directly relates to the health services, e.g., treatment adherence or follow-up to advice by service provider.
Outcome	Health outcomes	Health outcomes are features of the healthcare user's health. A variety of quite different health outcomes can be considered ranging from perceived health-related quality of life as reported by the health service user to specific clinical outcomes as reported by the healthcare provider.
	Service outcomes	Service outcomes regards both provider measures on service performance (such as waiting times) as well as health service users' perceptions of service provisioning, and the valuation of the service provisioning by health service users.

of the structure. Like the tangible resources they may have a type (e.g., general practitioner), availability (e.g., 32 hours per week), capacity and cost.

The elaborated generic framework encompasses two types of *outcomes*: *health outcomes* and *service outcomes*. Service outcomes refer to measurements and perceptions of the service provisioning by health service users, e.g., a service user's perceived timeliness or friendliness, or health service user satisfaction. Health outcomes may refer to generic health outcomes, such as patient-reported quality of life, or to disease-specific clinical outcomes such as HbA1c level (for T2D).

Behaviour encompasses two kinds of behaviour. Firstly, it relates to *generic health behaviour*, for instance referring to lifestyle or diet. Secondly, it may refer to *health service co-creating behaviour*, for instance to reporting measurements or therapy adherence (Riekert et al., 2013).

7.2.1.3 Operational model

Figure 7.2 illustrates how the elaboration of components and subcomponents can be used in an operational model to analyse the journeys of patients in different demand segments.

We see from Figure 7.2 that the demand from a population in a region can be disaggregated into demand locations and demand segments. A distinction in demand location might be, for instance, urban or rural – as patients living in a rural area typically have a further distance to travel or might be living more healthily. A 'demand segment' refers to a group of patients who have the same disease but are also comparable in the amounts of resources required. For chronic diseases this often requires a distinction between stages of the disease, as further stages often require more – and different – resources than the early stages.

For each of the demand segments services can be defined, consisting of service elements and a journey along the service elements. Demand segments and patient journey per segment result in expected patient flows, also taking into account patient behaviour impacts such as 'no-show' at a clinical appointment. As the resource requirements are defined at the level of service elements, we can calculate the amounts of resources required for each demand segment. Furthermore, we can calculate the annual output of the system under study, expressing this in the number of services produced and the number of resources required. We can then translate this into annual costs per patient in a demand segment (as the costs are defined at the level of service element).

The output of the system can be related to both health outcomes and service experience outcomes. When the same demand segments are used in all parts of the model, we can also differentiate outcomes between demand segments.

7.2.2 Case study

The operational models for diabetes, stroke, osteoarthritis and dementia were developed in case studies performed in six countries as part of the EU Managed

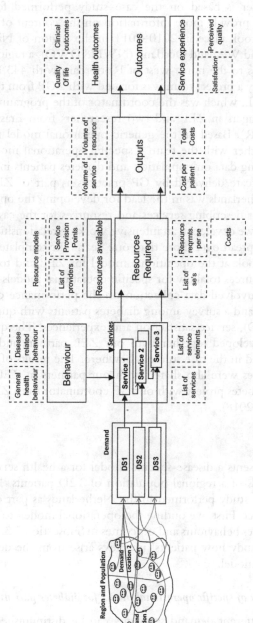

Figure 7.2 Generic operational model of patient journeys as used in Managed Outcomes.

Outcomes project. For detailed information on the methodology used in this project see (Elkhuizen et al., 2010; Mahdavi, 2015).

As this chapter is based on the case study performed for T2D in the Netherlands, we provide more information on the content of this case study. The case study took place in 2010–2011 in the region of Nieuwewaterweg Noord & Delfland Westland Oostland (NWN&DWO), a region covering 273 square kilometres to the north-west of Rotterdam with 443,109 inhabitants. For the case study a project team was formed with a GP from the primary care organisation, ZEL, which was the coordinator of the programme for diabetes, one of the managers in ZEL and two researchers from Erasmus University Rotterdam (EUR). Based on the generic operational model (Figure 7.2) we developed, together with the team a specific operational model for diabetes care in ZEL, using data on population and diabetes patients in the region and on the diabetes care delivered by GP practices as part of ZEL. As the case study in the Netherlands was in the lead for developing the operational model and templates for describing services and resources for the case studies in the other countries, we developed an intensive working relationship with our ZEL partners which spread over more than one year. The templates allowed other case studies to look at the operational model for ZEL and to change or add services and resources to allow for specific operational models elsewhere. The case study also involved data collection on the performance of diabetes care, such as HbA1c, and a survey among diabetes patients with questions on quality of life (EQ5D), service satisfaction and experiences. The questionnaire for diabetes was developed together with our ZEL partners and tested in ZEL before being used in the case studies elsewhere. The results of the case studies in other countries were also shared with our partners in ZEL, resulting in a paper on the diabetes project with our GP coordinator from ZEL as co-author (Mahdavi et al., 2018).

7.3 Results

This section presents a disease-specific model for a health service network to service the needs of a regional population of T2D patients. It uses data collected for a case study performed in the Netherlands as part of the Managed Outcomes project. First, we outline the operational model, to define demand, services, structures behaviours and outcomes in Subsection 7.3.1. In Subsection 7.3.2 we then study how patients' journeys arise from the demand segments included in the model.

7.3.1 Illustration of specific operational model for diabetes patients

For diabetes, different demand segments can be distinguished following the different stages of the disease (Mahdavi et al., 2015):

DS1: patients with high risk of developing diabetes.
DS2: patients with T2D treated with lifestyle advice.

DS3: patients with T2D treated with lifestyle advice and oral medication.

DS4: patients with T2D treated with lifestyle advice and insulin injections, sometimes also combined with oral medication.

DS5: patients with complicated T2D treated by a physician specialised in diabetes care.

Patients may proceed from one demand segment to the next. From all segments, patients can move to the final segment 5. Main movements between segments DS2–DS5 are shown in Figure 7.3. The transition probabilities to subsequent stages reflect the time per stage as well. For instance, a transition probability of 0.313 from stage DS2 to stage DS3, with an exit time probability of 0.012 and transition probability of 0.05 to stage DS5 imply a mean duration of DS2 of slightly less than three years.

For each demand segment, one or more health services (S) are defined (see Table 7.2):

Each service is comprised of a list of service elements, which form the fundamental units of services delivered. For T2D, the list of service elements is

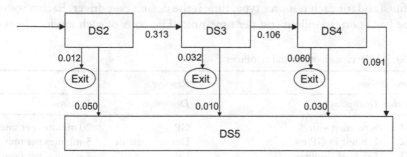

Figure 7.3 Movements between demand segments.

Table 7.2 Services

Service	Description	Delivered to demand segment
S1	Screening	DS1
S2	Diagnosis	DS2
S3	Chronic diabetes treatment with lifestyle advice	DS2
S4	Chronic diabetes treatment with lifestyle advice and oral medication	DS3
S5	Chronic diabetes treatment with insulin therapy and lifestyle advice and/or oral medication, first year with insulin stabilisation	DS4
S6	Chronic diabetes treatment with insulin therapy, lifestyle advice and oral medication, after first year	DS4
S7	Patients with complicated diabetes care treated with specialised care	DS5

depicted in Table 7.3, which also displays the resources required per service element, and the amount (in time or number) needed per resource per service element.

With the detailed resource use per service element specified (see Table 7.4), it is possible to relate the resources to the demand segments. By specifying the average percentage of patients actually using this service element and the frequency per user, the total resource requirement per service can be derived.

7.3.2 Differences in resource demand, costs and outcomes

The service journeys and transitions between disease stages enable us to derive 'expected service user journeys'. Moreover, they enable us to derive the expected services requirements per stage and the corresponding activity-based costs.

Costs are derived using *activity-based costing* (Kaplan and Porter, 2011), where the service elements form the activities. Cost objects are service elements, services, service journeys and ultimately service user journeys. Cost drivers include time, kits and medicine. For each service element required resource types are defined and for each resource type, time is the default cost driver. Each resource type has a corresponding cost per time unit. The costs of each service element

Table 7.3 Service elements and resources

Service element		Resource	
Number	Description	Description	Requirement
SE1	Screening visit	GP	20 minutes per unit
SE2	Lab test in GP office	Doctor assistant	5 minutes per unit
SE3	Lab test sampling	Lab	5 minutes per unit
SE4	Lab test analysis	Lab	1 minutes per unit
SE5	First visit	GP	20 minutes per unit
SE6	Visit for diagnosis and care plan	GP	20 minutes per unit
SE7	Follow-up visit	GP/practice nurse	20 minutes per unit
SE8	Diet consultation	Dietician	45 minutes per unit
SE9	Eye care	Optometrist	5 minutes per unit
SE10	Foot care	Practice nurse	5 minutes per unit
SE11	Self-test glucose monitoring	Test kit	1 kit per test
SE12	Oral medication	Medicine	1 pill per take
SE13	Insulin medication	Insulin	1 dose per injection
SE14	Education	Diabetic nurse	20 minutes per unit
SE15	Specialised care	Specialist	10 minutes per unit
SE16	Lifestyle programme	Lifestyle consultant	20 minutes per unit
SE17	Insulin injection by professional	District nurse	5 minutes per unit
		Insulin	Dose per injection
SE18	Delivering medication by professional	Pharmacist	5 minutes
SE19	Prescription medicine	GP	5 minutes
SE20	Education for using insulin	Diabetic nurse	20 minutes per unit

Table 7.4 Use of service elements per demand segment* (frequency recommended per year, utilisation rate (%))

Service element	Description	S1	S2	S3	S4	S5	S6
SE1	Screening visit	1					
SE2	Lab test in GP office						
SE3	Lab test sampling		1, 100%	1, 100%	1, 100%	1, 100%	1, 100%
SE4	Lab test analysis		1, 100%	1, 100%	1, 100%	1, 100%	1, 100%
SE5	First visit		1, 100%				
SE6	Visit for diagnosis and care plan		3, 100%				
SE7	Follow-up visit			4, 80%	4, 80%	4, 100%	4, 100%
SE8	Diet consultation			1, 10%	1, 1%	1, 1%	1, 1%
SE9	Eye care			1, 40%	1, 40%	1, 40%	1, 40%
SE10	Foot care			1, 10%	1, 65%	1, 65%	1, 65%
SE11	Self-test glucose monitoring					100, 100%	100, 100%
SE12	Oral medication				365, 100%	365, 90%	365, 90%
SE13	Insulin medication					365, 100%	365, 100%
SE14	Education		4, 100%				
SE15	Specialised care						
SE16	Lifestyle programme		12, 100%				
SE17	Insulin injection by professional					365, 2%	365, 2%
SE18	Delivering medication by professional				4, 100%	4, 100%	4, 100%
SE19	Prescription medicine				4, 20%		
SE20	Education for using insulin					8, 100%	

*As this chapter is focused on T2D care at primary healthcare settings, DS1–4 are further elaborated in terms of service elements, resources, behaviour and costs. We do not elaborate DS7 for DS5 since it was provided at hospital settings.

can therefore be calculated when the cost per time unit is specified for each resource type. For instance, a GP has a tariff per hour (or per minute), and the costs of a visit are the cost per minute times the number of minutes of the visit.

Cost calculations for the expected service journey S2 and S3 to service patients in DS2 are illustrated in Table 7.5.

On average patients remain in DS2 for three years, one year receiving service 2, and two years receiving service 3. The average cost per patient in DS2 is therefore €127.44 euros per year.

On a population level, the demand data as depicted in Table 7.6 enable the calculation of the number of patients in each demand segment, based on incidence (the number of new T2D patients), and the transition probabilities between the demand segments as shown in Figure 7.3.

Table 7.5 Illustration of cost calculation for service journeys S2 and S3 serving demand segment 2

	Resource type	S2				S3		
		Resource requirement per patient per year*	Unit cost	Cost per patient per year	Cost in ZEL region per year (911 patients)	Resource requirement per patient per year*	Unit cost	Cost per patient per year
SE3	Lab test sampling	Lab	5	€0.42	€2.10	€1,898	5	€0.42	2.10
SE4	Lab test analysis	Lab	1	€0.42	€0.42	€380	1	€0.42	€0.42
SE5	First visit	GP	20	€1.10	€22.00	€20,043			
SE6	Visit for diagnosis and care plan	GP	60	€1.10	€66.00	60,130			
SE7	Follow-up visit	GP & nurse					64	€0.71	€45.44
SE8	Diet consultation	Dietician					5	€0.53	€2.65
SE9	Eye care	Optometrist					2	€1.10	€2.20
SE10	Foot care	Practice nurse					1	€0.29	€0.29
SE14	Education	Diabetes nurse	80	€0.58	€46.40	€42,516			
SE16	Lifestyle programme	Lifestyle consultant	240	€0.58	€139.20	€127,549			
	Total per year				€276.12	€252,517			€53.10

Note: The above is rendered with Resource type in a shared column; per-row the columns are: code | name | Resource type | S2 resource req | S2 unit cost | S2 cost per patient | Cost in ZEL | S3 resource req | S3 unit cost | S3 cost per patient.

* Resource requirements are in minutes per year

Table 7.6 Patients in case study region (2009)

	Number/percentages
Population	443,281
Number of new diabetes patients	910
Incidence	0.21%
Number of diabetes patients	12.218
Prevalence	2.76%

Table 7.7 Main results per demand segment

Demand segment	Number of patients (2009) in segment	Hours of professional care per patient per year	Costs per patient per year	% Smokers	% Drinkers	Satisfaction with services* (1–7)	Own health** (0–100)	Satisfaction with own health** (1–7)	% Aware of HbA1c level**	% Patients with HbA1c in control
DS2	2687	3.1	127	7.0	72.0	5.9	77.1	4.9	42.4	84%
DS3	8084	1.5	419	11.4	66.8	6.3	77.8	5.0	56.1	87%
DS4	1451	2.6	1666	10.9	57.7	6.1	69.1	4.1	77.1	78%

* Significant $p < 0.10$; ** significant $p < 0.05$

In combination with resource requirements per service journey, the operational model then facilitates the determination of the expected total resource needs per demand segment and the corresponding expected total costs. Note that these cost calculations use the expected duration (in years) of patients' stay in a demand segment (three years in DS2, nine years in DS3 and ten years in DS4). Adding up the expected costs per segment yields the expected total cost of the service user journey (either per individual service user, or for the population at large).

For T2D the most relevant outcome parameter to examine health status is the HbA1c level. Patients with HbA1c of <53 mmol have balanced glucose levels. We also asked if the patient was satisfied with the services delivered (measured in a scale from 1–7), how they perceived their own health status (measured in a scale from 0–100), whether they were satisfied with their own health (measured in a scale from 1–7) and whether they knew their own HbA1c level.

In Table 7.7 we show the main results of these analyses.[2] As we focused in the case study on patients treated in primary care, the results are limited to the demand segments DS2–DS4.

Patients in DS2 (treatment with lifestyle advice) use the highest amount of professional care (3.1 hours) but cost the least per year. Their patient journey

2 Percentage of smokers, drinkers, satisfaction with services, perception of own health, satisfaction with own health, percentage awareness of HbA1c and percentage of patients with HbA1c in control are based on questions in the survey; the differences between demand segments were tested on significance with ANOVA.

includes, after the initial screening by the GP for the diagnosis, mainly lab tests and visits to the practice nurse for monitoring. However, in the first year there is much time invested in a lifestyle programme, to try and keep the patient for as long as possible in this demand segment. If we consider the behaviour of patients in DS2 we see the lowest level of smoking and the highest level of drinking. They are satisfied with the services delivered, but less so than in segments DS3 and DS4. They rate their health state as 77.1 on a 0–100 scale and are satisfied with their health, which is similar to DS3, but higher than DS4. The patients in DS2 are less aware of their HbA1c level. For 84% of the patients the HbA1c is in control, lower than for DS3, but higher than for DS4.

Patients in DS3 (treatment with lifestyle and oral medication) use on average about 50% less professional care than patients in DS2, but their annual costs are about three times as much. Their patient journey differs from DS2 mainly in visits to the GP for medication prescription and the daily intake of oral medication. In terms of behaviour, the percentage of smokers is higher than for DS2 and the percentage of drinkers is lower. They are slightly more satisfied with the services compared with DS2. They rate their health state as 77.8, which is slightly higher than for DS2, and their satisfaction with health is similar than for DS2 but higher than for DS4. The patients in DS3 are more aware of their HbA1c level than for DS2. For 87% of the patients, slightly more than for DS2, the HbA1c is in control.

Patients in DS4 (treatment with lifestyle, oral medication and insulin injections) use on average slightly less professional care than in DS2, but their annual costs are about four times the costs of patients in DS3. The main differences in terms of patient journey with DS3 are in the initial education they receive for using insulin to do with daily self-medication and regular self-testing to monitor their glucose levels. In terms of behaviour, the percentage of smokers is similar to that of DS3 while the percentage of drinkers is lower. The patients in DS4 are slightly less satisfied with the services received. They rate their own health lower compared to patients in DS3. They are more aware of their HbA1c level, which is in control for 78% of these patients.

If we concentrate on the significance of the differences between demand segments, we see that the differences for smoking ($p = 0.47$) and drinking ($p = 0.21$) are not significant. The difference in satisfaction with services is moderately significant ($p < 0.10$). We see moderately significant differences between patients in DS2 and DS3 ($p = 0.08$).

There are significant differences in the perception of patients of their own health, and the satisfaction with their own health ($p < 0.05$). Patients in DS4 feel less healthy compared with patients in DS2 ($p < 0.001$) and patients in DS3 ($p = 0.001$). Comparable differences can be seen in the satisfaction of patients with their own health. Patients in DS4 are less satisfied compared with patients in DS2 ($p = 0.008$) and patients in DS3 ($p = 0.001$).

There are significant differences in the awareness of patients of their HbA1c level ($p < 0.05$). Patients in DS2 are less likely to know their HbA1C level compared with patients in DS3 ($p = 0.061$) and patients in DS4 ($p < 0.001$). Patients in DS3 also differ significantly with patients in DS4 on this aspect ($p = 0.019$).

There are no significant differences between the demand segments concerning the percentage of patients within control for HbA1C.

7.4 Conclusion and discussion

In this chapter we investigated how we can model the journey of patients with a chronic condition, and address different needs, treatments and outcomes, as relevant in different stages of the condition, and for different subpopulations with the condition. We analysed the results of applying demand segmentation to T2D patients.

The chapter illustrates that patient journeys in chronic care and provider networks in a regional setting can be described, using standard operations management concepts and terminology. Distinguishing demand segments and using these demand segments throughout the different parts of the modelling and description of patient journeys and provider networks, makes it possible to look at the performance of regional healthcare delivery in transparent and verifiable detail.

The model enabled us to distinguish demand segments corresponding to stages of a chronic diseases, and subsequently to model operations (services, resources, behaviours) and outcomes for each of these disease stages. The model also enabled recognition of differences in service provisioning for each stage, and in addition captured the transitions between disease stages. The results illustrate that the use of resources (and consequent activity-based costs) show significant differences for patients in different demand segments. We also observed some of the outcomes to differ significantly between patients belonging to different demand segments.

Therefore, an important benefit of this approach is that we can relate demand, services, resource use, costs and outcomes at the more meaningful level of patient demand segments instead of only being able to consider the aggregate level of all T2D patients. This more differentiated insight at demand segment level can be used to develop solutions for problems in the delivery of health services for T2D patients.

Moreover, through modelling transitions between disease stages – and thus between demand segments and service journeys – we are able to model (expected) patient service journeys. For these complete service journeys, the model provides insight in overall performance, such as costs and quality of life over the full expected service user journey. This insight can help us to study the overall effects of interventions. For instance, one could study the effects of interventions aimed at keeping diabetes patients longer in DS2 with lifestyle advice or increasing the role of nurses (Mahdavi et al., 2018). The detailed underlying operational model facilitates the linking of interventions in patient journeys to outcomes, costs and detailed resource requirements. This illustrates the added value of the operations management-based approach to demand segmentation followed in this chapter.

One of the limitations of the approach followed is that the results of applying this modelling approach to T2D are based on a case study and that the results will be different in other applications. Another limitation is that the insights on diabetes and diabetes care which have taken place since, are not taken into account. The references used on diabetes and diabetes treatment may be outdated. Therefore, the contribution of the chapter is mainly methodological. The methodology, however, can be used to develop new specific operational models based on up-to-date scientific insight into diabetes as a complex chronic condition and treatment of diabetes, and – indeed – for other examples of chronic care as well.

7.5 Questions and exercises

Figure 7.3 describes the movement of patients between demand segments for T2D. This model can also be used for other chronic diseases (e.g., COPD, dementia), and for mental health diseases (e.g., schizophrenia). Select one of these diseases, find out what the disease stages are, and develop a similar model for the movement of patients between demand segments of the disease.

References

Cavanagh S and Bamford M (1997). Substitution in nursing practice: clinical, management and research implications. *Journal of Nursing Management*, 5, 333–339.

Clinical Guidelines Task Force (2005). *Global guideline for type 2 diabetes*. IDF, Brussels, 1–11.

Donabedian A (1966). Evaluating the quality of medical care. *Milbank Memorial Fund Quarterly*, 44, 166–206.

Elkhuizen S, Bowen T, Forte P, van de Klundert J, Konerding U, Mahdavi M, Torkki P and Vissers J (2010). *Operations management and demand-based approaches to healthcare outcomes and cost-benefits research*. Erasmus University Rotterdam, Rotterdam.

Ferlie E, Fitzgerald L, McGivern G, Dopson S and Exworthy M (2010). *Networks in health care: a comparative study of their management, impact and performance*. Department of Health and Social Care, London.

Institute of Medicine (2000). *To err is human; building a safer health system*. Institute of Medicine, Washington, DC.

Kaplan R and Porter M (2011). How to solve the cost crisis in health care. *Harvard Business Review*, 89(9), 47–64.

Kodner D and Spreeuwenberg C (2002). Integrated care: meaning, logic, applications, and implications--a discussion paper. *International Journal of Integrated Care*, 2(4), 2–12.

Mahdavi M (2015). *Building the bridge between operations and outcomes. Modelling and evaluation of health service provider networks*. PhD Thesis, Erasmus University Rotterdam, Rotterdam. https://repub.eur.nl/pub/ 77858/Mahdavi_THESIS_Final.pdf.

Mahdavi M, Vissers J, Elkhuizen S, Van Dijk M, Vanhala A, Karampli E, Faubel R, Forte P, Coroian E and Van de Klundert J (2018). The relationship between context, structure and processes with outcomes in 6 regional diabetes networks in Europe. *Plos One*, 13(2), 1–17.

Mahdavi M, Vissers J, Konerding U, Van Dijk M, Vanhala A, Elkhuizen S, Karampli E, Faubel R, Forte P, Coroian Eand Van de Klundert J (2015). Modelling and evaluation of diabetes provider networks in primary care. In Mahdavi M (ed.), *Building the bridge between operations and outcomes: modelling and evaluation of health service provider networks.* Erasmus University Rotterdam, Rotterdam, 79–118.

Makhni S (2017). Co-creation in health systems design. *American Medical Association Journal of Ethics*, 19(11), 1070–1072.

Montenegro H, Holder R, Ramagem C, Urrutia S, Fabrega R, Tasca R, … and Gomes M (2011). Combating health care fragmentation through integrated health service delivery networks in the Americas: lessons learned. *Journal of Integrated Care*, 19(5), 5–16.

Provan K, Beagles J and Leischow S (2011). Network formation, governance, and evolution in public health: the North American Quitline Consortium case. *Health Care Management Review*, 36, 315–326.

Raak AV, Mur-Veeman I and Paulus A (1999). Understanding the feasibility of integrated care: a rival viewpoint on the influence of actions and the institutional context. *International Journal of Health Planning and Management*, 14, 235–248.

Riekert KA, Ockene JK and Pbert L (2013). *The handbook of health behavior change.* Springer Publishing Company, New York.

Sampson S (2000). Customer-supplier duality and bidirectional supply chains in service organizations. *International Journal of Service Industry Management*, 11, 348–364.

Shojania K, Ranji S, McDonald K, Grimshaw J, Sundaram V, Rushakoff R and Owens D (2006). Effects of quality improvement strategies for type 2 diabetes on glycemic control: a metaregression analysis. *Journal of the American Medical Association*, 296, 427–440.

Struijs J and Baan C (2011). Integrating care through bundled payments - lessons from the Netherlands. *New England Journal of Medicine*, 364, 990–991.

Temmink D, Francke A, Hutten J, Van Der Zee J and Abu-Saad H (2003). Innovations in the nursing care of the chronically ill: a literature review from an international perspective. *Journal of Advances in Nursing*, 31, 1449–58.

Part II

Practice and improvement

Part II
Improving healthcare practice

Jan Vissers, Sylvia Elkhuizen and Nathan Proudlove

The cases that follow in this second part of the book illustrate Health Services Operations Management (HSOM) at work in different healthcare settings. The first part of the book offers a number of concepts that can be used to study the operations of a unit, a process chain or a network. We further made a distinction between levels of planning, i.e., strategic planning, tactical planning and operational planning. Also, we introduced modelling as a tool for studying the planning of a unit, process chain or network.

We now combine these three concepts in a framework that we can use for the setting, planning level and modelling technique, illustrated in cases. The first component of our framework (see Figure II.1) allows us to position the case in terms of the primary level of planning addressed, and in terms of unit OM, process OM or network OM. For the levels of planning, we distinguish five levels, which is a refinement of the three levels presented in Chapter 2.

We see that the strategic level is split into longer term (three years and more) capacity planning and annual volume planning (one to three years), and that the tactical level is split into capacity allocation to users/specialties/departments (three months to one year) and the detailed allocation to patient groups or pathways within a specialty or department. The operational level of planning (one day to three months) is focusing on the actual scheduling of patients for diagnosis or treatment).

To make it easier for the reader to position each contribution on these two dimensions, we use a visualisation as shown in Figure II.1. The illustration indicates that the case being presented is focusing on the second tactical level: allocation of resources to patient groups. A focus on unit, chain or network OM is represented by arrows. Arrows in a vertical direction refer to the prevalence of unit OM. The allocation and utilisation of resources play an important role in such case studies. Arrows in a horizontal direction refer to the prevalence of process chain OM. This means that the case study is focusing on processes for specific patient groups, and on ways to improve the performance of the chain in terms of service (waiting time) and throughput times. Arrows in both directions refer to a network OM approach: a combination of unit and chain OM. In the illustration the case study is characterised by a network logistics approach, implying that the objective of the case study is to improve

DOI: 10.4324/9781003020011-10

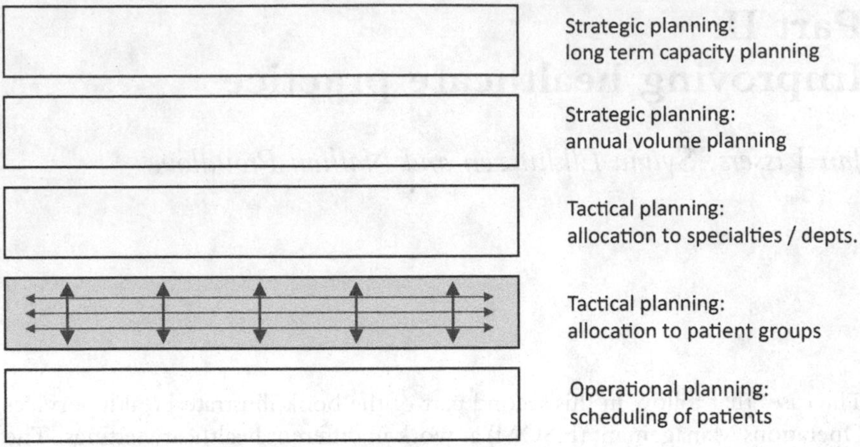

	Strategic planning: long term capacity planning
	Strategic planning: annual volume planning
	Tactical planning: allocation to specialties / depts.
	Tactical planning: allocation to patient groups
	Operational planning: scheduling of patients

Figure II.1 Positioning a case in level of planning and unit/chain/network OM approach

			Use of data				
			Rules of Thumb	Statistical analysis			
Type of model				Averages	Variation	Distribution	Benchmark
Descriptive	Flowchart						
	Spreadsheet						
Analytical	Deterministic						
	Stochastic	Queueing					
		Markov					
Simulation	Monte Carlo						
	Discrete event						
Heuristic	Simulated annealing						

Figure II.2 Technique of modelling and method of data analysis used in cases.

service performance in chains as well as the utilisation of resources by all chains combined.

The second component of our framework for the cases refers to the technique used for studying the problem or the solution of the problem. In Chapter 3 we presented different techniques for data analysis and modelling approaches. In Figure II.2 we summarise these techniques in a matrix that allows us to indicate what technique of modelling is used in a case and what method of data analysis.

In Figure II.2 we see that for the indication of the data used in the cases, we distinguish between a number of options:

- Making use of a rule of thumb (heuristic). For instance, we could use a rule of thumb for the target level of occupancy of beds for a surgical specialty with many emergency admissions, i.e., 80%.
- Making use of statistical analysis of data, using only averages, or also standard deviations, or the distribution (e.g., of durations of operations), or comparing with benchmark data.

For the use of modelling in the cases we distinguish between the following techniques:

- Descriptive modelling, i.e., making a flowchart of the patient journey or the unit process, using a spreadsheet model with data on operations and waiting times that allows different calculations.
- Analytical modelling, using mathematics, with a distinction between deterministic models (making use of averages) such as linear programming or stochastic models (including variation inside models) such as queueing models or Markov models (see Chapter 3).
- Simulation modelling, here focusing on Monte Carlo simulation or discrete event simulation approaches (see Chapter 3).
- Heuristic modelling, with one case (Chapter 16) being an example of use of the simulated annealing technique (see Chapter 3).

Each of the cases follows a similar format of elaboration. In principle, the following items are covered:

- An introduction to the context of the case, and a positioning of the case in our framework for cases in this book, as described above, making use of Figures II.1 and II.2.
- An introduction to the planning problem addressed. The problem is further elaborated in terms of level of planning and unit/chain/network OM. A short review of the literature on the planning problem is also provided.
- The elaboration of the planning problem, including data on operational characteristics of processes and resources.
- A description of the model developed, including positioning it in our framework.
- A discussion of the results obtained.
- A reflection on the strengths and weaknesses of the study and recommendations for the further development of the approaches used.

The cases are preceded by overview chapters for improving performance in unit OM, process OM and network OM. These chapters are meant for students of healthcare management or healthcare professionals and managers who want to study a specific HSOM problem for a unit, a process chain or a network, and develop a solution, following the design-oriented approach (Van Aken et al., 2012) as introduced in Chapter 1. This approach puts the problem studied in the middle of an iterative learning cycle of problem definition – analysis and diagnosis – solution design – implementation – evaluation. In each of the three following chapters, we place ourselves in the position of these students, professionals or managers, to help them in their efforts to improve the OM performance. We provide an overview of the state of art for each area, and different steps that can be undertaken to improve the level of performance, starting with simple approaches and adding ideas for more sophisticated approaches using modelling.

Reference

Van Aken J, Berends H and Van der Bij H (2012). *Problem solving in organizations: a methodological handbook for business and management students*. Cambridge University Press, Cambridge, UK.

8 Improving operations management of units

Jan Vissers, Sylvia Elkhuizen and Nathan Proudlove

8.1 Introduction

Unit operations management (OM) is the basis for a good performance of healthcare providers. Making the best use of limited resources can only be realised through well-developed unit OM. Taking care that the service contribution of the unit meets the standards for service delivery while at the same time resources are used efficiently, is the daily challenge for unit OM. This applies for all units in a healthcare provider organisation, whether a hospital, a GP practice, a nursing home, a rehabilitation centre, a mental health provider, a home for the elderly or a homecare provider. Though the type of care differs, as well as the complexity of the provider organisation, the task of well-developed unit OM is – broadly – the same. In Section 8.2, we follow the steps taken in a design-oriented approach to an OM problem in the context of a unit and provide suggestions for evidence-based research for each of the steps.

First, we provide a selective overview of possible OM topics of research within a unit, see Figure 8.1. In Figure 8.1 we present a number of topics that might be of interest when improving the OM performance of units. We arranged the topics according to the primary level of planning addressed. At the operational level there may be difficulties with the daily use of resources, for instance 'peaks and troughs' in the workload of a unit, or much waste of capacity. Another problem at this level might be a throughput time that is too long or the waiting time for patient access. A third topic at this level might be the day-to-day scheduling of patients and staff.

At the tactical level the way the resources are allocated in a capacity plan might be a topic of OM improvement. Another related topic would be the staffing of activities in the unit, as staff would like to know in advance when they will be required. A third topic at tactical level would be the design of the delivery process if daily problems in service delivery are becoming regular and suggest a redesign of processes.

At the strategic level the setting of targets for the performance of the unit might be a topic of research. A second topic might be the size of the unit, and a third its long-term resource requirements.

DOI: 10.4324/9781003020011-11

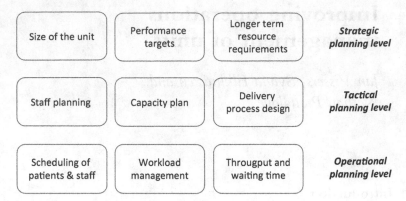

Figure 8.1 Topics for unit OM improvement.

It may be clear that this is a selection of topics that are most common. There will, of course, also be other topics that may be of interest for unit OM improvement (Hulshof et al., 2012).

In Section 8.3 we provide a number of elaborations of cases for topics mentioned in Figure 8.1. Some of these topics are further illustrated by fully elaborated case studies.

8.2 Stepwise approach for design–oriented study of a unit problem

8.2.1 Problem definition

For a problem-solving approach for a unit, it is of utmost importance to have a well-elaborated description of the problem and the unit. Though still in an orientation phase, we need to find out that we are dealing with a genuine problem, and what the size of the problem is. In this section we take the perspective of a student of healthcare management who is not familiar with the provider organisation and the problem.

The first step is to describe the unit of investigation, and its OM characteristics. In Chapter 4 we have elaborated the OM perspective of a unit, now we have to interpret that for the case.

- We have to know the type of services the unit delivers and the annual service demand.
- We need to know the capacity of the unit, and to have an idea of the configuration of resources that the unit uses for delivering its service, and of the amounts of resources that are available.
- We need to know where the demand for services of the unit originates from: requests from inside the provider organisation (e.g., for a

radiology department) or direct access from outside (e.g., for an emergency department).

- We need to have an idea what the delivery process of the unit looks like.
- We need to know how patients are scheduled for services (appointment, walk-in, waiting list).
- We need to know how performance is measured and what the targets for performance are.
- We need to know what data is available for analysis.

Of course, we also need to know the management structure of the unit, and how the unit is positioned in the organisational structure of the hospital.

When we are more familiar with the unit and its setting, we can focus on the problem under investigation. Suppose a nursing ward for general surgery reports regular problems with bed shortages. Patients for the ward are then admitted to a different ward ('outlying' or 'boarding'). The nursing staff of the ward, and the doctors who admit patients to it, are not happy with this, as it affects the quality of care delivered and it leads to longer length of stay.

To develop a clear idea of the problem, and its size, a number of things should be checked during the initiation of the study with contact people in the provider organisation.

- Do stakeholders have a common perspective on the problem, and its possible underlying causes (e.g., growth in demand, increase in complexity of cases, lengthening waits for follow-up care and so discharge, etc.)?
- What is the average occupancy of the ward? How often are all beds occupied? How often are patients then admitted to other wards? What are the consequences of admissions being redirected elsewhere on quality of care and length of stay? Are there patterns in bed use during the week?
- What are the stakeholders' ideas for solving the problem? What has been tried before, and with what results?

As we are still in an orientation phase of the study, we have to rely on our contact staff for information on the unit and the problem. It would be nice if there were written evidence for the problem, for instance information from a nursing ward's bed occupancy dashboard, but in this phase of the study it is not necessary to gather detailed information or send out questionnaires. The objective of this step is to identify the problem, gain insight into its impact, and be able to formulate an initial problem statement, the objective of the research project and research questions that need to be answered.

Though this might be sufficient for the first step of identifying the problem, we assume that a student of healthcare management, for example involved in a master's thesis project, has to develop in parallel his or her skill in writing and knowledge about the problem. We suppose that the material collected about the problem in this initial phase in the provider organisation and from the papers found in a literature search on the research topic, have to be 'digested' by the student. This can be done through a number of tasks in which the student can practice these skills.

We have a number of suggestions for this initial phase of the project to ground the project in evidence-based research and aim for scientific quality.

- Often problems have multiple causes. It can be worthwhile to develop a cause-and-effect diagram of the problem, in which one can see how the problem may have developed through contributions of different causes (see Section 6.2). This can create an overview and structure for the study of the problem. Sometimes, in cases where the problem has been studied before and reported in literature, it is possible to find such a structured cause-and-effect diagram in a published paper. However, creating such a diagram as a student yourself helps to understand the problem and the mechanisms that play a role in causing the problem in the specific setting of the study.
- Formulating an initial problem statement, the research objective and the research questions to be answered, requires careful wording but can help to find a focus for the study. The objective should be clear and realistic and follow logically from the problem statement. Take care that you do not use the term 'optimal' in situations where you cannot claim a (mathematically) optimal solution, but rather go for an 'improvement' objective.
- The set of research questions for a design-oriented case study may typically consist of the following questions:
  1. What is the current planning method applied to this problem area in the organisation?
  2. What is the performance of this current method?
  3. What are the requirements that a new design for planning should meet?
  4. What are possible interventions and what are their expected effects (considering the various stakeholders)?
  5. What does the design for the new way of planning look like?
  6. What is the expected performance of the new design?
  7. How will the new way of planning be implemented?
  8. What are the effects of the new way of planning, after implementation?
  For a master's thesis project, often the study ends with predicting the expected performance of the new design, as often the lead time of implementation does not make it possible to include this stage in the timeframe for the study.
- It would be good to capture the topic of research or the solution in the short main title, and the type of research (e.g., a design-oriented case study into …) in the subtitle. This is, of course, a working title that can be adapted during the study, but it is important to try to formulate this from the beginning, as it is the shortest 'summary' of your research.

- Start reading literature that helps you to learn about the problem being investigated. To start with, look for a few review papers that help you to develop an overview of the area of research. Do not expect to find a paper that exactly matches your study. See the topic of your study as a representative of a broader type of problem area and use review papers on the broader area to find papers that can help you with finding directions for possible solutions.
- Try to capture what you learn about the problem in a conceptual model that provides an OM perspective of the unit and the problem, which you can use during your study as a framework for presenting results and insights developed.

8.2.2 *Analysis and diagnosis*

In this second step of the problem-solving cycle we are going to analyse the current situation of the unit, the current planning method, and come to a diagnosis of the problem. First, we elaborate the current situation of the unit from an OM perspective, using different concepts of unit OM, and descriptive modelling techniques (Subsection 8.2.2.1). Then we analyse the performance of the unit in the current situation (Subsection 8.2.2.2) and draw conclusions on the diagnosis of the problem (Subsection 8.2.2.3).

It is worthwhile to think about the way you would like to involve the staff of the unit and other stakeholders in your study. A focus group, with representatives of different parts of the provider organisation that play a role in your study, can help to discuss data gathering for the study, interpret results of analysis, discuss possible solutions and evaluate the proposal for a new way of planning.

8.2.2.1 *Description of current situation*

We now describe the current planning situation of the unit in more detail, using an OM perspective. In Chapter 4 we have elaborated the concepts for describing a unit with OM terminology.

The conceptual model of the unit now needs to be elaborated in a more detailed way. How many workstations does the unit have? What is the configuration of resources in each workstation? What is the flow of patients in the unit?

What are the amounts of resources available for the unit? What are the characteristics of these resources (continuously/intermittently available, leading or following, dedicated or shared)? and does one of these resources often act as bottleneck for the output of the unit?

What does the delivery process of the unit look like? Are services of the unit delivered on request or can patients access the unit directly (e.g., for an emergency department)? What types of services are performed? And what are their characteristics? What are the average durations of the different services and the variations? Which unit has the patient – as a rule – visited before or after the visit to the unit under investigation?

What are the patterns in demand for services, during the year, within the week, and within a day?

How is the planning of services and resources organised at the different levels? What is the long-term capacity plan for the unit? What are the amounts of resources available for the current year in comparison with the volume of services expected? How are resources allocated to the workstations and how far ahead is that known? What type of planning system is used for scheduling services (appointments, walk-in, waiting list), and how far ahead are patients scheduled?

8.2.2.2 *Analysis of current performance*

Having described the current situation, we now describe how measuring the performance of the unit takes place, and then using this data to calculate the performance of the unit in the current situation.

What are the measures used to express the performance of the unit? Are definitions provided for each of the measures? How does measurement of a performance measure take place? What are the data used for measuring performance?

What are the results on the various performance measures of the unit? What analyses of data would enhance insight into the performance of the unit? For a ward, for instance, it would be interesting to show a run chart (see Section 6.2) of the number of admissions for each day of the year, apart from calculating average occupancy and measures of variation.

What further analyses can be performed to find out what the causes are for a possible loss of capacity from the unit? For instance, analysis of no-shows, cancellations of appointments, patterns of availability of staff during the days of the week, etc.

8.2.2.3 *Diagnosis of the problem*

The results of the different analyses can now be used to draw conclusions on the diagnosis of the problem. Perhaps a Pareto analysis (see Section 6.2) can be used to find out what the most important causes are for the performance of the unit.

Now we have developed more insight into the problem and its effect on current performance, it would be good to check whether the original problem formulation needs adaptation.

8.2.3 Solution design

To design a solution for the problem in an evidence-based way, we need first to define the requirements that need to be fulfilled by the design (Subsection 8.2.3.1), next we have to find possible interventions that will improve the performance (Subsection 8.2.3.2), then we need to combine the most promising interventions in an elaborated design of a new way of planning (Subsection 8.2.3.3) and finally we have to predict the expected performance of the new planning (Subsection 8.2.3.4).

8.2.3.1 *Design requirements*

The design requirements form an essential part of a design study to make the design evidence-based, and not just an idea of a researcher. Van Aken et al. (2012) distinguish between four categories of requirements:

- Functional requirements: these are the most important requirements as they define the targets that the new design must meet, or the level of improvement of a problem required. Preferably, the functional requirements would be based on documents (if standards for the performance level of the unit are available) or papers in literature on such standards, or they might be derived from a questionnaire or discussions among stakeholders.
- User requirements: users of a planning system may have preferences for a solution direction or the way the system can be used in practice.
- The user requirements can be based on interviews with representatives of different user groups.
- Boundary restrictions: external limitations that are imposed on the solution. These can – as a rule – be based on documents.
- Design restrictions: constraints from the provider organisation in terms of budget for the implementation of the solution or in the time available for developing the solution.

When these requirements are complete, they can be prioritised by, for instance, asking members of a focus group to express the importance of each requirement in a score on, for instance on a five-point Likert scale (very important, important, uncertain, less important, not important). The scores may help to evaluate alternative solutions in terms of meeting these requirements.

8.2.3.2 *Possible interventions*

A very important step is the search for possible interventions that can contribute to a solution for the problem. An intervention is not just an idea but an evidence-based way to solve a problem or reduce the negative effects of a problem if it cannot be solved completely. There are different ways to find such interventions:

- Standard solutions to types of problems.
  If the problem under investigation belongs to a class of problems that has been studied before and has resulted in standard solutions, then this is, of course, very strong evidence for an intervention. An example of this is the

determination of the size of nursing ward, given the average and standard deviation of the number of admissions, and the acceptance of a particular risk that all beds are occupied (see the case study in Chapter 11 and De Bruin (2010)).

- Literature.

  If the problem investigated has been studied before and solutions or improvements have been published in the literature, then this can be used as an inspiration for an intervention. Of course, it requires careful checking whether the conditions of the interventions reported in literature can be met. An example of this is the substitution of work performed by physician assistants for work done by medical doctors. Again, it requires careful checking to what extent the intervention reported in literature can be applied to the case investigated.

- Benchmark.

  Another source of inspiration can be a benchmark of the type of unit among similar organisations, regarding the problem investigated. This could be a regularly reported benchmark, or a one-time small-scale 'benchmark' in which a few organisations are approached to participate in a reference study for a specific healthcare provider organisation on an OM problem of a type of specific unit. The evidence from the regularly organised benchmark is, of course, stronger, but the evidence of a small-scale can be very inspiring as it offers great possibilities to learn from differences in the way organisations handle specific OM problems.

- Empirical data.

  In case of abundant empirical data on the performance of a unit, it is possible that the analysis of the data may comprehensively reveal issues behind the problem investigated and may also suggest what can be gained if certain wastes can be avoided.

- Questionnaire/interviews

  If the aforementioned options are not available, it is always possible to seek to interview stakeholders on their opinion on the problem and how it can be solved. To improve the methodological quality, starting with a few interviews before constructing a questionnaire is useful, and then piloting the first draft before sending it out to all targeted recipients. A follow up could be to send the list of possible solutions to the staff or members of a focus group that helped the researcher with the study and ask them to score the options in terms of importance, expected impact and implementability on, for instance, a five-point Likert scale.

It may be clear that the order of the above options also corresponds with the weight of the evidence obtained.

8.2.3.3 New design

For the design of a new method of planning for a unit, it would be advisable to include a few interventions that look most promising in terms of scores on the different dimensions. It would be logical to include, especially, options that are having high impact and can be realised at a short term.

The idea is then to include these options in an adapted description for the new planning method for the unit, and to elaborate this in a detailed manner.

8.2.3.4 *Expected performance of new design*

As implementation of the new design is often not possible within the time-frame of the study, the design of the new planning method can be evaluated in terms of the performance that one may expect from implementing the new design.

A quantitative approach that underpins the expected performance of the unit may be based on the expected effect from implementing an intervention found in literature, or a calculation of the gain in performance using a model of the unit's delivery process (e.g., built in Excel).

Also, the final design could be evaluated by staff or members of a focus group, again using a scoring system on the different aspects of the new design.

8.2.4 *Implementation and evaluation*

The last two steps in the design cycle are 'implementation' and 'evaluation' and closing the loop to the 'problem definition' to see whether the problem has been solved.

8.3 Case elaborations for unit OM improvement

We started this chapter on unit OM improvement with an overview of topics that might be of interest for an OM study (see Figure 8.1), now we will provide suggestions for finding evidence in literature for these topics and for choosing the level of sophistication of modelling support. We start with simple solutions and then make suggestions for stepping up the level of model support.

At the end of a case described under a topic, we will sometimes refer to a more detailed case study appearing in Chapters 11–17. These case studies are added to illustrate in more detail solutions and approaches reported in literature. However, the format used in these case studies is of the more common general case study type, and not based on the design approach adopted for this textbook.

8.3.1 *Size of a unit*

This topic of research refers to determining the size of a unit. In a hospital setting it may refer to the number of beds in a ward or the number of operating theatre rooms required to be able to deliver services to the number of patients requiring those services.

The simplest way to approach this problem is making use of a standard methodology in OM theory, called 'Rough Cut Capacity Planning' (RCCP). This method allows us to generate in a simple intuitive way a rough estimate of the amounts of resources required to produce a certain amount of output.

For a nursing ward, for instance, the number of beds required for providing nursing care for an annual demand of 3000 patients, who stay on average four days, and assuming an average bed occupancy level of 85%, would be:

$$\text{Required number of beds} = (3000 \times 4)/(365 \times 0.85) = 38.67$$
$$\text{or about 39 beds.}$$

The RCCP method does not take into account the variation in bed demand over time (days, weeks and months), nor the possibility for using overflow beds in another ward. A more sophisticated method is making use of standard queueing theory model (such as the Erlang loss model), as used in De Bruin et al. (2010) to determine the number of beds needed for a ward to cope with a patient flow at a certain risk of running out of beds. See also the case study in Chapter 11. Instead of using a theoretical queueing model, an approach based on historical data analyses may be appropriate (see for example Elkhuizen et al., 2007).

In Chapter 11 a case study is presented on the use and misuse of queueing theory for bed capacity decisions in hospitals.

8.3.2 Performance targets

This topic concerns the determination of targets for the performance of a unit. Performance of a unit is, generally, expressed in terms of occupancy level (percentage of available capacity that is used by services, average and standard deviation), risk that the unit is fully occupied so a request for service cannot be met, throughput time and waiting time (average and standard deviation).

The setting of targets for these performance measures can be based on benchmark studies for specific units (e.g., for a benchmark for operating theatres, see Van Veen-Berkx et al., 2016), or derived from studies on the size of units (see Subsection 8.3.1.1).

8.3.3 Longer-term resource requirements

This topic of research concerns the determination of resource requirements of a unit in the longer term, say 5–10 years ahead. These questions often become relevant when building or extending facilities. At this timescale it is important to consider trends in use of health services and the factors that influence this use. Developments of interest could concern population, incidence of diseases, technology and the influence it may have on the use of health services. An important variable that is influenced by these developments is, for instance, the length of stay. Length of stay has decreased for many diseases substantially, due to increased medical knowledge and improved technology. Though each of these developments should first be analysed separately, it is the impact of the combination of developments that we are after. Though the topic has not been addressed much in Chapter 4, a simple approach for a projection of scenarios of longer-term resource requirements can be easily put into practice with Excel modelling.

8.3.4 Staff planning

This topic refers to the planning of healthcare professional staffing for a unit. While the target for the number of staff necessary for a unit is determined at the strategic level of planning, at the tactical level decisions have to be made about how much staff resource capacity should be available at what times. This requires an analysis of aggregated demand per (part) day of the week (services provided in office hours), or per hour of the day (24/7-based services), and translating these demands into staff hours, and checking whether this level of staffing is sufficient to handle the variations in demand within the period of time considered. Staff planning can also be part of a capacity plan (see Subsection 8.3.5).

8.3.5 Capacity plan

This topic of research refers to the planning of resources of the unit at the tactical level. This concerns the allocation of the available capacity of the unit to groups of users of the unit. In hospitals, clinics in the outpatient department and surgery sessions in the operating theatres department have weekly or biweekly schedules in which capacity is allocated for each (part) day of the week. These master schedules are very important for the expected use of resources, for the leading units (before them in the chain), but also for the following units.

A simple approach to investigate these schedules on their expected performance, for leading and following resources, is a spreadsheet model that allows for analysis of performance and for what-if scenarios. See Elkhuizen et al. (2007) for an example concerning different levels of nurse capacity planning.

More sophisticated methods for master surgical schedules make use of mathematical programming and simulation to investigate optimality of performance measures or trade-offs.

There is a vast number of papers published on master surgery scheduling. To become familiar with this area of Health Services Operations Management research one can start with one or more review papers (e.g., Cardoen et al., 2010; Zhu et al., 2019). Then, there are many papers, requiring more mathematical knowledge, that look at optimal master schedules, sometimes focusing only on use of operating theatre resources, but often also in combination with use of Post Anaesthesia Care Units and Intensive Care Units or Wards (for instance Heider et al., 2022).

In Chapter 16 a case study is presented in which a master schedule for a specialty is investigated on its performance in terms of spreading of operating theatre sessions and clinic sessions.

Though the case studies in Chapters 12 (admission planning) and Chapter 17 (cardiology patient flow management) are examples of a network approach (see Chapter 10), the focus is on the unit perspective, so they might also be relevant for improving the OM performance of the unit considered.

8.3.6 Delivery process design

This topic refers to the design of the process of delivering services of a unit. When a process is structurally underperforming, it might be necessary to redesign the process fundamentally. This topic has been covered in Section 6.3.

8.3.7 Scheduling of patients

This topic concerns the scheduling of individual patients for the services of a unit. This may concern the scheduling of appointments for a GP or visits to the outpatient department of a hospital, diagnostic or therapeutic procedures in a hospital, or admissions to a hospital, rehabilitation centre or nursing home. There is much literature on advanced-access scheduling and outpatient appointment scheduling and also on operating theatre scheduling and admission planning. For literature suggestions, see Chapter 4.

8.3.8 Workload management

This topic of research refers to the balancing of workload of (scheduled) services for the healthcare professionals who deliver the services to patients in the unit. Typical examples are the handling of workload for nurses resulting from admissions of patients, but also the handling of workload in an emergency department resulting from unscheduled patient arrivals. This type of problem requires a thorough analysis of workload patterns by days of the week, parts of the day and sometimes hours of the day. For further suggestions, see Chapter 4.

8.3.9 Throughput and waiting time

This topic concerns the performance of the unit in terms of throughput time and waiting time for patients using the unit. When the throughput time (the time the patient spends in the unit for delivery of the service), or the time that patients have to wait for delivery of a service by the staff of the unit (external waiting time, before entering the unit; or internal waiting time within the unit) are too long – and the current design of the process is considered as appropriate – then improvement in OM performance can be realised by use of one of the improvement approaches discussed in Chapter 6.

References

Cardoen B, Demeulemeester E and Beliën J (2010). Operating room planning and scheduling: a literature review. *European Journal of Operational Research*, 201, 921–932.

De Bruin AM, Bekker R, Van Zanten L and Koole GM (2010). Dimensioning hospital wards using the Erlang loss model. *Annals of Operation Research*, 178, 23–43.

Elkhuizen SG, Bor G, Smeenk M, Klazinga NS and Bakker PJM (2007). Capacity management of nursing staff as a vehicle for organizational improvement. *BMC Health Services Research*, 7. https://doi.org/10.1186/1472-6963-7-196.

Heider S, Schoenfelder J, Koperna T and Brunner JO (2022). Balancing control and autonomy in master surgery scheduling: benefits of ICU quotas for recovery units. *Healthcare Management Science*. https://doi.org/10.1007/s10729-021-09588-8.

Hulshof PJH, Kortbeek N, Boucherie RJ, Hans EW and Bakker PJM (2012). Taxonomic classification of planning decisions in health care: a structured review of the state of the art in OR/MS. *Health Systems*, 1(2), 129–175. https://doi.org/10.1057/hs.2012.18.

Van Aken J, Berends H and Van der Bij H (2012). *Problem solving in organizations: a methodological handbook for business and management students*. Cambridge University Press, Cambridge.

Van Veen-Berkx E, De Korne DF, Olivier OS, Bal RA, Kazemier G (2016). Benchmarking operating room departments in the Netherlands: Evaluation of a benchmarking collaborative between eight university medical centres. *Benchmarking: An International Journal*, 23(5), 1171–1192.

Zhu S, Fan W, Yang S, Pei J and Pardalos P (2019). Operating room planning and surgical case scheduling: a review of literature. *Journal of Combinatorial Optimization*, 37, 757–805.

9 Improving operations management of process chains

Jan Vissers, Sylvia Elkhuizen and Nathan Proudlove

9.1 Introduction

When the operations management (OM) of units has reached a reasonable level of maturity, the next challenge is to develop the OM of process chains. This can be very rewarding as improved OM of process chains creates value for patients, as it takes the patient journey as the point of view for improvement. Regardless of the scale of improvement – whether solving a long access waiting time, or a complete redesign of all the steps in the process chain – this requires thinking about what constitutes value for the patient making use of this service, and there is the possibility to take the ideal process design as the ultimate objective. Therefore, if we define unit OM as the necessary basis for OM performance, we can see process OM as the next level of OM maturity for healthcare providers.

We again follow the steps of the design-oriented approach to an OM problem in a process chain and provide suggestions for evidence-based research for each of the steps in Section 9.2, but first provide a selective overview of possible OM topics of research of a process chain, see Figure 9.1.

In Figure 9.1 we present a number of topics that might be of interest when improving the OM performance of process chains. We arranged the topics according to the primary level of planning addressed. At the operational level there may be difficulties with a throughput time or the waiting time for patients that is too long. Another topic might be that the costs of services need to be reduced. A third topic at this level concerns the scheduling of patients and staff.

At the tactical level the amounts of resources required for delivering the services might be a topic of concern for OM improvement. Another topic at tactical level would be the design of the delivery process, if daily problems in service delivery are becoming structural and suggest a redesign is required.

At the strategic level, the setting of targets for the performance of the process chain might be a topic of research. These targets are already partially known if a care pathway for the delivery process exists, based on medical evidence.

It may be clear that this is a selection of topics that are most common. There will, of course, be also other topics that may be of interest for process chain OM improvement. For more topics, see Hulshof et al. (2012).

DOI: 10.4324/9781003020011-12

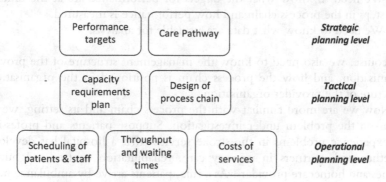

Figure 9.1 Topics for process chain OM improvement.

9.2 Stepwise approach for a design-oriented study of a process chain

9.2.1 Problem definition

The first step is to describe the process chain that we want to investigate, its demarcation and its OM characteristics. In Chapter 5 we elaborated the OM perspective of a process chain, now we have to interpret that for our process chain under study.

- We have to know the type of services delivered by the process chain and the demand for services at an annual level.
- We need to know whether a care pathway is used for organising the services, monitoring its performance and improvement of quality.
- We need to know which units are involved in the service delivery of the process chain, which units are key in the process delivery and which units are delivering services on request, and to have an idea of the configuration of resources that the key units need for delivering their services, and of the amounts of resources that are available for these key units.
- We need to know where the demand for services of process chain originates from: referrals from GPs, internal referrals or emergency patients.
- We need to have an idea what the delivery process of the process chain looks like, but also know about the steps taken by the patient before arrival at the provider organisation, and the steps followed by the patient after discharge in follow-up treatment with the provider organisation or in another provider.
- We need to know what the current way is of managing the process chain, and how the coordination of the process chain is arranged in the case of collaboration with different provider organisations.
- We need to know how patients are scheduled for services (appointment, walk-in, waiting list).

- We need to know what the targets for performance are at the different steps in the process chain and how performance is measured.
- We need to know what data are available for analysis.

Of course, we also need to know the management structure of the provider organisation, and how the process chain is positioned in the organisational structure of the provider organisation.

Now we are more familiar with the process chain and its setting, we can focus on the problem under investigation. Suppose patients and professionals experience problems in the stroke services that a hospital has developed together with partners in primary care, rehabilitation centres and nursing homes and homecare providers. As a rule, patients arrive by ambulance in the emergency department (ED), are seen by a neurologist at the ED, have a CT scan, are diagnosed and receive initial treatment in the ED, stay in the stroke unit until they are stabilised, and are then moved to a regular neurology ward for further treatment and recovery. When the treatment in the hospital is finished, patients either return home and receive homecare, go to a rehabilitation centre or to a nursing home for further rehabilitation. The problems experienced are mainly waiting times and throughput times, in the first part of their stay in the ED, as well as in the phase of discharge from the hospital.

To develop an idea of the problem, and its size, a number of things should be checked during the initialisation of the study with contact staff in the provider organisation.

- What are the views of stakeholders of the problem, and the possible underlying causes for the problem (growth in demand, complexity of cases, waiting for follow-up care, etc.)?
- What are the approximate waiting times and length of stay in the ED, and the ward? What is the availability of CT scan services for stroke patients? What is the average occupancy of the neurology ward? What are the arrangements with follow-up services after the stay in the hospital?
- What are the ideas for solving the problem, according to the stakeholders? What has been tried before, and with what result?

As we are still in an orientation phase of the study, we have to rely on the contact staff for information on the process chain and the problem. As there are different providers involved in the stroke service, it will be necessary to speak with them and understand their views. It would be nice if there is written evidence about the problem, for instance information from a stroke services monitoring tool, but in this phase of the study it is not necessary to gather detailed information or send out questionnaires. The objective of this step is to identify the problem, and have insight about the size of the problem, and be able to formulate an initial problem statement, objective of the research project and research questions that need to be answered. As this concerns a complex chain, and the problems indicated concentrate on the initial phase at the ED and the discharge phase at the ward, this requires careful consideration and demarcation. The OM of the initial phase (the hyper-acute and acute phase) is very different from the OM in the discharge phase.

Similar to unit OM improvement, we assume that a student of healthcare management, involved in a master's thesis project on this topic, will develop in parallel his or her skill in writing and knowledge about the problem. We refer to Subsection 8.2.1 for suggestions to improve the quality of research in this phase of the project.

9.2.2 *Analysis and diagnosis*

In this second step of the problem-solving cycle we analyse the current situation of the process chain, and the current way of planning, and come to a diagnosis of the problem. First, we elaborate the current situation of the process chain from an OM perspective, using different concepts of process chain OM, and descriptive modelling techniques (Subsection 9.2.2.1). Then we analyse the performance of the unit in the current situation (Subsection 9.2.2.2) and draw conclusions on the diagnosis of the problem (Subsection 9.2.2.3).

It is worthwhile thinking about the way you would like to involve different disciplines that are involved in the services provided by the process chain in your study. A focus group, with representatives of the different disciplines, can help to discuss data gathering for the study, interpret the results of the analysis, discuss possible solutions and evaluate the proposal for a new way of planning (Elkhuizen et al. 2007). If it concerns a complex chain, with the involvement of different providers, it might be more logical to include team leaders and managers in the focus group instead of healthcare professionals.

9.2.2.1 *Description of current situation*

We now describe the current situation of planning of the process chain in more detail, using an OM perspective. In Chapter 5 we elaborated the concepts for describing a process chain with OM terminology.

If a care pathway is used for the process being investigated, this functions as a point of departure for the description, as it provides the specifications of the process and targets for its performance (Van Vliet et al., 2010). However, a description of the process chain involves more than that.

For the description of the process in OM terminology we can start with developing a detailed process flow chart of the chain (see Subsection 5.3.1) and an Excel-based description of all the steps in the process, the use of resources for each step, duration and waiting time (see Section 5.5).

We need to describe the patient flow in the process chain, with the annual numbers of patients in each step. For the inflow to the chain, we need to know the different channels patients use to enter the services of the process chain. For the stroke example, we need to know how many patients arrive at the ED by ambulance, or by other entry routes, to get a complete overview of the way patients enter the chain. As it concerns emergency patients that can arrive during the whole day, we also need to know arrival times, to gain insight into arrival patterns over the days of the week and during the day. If part of the patient flow regards elective patients, we need to know the share of electives in the total flow.

For each step in the process we need to know what the arrangements are for access to resources for the process chain. Are there dedicated units for the chain (such as a stroke unit for stroke patients) or are resources shared with other patient groups or specialties, but a specific amount of capacity is made available for the process chain?

We need to know the duration of each step in the process (average and standard deviation) and the waiting time before each step (average and standard deviation).

We need to know how each step is scheduled. Is it on request? Is it on a walk-in basis or with appointment? is there a waiting list? Who is responsible for scheduling a step?

We need to know how many patients leave the chain to various destinations, and when, and what is the follow-up service they use? How much time do patients have to wait before they leave the hospital, and what is the reason for this delay?

How is the overall coordination of the chain arranged?

After this detailed description of the process chain, it is also useful to reflect on the qualitative characteristics of the process chain (see also Section 2.5). Does it treat elective/emergency patients? Is the volume of the inflow of patients high or low? Is the urgency high or low? Does it concern a long or short process chain? Does the chain exhibit complexity? Is its predictability high or low? What step in the process chain often causes delay because it acts as a bottleneck?

9.2.2.2 *Analysis of current performance*

Having described the current situation, we now describe how measurement of the performance of the process chain takes place, and how we use data to calculate the performance of the process chain in the current situation.

What are the measures used to express the performance of the process chain? What are the definitions of each of the measures? How does measurement take place? What are the data used for measuring performance?

What are the results on the different performance measures of the process chain? What analyses of data could be provided to enhance insight into the performance of the process chain? For the stroke services case, what are the key performance measures in the hyper-acute and acute phase? What are the key performance measures in the discharge phase?

What further analyses can be performed to find out what the causes are for a possible loss of capacity in the process chain unit (cancellations, no-shows)?

9.2.2.3 Diagnosis of the problem

The results of the different analyses can now be used to draw conclusions on the diagnosis of the problem. Perhaps a Pareto analysis can be used to find out what the most important causes are for the performance of the unit (see Section 6.2).

Now we have developed more insight into the problem and its effect on the current performance, it would be good to check whether the original problem formulation needs adaptation.

9.2.3 Solution design

9.2.3.1 Design requirements

For the four categories of design requirements, see Subsection 8.2.3.1.

9.2.3.2 Possible interventions

For ways to find possible interventions that help to solve the problem, see Subsection 8.2.3.2.

9.2.3.3 New design

For the design of a new way of planning for a process chain, it would be advisable to include a few interventions that look most promising in terms of score on the different dimensions. It would be logical to include, in particular, options that are expected to have high impact and that can be realised in the near term.

The idea is then to include these options in an adapted description for the new planning of the process chain, and to elaborate this new way of planning in a detailed manner.

9.2.3.4 Expected performance of the new design

As implementation of the new design is often not possible within the timeframe of the study, the design of the new planning method can be evaluated in terms of the performance that one may expect from implementing the new design.

A quantitative approach that underpins the expected performance of the process chain may be based on the expected effect from including an intervention that is found in literature, or a calculation of the gain in performance in an Excel model of the delivery process of the process chain.

Also, the final design can be evaluated by employees or members of a focus group by again using a scoring system on the different aspects of the new design.

9.2.4 Implementation and evaluation

The last two steps in the design cycle are 'implementation', 'evaluation' and closing the loop to the 'problem definition' to see whether the problem has been solved.

9.3 Case elaborations for process chain OM improvement

In Figure 9.1 we presented an overview of topics that might be of interest for a study on process chain OM improvement, now we provide suggestions for finding evidence in literature for these topics and for choosing the level of sophistication of modelling support. We start with simple solutions and then make suggestions for stepping up the level of model support.

9.3.1 Performance targets

This topic concerns the determination of targets for the performance of a process chain. The performance of a process chain is, generally, expressed in terms of waiting times (access time, in-process waiting times, time on waiting list, lead times), throughput times (diagnostic phase, treatment phase, follow-up phase) and durations of operations. But also 'drop-outs' (patients leaving the process chain) can be a performance measure if it concerns a patient who is not satisfied with the treatment. From the patient journey point of view the satisfaction with the services and its organisation are important performance measures.

The setting of targets for these performance measures can sometimes be based on national standards (for instance waiting times), or international publications (e.g., patient satisfaction studies).

9.3.2 Care pathway

When a care pathway is in use for the process chain considered, it is important to find out if the pathway is well established and actively monitored and managed. The care pathway is a strategic level input for the OM of the care process as it defines the specifications for the process chain and its OM. What is the quality of resources required for the pathway? What are the objectives for the pathway and its planning? What needs to be monitored in the OM of the process chain from the pathway perspective?

9.3.3 Capacity requirements plan

This topic of research refers to the arrangements of resources for the process chain at the tactical level. The first question to be answered is how much resource is required for proper functioning of the process chain. The next question would be, how are arrangements made with units that contribute to the services of the pathway so that these resources are available for a smooth flow of patients through the care pathway.

A simple approach to investigate the resource requirements of a process chain is to use the care pathway, if that is available, and develop a process flowchart combined with an Excel model of the process (see case study in Chapter 13).

The management of the pathway, insofar as it exists, should check with the management of the units for the conditions required for a smooth flow of patients. Forms of operational and structural coordination (see Section 2.8) should be discussed, and arrangements for these forms of lateral coordination between pathways and units should be established. For instance, if patients from the pathway should be seen on a walk-in basis in a radiology department, then a check should be made that the department has defined a capacity for walk-in patients on the specified days of the week of the specialty concerned, that takes into account the patient flow that can be expected for radiology from the clinic.

9.3.3.1 Case studies

In Chapter 13 a case study is elaborated on how a care pathway can be considered with a process flowchart and an Excel-based model that allows for calculation of resource requirements of the pathway.

9.3.4 Design of the process chain

This topic refers to the design of the process of delivering services in a process chain.

In Chapter 14 a case study is presented on a comparison of stroke services in six EU countries. One of the research questions was whether there were differences in the design of the stroke service between the six countries and whether these differences could explain differences in performance.

9.3.5 Scheduling of patients and staff

This topic concerns the scheduling of individual patients for the services of a process chain, and the scheduling for healthcare professional staff for delivering these services. Generally, the scheduling of staff for the process chain is included in the scheduling of services for patients.

The current level of sophistication of planning systems in healthcare does not yet allow scheduling of the complete patient journey in advance. Rather, parts of the whole process are scheduled together, such as the combination of visits and examinations in the diagnostic phase, or the combination of surgery, pre-operative screening and admission. This planning is not controlled by the management of a pathway, but performed by a unit (clinic staff, admission planning). Forms of pull planning (see Subsection 5.6.2) should be installed where possible.

9.3.6 Throughput and waiting time

This topic concerns the performance of the unit in terms of throughput time and waiting time for patients using the unit. This topic can well be researched with a Lean Management approach, see Van Vliet et al. (2010), Elkhuizen et al. (2007) and Chapter 7.

9.3.7 Costs of services

The case study in Chapter 14 on stroke services in six EU countries provides insights into the costs of stroke services and provides an explanation for differences in costs between them.

References

Elkhuizen SG, Burger MPM, Jonkers RE, Limburg MM, Klazinga NS and Bakker PJM (2007). Using business process redesign to reduce wait times at a University Hospital in the Netherlands. *Joint Commission Journal on Quality and Patient Safety*, 33(6), 332–341. https://doi.org/10.1016/S1553-7250(07)33038-9.

Hulshof PJH, Kortbeek N, Boucherie RJ, Hans EW and Bakker PJM (2012). Taxonomic classification of planning decisions in health care: a structured review of the state of the art in OR/MS. *Health Systems*, 1(2), 129–175. https://doi.org/10.1057/hs.2012.18.

Van Vliet EJ, Sermeus W, van Gaalen CM, Sol JCA and Vissers JMH (2010). Efficacy and efficiency of a lean cataract pathway: a comparative study. *Quality and Safety in Health Care*. https://doi.org/10.1136/qshc.2008.028738.

10 Improving operations management of networks

Jan Vissers, Sylvia Elkhuizen and
Nathan Proudlove

10.1 Introduction

In Section 2.7 we introduced network operations management (OM) as the combination of unit OM and process chain OM. We illustrated this with examples of a hospital setting, representing the hospital as a network of units and process chains. The unit logistics perspective is required to optimise the use of resources, as resources are often shared between specialties or between different pathways within a specialty. The chain logistics perspective is necessary to optimise the throughput volume and throughput time of a process chain. To be able to strike a balance between efficiency of resources and service performance of the process chains we often need to adopt a network logistics perspective.

Another form of network logistics is the application of logistics approaches to a network of collaborating providers. From an organisational sciences perspective a network organisation can be defined as a system of delegating and coordinating tasks among a number of providers that work together for a common goal. An example of such a network organisation in healthcare can be found in stroke services. In stroke services a number of organisations that provide services for stroke patients in a regionally defined area can work together. This may involve one or more hospitals, one or more ambulance services, primary care providers, nursing homes, rehabilitation centres, homecare providers, etc. For an effective operation of the stroke network the different providers have to make clear how much resource they have available for stroke patients. However, all of these providers also have to treat many other types of patients. Many of the resources used for stroke patients are shared with other patients in the hospital, nursing home or rehabilitation centres. So, the running of an effective and efficient network for stroke services is another challenge that requires a network logistics perspective.

As we have already discussed, the design study steps for a unit OM improvement (Chapter 8) and for process chain OM improvement (Chapter 9) and having defined network OM as a combination of unit OM and process chain OM, we refer to these chapters for suggestions for the steps in a network OM project. We also won't present an overview of research topics of network OM

DOI: 10.4324/9781003020011-13

as these would overlap with the topics in Figures 8.1 and 9.1. Therefore, our approach to network OM problems in healthcare in this chapter is different. We first discuss the typical difficulties of a network OM approach to a problem (Section 10.2). Then we first elaborate the two most common forms of network logistic approaches, i.e., network logistics problems within a single healthcare provider's organisation such as a hospital (Section 10.3), and logistic problems in a network of collaborating healthcare providers such as a stroke service (Section 10.4). We conclude with some final remarks (Section 10.5).

10.2 Challenges of network OM approaches

Having labelled unit OM as a basis for good OM performance of healthcare providers, and process OM as the next challenge for Health Services Operations Management (HSOM), it is evident that we see network OM as the ultimate objective for improving the OM performance of healthcare organisations. For instance, in a hospital with its many shared resources and dependencies between units, very often a network OM approach would have been justified for the problem investigated. However, for reasons of manageability of the research or improvement project, assumptions are made to isolate the problem and its setting from the wider system context. This is understandable, as a network OM approach is more complicated for several reasons. A first reason is that the wider network context requires the involvement of more stakeholders, who all have an interest in the solution of the problem, and the trade-offs that often have to be made. A second reason is that the larger scope also requires more data (often from different systems) and more analyses. A third is that the type of solution requires more abstract thinking, and a broader perspective that is not always appealing to an individual healthcare professional who wants to improve the pathway he or she is involved with.

Nevertheless, there are situations in which a broader systems perspective is required in order to do justice to the setting and to use an adequate solution approach for the problem. If a specific pathway is investigated, the OM approach strongly suggests we should include other pathways or process chains that make use of the same resources, and to demarcate the relevant context as that of the specialty concerned, to be able to make trade-offs between throughput improvement and use of resources. From a healthcare management point of view the challenge is not to improve the performance of one single pathway but to ensure that the other pathways of process chains are also performing as intended.

10.3 Network logistics within a single healthcare provider organisation

Most healthcare providers have to treat or care for different types of patients. In an acute hospital with 15–20 specialties, each having 5–10 main patient groups with different conditions, the number of main patient groups can easily reach

150, each having their own journey through the hospital. In a nursing home, patients can be grouped in wards for rehabilitation or for dementia care, and in terms of the levels of care required. In a mental healthcare provider, patients can be grouped in terms of the mental health condition (depression, anxiety, etc.) they are being treated for. As healthcare providers have limited resources, these patient groups all 'compete' for the resources they share. In a hospital this may involve beds, operating theatres, intensive care or diagnostic resources. In a nursing home this may concern beds, nurses and physiotherapy. In a mental health hospital this may involve psychiatrists, diagnostic services or specific treatment staff.

When a care pathway or process for a single patient group is being optimised in such a setting, there is a high chance of sub-optimisation, i.e., the one process considered is improved but at the expense of other processes. This is due to the fact that these processes share resources, and that more resources for one process imply fewer resources for others. Therefore, it is important to adopt a wider system perspective (Winasti et al., 2018). It is, of course not practicable or advisable to include the whole hospital in this perspective, when dealing with the effects of optimising a pathway that shares resources with other pathways. But for in hospital setting, it would be logical to consider a specialty as the frame for a systems perspective for optimising one specific pathway, as most of the resources used are shared within a specialty. To illustrate such a systems approach, we will elaborate it further for a specialty in a hospital, i.e., ophthalmology.

Suppose ophthalmology faces problems of long access times (waits) for patients who are referred for diagnosis and treatment of their eye problem. The main patient groups within ophthalmology are cataract, strabismus, glaucoma and retina – for which defined care pathways often already exist. Patients are referred by their GP and visit a general or a specific clinic. Often, all the ophthalmologists see the main patient groups but in addition have special interest areas. Clinics for strabismus, glaucoma and diabetes are held by orthoptists. Ophthalmic examinations are performed by optometrists and technical ophthalmic assistants, who work with the ophthalmologists. Surgery for cataract and strabismus is performed in a day-care setting, surgery for retinal detachment and other more complicated surgery are performed in an inpatient setting.

The first step in an OM network approach would be to describe the current situation in such a way as to be able to look at the impact on access times and throughput times on all the care pathways (the process perspective) as well as the use of shared resources (unit perspective). In Figure 10.1 we illustrate the network logistics approach for this ophthalmology setting.

The conceptual model in Figure 10.1 is built up in three layers. In the bottom part we see the different pathways, represented in the format of a flowchart with activities and waiting times. By analysing data on past performance, it would be possible to determine timelines, and calculate average access time, average waiting time on the waiting list for surgery or treatment, and average

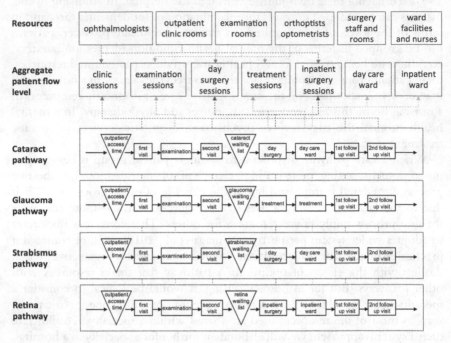

Figure 10.1 Conceptual model for network OM analysis of ophthalmology.

throughput time for diagnosis and treatment. See Chapter 5 for more information on how process chains can be analysed.

For each of these pathways, resources are required to perform activities. In
the upper part of Figure 10.1 the most important resources used by ophthalmology are listed. For each of the resources the amount of capacity available
needs to be defined. Chapter 4 on unit OM provides information on how the
amounts of resources available can be defined.

In the middle part, configurations of resources are illustrated for the workstations in the service delivery structure of ophthalmology. Ophthalmologists
see patients in clinic sessions that require a physician, a doctor's assistant and a
consultation room with equipment. Operating theatre sessions require a surgeon
and operating assistant, an anaesthetist and anaesthesia assistant and an operating
room. At this aggregate level it is possible to define in a master production schedule the number of sessions available per week at each workstation which determines the number of patients that can be seen and treated in an average week.

We now have a network perspective of ophthalmology, and we can describe
and analyse the different pathways on their performance (process logistics), but
we also can see how much resource is required for the mix of patients that
needs to be seen, and therefore the workload for units (unit logistics). This
allows us to strike a balance between the service quality realised in pathways
and the efficiency in the use of resources.

The network perspective on ophthalmology makes it possible to consider the impacts of different options to reduce the long access time for cataract patients, for instance:

- Increasing the capacity of the cataract pathway by allocating more resources. Allocating more clinic sessions and operating theatre sessions to cataract treatment – without expanding the total amounts of resources for ophthalmology – implies fewer resources available for other patient groups. The network logistics analysis allows us to calculate the impact of the changes on the performance of pathways and units.
- Redesigning the care pathway for cataract patients.
  An alternative would be to redesign the current care pathway to make it more efficient. This could be done, for instance, by saving time for ophthalmic surgeons if follow-up appointments can be dealt with by ophthalmic technician assistants, or by organising the care pathway for cataract patients as a focused factory with dedicated resources.

Above, we have sketched an initial elaboration of a network approach for solving a problem with waiting and throughput time in a pathway. A full elaboration would require more detailed descriptions of the pathways, and analysis of the available resources. Chapters 4 and 5 provide support for these elaborations.

However, there are also complications encountered when attempting a full elaboration for the case considered. The number of different diagnoses in ophthalmology can easily be as many as 150–200. This implies that the first problem for such a network OM approach would be to define the most important patient groups for the OM analyses. It must be clear that the number of patient groups that can be included in the analyses to make the results meaningful and manageable, should be not more than five to ten patient groups. Of course, the patient groups for an OM analysis can be less refined than a medical classification based on diagnosis (see also Section 5.2). To find a meaningful classification grouping for a specialty for OM purposes, would be a separate project and take much time. The best way to make progress from a practical perspective, would be to start with an initial grouping based on expert knowledge and supported with data. Using the rule of thumb, that often around 80% of the services provided can be covered with the most frequent 20% of diagnoses, can help decide which pathways need to be elaborated in an OM way, with the others aggregated as an 'other patients' group.

10.4 Network logistics of collaborating healthcare providers

We now provide a first elaboration of a network logistics approach for a network of collaborating healthcare providers, taking stroke services as an example.

Suppose we are considering a stroke network within a regional setting, with one hospital, a number of GP practices, one ambulance service, one rehabilitation centre, two nursing homes, three homes for the elderly and two homecare providers. The partners in the stroke network have agreed to work together for the benefit of stroke patients and have made several arrangements to make it easy to transfer a stroke patient who has finished treatment at a stage and needs follow-up care from another healthcare provider.

Figure 10.2 shows the configuration of healthcare providers that contributes to the care of stroke patients in the region.

From Figure 10.2 we see the first contact for a stroke patient will be the GP or the ambulance. The patient will be transported to the emergency department of the hospital and will be seen there by a neurologist. After some tests and a CT scan, the patient will be moved to the stroke unit where they will be further stabilised. After a few days the patient will be moved to the regular neurology ward for further treatment. When the treatment of the patient is finished, they will be made ready for discharge from the hospital. One possibility is that the patient can go home, possibly with support from one of the two homecare organisations. The other possibility is that the patient needs follow-up care at the rehabilitation centre, one of the two nursing homes (which may have rehabilitation facilities for stroke patients), or one of the three homes for elderly (which might have a special unit for stroke follow-up care). Figure 10.3 illustrates the patient flows between the healthcare providers.

When the patient has finished treatment in the rehabilitation centre, the patient might then go to home (with homecare) or to a nursing home or a home for the elderly.

Each of these healthcare providers has to take into account that beds/places can be required for treatment and care for stroke patients. Based on average figures of patient flows in the past, the provider may use a target level of beds that should be kept available for treatment and care for stroke patients in the network. This is illustrated in Figure 10.4.

Figure 10.4 illustrates that the amount of capacity reserved for stroke patients may vary considerably between providers. While in the neurology ward of the hospital the target level of beds for stroke patients may be 50%, the levels

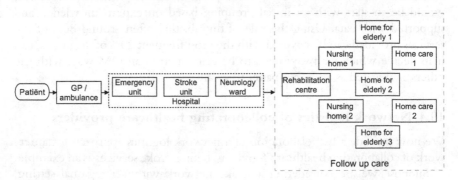

Figure 10.2 Configuration of healthcare providers for stroke patients.

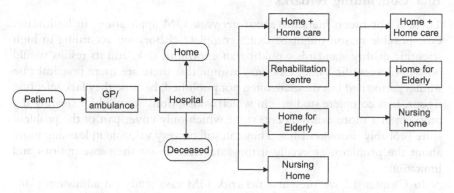

Figure 10.3 Patient flow between healthcare providers in a regional stroke network.

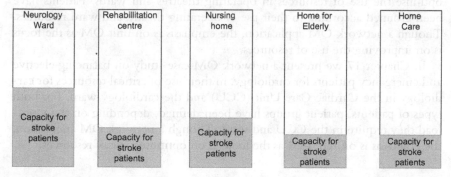

Figure 10.4 Resource availability for stroke patients for different healthcare providers in a network.

of capacity required of other providers may be much less, depending on the patient flow in their part of the network.

For all these parts of the network the resources involved are, in principle, shared resources. It may be that there are target levels for availability for stroke patients, but the healthcare provider has to be flexible in the use of resources by all patients that could be treated with the resources involved. The only resource in the stroke service network that is dedicated is the stroke unit, the other resources will be shared.

The stroke service network will probably have a steering group with representatives of all partners involved which discusses the arrangements made for the flow of stroke patients. These arrangements will be in line with the autonomous positions that the partners have, i.e., they will probably not accept a central body that controls the stroke patient flow for the whole network. The arrangements will probably be in terms of a guarantee that the transfer of a stroke patient from a hospital to a follow-up care provider has to take place within one to two days.

10.5 Concluding remarks

There is not much literature about network OM applications in healthcare. One possible reason might be that a complete elaboration according to high scientific quality standards would be an enormous task, and its results would only have scientific value. One may assume that there are more practical case studies performed but these are often not published, because they lack scientific rigour. Less complete studies – in which assumptions are used for treating the problem in a more isolated context, or which only cover part of the problem – are probably more available. They can still be very valuable in learning more about the problem, especially if they are clear about their assumptions and limitations.

In Chapter 12 we present a network OM case study on admission planning for a surgical specialty, in which we developed an approach to determine the numbers of patients that need to be admitted each day of the week to optimise the use of resources in operating theatres and wards. Patients have been grouped according to their use of operating theatre and ward resources. Though a network OM application, the emphasis is on unit OM as the focus is on improving the use of resources.

In Chapter 17 we present a network OM case study on balancing elective and emergency patients for cardiology, in their use of critical resources for cardiology in the Cardiac Care Unit (CCU) and the cardiology ward. For both types of patients, patient groups have been defined, depending on the workload they require in the CCU and ward. Though a network OM application, the emphasis is on unit OM as the focus is on optimised use of resources.

Reference

Winasti W, Elkhuizen S, Berrevoets L, Merode F and Berden B (2018). Patient flow management for inpatient units: a systematic review. *International Journal of Health Care Quality Assurance*, 31(7), 718–734. https://doi.org/10.1108/IJHCQA-03-2017-0054.

11 Use and misuse of Queueing Theory for hospital capacity decisions

Nathan Proudlove

Case positioning

This is a real case using real data, based on experience with a hospital in the UK, plus extending the ideas by using published data from a hospital in the Netherlands. The case involves using queueing theory models to consider the impact of the size of a unit (a hospital inpatient ward) on service levels (patient access). In Figure 11.1 we have positioned the case in the framework we use for case studies in this book.

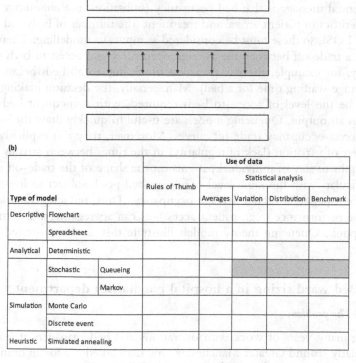

Figure 11.1 Position in case framework.

DOI: 10.4324/9781003020011-14

In Figure 11.1(a) we indicate that the case is about tactical planning: allocation of resources to specialties/departments, and with a unit focus. In Figure 11.1(b) we indicate that the type of model used in the case is from queueing theory (from the class of stochastic-analytical models) and the use of data analyses variation, with some comparisons with and assumptions about its distributions, and we also pull in some benchmarks.

11.1 Introduction

This chapter is based on experience at an NHS acute hospital trust in Greater Manchester in the UK, as written up academically in Proudlove (2020).

Queueing theory can and has been used to inform decision making about the size of units, for example hospital bed pools (e.g., wards), though rarely by managers themselves. The insights queueing theory brings are also not widely and properly understood by healthcare managers. In the UK, these two short-comings have led to the persistent fallacy that there is a globally applicable opti-mum average bed occupancy level, for example 85%, for all wards. If applied, this can lead to under- or over-provision of resources (beds), with consequent excessive risk of all beds being full or the waste of treatment potential, respec-tively. This chapter aims both to make queueing models more accessible and to provide visual demonstrations of the general insights managers should absorb from queueing theory.

A central message is that bed occupancy (utilisation) is a *consequence* of the characteristics of patient arrival and treatment (the number of beds and length of stay, LOS), so these must be considered as inputs to modelling. There is, of course, a trade-off between the average occupancy and access to beds (meas-ured by, for example, the risk of access block due to all beds being full or the average waiting time for a bed). Managerially, the decision making target should be the level of access to beds required, with consequent bed occu-pancy as an output. Queueing models are useful to quickly draw the shape of these access–occupancy trade-off curves. Moreover, they can explicitly show the effect of variation (lack of regularity) in the times between arrivals and in the lengths of stay of individual patients on the shape of the trade-off curves. In particular, with the same level of access, bed pools subject to lower vari-ation can operate at higher average occupancy. Thus, reducing variation can improve performance (e.g., patient access), as can aggregating wards to make larger pools. Queueing theory models illustrate this, as demonstrated in this chapter.

11.2 Bed ward sizing in a hospital paediatrics department

11.2.1 The problem

During many years of work with operations and bed managers at hospitals, particularly around Greater Manchester, one trust asked me for an opinion on the potential to resize its paediatric inpatient department. The bed managers' performance data reported a usual bed pool (ward) size of 34 beds and an average occupancy of around 54%. As this was below 'the recommended level of around 85% occupancy' they saw potential to close beds and so move resources elsewhere.

This 85% 'target' originated in a Monte Carlo computer simulation study (see Chapter 3 for an introduction to the technique). That study was summarised in a paper in the *British Medical Journal* (BMJ) (Bagust et al., 1999) and became very influential in the NHS (National Audit Office, 2000), finding its way into some acute hospital trusts' strategy documents as a target across inpatient activity areas.

For this paediatrics department, we can use the basic relationship in Equation 11.1 to do back-of-the-envelope calculations to get the 'simple' answer, where m is the number of beds.

$$\text{Average utilisation}\,(\text{bed occupancy}) = \lambda \times ALOS\,/\,m \qquad \text{Equation 11.1}$$

The average workload (average patients in the ward) $= \lambda \times ALOS$, where λ is the average number of patients admitted per day, and ALOS is their average length of stay.

$$\text{Currently}: \lambda \times ALOS\,/\,34 = .54$$

Changing to X beds would take occupancy up to 0.85 if $\lambda \times ALOS/X = 0.85$. Thus, $X = 34 \times 0.54/0.85 = 21.6$, so the ward should have about 22 beds, meaning 12 could be closed.

However, averages ignore what is really important in this real situation. If there were no variation at all, the ward could run like clockwork, with exactly, say, ten patients arriving each day (at the same times each day) and everyone staying exactly, say, two days – then the hospital could house them with 20 beds and have 100% occupancy with no delays or blockages to admission. It's the variation in admissions and LOS that makes this impossible. The conceptual reason is that quiet periods cannot be averaged with busy periods because the hospital cannot 'store' the empty bed time from these quiet periods to use at busy times. At quiet times some beds are empty; the resource that they represent is 'starved' of work and this capacity is said to 'perish'. The larger the variation, the larger the peaks and troughs in workload, so the more will be lost in quiet periods, and the poorer performance will be (poor performance here meaning higher chance that all the beds will be full at any particular instant).

This is particularly important in this case since this is a relatively small bed pool, dominated by emergency admissions. Paediatrics is ring-fenced: children should not be transferred to (or be 'outliers' or 'boarders' on other (i.e., adult) wards, and transporting them to a different hospital should be very much avoided.

As introduced in Chapter 3, queueing models build in the random variation in arrivals and service times around their averages to provide some metrics on how such systems perform, including the probability (and so risk) of various states such as all beds being full and so access being blocked for newly arriving patients. Study of queueing systems goes back over 100 years to Erlang's analysis of the telephone system in Copenhagen (Tanner, 1995), and queueing theory is now an established operational research technique, which has been applied to industrial and health systems for many decades, though largely by academics and consultants. Figure 11.2 shows the two basic situations considered by Erlang, translated to the hospital bed pool context. The differences arise in what happens to new arrivals if the bed pool (all the 'servers') are full.

i. **Patients Wait** in a queue (the circle) for an appropriate bed. In practice they are held 'upstream' (e.g., in the emergency department or a receiving area, or *temporarily* 'board' or 'outlie' in a less-appropriate bed) until a bed in the appropriate pool becomes available, *or (models are built under one assumption or the other)*.

ii. **Patients Transferred** to an alternative treatment process (bed pool, hospital or service) instead of waiting; being 'lost' from the system at the decision point (the diamond).

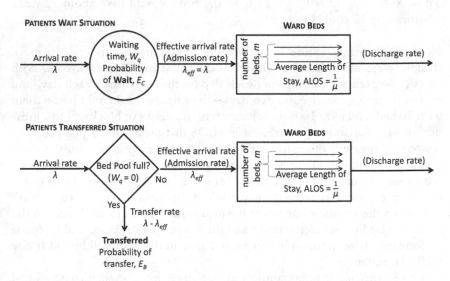

Figure 11.2 Characteristic of basic queueing models.

Queueing theory provides a number of stochastic analytical (random probability-driven mathematical) models which describe the behaviour of such systems under a set of simplifying assumptions to make the mathematics tractable. The most important simplifying assumptions are that the system is in steady state (long-run equilibrium, so not systematically getting busier or quieter) and that all arrival and exit (discharge) events are independent of each other. With figures for the average arrival rate (λ, as above) and average potential service rate ($\mu = 1/ALOS$), and assumptions about the distributions around these means, the models allow the calculation of expected (long-run average) values of performance metrics including the average utilisation of the servers (bed occupancy) and the waiting time in the queue, W_q, and risk of having to wait, E_C, or of being transferred, E_B.

Though it is necessarily a great simplification of complex reality, first-cut answers can be obtained in some situations where the simplifying assumptions, always necessary in mathematical modelling, are reasonably acceptable. In this chapter we show that is relatively easy to apply the models, and so for managers to derive context-specific results.

The key equations of interest to us in this case are Equations 11.2 and 11.3.

$$P(\text{Delay}) = E_C = \frac{\dfrac{A^m}{m!}}{\dfrac{A^m}{m!} + (1-u)\sum_{i=0}^{m-1}\dfrac{A^i}{i!}} \qquad \text{Equation 11.2}$$

Equation 11.2 is known as Erlang-C (or Erlang's Delay Function), E_C, and depends on the number of servers (e.g., beds), m, and a measure of congestion or 'traffic intensity', $A = \lambda/\mu$. (It is also categorised as the M/M/m/∞ queueing theory model – see online supplement for more detail on queueing models.) It applies to the Patients Wait situation. It is the risk that a patient arriving at any particular instant finds the beds all full, so has to wait, i.e., $W_q > 0$.

The equivalent to Equation 11.2 for the Patients Transferred situation is Erlang-B (or Erlang's Loss Function):

$$P(\text{Transferred}) = E_B = \frac{\dfrac{A^m}{m!}}{\sum_{i=0}^{m}\dfrac{A^i}{i!}}\,sd \qquad \text{Equation 11.3}$$

Here, patients arriving when all beds are full are transferred, they are not delayed, so W_q has to always be 0. The formula gives us the risk that a patient arriving at any particular instant finds all the beds full, so would have to be transferred (for good – they do not come back to these systems when it is quieter).

The formulae may look complicated but can be set up in a spreadsheet (see the Excel file in the online supplement; this and the text file also cover a few generalised and simpler approximate models).

The basic model of variation is that both the time between arrivals and the service durations (LOS) reasonably fit exponential theoretical probability distributions or, equivalently, the numbers of both arrivals and discharges in an interval of time follow Poisson distributions. These are called Markovian models; they are often adequate for bed modelling (McManus et al., 2004). Some of these assumptions can also be relaxed, at the cost of being able to estimate fewer system performance metrics (see online materials), and in fact the probability that an arriving patient is transferred, P(Transferred), E_B, does not depend on the service times being Markovian, so is valid whatever the LOS distribution might be. The online materials consider the fits of real data from this case to exponential/Poisson distributions.

Assuming that a patient arriving when the unit is full will generally wait (e.g., in the emergency department) until a bed is available, rather than being transferred elsewhere (and so ceases to be the responsibility of this paediatric ward to accommodate as soon as a bed becomes available), then this situation fits the assumptions of the Patients Wait model. (However, the Patients Transferred model results are shown too.)

11.2.2 Results

Data from the hospital trust's patient administration information system showed an ALOS of 1.61 days. The relationships in Equation 11.1 gave a quick estimate of the arrival rate of 11.56 per day. Using this, the model predicts that the consequences of 85% average bed occupancy would be very undesirable (Figure 11.3), with an E_C (risk of all beds being full) of about 33%. (See the online supplement for the Excel spreadsheet containing these calculations.)

Another useful relationship from queueing theory for the Patients Wait model is that the expected (long-run average) waiting time in the queue is:

$$W_q = \frac{E_C}{m\mu - \lambda}$$

Equation 11.4

For $m = 22$ beds this gives 0.17 days, i.e., about four hours average wait for a bed.

It is this access risk that is the more appropriate performance metric. Healthcare management thinking should start with the purpose in mind, i.e., achieving a suitable level of service. Data for English hospitals suggests that

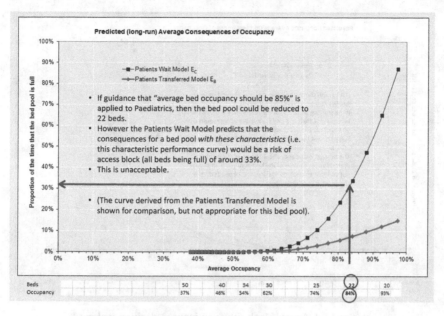

Figure 11.3 Consequences of increase in bed occupancy.

in paediatrics, most units operate at around a 0.1% risk of all beds being full (Jones, 2003). (Incidentally, the BMJ modelling (Bagust et al., 1999) produced the result that at 85% average occupancy the risk of all beds being full would be 0.1%, but this result came from the particular *context* that they studied which was very different from paediatrics.)

Using the same model, but now with the input to decision making being that the risk of there being no bed available when needed should be only 0.1%, the outcome (as shown graphically in Figure 11.4) is that the average occupancy should be around 55%, and so *no* bed reduction would be recommended! (National data also show paediatrics units running at around 40–60% occupancy (Jones, 2003).) These graphs were used to demonstrate performance characteristics of this type of system to bed and operations managers at the trust.

11.3 Illustration of ward sizing for other hospital departments

The point that appropriate average occupancy depends on the characteristics of a particular bed pool can be made powerfully by comparing a set of pools. In this section the parameters tabulated for a Dutch hospital (de Bruin et al., 2010) (bed pool sizes, ALOS, arrival rates, average occupancy – see online materials) are used to illustrate this graphically. In the Dutch situation, if a bed pool is full then patients are transferred to another pool or hospital, introducing the complication that the actual admission rate is not the 'actual' arrival rate

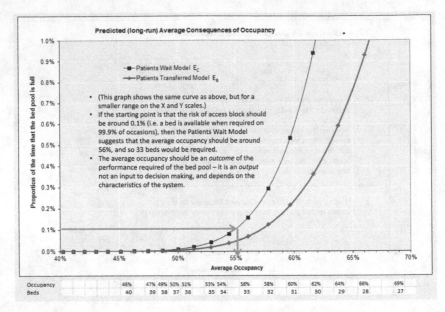

Figure 11.4 Access-block risk as an input to decision making.

(the difference being the rate at which patients are transferred, E_B, (i.e., turned away) – see Figure 11.2. It is the (unknown) arrival rate that is needed for the models, so the Dutch analysts used the admission rate and the average occupancy to 'reverse engineer' the algebra and so infer this arrival rate parameter (de Bruin et al., 2010). They then used the Patients Transferred model to calculate and tabulate the required numbers of beds in each pool to meet various levels of risk of patient transfer.

Here, we use their parameters to calculate the shapes of the performance curves for each ward (Figure 11.5) to demonstrate visually their behaviours and so reinforce the *non*-universality of the 85% 'gold standard' occupancy. For comparison, we have also added the corresponding curve from the BMJ paper through which the 85% figure gained so much currency in the UK NHS; the characteristics of the bed pool modelled in that study are very different.

Beyond simply calculating the numbers of beds required to achieve a certain threshold of risk performance, we argue that it is important for healthcare managers to grasp the insight that different pools behave differently, with some requiring low average occupancy and being subject to rapidly increasing risk as average occupancy increases to even relatively low levels. This is an important and rarely illustrated point, since academics tend to concentrate on algebra and numerical results, clinicians investigating queueing models have tended to focus on a single bed pool, and healthcare managers tend to have little access to models.

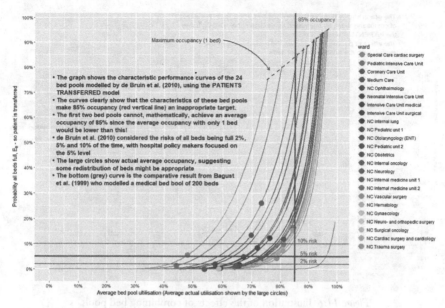

The graph shows the following embedded text:

- 100%
- 90%
- 80%
- 70%
- 60%
- 50%
- 40%
- 30%
- 20%
- 10%
- 0%

85% occupancy

Maximum occupancy (1 bed)

- The graph shows the characteristic performance curves of the 24 bed pools modelled by de Bruin et al. (2010), using the PATIENTS TRANSFERRED model
- The curves clearly show that the characteristics of these bed pools make 85% occupancy (red vertical line) an inappropriate target.
- The first two bed pools cannot, mathematically, achieve an average occupancy of 85% since the average occupancy with only 1 bed would be lower than this!
- de Bruin et al. (2010) considered the risks of all beds being full 2%, 5% and 10% of the time, with hospital policy makers focused on the 5% level
- The large circles show actual average occupancy, suggesting some redistribution of beds might be appropriate
- The bottom (grey) curve is the comparative result from Bagust et al. (1999) who modelled a medical bed pool of 200 beds

Probability all beds full, E_n - so patient is transferred

10% risk
5% risk
2% risk

0%   10%   20%   30%   40%   50%   60%   70%   80%   90%   100%
Average bed pool utilisation (Average actual utilisation shown by the large circles)

ward
- Special Care cardiac surgery
- Pediatric Intensive Care Unit
- Coronary Care Unit
- Medium Care
- NC Ophthalmology
- Neonatal Intensive Care Unit
- Intensive Care Unit medical
- Intensive Care Unit surgical
- NC Internal lung
- NC Pediatric unit 1
- NC Otolaryngology (ENT)
- NC Pediatric unit 2
- NC Obstetrics
- NC Internal oncology
- NC Neurology
- NC Internal medicine unit 1
- NC Internal medicine unit 2
- NC Vascular surgery
- NC Hematology
- NC Gynaecology
- NC Neuro- and orthopedic surgery
- NC Surgical oncology
- NC Cardiac surgery and cardiology
- NC Trauma surgery

Figure 11.5 Bed pool risk-occupancy characteristic performance curves for a range of types of hospital wards

The models can also be used to convey further, deeper, insights into the behaviour of queueing systems, including policies sensible for healthcare managers to pursue.

11.4 Illustration of the impact of pooling of wards

Staying with the Dutch example, de Bruin et al. (2010) suggest combining three of the small bed pools. Using the Patients Transferred model again, we can graph the results to show how dramatically improved (lower) the characteristic performance trade-off curve is for the resultant combined pool (Figure 11.6).

The total number of beds in the combined pool is the same, so the average utilisation would be the same as the (weighted) average of the three separated pools, but the risk of transfer would be very much lower. Combining the previous system of three queues reduces the risk of transfer (or, in other systems, wait) by reducing the risk of a patient being 'stuck' in a queue to access an unusually busy pool when another has capacity. This is a general insight of queueing systems: pooling of queues produces better performance, often dramatically so. Another term for this is reducing capacity carve-out.

There is, of course, a tension in managing operational systems between the economies of scale from pooling and the economies of focus from greater specialisation (Bekker et al., 2017). In general, there has often been found

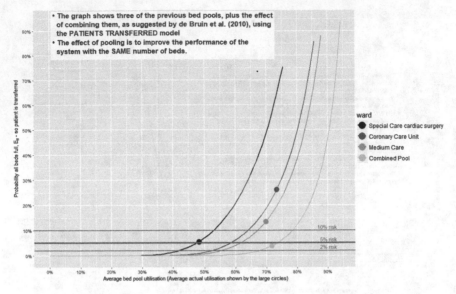

Figure 11.6 Illustration of the effects of combining bed pools.

to be more carve-out of healthcare capacity than can be justified (Walley et al., 2006). There are, however, human considerations in designing queueing systems (Walley et al., 2006), and the pure mathematical relationships neglect behavioural phenomena. Some hospital staff feel the ability to overflow the limits of some areas (particularly medicine) by outlying excess patients in others (particularly surgical specialisms) provides too easy an escape from dealing with an area's own flow problems as well as leading to further degradations in efficiency as noted in the introduction. This is leading some trusts to limit, or at least make harder, such overflowing, forcing areas to 'consume their own smoke' to a greater extent (Proudlove et al., 2003).

11.5 Illustration of the impact of reducing variation of wards

The modelling in this chapter so far has used the stereotypical (and default) Markovian models of variation in arrival rate (Poisson distribution, or equivalently the exponential distribution of times between arrivals) and LOS times (exponential distribution). Whilst these have often been found to be good approximations (de Bruin et al., 2010), they do not always hold. While unplanned care is closer to having expected levels of randomness, variation is often actually larger unplanned care (McManus et al., 2003; Fusco et al., 2003; Proudlove et al., 2007a; de Bruin et al., 2010; Harrison et al., 2005).

More importantly, assuming the 'benchmark' degree of variation implicit in the standard (Markovian) queueing models hides another fundamental insight important for healthcare managers: the effect of the size of the variation in patient flows. One extreme would be a system in which all jobs (e.g., patients) arrive exactly when managers plan, and all jobs take exactly the predicted amount of time to complete. Such a zero variation (deterministic) system could operate at 100% utilisation with no waits or transfers; conversely, the greater the variation in arrivals and/or services the worse the performance of the queueing system, i.e., the greater the risk of a wait or transfer at any given level of utilisation (e.g., bed occupancy). Again, queueing models can illustrate this. As noted earlier, the general (non-Markovian) version of the Patients Wait model has the powerfully intuitive approximation for the expected waiting time in a queue: W_q = **V**ariation term × **U**tilisation × service **T**ime (see Equation A5 in the online materials). This so-called 'VUT' relationship produces the same form of characteristic performance trade-off curves as for the examples shown earlier, but now we can easily investigate the impact of different degrees of variation in arrivals and/or service (LOS).

We return to the Greater Manchester hospital for our illustration, this time to the 28-bed urology bed pool, in which the arrival rates and service times both have higher variation than the benchmark (Markov) model. Data from the hospital information system were used to analyse the arrival rates (and inter-arrival times) and LOS for inpatients. The distributions and calculated parameters are in the online materials. The pool handles both elective and emergency admissions and as the Dutch analysts did (de Bruin et al., 2010), we considered these together. We also used the bed managers' occupancy performance reports to check overall fit. The insight of particular interest here is the effect of the size of the variation. Figure 11.7 illustrates this showing the effect of varying the variation term in the VUT equation.

Left to its natural behaviour, there would be long waits for beds in the urology bed pool. To mitigate such effects requires much effort, particularly by operational and bed managers to 'juggle' patients and beds, temporarily outlie them to other wards or transfer patients to other hospitals (Proudlove et al., 2003; Boaden et al., 1999; Dodds, 2018, 2014). This is not a desirable way to work (Proudlove et al., 2007b).

Qualitative and conceptual consideration has been given to how operations management principles for reducing variation and improving flow can and might be applied in healthcare (Allder et al., 2010), and reducing variation is the core focus of many improvement methodologies developed in manufacturing and gradually being adapted and applied in healthcare, including Lean Management and Six Sigma, along with a focus on flow (Boaden et al., 2008). It is notable that much of the large variation in healthcare activity, as noted earlier for planned care, is artificially or systemically caused variation and so there is great scope to understand root causes, and so reduce it in order to increase productivity and improve patient experience (Proudlove et al.; 2007a, McManus *et al.*, 2003; Proudlove et al., 2003; Fusco et al., 2003). Other approaches include forecasting and planning around peaks and troughs to level the workload (Slack et al., 2016; Proudlove et al.; 2003, Fusco et al.,

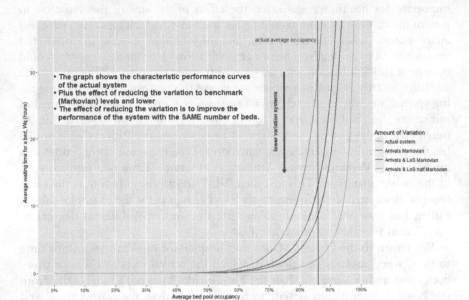

Figure 11.7 Illustration of the effects of reducing variation.

2003; Proudlove et al., 2007a). However, after reducing all systemic and special cause variation, common cause (randomness) will remain (Boaden et al., 2008), and systems must be designed to absorb this, including through lower utilisation, than calculations based on averages would suggest, even in booked inpatient systems (Gallivan et al., 2002).

11.6 Discussion

The literature (Jones, 2003; Green, 2002; Green and Savin, 2008) is in accordance with our personal experience that healthcare managers generally consider capacity requirements based on *averages*: ALOS and average occupancy. However, ignoring variation can both produce erroneous numbers and miss the opportunities to improve performance without increasing capacity (Mackay and Lee, 2005; Rutherford et al., 2017; Hulshof et al., 2012). Central guidance on bed occupancy targets, such as 85% and 92% (NHS Improvement and NHS England, 2017), is intended to accommodate variation, but ignores the contexts hospital managers face, so may also produce inappropriate results and bypass service improvement thinking.

The Patients Wait model has been applied to examples of representative obstetrics and intensive care units (ICUs) (Green, 2002). The Patients Transferred model has been used to estimate bed pool sizing in a Dutch hospital (de Bruin et al., 2010), and bed requirements for a particular stroke unit

(Boulton et al., 2016) and a small paediatric ICU (McManus et al., 2004). Unusually, in the last of these examples, the bed pool operated at very high bed occupancy (as high as 91% over one particular month) with correspondingly high numbers of patient transfers (up to 47%), and they were able to gather this outcome history and validate the adequacy of their queueing model this way.

Operational research academics have done a stream of work with more complex models but have found that complex models are likely to over-fit data, and without a practitioner-user caring or understanding this risk (Mackay, 2001; Mackay and Lee, 2005; Harrison et al., 2005). If the assumptions of queueing theory are too simplistic, in particular if we are interested in systems which are not in non-steady state or arrivals and/or LOS are dependent on other processes (e.g., dependent on the state of other resources in other systems), then we would often turn to discrete-event simulation to model such complex flow systems (Proudlove et al., 2007a; Harper and Shahani, 2002; Pitt et al., 2016). However, such modelling is very time consuming, data hungry, requires specialist knowledge and software and can rapidly become too complex or protracted to be of practical value (Proudlove et al., 2017).

In summary, whilst the literature contains quite a few examples of the use of queueing theory to model bed pools, the emphasis has been i) in the healthcare management literature to answer questions about specific one-off situations and to demonstrate that it is useful, and ii) in the operational research literature to extend the queueing models themselves (at the expense of greater complexity). Neither goes far into how to apply the fundamentals in a way that a reasonably quantitative healthcare manager could use and see (and so trust) the workings of, or much consider the general insights that queueing theory convey. This may partly explain the observations in the literature and of this author that use in practice is, at best, very limited.

Queueing models can seem inaccessible to healthcare managers due to apparent mathematical and computational complexity. There is a variety of algebraic notation and routes through the algebra across operational research/ management science (Winston, 2004), operations management (Slack et al., 2016; Hopp and Spearman, 2011) and specialist queueing theory texts (Tanner, 1995). The operational research texts tend to focus heavily on algebraic derivations and calculation of 'answers' from them rather than the insight the algebraic relationships imply, whereas operations management texts tend to make very partial use of the many metrics and relationships. A good mixture is *Factory Physics* (Hopp and Spearman, 2011), but it still does not contain some of the relationships we would want for modelling a bed pool or guidance on practical implementation. In the online additional materials, we pull together a set of the most useful analytical relationships for considering bed pools from a range of sources, imposing a consistent system of notation. We show that they can be implemented fairly easily and transparently in a spreadsheet.

For the Patients Wait model we can get directly to the probability that all beds are full when a patient wants one using Equation 11.2, which depends on the number of servers (e.g., beds) and the busyness (congestion) of the system

(Tanner, 1995). The mathematical properties of the Markovian processes make the algebra tractable to derive exact solutions, but few texts make the point that this complex-seeming equation can be implemented fairly easily and compactly in a standard spreadsheet as shown in the online materials.

A particularly useful extension is to relax the assumption of the Markovian arrivals and service (LOS) distributions to any 'general' probability distributions in the form of approximations, with the Markovian models as special exact cases. Equation A5 in the online materials is highlighted in some operations management texts (Hopp and Spearman, 2011; Slack et al., 2016) as being particularly conceptually powerful since it shows that

Delay ≈ **V**ariation term × **U**tilisation term × service **T**ime term

This is the 'VUT' relationship (Slack et al., 2016; Hopp and Spearman, 2011) which makes it very clear that the performance of a queueing process depends on these three components:

- The *variation* in arrivals and service (LOS).
- The utilisation of the servers, i.e., average bed occupancy, which for a given demand and service (LOS) situation depends on *the number of beds*.
- The mean service time (*ALOS*).

This prompts the impact of each to be examined explicitly, independently and jointly. The variation term uses the coefficient of variation (standard deviation divided by the mean) of both the arrivals and service times distributions. A property of the Markovian process is that the standard deviation and the mean are equal, thus the coefficients of variation of arrivals and service are both 1, and so the Markovian can be considered to have a benchmark amount of variation (=1). Most valuable from a healthcare service improvement point of view is the opportunity to stress the trade-off between variation and utilisation, which has been illustrated in this chapter. It is hard to find discussion or examples of this and the insights it brings in healthcare queueing applications.

As noted, these equations are expressed in various forms and different combinations in texts, but the ease of implementation of even the most common ones in a user-friendly way is not made apparent. Some texts implement some of these in accompanying spreadsheet files, but these can be hard to obtain, use very old software or versions, and from our investigations it is not uncommon for them to contain bugs or errors. There are a few freestanding 'Erlang' or queueing calculators available online, but many of these are cumbersome to use, black-box, very complex and/or are aimed at call-centre traffic analysis and difficult or impossible to use in the bed pool context. Therefore, we developed the fairly simple spreadsheet shown in Figure A2 and made available (see online materials). We have tested it against examples and tables of results from a range of texts, including those cited in this chapter.

11.7 Conclusions

Despite some groups of healthcare managers claiming familiarity with queueing theory (Esan et al., 2016), in decades of running national training programmes for NHS clinical, non-clinical and scientific leaders and working with a large number of trusts, we have found very little use of the results or true insights it brings. Instead, we find both inadequate approaches to planning the configuration and operational management of bed pools and misunderstanding of some high-publicised results. These managerial shortcomings continue to waste and/ or overburden this valuable resource (Fusco et al., 2003).

Approaches based on rules of thumb and average length of stay (ALOS) continue to be used in practice by hospital managers despite their shortcomings (Awad et al., 2017; Mackay, 2001; Mackay and Lee, 2005; Harrison et al., 2005). These approaches disregard the variation in patient arrivals and service durations that lead to queues or access block, even with utilisation considerably less than 100%. In contrast, queueing theory models have been used since the mid-1970s in the US to suggest average bed occupancy rates appropriate to absorb this variation, with 85% or thereabouts being the typical result (Green, 2002). The computer simulation study of a generic UK NHS acute hospital published in the BMJ (Bagust et al., 1999) produced the same sort of figure and became very influential in the NHS (National Audit Office, 2000), finding its way into some acute hospital trusts' strategy documents as a target across inpatient activity areas. However, regarding '85%' as a universal target ignores the contextual assumptions behind this modelling study which can make it inappropriate, even dangerous. Nonetheless it still has currency, including in the UK (National Audit Office, 2013; The King's Fund, 2014), as 'a gold standard' in the Netherlands (de Bruin et al., 2010), the Gulf (Boulton et al., 2016) and in academic reviews (He et al., 2019). As service improvement educators and facilitators in the NHS, we and others (Dodds, 2018, 2014) continue to attempt to counter fallacious understandings and consequent potentially deleterious 'improvement' planning.

Motivated by discussion with NHS hospital managers, this chapter is an attempt to clearly address these twin shortcomings: ignorance about how to use queueing theory, and lack of awareness of the true insights and principles it brings, including the fallacy of the 85% occupancy target. In particular, managers at a hospital trust aware of the 85% occupancy level guidance enquired about how many beds could be closed in order to increase occupancy in their acute paediatric service to 85% from a much lower level. In fact, since the variation is relatively high, this would result in very high risk of access block: it is actually appropriate that the average occupancy should be lower. Similarly, at a national workshop for 'exemplar' trusts, managers from another hospital trust proposed to considerably reduce occupancy in wholly-elective (planned care) units to 85% from a considerably higher level. In this low-variation context the likely consequence would have been considerable waste of resources.

This chapter shows that queueing models can be used fairly easily to produce first-cut information on the trade-off between patient access performance (risk of access block or the expected waiting time for access) and bed occupancy for planning decisions and emphasises that it is more appropriate to use access performance as the target than occupancy. We use data from a UK and a Dutch hospital to illustrate that the characteristic trade-off curves depend on bed pool characteristics, and the consequent deeper insights that pooling queues and reducing variation can produce dramatically better performance from the same resource. In this chapter (together with the online materials), we have shown these queueing theory models can be accessible with nothing more than a spreadsheet (online materials) and so can be used to produce first-cut answers to questions about capacity versus patient occupancy trade-offs.

Access to models is a powerful way to demonstrate that the common figure of '85%' is not a universal goal (Figures 11.1 and 11.5). Despite several academic papers noting that this has been a misunderstanding, the myth or fallacy lives on. Instead, utilisation should be an output of modelling and not an input: it is a consequence of a desired service level, e.g., risk of access block or acceptable waiting time (Figure 11.4). The characteristic performance curves are also very valuable to convey the insight that the trade-off is sharply non-linear above some critical level of utilisation (e.g., bed occupancy).

Comparing the curves for different bed pools (e.g., Figure 11.5) shows the importance of context and can show the dramatic improvements that combining bed pools can have (e.g., Figure 11.6). Further, the 'VUT' relationship brings home the impact of variation on performance (e.g., Figure 11.7). These are intuitions that operational and planning managers should absorb, and we suggest that graphical illustrations such as those in this chapter are a powerful way of promoting this.

These are tools to which healthcare managers should have access to when planning unit capacity to obtain quick ballpark figures. The stereotypical application is to bed pools, but the principles are the same with other service systems. Of course, many systems have more complex features, which would require much more detailed modelling, perhaps computer simulation, though this is a major leap in the level of modelling tool, expertise and time required.

11.7.1 Conclusions for hospital managers

Though queueing theory may appear mathematically complex, it offers important qualitative insights, and first-cut quantitative results can be produced without very advanced mathematical skills or software. There are many queueing situations in healthcare, whether hidden or readily apparent. Inpatient bed pools are chosen here to illustrate the insights and models as the situation is readily apparent, and this application has been a frequent subject for academics and consultants. The aim of this chapter is to make the qualitative insights and mechanics more widely accessible and understood.

The take-aways for practising managers are:

- The simplest back-of-the-envelope calculation of bed requirements for a particular pool would be beds required = average demand (patients per day) × ALOS (in days) (Equation 11.1). This, though, takes no account of providing some 'headroom' to absorb peaks from the inevitable *variation* around these averages, so is an underestimate of requirements.
- An improvement would be to divide this first estimate by the average bed occupancy desired (e.g., 0.85, the 85% 'target'). But what occupancy figure should we use? Important insights are that:
  - It is the *service level* (access to beds – a low risk of there being no bed available or that the patient has a material waiting time) that is our true goal, and the relationship between them has the characteristic performance curve shape illustrated in Figure 11.4.
  - The actual position of the performance curve we should aim to be at (on average) depends on the context, notably the size of the resource pool and the degree of variation, examples are shown in Figure 11.5.
- In particular, '85%' bed occupancy carries a high risk of access block (all beds being full), except for pools that are very large (e.g., 200 beds) or have very low variation (e.g., some highly standardised elective-only pools).
- Since the performance curve depends on this context, performance could be improved without adding more beds (i.e., we could deal with more patients with the same access level) by:
  - Combining bed pools, as illustrated in Figure 11.6, though the improvements the mathematics suggest have to be balanced against the faster and better treatment that greater specialisation might bring (in operations management terms this is called segmentation) and staff-capability and patient-experience issues, as discussed elsewhere (Bekker et al., 2017).
  - Reducing variation, as illustrated in Figure 11.7, which is a key theme of many improvement initiatives, as noted earlier.
- An analyst, or quantitatively able manager, can generate such performance curves using the equations and a spreadsheet (as shown in the online materials). This is fairly quick and requires relatively little data – as illustrated here with the UK and Dutch examples. Much more complex situations and patient-flow logic can be modelled using networks of queues using much more complex mathematics or specialist simulation software (see Chapter 3) and expertise.

11.8 Questions and exercises

See online supplement.

References

Allder S, Silvester K and Walley P (2010). Managing capacity and demand across the patient journey. *Clinical Medicine*, 10(1), 13–15. https://doi.org/10.7861/clinmedicine.10-1-13.

Awad A, Bader-El-Den M and McNicholas J (2017). Patient length of stay and mortality prediction: a survey. *Health Services Management Research*, 30(2), 105–120. https://doi.org /10.1177/0951484817696212.

Bagust A, Place M and Posnett J (1999). Dynamics of bed use in accommodating emergency admissions: stochastic simulation model. *British Medical Journal*, 319, 155–158. https:// doi.org/10.1136/bmj.319.7203.155.

Bekker R, Koole G and Roubos D (2017). Flexible bed allocations for hospital wards. *Health Care Management Science*, 20(4), 453–466. https://doi.org/10.1007/s10729-016 -9364-4.

Boaden R, Harvey G, Moxham C and Proudlove NC (2008). *Quality improvement: theory and practice in healthcare*. NHS Institute for Innovation and Improvement, Coventry. www.england.nhs.uk/improvement-hub/wp-content/uploads/sites/44/2017/11/ Quality-Improvement-Theory-and-Practice-in-Healthcare.pdf.

Boaden R, Proudlove NC and Wilson M (1999). An exploratory study of bed management. *Journal of Management in Medicine*, 13(4), 234–250. https://doi.org/10.1108 /02689239910292945.

Boulton J, Akhtar N, Shuaib A and Bourke P (2016). Waiting for a stroke bed: planning stroke unit capacity using queuing theory. *International Journal of Healthcare Management*, 9(1), 4–10. https://doi.org/10.1080/20479700.2015.1101910.

de Bruin AM, Bekker R, van Zanten L and Koole GM (2010). Dimensioning hospital wards using the Erlang loss model. *Annals of Operations Research*, 178(1), 23–43. https:// doi.org/10.1007/s10479-009-0647-8.

Dodds S (2018 and 2014). The 85% optimum occupancy myth. *The Improvement Science Blog*.

Esan OT, Akanbi CT, Esan O, Fajobi O and Ikenebomeh PI (2016). Application of quantitative techniques in decision making by healthcare managers and administrators in Nigerian public tertiary health institutions. *Health Services Management Research*, 29(3), 50–61. https://doi.org/10.1177/0951484816662490.

Fusco D, Saitto C, Arcà M, Ancona C and Perucci CA (2003). Cyclic fluctuations in hospital bed occupancy in Roma (Italy): supply or demand driven? *Health Services Management Research*, 16(4), 268–275. https://doi.org/10.1258/095148403322488964.

Gallivan S, Utley M, Treasure T and Valencia O (2002). Booked inpatient admissions and hospital capacity: mathematical modelling study. *British Medical Journal*, 324, 280–282. https://doi.org/10.1136/bmj.324.7332.280.

Green LV (2002). How many hospital beds? *Inquiry*, 39, 400–412. https://doi.org/10.5034 /inquiryjrnl_39.4.400.

Green LV and Savin S (2008). Reducing delays for medical appointments: a queueing approach. *Operations Research*, 56(6), 1526–1538. https://doi.org/10.1287/opre.1080 .0575.

Harper PR and Shahani AK (2002). Modelling for the planning and management of bed capacities in hospitals. *Journal of the Operational Research Society*, 53(1), 11–18. https://doi .org/10.1057/palgrave/jors/2601278.

Harrison GW, Shafer A and Mackay M (2005). Modelling variability in hospital bed occupancy. *Health Care Management Science*, 8(4), 325–334. https://doi.org/10.1007/ s10729-005-4142-8.

He L, Madathil SC, Oberoi A, Servis G and Khasawneh MT (2019). A systematic review of research design and modeling techniques in inpatient bed management. *Computers & Industrial Engineering*, 127, 451–466. https://doi.org/10.1016/j.cie.2018.10.033.

Hopp WJ and Spearman ML (2011). *Factory physics*. 3rd ed. Waveland Press, Long Grove, IL.

Hulshof PJH, Kortbeek N, Boucherie RJ, Hans EW and Bakker PJM (2012). Taxonomic classification of planning decisions in health care: a structured review of the state of the art in OR/MS. *Health Systems*, 1(2), 129–175. https://doi.org/10.1057/hs.2012.18.

Jones R (2003). *Bed management (tools to aid the correct allocation of beds)*. Camberley, Surrey. www.hcaf.biz/Hospital%20Beds/Microsoft%20Word%20-%20Bed%20planning %20HMC.pdf.

Mackay M (2001). Practical experience with bed occupancy management and planning systems: an Australian view. *Health Care Management Science*, 4(1), 47–56. https://doi.org /10.1023/A:1009653716457.

Mackay M and Lee M (2005). Choice of models for the analysis and forecasting of hospital beds. *Health Care Management Science*, 8(3), 221–230. https://doi.org/10.1007/s10729 -005-2013-y.

McManus ML, Long MC, Cooper A and Litvak E (2004). Queuing theory accurately models the need for critical care resources. *Anesthesiology: The Journal of the American Society of Anesthesiologists*, 100(5), 1271–1276.

McManus ML, Long MC, Cooper A, Mandell J, Berwick DM, Pagano M and Litvak E (2003). Variability in surgical caseload and access to intensive care services. *Anesthesiology*, 98(6), 1491–1496.

National Audit Office (2000). Inpatient admissions and bed management in NHS acute hospitals. National Audit Office, London. www.nao.org.uk/report/inpatient-admissions -and-bed-management-in-nhs-acute-hospitals.

National Audit Office (2013). Emergency admissions to hospital: managing the demand. www.nao.org.uk/wp-content/uploads/2013/10/10288-001-Emergency-admissions.pdf.

NHS Improvement and NHS England (2017). A review of winter 2016/2017. https:// nhsicorporatesite.blob.core.windows.net/green/uploads/documents/Winter_review _final_f4jPBJO.pdf.

Pitt M, Monks T, Crowe S and Vasilakis C (2016). Systems modelling and simulation in health service design, delivery and decision making. *BMJ Quality & Safety*, 25, 38–45. https://doi.org/10.1136/bmjqs-2015-004430.

Proudlove NC (2020). The 85% bed occupancy fallacy: the use, misuse and insights of queuing theory. *Health Services Management Research*, 33(3), 110–121. https://doi.org/10 .1177/0951484819870936.

Proudlove NC, Bisogno S, Onggo BSS, Calabrese A and Levialdi Ghiron N (2017). Towards fully-facilitated discrete event simulation modelling: addressing the model coding stage. *European Journal of Operational Research*, 263(2), 583–595. https://doi.org /10.1016/j.ejor.2017.06.002.

Proudlove NC, Black S and Fletcher A (2007a). OR and the challenge to improve the NHS: modelling for insight and improvement in in-patient flows. *Journal of the Operational Research Society*, 58(2), 145–158. https://doi.org/10.1057/palgrave.jors .2602252.

Proudlove NC, Boaden R and Jorgensen J (2007b). Developing bed managers: the why and the how. *Journal of Nursing Management*, 15(1), 34–42. https://doi.org/10.1111/j.1365 -2934.2006.00632.x.

Proudlove NC, Gordon K and Boaden R (2003). Can good bed management solve the overcrowding in A&E? *Emergency Medicine Journal*, 20(2), 149–155. https://doi.org/10 .1136/emj.20.2.149.

Rutherford P, Provost L, Kotagal U, Luther K and Anderson A (2017). *Achieving hospital-wide patient flow*. Institute for Healthcare Improvement, Cambridge, MA. www.ihi.org/ resources/Pages/IHIWhitePapers/Achieving-Hospital-wide-Patient-Flow.aspx.

Slack N, Brandon-Jones A and Johnston R (2016). *Operations management*. 8th ed. Pearson Education, Harlow.

Tanner M (1995). *Practical queueing analysis*. McGraw-Hill, New York.

The King's Fund (2014). *What's going on with A&E waiting times?* The King's Fund. www .kingsfund.org.uk/projects/urgent-emergency-care/urgent-and-emergency-care -mythbusters.

Walley P, Silvester K, Steyn R and Conway JB (2006). Managing variation in demand: lessons from the UK National Health Service. *Journal of Healthcare Management*, 51(5), 309–322. https://doi.org/10.1097/00115514-200609000-00007.

Winston WL (2004). *Operations research - applications and algorithms*. 4th ed. Thompson Learning, Belmont, CA.

12 Surgical admission planning and patient mix optimisation

Jan Vissers[1]

Case positioning

The case refers to the planning of patients for orthopaedics in a 400-bed hospital in the Netherlands. We investigated what the mix of patients should be to be admitted each day of the week to optimise the use of resources in the operating theatre department and at the nursing ward. In Figure 12.1 we have positioned the case in the framework we use for case studies in this book.

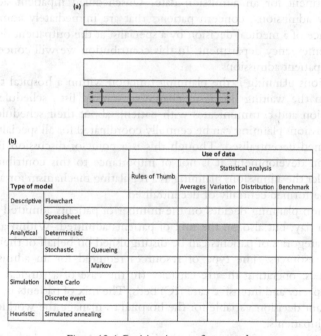

Figure 12.1 Position in case framework.

---

1 The case is based on a case study in (Vissers et al., 2005), authored by Jan Vissers, Ivo Adan and Miriam Eijdems. Though the case makes use of data from before 2000, and length of stay has since then dropped considerably, we think the case has still value for a textbook because it illustrates in a simple way what can be gained if admission planning makes use of the principles applied in this case study.

DOI: 10.4324/9781003020011-15

In Figure 12.1(a) we have indicated the planning levels addressed in the case and whether the focus is on unit, chain or network operations management (OM), and in Figure 12.1(b) the type of model used in the case and the use of data. We see that the case addresses a tactical level of planning, i.e., the detailed allocation of resources to patient groups. It is a network OM problem as we include delivery processes for all patient groups and use of resources in units. The emphasis is, however, on unit OM as we focus on improving the use of resources. In the case a form of deterministic analytical modelling is used, i.e., integer linear programming. Data wise, the case makes use of data, based on averages and standard deviations for operating theatre use and bed use.

12.1 Introduction

Patients can enter a hospital in three ways: as an outpatient after a referral from a general practitioner, as an emergency patient in case of immediate need of specialist treatment and as an inpatient. Inpatient admissions can be distinguished by two types: scheduled or unscheduled. Scheduled inpatient admissions, also called elective patients, are selected from a waiting list, or are given an appointment for an admission date. Unscheduled inpatient admissions, emergency admissions, concern patients that are immediately admitted as a consequence of a medical decision by a specialist at the outpatient department or at the emergency department. In this contribution we will concentrate on elective inpatient admissions.

Admissions planning is the planning function within a hospital that places patients on the waiting list, is in charge of waiting lists, schedules patients for admission and communicates with patients about their scheduled admission. Admissions planning can be centrally coordinated for all specialties or can be performed decentralised. Though this is a point of discussion in hospital organisation development, it is not of importance to this contribution. We will consider the admissions planning as a regulating mechanism for a specialty, whether performed centrally or decentralised.

Admission planning decides on the number of patients admitted for a specialty each day, but also on the mix of patients admitted. Within a specialty, different categories of patients can be distinguished on behalf of their requirements of resources. The type of resources required for an admission may involve beds, operating theatre capacity (in the case of a surgical specialty), nursing capacity and intensive care (IC) beds. The mix of patients is, therefore, an important decision variable for the hospital to manage the workload of the inflow of inpatients.

The current way of dealing with this issue is based on experience of planners rather than on a formal procedure. Often the only focus is the operating theatre capacity because it is important that this resource is used to its maximum capacity. Admission planning in such a case comes down to operating theatre planning, as the other resources involved are not considered. Most hospitals do not have a tool available to evaluate the patient admission profile (i.e., the number and the mix of patients to be admitted) on their consequences for the combined resources involved.

BOX 12.1 THE CASE-STUDY HOSPITAL

The case-study hospital – that acted as pilot-setting for the development of the model – is a 400-bed hospital in the southeast of the Netherlands. The pilot concerned the specialty of orthopaedics. We use data from this specialty to illustrate the model.

The orthopaedic surgeons as a group were very concerned to improve the planning of inpatient admissions. The number of surgeons was on a stable level again, after a few years of ups and downs, and the number of admissions had been rising since the previous year. The questions raised in the group were, amongst others:

- *How many resources do we need to fulfil the contracts agreed with hospital management?*
- *What is a good balance between beds, operating theatre hours and nursing staff to effectively accommodate the planning of admissions as well as the efficient use of resources?*
- *What is the mix of patients to be admitted each day of the week to optimise the use of available resources?*

The orthopaedic surgeons discussed this problem with the hospital management. Together they decided to start a pilot project to develop a tool to support this problem.

Section 12.2 provides further information on the planning problem and a short review of literature. In Section 12.3 the planning problem is further elaborated by providing data for the orthopaedics specialty. Section 12.4 describes the model that has been developed for this planning problem. In Section 12.5 we discuss the application of the model to orthopaedics and the results, illustrating the functioning of the model and the contribution to the planning problem of orthopaedics. Finally, in Section 12.6 we reflect on our contribution to this planning problem, by formulating conclusions and recommendations for further research.

12.2 Planning problem

For the development of the model, we concentrated on the third question of the group of orthopaedic surgeons, as the first two questions are included in providing an answer for the optimal mix of patients to be admitted (see Box 12.1). In this contribution we therefore concentrate on the following planning problem: how can one generate a patient admission profile for a specialty, given targets for patient throughput and utilisation of the resources while satisfying given restrictions?

12.2.1 Position in planning framework

As shown in Figure 12.1 the planning problem addressed in this case study, is positioned at the second level of the framework, i.e., patient group management. The approach followed is defined as a network OM approach, though the emphasis lies on unit OM. We will provide some further information on the position of the case study in the framework.

The main focus of the planning problem and approach followed in the case study is on the level of *patient group management*. A key issue is to define the mix of patients, selected from different patient groups, which need to be admitted for each day of the week to realise targets for resource utilisation and throughput. This is a relevant planning issue at a weekly or monthly planning level. It uses aggregate information on patient groups and their resource profiles. Though the resource profiles of the patient groups provide information on the use of different resources (regular beds, operating theatres, IC beds, nursing staff), the resource profile cannot be used for scheduling individual patients. Its main function is to allow for visualisation of the impact of different admission profiles on the use of resources. Though a combination of process chain OM (patient groups and multiple resources) and unit logistics (resource use), the emphasis lies on the unit logistics perspective, as we are most interested in a balanced use of resources that is optimal with respect to targets set.

The emphasis lies on the second level of the framework, but there are also links with the other levels. At the level of *Strategic Planning* the categories of patients distinguished for admission planning need to be checked with the profile of the hospital. The throughput used for admission planning needs to be checked with the annual volumes agreed upon at the level of *Annual Volume Planning*. At this level, where annual patient volumes are translated into capacity allocations, also the amounts of resources available to a specialty needs to be checked. It is also at this level where decisions are taken to set beds aside or reserve beds for emergency admissions. The link with the level of *Tactical Planning – allocation to specialties* is clear, as the planning of patient groups needs to be performed within the restrictions of the available capacity for the sum of patient groups served by the specialty. The admission profile developed at the level of patient groups can be of guidance to the level of *Operational Planning*. When admission planning uses the admission profiles as a target mix to be filled in with daily admissions, one may expect results similar to the projections.

12.2.2 Literature review

The literature on admission planning and patient classification is rather extensive. See Gemmel and Van Dierdonck (1999) for a state of the art on admission planning. Though many studies are concerned with scheduling of admissions and resources (see for instance Fetter and Thompson, 1969; Roth and Van Dierdonck, 1995), developing policies for admission based on the mix of different categories of patients within a specialty has not been investigated much before (Vissers et al., 1999; Adan and Vissers, 2002). Patient classification studies and patient mix studies are mostly used for marketing and finance purpose (see, for instance, Barnes and Krinsky, 1999) and not so much for patient flow planning.

Since the case study execution (1999) many more papers have been published on admission planning for surgical patients. See, for instance, Cardoen et al. (2010), Hulshof et al. (2012), Zhu et al. (2018) and Heider et al. (2021).

12.3 Elaboration

The model has been applied to the specialty of orthopaedics in a general hospital setting. We will discuss in this section the different data required to analyse the problem and to develop a model.

12.3.1 Patient inflow and throughput

In 1998 about 760 inpatients and 700 day cases were admitted. About 15% of the inpatients were admitted as emergencies, while the remainder were admitted on an elective basis using a waiting list. Day cases are always elective admissions. The average length of stay of inpatients (excluding day cases) was 12.4 days. There were 11 categories of patients that could be distinguished in orthopaedics.

We recorded the actual admissions over a number of weeks and use the inflow of week 12 in 1998, which was considered as a representative inflow pattern, to illustrate the model. We also use the average inflow, based on the annual output, as a reference inflow pattern. Table 12.1 provides information on the number of admissions per category of patients in the sample week and the average week.

12.3.2 Demand requirements

The patient groups can be characterised on a number of features, such as length of stay, nursing workload, day and duration of operation, use of IC beds and days of using IC bed. These features are given in Table 12.2 and Box 12.2.

Table 12.1 Number of admissions per category
of patients in the sample week and
the average week

Patient category	Patient mix week 12	Patient mix average
1	14	13
2	2	1
3	0	1
4	1	2
5	0	1
6	0	1
7	1	2
8	3	1
9	2	2
10	1	1
11	2	1
Total	26	26

Table 12.2 Characteristics per category of patients

Patient category	Length of stay (days)	Nursing workload	Day of operation	Operation duration (min.)	Use of IC beds	Days IC bed start	duration
1	1	L1	0	20	N		
2	1	M1	0	30	N		
3	2	M1L1	0	38	N		
4	3	M2L1	0	40	N		
5	4	M2L2	0	50	N		
6	5	M3L2	0	46	N		
7	9	Z4M4L1	1	77	N		
8	14	Z6M6L2	1	70	N		
9	18	Z6M8L4	1	80	N		
10	24	Z24	1	120	Y	0	1
11	29	Z29	1	92	N		

(nursing workload profile is expressed in number of days with Z workload (5 points),
number of days with M workload (2 points) and number of days with L workload (1
point); if a patient is operated on the day of admission it is labelled as day 0; IC days are
counted with the day of the operation as starting point).

BOX 12.2 CATEGORIES OF PATIENTS

There are 11 categories of patients distinguished. Each of the groups is described below and examples of procedures are given.

Category 1: day surgery procedures that generate little nursing workload. Patients can take care of themselves. Example procedures are arthroscopy of the knee and small procedures on hands or feet. The procedures do not take more than 20 minutes.

Category 2: day surgery procedures that generate medium nursing workload because these patients can't use an arm or leg after the operation. Example procedures are carpal tunnel syndrome, arthroscopy of the knee and removing osteosyntheses.

Category 3: surgical procedures in short stays with a length of stay of two days. The nursing workload is medium for the day of operation, usually because the patient can't move a hand or foot for a couple of hours. Examples in this category are menisectomy by arthroscopy and small operations on the hands and feet.

Category 4: surgical procedures in short stays with a length of stay of three days. Operations are osteotomy of the toes and osteotomy of the hand or foot and a classical menisectomy.

Category 5: operations in short stays with a length of stay of four days. Examples are minor osteotomy of the leg or elbow.

Category 6: operations with a length of stay of five days. Examples are osteotomy of the ankle or shoulder.

Category 7: operations with an average length of stay of nine days. Operations are extensive osteotomies of the thigh or hip, and operations to repair the rupture of the knee ligament. The nursing workload for these patients is high for the first four days because they are not allowed to leave their bed.

Category 8: operations with an average length of stay of 14 days. Examples are surgical procedures for a total hip replacement.

Category 9: operations with an average length of stay of 18 days. Examples are surgical procedures for a total knee replacement.

Category 10: operations with an average length of stay of 24 days. This group of patients contains spine operations. These patients need to go to the IC unit the night after the operation because of the high risks.

Category 11: the last category is a mixture of different types of procedure. A characteristic of the patients in this group is that most of them are older than 60 and end up in a nursing home. It usually takes a while before they have a place in a nursing home.

12.3.3 Available resources

Orthopaedics has 28 beds allocated on a ward, including short-stay beds. There are also beds for day-surgery patients, shared with other specialties, but we concentrate on inpatients. The four orthopaedic surgeons have daily operating theatre sessions, in total six hours a day. There are about 12 full-time equivalent nurses available for the ward, but nursing capacity is expressed in terms of nursing points. On Wednesday one IC bed is reserved for elective admissions from category 10. Table 12.3 summarises the available resources for orthopaedics.

As can be seen, the availability of resources can be less during the weekend. During the weekend there is no operating theatre capacity available and no IC beds; there are also no short-stay beds available, and the nursing staff is less.

12.3.4 Capacity load factors and resource importance

The different resources each have a target occupancy level, which defines the level of occupancy that reflects a realistic target workload. This can be different during the weekend. Table 12.4 provides information on the target occupancy level for each type of resource.

The above-mentioned data are required to describe the service delivery system of the specialty. It is further required to specify the relative importance of the different resources. Table 12.5 gives the weights used to reflect the relative importance of the different resources involved, according to the participants in the hospital.

Table 12.3 Available resources for orthopaedics

Day of the week	Operating theatres (minutes)	Beds (number)	Nursing (points)	IC beds (number)
Monday	360	28	80	0
Tuesday	360	28	80	0
Wednesday	360	28	80	1
Thursday	360	28	80	0
Friday	360	28	80	0
Saturday	0	20	70	0
Sunday	0	20	70	0

Table 12.4 Target occupancy levels per type of resource

Day of the week	Operating theatres	Nursing	Beds	IC bed
1	85%	95%	90%	0%
2	85%	95%	90%	0%
3	85%	95%	90%	100%
4	85%	95%	90%	0%
5	85%	95%	90%	0%
6	0%	95%	80%	0%
7	0%	95%	80%	0%

Table 12.5 Relative weights per type of resource

Resource type	Weight
Operating theatres	5
Nursing	3
Beds	4
IC beds	5

(weight range: 0 = ignore, 1 = not important, 2 = barely important, 3 = medium importance, 4 = important, 5 = very important).

As one can see, operating theatres and IC bed use are considered very important, bed use is considered important, and nursing workload is considered of medium importance.

12.3.5 Restrictions

It is also important to be aware of any restrictions imposed on the planning problem. In reality, many restrictions can play a role that will make it difficult to realise a feasible admission profile. We will illustrate this with two examples of restrictions in the case of orthopaedics. The first restriction that plays a role in the planning problem is that category 6 patients, having a length of stay of five days, need to be admitted on Monday in order to have them discharged before the weekend. Furthermore, the number of category 1 patients is limited to six patients a day from Monday to Friday in order to avoid a concentration of day-surgery patients (leading to extra handling for the nurses) on one day.

12.4 Model

In this section we translate the planning problem into a mathematical model in the form of an integer linear programme (ILP). In the following section we first describe the various factors that are relevant to the planning problem (Subsection 12.4.1). Then, in Subsection 12.4.2 the mathematical model is formulated.

12.4.1 Relevant factors

It is clear from the discussion in the previous sections that the following factors play an important role in the planning problem.

- Planning period.
  This is the complete time period (typically several months or a year) over which the admittance of patients has to be planned.
- Patient categories.

There is usually such a wide variety of patients that they need to be categorised to make the planning problem more manageable. Patients are categorised according to their utilisation of resources. Patients in the same category have a similar length of stay and require, on average, the same amount of nursing and operating theatre time.

- Resources.
  The relevant resources are beds, IC beds, operating theatres and nursing staff.

- Available capacity of the resources.
  The bed and IC bed capacity are the total number of beds available to the speciality in the wards and IC unit, respectively. The operating theatre capacity is the total operating time available per day. Nursing workload is measured in points; the nursing capacity is the number of points that is available per day. Typically, the availability of resources varies over the planning period, and the capacities will be allocated in a cyclic (e.g., weekly) pattern.

- Planning cycle.
  Since the capacities are allocated cyclically, it is natural to also consider cyclic admission patterns. On one hand, the cycle length should not be too short, because then patients with a low admission occurrence cannot be included in the admission cycle. On the other hand, a long cycle length results in a planning problem that is computationally too big to handle. In practice, the cycle length typically varies from one week to four weeks.

- Admission profile.
  The admission profile describes the inflow of patients, i.e., the number and mix of patients admitted on each day within the planning cycle.

- Target patient throughput.
  The target number of patients that should be admitted within the planning cycle. Of course, this number can be easily deduced from the target number of patients set for the whole planning period.

- Target utilisation of the resources.
  This is the desired utilisation (or occupancy rate) of the resources on each day of the planning cycle. It should be realised as close as possible.

- Restrictions on admission profiles.
  An admission profile realising the target throughput and resource utilisation may still be unacceptable for the specialty for a number of reasons. The specialty may want to fix the number of patients from a specific category admitted at a specific day in the admission cycle, or the number of patients from a certain combination of categories who can be nursed (or operated) on a single day is limited.

These options will be treated as additional restrictions for admission profiles.

This completes the description of the relevant factors. Clearly, the important decision variable is the admission profile, and the planning problem can now be reformulated as follows: find an admission profile for a given planning cycle such that the desired target utilisation of the resources is realised as close as possible, while satisfying the target patient throughput and restrictions.

12.4.2 *Mathematical model*

In this section we translate the planning problem into a mathematical model. Let T denote the length (in days) of the planning cycle, and let M denote the number of patient categories. The patients are categorised according to their workloads for the resources. To describe the workloads of patients from category i, $I = 1, \ldots, M$, we introduce the following variables:

- b_i = number of days that a patient from category i stays in the hospital and needs a bed.
- p_i = number of pre-operative days for a patient from category i.
- C_i = number of days that a patient from category i needs an IC bed.
- O_i = the operation time (in minutes) for a patient from category i.
- N_{it} = the nursing workload (in points) for a patient from category i on day t of his stay in the hospital, where t runs from 1 to b_i.

On each day of their stay in the hospital a patient needs a nursing bed at the wards. Here we assume that a nursing bed is also reserved while the patient is in the IC unit. The number of IC days are counted with the day of operation as the starting point. Typically, the nursing workload is high on the day of the operation, after which it gradually diminishes. Finally, the target throughput of patient category i over the planning cycle is denoted by THR_i.

It is convenient to number the resources operating theatre, nursing, beds and IC beds from 1 to 4. For resource r, $r = 1, \ldots, 4$, we then introduce the following quantities:

- C_{rt} = available capacity of resource r on day t of the planning cycle.
- U_{rt} = target utilisation of resource r on day t of the planning cycle.

The important decision variables in the planning problem are the number and mix of patients admitted on each day of the planning cycle. Let X_{it} denote the number of patients from category i admitted on day t of the planning cycle. Clearly, X_{it} is a non-negative integer. Thus:

$$X_{it} \in \{0, 1, 2, \ldots\}, \ i = 1, \ldots, M, \ t = 1, \ldots, T,$$

and they should satisfy the target patient throughput, i.e.,

$$\sum_{t=1}^{T} X_{it} = THR_i, \ i = 1, \ldots, M.$$

We now want to find X_{it}s for which the absolute deviation of the realised and target utilisation of the resources is minimised. For this problem we introduce the auxiliary variables V_{rtk} satisfying:

$$V_{rtk} \geq 0,\ r = 1, \ldots, 4,\ t = 1, \ldots, T,\ k = 1, 2;$$

and formulate linear constraints forcing these variables to be equal to the absolute deviation of the realised and target utilisation. Below we first explain this for resource 1, i.e., the operating theatre. Since patients of category i are operated after being p_i days in the hospital, the realised utilisation of the operating theatre on day t is equal to:

$$\sum_{i=1}^{M} O_i X_{it-p_i}.$$

Here we adopt the convention that subscript t in X_{it} should be read modulo T (so, e.g., $X_{iT} + 1 = X_{i1}$). Hence, if we require that:

$$\sum_{i=1}^{M} o_i X_{it-p_i} \leq U_{1t} + V_{1t1},\ t = 1, \ldots, T,$$

$$\sum_{i=1}^{M} o_i X_{it-p_i} \leq U_{1t} - V_{1t2},\ t = 1, \ldots, T,$$

and minimise the sum:

$$\sum_{t=1}^{T} \left(V_{1t1} + V_{1t2} \right),$$

then it is readily verified that the minimum is realised for:

$$V_{1t1} = \max \left(\sum_{i=1}^{M} o_i X_{it-p_i} - U_{1t}, 0 \right),\ V_{1t2} = \max \left(U_{1t} - \sum_{i=1}^{M} o_i X_{it-p_i}, 0 \right).$$

So, indeed, $V_{1t1} + V_{1t2}$ is equal to the absolute deviation of the realised and target utilisation of the operating theatre on day t of the planning cycle. For the other resources we formulate constraints similar to the ones above. That is, for nursing staff, beds and IC beds we subsequently obtain:

$$\sum_{i=1}^{M} \sum_{d=1}^{b_i} n_{id} X_{it-d+1} \leq U_{2t} + V_{2t1},\ t = 1, \ldots, T,$$

$$\sum_{i=1}^{M}\sum_{d=1}^{b_i} n_{id} X_{it-d+1} \le U_{2t} - V_{2t2}, \quad t = 1,\ldots,T,$$

$$\sum_{i=1}^{M}\sum_{d=1}^{b_i} X_{it-d+1} \le U_{3t} + V_{3t1}, \quad t = 1,\ldots,T,$$

$$\sum_{i=1}^{M}\sum_{d=1}^{b_i} X_{it-d+1} \le U_{3t} - V_{3t2}, \quad t = 1,\ldots,T,$$

$$\sum_{i=1}^{M}\sum_{d=1}^{c_i} X_{it-p_i-d+1} \le U_{4t} + V_{4t1}, \quad t = 1,\ldots,T,$$

$$\sum_{i=1}^{M}\sum_{d=1}^{c_i} X_{it-p_i-d+1} \le U_{4t} - V_{4t2}, \quad t = 1,\ldots,T.$$

The realised utilisation of the resources may, of course, not exceed the available capacity. Thus:

$$U_{rt} + V_{rt1} \le C_{rt}, \quad r = 1,\ldots,4, \quad t = 1,\ldots,T.$$

Then, minimising the absolute deviation of the realised and target utilisation of the resources amounts to minimising the sum:

$$\sum_{r=1}^{4} w_r \sum_{t=1}^{T} \left(V_{rt1} + V_{rt2} \right). \tag{12.1}$$

In this sum, the absolute deviation of the utilisation of resource r is weighted with coefficient w_r, defined as:

$$w_r = \frac{a_r}{\sum_{t=1}^{T} U_{rt}}. \tag{12.2}$$

Where a_r is some non-negative number. The coefficients w_r are introduced (*i*) to make the sum dimensionless (i.e., independent of the units used) and (*ii*) to control the relative importance of the resources (by means of a). Finally, we have to take into account the restrictions on admission profiles mentioned in the previous section. The first restriction just means that we fix certain variables X_{it} to prescribed values. For the second restriction we introduce B indicating the maximum number of patients from categories $i \in S$ that can be nursed on a single day, where S is a subset of $\{1,\dots,M\}$. Then, the second restriction translates to:

$$\sum_{i \in S} \sum_{d=1}^{b_i} X_{it-d+1} \leq B, \ t = 1, \dots, T.$$

Summarising, our planning problem can be formulated as the following ILP:

$$\min \sum_{r=1}^{4} w_r \sum_{t=1}^{T} \left(V_{rt1} + V_{rt2} \right)$$

subject to the following constraints:

$$\sum_{t=1}^{T} X_{it} = THR_i, \ i = 1, \dots, M,$$

$$U_{1t} - V_{1t2} \leq \sum_{i=1}^{M} o_i X_{it-p_i} \leq U_{1t} + V_{1t1}, \ t = 1, \dots, T,$$

$$U_{2t} - V_{2t2} \leq \sum_{i=1}^{M} \sum_{d=1}^{b_i} n_{id} X_{it-d+1} \leq U_{2t} + V_{2t1}, \ t = 1, \dots, T,$$

$$U_{3t} - V_{3t2} \leq \sum_{i=1}^{M} \sum_{d=1}^{b_i} X_{it-d+1} \leq U_{3t} + V_{3t1}, \ t = 1, \dots, T,$$

$$U_{4t} - V_{4t2} \leq \sum_{i=1}^{M} \sum_{d=1}^{c_i} X_{it-p_i-d+1} \leq U_{4t} + V_{4t1}, \ t = 1, \dots, T,$$

$$\sum_{i \in S} \sum_{d=1}^{b_i} X_{it-d+1} \leq B, \ t = 1, \dots, T,$$

$$U_{rt} + V_{rt1} \leq C_{rt}, \ r = 1, \dots, 4, \ t = 1, \dots, T,$$

$$V_{rt1} \geq 0, \ V_{rt2} \geq 0, \ r = 1, \dots, 4, \ t = 1, \dots, T,$$

$$X_{it} \in \{0, 1, 2, \dots\}, \ i = 1, \dots, M, \ t = 1, \dots, T.$$

This completes the description of the mathematical model.

12.4.3 Solution approach

To solve the above ILP problem we used the solver MOMIP. This is an optimisation solver for middle-sized mixed integer programming problems, based on the branch-and-bound algorithm. It was developed by Ogryczak and Zorychta (1996). A nice feature of this solver is that it allows the user to control the computation time (by limiting the number of nodes examined), of course, without a guarantee of finding the optimal solution. In the application presented in the next section we bounded the computational effort for each scenario, and always found a good (but maybe not optimal) solution in a few minutes' computer time on an ordinary PC. The model has been implemented in a decision support system called OptiMix.[2]

12.5 Results

The results presented are twofold. The results in the following subsection (12.5.1) illustrate the behaviour of the model on different parameter settings of the weighting function using data on orthopaedics. The results in Subsection 12.5.2 illustrate the contribution of the model to the planning problem in the case of orthopaedics.

12.5.1 Sensitivity analysis

This section contains results produced by the model to illustrate the behaviour of the model on the use of the weighting function for the relative importance of the different resources. The outcomes of the model provide evidence that the model does what it should do.

We start with the current settings for the weighting function provided in Table 12.5, and use the average weekly throughput of patients in Table 12.1. The other parameters are set according to the settings in the current situation described before. The output of the model for the current setting is shown in Table 12.6. The numbers between brackets (following the resource type) indicate the weights used in the objective function.

As can be seen from Table 12.6, operating theatre utilisation shows the least performance due to an overcapacity that is made available to orthopaedics. The use of beds follows the target utilisation reasonably well and the nursing workload and the IC use are according to their targets. The score of the solution, based on the objective function, is 1.56. The score is the outcome of Equation (12.1) and represents the weighted sum of the deviations between the realised and the target utilisation of the resources involved per day of the week. A lower score represents a better fit between realisations and target. The admission profile suggested by the model is shown in Table 12.7.

---

2 A later version of OptiMix is available as online material.

Table 12.6 Occupancy levels for the current setting

Day no.	Operating theatres (5) (minutes)		Nursing (3) (points)		Beds (4) (number)		IC beds (5) (number)	
	Target	Realised	Target	Realised	Target	Realised	Target	Realised
1	306	293	76	76	25	25	0	0
2	306	272	76	77	25	25	0	0
3	306	200	76	76	25	22	1	1
4	306	90	76	76	25	23	0	0
5	306	245	76	75	25	25	0	0
6	0	0	66	64	16	16	0	0
7	0	0	66	65	16	16	0	0

Table 12.7 Admission profile for current setting

Day Category	1	2	3	4	5	6	7
1	4	3	0	1	5	0	0
2	0	0	0	0	1	0	0
3	0	0	0	0	1	0	0
4	1	1	0	0	0	0	0
5	1	0	0	0	0	0	0
6	1	0	0	0	0	0	0
7	1	0	0	0	1	0	0
8	0	0	0	1	0	0	0
9	0	1	1	0	0	0	0
10	0	0	1	0	0	0	0
11	0	1	0	0	0	0	0

Table 12.8 Occupancy levels for the current setting with reduced operating theatre capacity

Day no.	Operating theatres (5)		Nursing (3)		Beds (4)		IC beds (5)	
	Target	Realised	Target	Realised	Target	Realised	Target	Realised
1	221	243	76	73	25	22	0	0
2	221	220	76	77	25	24	0	0
3	221	200	76	78	25	23	1	1
4	221	227	76	77	25	25	0	0
5	221	210	76	74	25	25	0	0
6	0	0	66	64	16	16	0	0
7	0	0	66	64	16	17	0	0

As can be seen from Table 12.7, the restrictions regarding patient categories 1 and 6 have been dealt with properly. Also, the category 10 patient is admitted on Tuesday and in need of an IC bed on Wednesday.

Suppose we want to reduce the operating theatre resources to find a better fit between demand for and supply of resources. Table 12.8 shows the utilisation figures with a reduction in operating theatre resources available to orthopaedics to 260 minutes a day.

As can be seen from Table 12.8, the reduced operating theatre capacity is sufficient to handle the demand, and the occupancy levels follow the target levels reasonably well. The objective function score of this solution is 0.53. This shows that the deviations from the target utilisation levels in Table 12.8 are less than the deviations in Table 12.6.

Suppose we change the weight function, focussing on optimising one resource type, say operating theatres; we give operating theatres capacity a maximum weight of 5 and the other resources a minimum weight of 1. Table 12.9 shows the utilisation figures of this change in the parameter setting of the weight function.

As can be seen from Table 12.9, the use of operating theatre capacity has improved, and the use of beds and nursing workload had slightly worsened; the use of the IC beds is unaltered.

12.5.2 Application to orthopaedics

Focussing on the contribution of the mathematical model to the planning problem of orthopaedics, we illustrate this with output of the model for the following situations:

- What if we use the programme of week 12, the sample week, in combination with the original settings?
- What is an adequate availability of resources for the average week programme?

We first evaluate the feasibility of the programme of week 12 (see Table 12.1). The total number of patients is the same as for the average week programme, but there is a substitution towards patient groups requiring more resources (groups 8 and 11). Using the model for this inflow of patients results in no feasible solution found within the restrictions defined for the planning problem. Looking at Table 12.6, one may suspect that the nursing capacity and the bed

Table 12.9 Occupancy levels with maximum weight for operating theatre use

Day no.	Operating theatres (5)		Nursing (1)		Beds (1)		IC beds (1)	
	Target	Realised	Target	Realised	Target	Realised	Target	Realised
1	221	206	76	69	25	21	0	0
2	221	222	76	76	25	25	0	0
3	221	220	76	79	25	24	1	1
4	221	232	76	80	25	24	0	0
5	221	220	76	78	25	25	0	0
6	0	0	66	65	16	16	0	0
7	0	0	66	62	16	17	0	0

capacity have acted as bottlenecks obstructing a solution, and not the operating theatre capacity. The conclusion is that the programme of week 12, though the number of patients is adequate, has a mix of patients that does not fit within the capacity constraints for orthopaedics. Probably, the orthopaedic surgeons have only considered the operating theatre capacity, when deciding the week programme, and not bed and nursing capacity.

So, the first decision orthopaedics has to make is the week programme that reflects the maximum number and mix of patients that can be admitted as elective patients, given the capacity constraints. This can be calculated from the target volumes at annual level, given the number of weeks operating theatres are available to orthopaedics. Perhaps it is necessary to make different week programmes for each season, but in total it has to result in the annual target volumes.

Suppose we use the average week programme as given in Table 12.1, how many resources do we then need to adequately fit the demand of resources? We follow a stepwise procedure. First, we observe in Table 12.8 that operating theatre capacity is, on average, at the target level, so further reduction will not be wise. The only resource worthwhile to consider is the bed capacity. By reducing the bed capacity during the week to 27 beds, we arrived at the results as shown in Table 12.10.

Clearly, there are different answers possible to the question put forward on the amounts of resources that would adequately fit to the demand required for the average week programme, but the solution presented does show off good results. The objective function produces a score of 0.21. This is a better fit, compared to the fit in Table 12.8 with a score of 0.53.

Up to now we only have considered constant target levels during the week, with a shift of level during the weekend. One step further would be to consider solutions with different amounts of resources allocated within the days of the week. Suppose we increase the operating theatre capacity in the beginning of the week and decrease the capacity at the end of the week. See Table 12.11 for the allocations used per day, and Table 12.12 for the utilisation results.

As can be seen from Table 12.12, by allocating more operating theatre resources and bed resources in the beginning of the week but increasing the

Table 12.10 Finding the proper allocation of resources

Day no.	Operating theatres (5)		Nursing (3)		Beds (4)		IC beds (5)	
	Target	Realised	Target	Realised	Target	Realised	Target	Realised
1	221	216	76	77	24	24	0	0
2	221	227	76	75	24	23	0	0
3	221	220	76	77	24	24	1	1
4	221	217	76	79	24	24	0	0
5	221	220	76	74	24	24	0	0
6	0	0	66	66	16	17	0	0
7	0	0	66	61	16	16	0	0

Table 12.11 Allocated resources per day of the week

Day of the week	Operating theatre (minutes)	Beds (number)	Nursing (points)	IC beds (number)
Monday	280	27	80	0
Tuesday	280	27	80	0
Wednesday	260	27	80	1
Thursday	240	25	80	0
Friday	240	25	80	0
Saturday	0	23	70	0
Sunday	0	23	70	0

Table 12.12 Occupancy levels with varying amounts of allocated capacity per day

Day no.	Operating theatres (5)		Nursing (3)		Beds (4)		IC beds (5)	
	Target	Realised	Target	Realised	Target	Realised	Target	Realised
1	238	243	76	75	24	24	0	0
2	238	230	76	76	24	25	0	0
3	222	220	76	76	24	23	1	1
4	204	197	76	74	22	22	0	0
5	204	210	76	73	22	22	0	0
6	0	0	66	68	18	18	0	0
7	0	0	66	67	18	18	0	0

number of beds available during the weekend, we seem to get a better fit between demand and supply. The objective function score is 0.24, showing even that this solution is slightly worse than Table 12.10. As both scores are almost equal, one could say that both solutions result in a similar performance.

The total amount of resources used in Table 12.12 is almost similar to Table 12.10: the total amount of operating theatre capacity used is the same, the total number of beds used is slightly better (one bed less on three days) and the nursing capacity is unaltered. Perhaps a similar approach to the allocation of nursing capacity (following the availability of beds) would result in a small improvement in the use of nursing capacity. The day-dependent allocation makes it possible to reflect better the resource demands caused by the short-stay policy followed for many orthopaedic patients. On the other hand, the fixed allocation is perhaps easier to implement, and does not result in a loss of performance, providing the right level of availability of resources.

12.6 Discussion and reflection

Based on the results described in Section 12.5, we can conclude that the model is able to generate an optimal admission profile per category. With an optimal admission profile, we mean a profile which results in the smallest possible deviation between the realised and the target resource utilisation, while the total available capacity of the different resources is not exceeded, the target patient throughput is met, and the given restrictions are not violated.

The model has been implemented in a decision support system called OptiMix. It has been developed primarily to support the tuning of the demand on and the availability of capacities at a tactical level of decision making, but it can also be used at the strategic and operational level. Determining how many resources are required for the coming years is a strategic decision. If the volumes of patients per category for the next couple of years can be predicted, then OptiMix can calculate the minimum amount of capacity that is required to treat these patients. Although OptiMix doesn't use detailed information, it can still be used to balance the demand on and the availability of capacities in the short term. If in the short run patients are already scheduled for the dates in the planning period, OptiMix can be used to define an optimal mix for the remaining admissions, while fixing the already scheduled admissions and treating these as restrictions for the planning problem.

The current model is a fairly simple deterministic linear model, using only averages of duration of operations. A serious limitation of this work is that it excludes the emergency flow. A model with this limitation is, therefore, more supportive for a specialty with a low percentage of emergency (e.g., orthopaedics) than for a specialty with a high percentage of emergency (e.g., general surgery). In a follow-up project we have developed a model for thoracic surgery planning that deals with both flows, the elective and emergency flow (see Adan et al., 2005). In another follow-up project for thoracic surgery we also included stochastic resource requirements in our mixed integer programming model (Adan et al., 2009), which improved the quality of the model and its projections. A final extension of our work on this topic is published in (Adan et al., 2011), where we evaluated the use of tactical master schedules for elective and emergency patients on the effects in operational performance, with a mixed integer programming model and a simulation.

Since then, many authors have worked on this topic, leading to many publications, but often only interesting for an academic audience. For an overview see (Abdalkareem et al., 2021).

Reflecting on the case and the modelling used, we have seen a linear programming model that is fairly easy to understand (mainly summations, restrictions and an objective function), and an application of the theory on linear programming, as presented in Chapter 3. The data used are averages of durations of operations, which is in line with a deterministic approach. The grouping of patients within orthopaedics, based on the use of resources of patients, is interesting. As we cover, all inpatient trajectories, in principle we have a complete view on the patient flow of orthopaedics and their use of resources of the units involved. So, this is an example of a network OM approach to unit problems to realise a high, but balanced, use of resources.

If we link the case to the theory presented in the theory part of the book, we see that we use the principles of leading and following resources to take account of the effects of master surgery schedules on the use of resources in following units such as wards and intensive care units. By making use of the patterns in the resource use of patient groups, we are able to control the effects of forms of artificial variability that is introduced in hospital operations by lack of coordination in managerial decision making.

12.7 Questions and exercises

Verify the score of the current setting in Subsection 12.5.1 by using the information in Table 12.6 and Equations (12.1) and (12.2).

Formulate the basic assumptions underlying the mathematical model and investigate the degree to which the model fits reality.

Formulate one or more scenarios as a follow up of the scenarios presented in Subsection 12.5.2 that would be interesting to investigate to improve the performance of orthopaedics.

Reflect on the wider applicability to other specialties or other planning issues in a hospital. How should the model be adapted to these alternative circumstances?

A later version of the OptiMix model is available as online material. See there for further exercises with the model.

References

Abdalkareem ZA, Amir A, Azmi Al-Betar M, Ekhan P and Hammouri AI (2021). Healthcare scheduling in optimization context: a review. *Health and Technology*, 11, 445–469. https://doi.org/10.1007/s12553-021-00547-S.

Adan I, Bekkers J, Dellaert N, Vissers J and Yu X (2009). Patient mix optimisation and stochastic resource requirements. A case study in cardiothoracic surgery planning. *Health Care Management Science*, 12, 129–141.

Adan I, Bekkers J, Dellaert N, Jeunet J and Vissers J (2011). Improving operational effectiveness of tactical master pland for emergency and elective admissions under stochastic demand and capacitated resources. *European Journal of Operational Research*, 213, 290–308.

Adan IJBF and Vissers JMH (2002). Patient mix optimisation in hospital admission planning: a case study. Special issue on 'Operations Management in Health Care' of the *International Journal of Operations and Production Management*, 22(4), 445–461.

Barnes C and Krinsky T (1999). Classification systems, case mix and data quality: implications for international management and research applications. *Case Mix*, 1(2).

Cardoen B, Demeulemeester E and Beliën J (2010). Operating room planning and scheduling: a literature review. *European Journal of Operational Research*, 201, 921–932.

Fetter RB and Thompson JD (1969). A decision model for the design and operation of a progressive patient care hospital. *Medical Care*, 7(6), 450–462.

Heider S, Schoenfelder J, Koperna T and Brunner JO (2021). Balancing control and autonomy in master surgery scheduling: benefits of ICU quotas for recovery units. *Healthcare Management Science*. https://doi.org/10.1007/s10729-021-09588-8.

Hulshof PJH, Kortbeek N, Boucherie RJ, Hans EW and Bakker PJM (2012). Taxonomic classification of planning decisions in health care: a structured review of the state of the art in OR/MS. *Health Systems*, 1(2), 129–175. https://doi.org/10.1057/hs.2012.18.

Ogryzak W and Zorychta K (1996). *Modular optimizer for mixed integer programming - MOMIP version 2.3. WP-96-106.* IIASA, Laxenburg, Austria.

Roth A and Van Dierdonck R (1995). Hospital resource planning: concepts, feasibility, and framework. *Production and Operations Management,* 4(1), 2–29.

Van Gemmel P and Van Dierdonck R (1999). Admission scheduling in acute care hospitals: does the practice fit with the theory? *International Journal of Operations & Production Management,* 19(9), 863–878.

Vissers JMH, Adan IJBF and Bekkers JA (2005). Patient mix optimization in tactical cardiothoracic surgery planning: a case study. *IMA Journal of Management Mathematics,* 16, 281–304. https://doi.org/10.1093/imaman/dpi023.

Vissers JMH, Eydems-Janssen M, De Kok R and Myburg F (1999). Optimisation of the patient mix for hospital admission planning. In Mikitis E (ed.), *Information, management and planning of health services. Proceedings ORAHS99,* 161–178.

Zhu S, Fan W, Yang S, Pei J and Pardalos P (2018). Operating room planning and surgical case scheduling: a review of literature. *Journal of Combinatorial Optimization,* 37, 1–49.

13 Using pathways to model care processes and analyse performance

Jan Vissers

Case positioning

The case is a virtual case with virtual data but based on experiences with a number of student projects. The case regards an investigation of the use of a care pathway to develop a process model that allows calculation of the resources required for the services provided by the process chain and other performance measures. In Figure 13.1 we have positioned the case in the framework we use for case studies in this book.

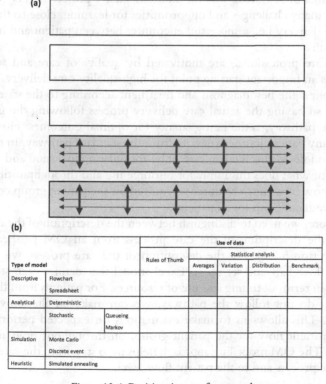

(a)

(b)

Type of model			Use of data				
			Rules of Thumb	Statistical analysis			
				Averages	Variation	Distribution	Benchmark
Descriptive	Flowchart						
	Spreadsheet						
Analytical	Deterministic						
	Stochastic	Queueing					
		Markov					
Simulation	Monte Carlo						
	Discrete event						
Heuristic	Simulated annealing						

Figure 13.1 Position in case framework.

DOI: 10.4324/9781003020011-16

In Figure 13.1(a) we have indicated the planning levels addressed in the case and whether the focus is on unit, chain or network operations management (OM), and in Figure 13.1(b) the type of model used in the case and the use of data.

We see that the case addresses two levels of planning. The focus is on the operational level of planning (a description of the operational process), but the combination with an Excel-based model of the process allows us to calculate the resources required for the pathway to deliver the services projected at an annual level. It is a chain OM approach as only one patient group is included. In the case, forms of descriptive modelling are used, i.e., a process flowchart and an Excel model of the process. Data wise, the case makes use of data mainly based on averages of waiting times, durations of operations and average workloads on resources.

13.1 Introduction

Many student projects in healthcare management concern improvement of a pathway in a hospital setting. The reason for this is the importance for patients, healthcare professionals and hospital management of a smooth-running care process that delivers the best outcomes at the shortest notice and with the least amounts of resources. For the student, such a project is very rewarding as it offers many challenges and opportunities for learning, close to the core of healthcare delivery i.e., a successful encounter between patient and healthcare professional.

Healthcare professionals are motivated by quality of care and see a care pathway as an important starting point for high-quality care delivery. The care pathway offers the best diagnosis and treatment according to the state of art in medicine, so having the actual care delivery process following the guidelines of the care pathway, is the best guaranty for optimal outcomes. However, in reality, many patient journeys deviate from the standard pathway. In the 'pathway methodology' this is taken care of by formulating inclusion and exclusion criteria. But what does this imply for resource use and throughput time? If we want to know how much resource is required for the patient group concerned, how do we handle this for all patients?

Therefore, we need to distinguish between the description of the care pathway and the description of the care process from an OM perspective (see also Subsection 5.2.3). For the description of the care process, we can draw a process flowchart and set up an Excel model that defines each step in the flowchart in terms of timing and use of resources. For patients from the patient group that do not follow the pathway, we can make an alternative process flowchart. This allows us to make calculations on expected performance of the total patient flow for the patient group, on throughput time and use of resources. The OM modelling approach helps us to step from the care pathway to the care process and to the patient flow level.

An important issue for this approach is where to get the data from for the care process model. What can we base on estimates from experts, i.e., health-care professionals, and what do we have to extract from data on actual health-care delivery?

So, the research questions for this case study are:

- How can we model the patient care process of a patient group, given a description of their care pathway?
- What are the best sources of the data required for the OM description of the care process?
- How can we use the OM description of the care process to calculate the expected performance of the patient flow for the whole patient group?
- What are the possibilities for using more advanced modelling approaches reported in the literature?

The case study is based on a virtual setting and uses virtual data but is based on experiences in a number of student projects. We first clarify the methods used for this case study in Section 13.2. Then we present, in Section 13.3, the results of this case study to answer the research questions. In Section 13.4 we reflect on the case study and its modelling approach.

13.2 Methods

We make use of descriptive modelling techniques for this case, i.e., a process flowchart and an Excel-based model that describes, for each step in a path-way, the number of patients requiring this step, the operation taking place, the amount of resource used for the operation and the time until the next step in the process. For a description of these techniques, see Chapter 5.

13.3 Results

13.3.1 Process description

We start with a description of the care pathway, concentrating on the care process of the patient. The process description of a care pathway often takes the form of a decision tree that describes what healthcare professionals should do according to the most recent medical guidelines, depending on results of diagnostic tests or effects of treatment. The care pathway process for a patient with hip problems could look as depicted in a simplified manner in Figure 13.2.

Following referral by a general practitioner, the patient is first seen by an orthopaedic surgeon. For a diagnosis an X-ray examination is required. The

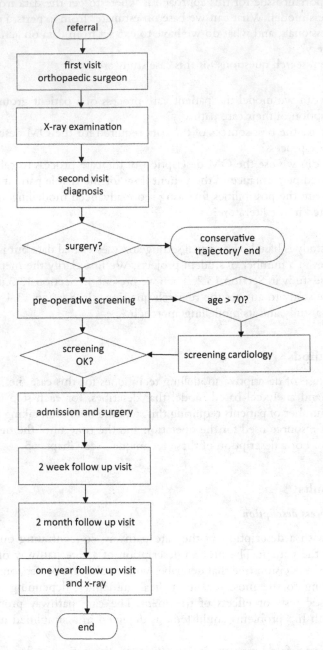

Figure 13.2 Total hip prosthesis pathway.

X-ray procedure is performed in a visit to the radiology department, and the patient returns to the orthopaedic surgeon for a diagnosis and a discussion of the treatment options. If the patient and orthopaedic surgeon agree on surgery, the patient is referred to pre-operative screening to check whether the patient is fit for surgery. For patients older than 70 years an extra cardio-vascular check is necessary. Then the patient has to wait until their surgery date to be admitted to a ward and be operated on. After recovery from the surgery in the hospital and the start of their rehabilitation, the patient is discharged for further rehabilitation at home. There are follow-up appointments with the orthopaedic surgeon after two weeks, after two months and after one year.

The pathway is an important point of departure for the description of the process. It defines the specification of the content of the process: what needs to be done in each step of the process, who is performing the work, which resources are required to perform a step and, in cases of medical urgency, restrictions on the timing of steps. However, in terms of an OM perspective, the picture of the process is incomplete. It is not clear how many patients require each step. The amount of resource required for each step is not specified and the timing of steps is missing.

To provide a more detailed description we translate the pathway process description into an OM description, using a flowchart. We also add information to the flowchart to make the description more complete.

We start with a flowchart description of the process. To emphasise the flow of the patient, we rotate the decision tree 90 degrees, and draw the chart from left to right (see Figure 13.3).

In Figure 13.3 we see the flow of the patients following the care pathway of hip surgery. We see also two periods of waiting time, the access time for the first appointment and the time on the waiting list before the date of the surgery.

Now we would like to add some information on the proportion of patients proceeding to each step, duration of the steps, and the use of resources. Therefore, we complement the graphical presentation of the flowchart with an Excel table with data on each step (see Table 13.1).

We see in Table 13.1 for each step the percentage of patients that proceed to this step, the average duration of the step and the use of resources. We see that in step 4, 10% of the patients decide not to continue to surgery (and may stay in conservative treatment). Ninety percent of the patients continue to surgery by visiting the pre-assessment unit for a screening. Ten percent of the flow at this point needs an extra cardiac check. After screening, 100% continue to surgery, but have to wait for the surgery date. After surgery and recovery in the operating theatre department, the patient stays in a ward for five days. After the discharge from the ward, the patient returns after two weeks, two months and one year.

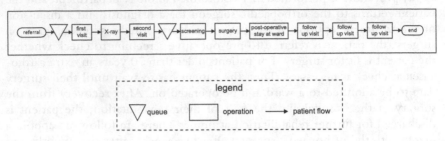

Figure 13.3 Flowchart of the hip surgery process.

The data for the patient flow movement can be based on an assumption or an expert input (judgements and experience). This might lead to an inaccurate estimate that needs further refinement. An alternative approach might be to deduce this from delivery data. However, the experience with 'production' data on the delivery of services is that this can be a difficult and time-consuming task. The data on the delivery of services (and coding of activities) as registered in the hospital information systems is often based on financial criteria and not on a proper representation of the patient journey. No business or commercial service organisation would make such a mistake, as everybody knows that a proper description of your core process is a prerequisite for a sound business model.

The description presented in these Excel tables is reasonably reliable in terms of an adequate description of the patient process and quite versatile in use. If, for instance, some of the patients in a clinic session are seen by the medical specialist and others by a junior doctor, this can be easily taken into account. Even the extra time for supervision of the junior doctor by the specialist can be modelled.

The data on the use of resources can easily be collected via planners, as it is based on planning rules. The data on waiting times and lead times can again be based on the expert knowledge of planners, but most of the time it is also possible to base these data on the analysis of care delivery data.

Suppose about 500 patients are following this standard trajectory, but another 250 are using a similar trajectory and their surgical procedure takes a bit more time, requiring an extra day on the ward to recover, and two extra visits (see Table 13.2).

We now have a model[1] that can be used for making calculations.

---

1 See the Excel model in the online material

Table 13.1 Excel table with data on patient flow, timing and resource use in hip surgery process

OM description of a care process: example for patient for orthopaedic hip surgery

Step	Percentage of patients following this step	Content	Average duration of step (minutes)	Use of resources						Waiting / lead time till next step (days)
				Resource 1		Resource 2		Resource 3		
				Type	Workload (minutes)	Type	Workload (minutes)	Type	Workload (minutes)	
1	100%	Referral	PM							14
2	100%	First visit	15	OPD assistant	5	Orthopaedic surgeon	15	OPD room	15	0
3	100%	X-ray	15	Radiographer	15	X-ray room	15			5
4	100%	Second visit	15	OPD assistant	5	Orthopaedic surgeon	15	OPD room	15	0
4a	10%	No surgery	PM							0
5	T	Pre-operative screening	20	Anaesthetist	20	OPD room	20			10
5a	10%	Cardiac screening	15	Cardiologist	15	OPD room	15			42
6	100%	Surgery	120	Orthopaedic surgeon	100	OT team	120	OT room	140	0
7	100%	Stay at ward	7200	Nurse	300	Bed	7200	Orthopaedic surgeon	30	14
8	100%	Two weeks follow up	20	OPD assistant	5	Orthopaedic surgeon	20	OPD room	20	49
9	100%	Two month follow up	15	OPD assistant	5	Orthopaedic surgeon	15	OPD room	15	302
10	100%	One year follow up	15	OPD assistant	5	Orthopaedic surgeon	15	OPD room	15	

Table 13.2 Variant hip surgery process

Step	Percentage of patients following this step	Content	Average duration of step (minutes)	Resource 1 Type	Workload (minutes)	Resource 2 Type	Workload (minutes)	Resource 3 Type	Workload (minutes)	Waiting/ lead time till next step (days)
1	100%	Referral	PM							14
2	100%	First visit	15	OPD assistant	5	Orthopaedic surgeon	15	OPD room	15	0
3	100%	X-ray	15	Radiographer	15	X-ray room	15			5
4	100%	Second visit	15	OPD assistant	5	Orthopaedic surgeon	15	OPD room	15	5
extra	75%	Extra visit	15	OPD assistant	5	Orthopaedic surgeon	15	OPD room	15	0
4a	10%	No surgery	PM							0
5	90%	Pre-operative screening	20	Anaesthetist	20	OPD room	20			10
5a	10%	Cardiac screening	15	Cardiologist	15	OPD room	15			42
6	100%	Surgery	150	Orthopaedic surgeon	130	OT team	150	OT room	170	0
7	100%	Stay at ward	8640	Nurse (ward)	360	Bed	8640	Orthopaedic surgeon	30	14
8	100%	Two weeks follow up	20	OPD assistant	5	Orthopaedic surgeon	20	OPD room	20	14
extra	75%	Extra visit	15	OPD assistant	5	Orthopaedic surgeon	15	OPD room	15	49
9	100%	Two month follow up	15	OPD assistant	5	Orthopaedic surgeon	15	OPD room	15	288
10	100%	One year follow up	15	OPD assistant	5	Orthopaedic surgeon	15	OPD room	15	

13.3.2 Output

The Excel model of the standard and alternative process can be used to compare the performance of the two processes, to calculate patient flow volumes at the annual level, and to calculate the resource required for delivering the services of the care pathway during a year. See Table 13.3.

We see in Table 13.3 that the two variant processes have similar performance levels in terms of throughput and waiting time, and only differ a little in the use of resources. We now have an indication of the amounts of resources required for delivering the services for the hip surgery pathway for one year.

Table 13.3 Output of Excel model of the hip surgery pathway

Results of expected performance of the care pathway for hip surgery

Item	Current situation		
	Pathway	*Variant*	*Total*
	Annual inflow of 500 patients	*Annual inflow of 250 patients*	
Access time (days)	14	14	
Waiting time for surgery (days)	42	42	
Throughput time diagnostic phase (days)	19	24	
Throughput time therapeutic phase (days)	47	48	
Throughput time therapeutic phase in case of cardiac screening	57	58	
Throughput time follow-up phase (days)	365	365	
Total throughput time (days)	431	437	
Total throughput time in case of cardiac screening (days)	441	447	
Number of patients treated	450	225	675
Number of first visits	500	250	750
Number of return visits	1850	1281.3	3131
Amounts of resources used (hours)			
1 Orthopaedic surgeon	1600	1001.6	2602
1a Nurse OPD			
2 OPD assistant	195.8	127.6	323
3 OPD room (for orthopaedics)	625	401.6	1027
4 OT team	900	562.5	1463
5 OT room	1050	637.5	1688
6 Radiographer	125	62.5	188
7 X-ray room	125	62.5	188
8 Anaesthetist	150	75	225
9 OPD room (for anaesthesiology)	150	75	225
10 Cardiologist	11.25	5.6	17
11 OPD room (for cardiologist)	11.25	5.6	17
12 Bed (days)	2250	1350	3600
13 Nurse (ward)	2250	1350	3600

13.3.2.1 Calibration

Though we have carefully built up the model with expert knowledge, it might be that there are differences between the calculation of the annual volume of patients, based on the model, and the actual reality of services as registered in production systems. Suppose we have a difference in patient volumes as indicated in Table 13.4.

When we consider the differences between the projection of annual volumes by the model and data on actual services delivered, as registered in IT systems, we notice that the main difference is the number of return visits. Apparently, our model approach underestimates the number of return visits made by patients. An explanation for this could be that the experts tend to describe the normative process, and do not take into account the extra visits required because of incomplete tests or not being asked for by patients who perhaps have doubts about the procedure. The difference of about 400 visits can, however, not be ignored. Therefore, we need to calibrate the model and increase the frequencies of extra visits for the standard process and the variant process in such a way as to generate 400 extra return visits.[2]

13.3.3.2 Scenarios for process design improvement

We can now use the calibrated model to develop a number of what-if scenarios to investigate the effects of plans to improve the throughput of the hip surgery process. Suppose we want to investigate the effect of the following scenarios:

- Shortening the diagnostic phase by combining first visit, X-ray examination and second visit on the same day.
- Reduction of workload for the orthopaedic surgeon by having the follow-up visits done by a nurse.
- Increase of inflow from 750 to 900 patients annually.

After having the suggested changes implemented in the calibrated models of the hip process,[3] we can see the results of these scenarios in Table 13.5.

Table 13.4 Comparison model – production

Number of	Model	Production
Patients	675	670
Surgeries	675	680
First visits	750	740
Return visits	3131	3500

2 In the online supplement for this chapter the manipulations for calibrating the model are shown, leading to in total 3500 return visits in the calibrated model which is in line with the volume of return visits in the production systems.
3 See the changes in the models in the online appendix.

Table 13.5 Scenario results for hip surgery process improvement

Item	Shortening diagnostic phase			Follow-up by nurse			Increased inflow 900		
	Pathway Annual inflow of 500 patients	Variant Annual inflow of 250 patients	Total Annual inflow of 750 patients	Pathway Annual inflow of 500 patients	Variant Annual inflow of 250 patients	Total Annual inflow of 750 patients	Pathway Annual inflow of 600 patients	Variant Annual inflow of 300 patients	Total Annual inflow of 900 patients
Access time (days)	14	14		14	14		14	14	
Waiting time for surgery (days)	42	42		42	42		42	42	
Throughput time diagnostic phase (days)	14	19		14	19		14	19	
Throughput time therapeutic phase (days)	47	48		47	48		47	48	
Throughput time therapeutic phase in case of cardiac screening	57	58		57	58		57	58	
Throughput time follow-up phase (days)	365	365		365	365		365	365	
Total throughput time (days)	426	432		426	432		426	432	
Total throughput time in case of cardiac screening (days)	436	442		436	442		436	442	
Number of patients treated	450	225	675	450	250	675	540	270	810
Number of first visits	500	250	750	500	250	750	600	300	900
Number of return visits	2100	1400.0	3500	2100	1400.0	3500	2520	1680.0	4200
Amounts of resources used (hours)									
1 Orthopaedic surgeon	1662.5	1031.3	2694	1287.5	787.5	2075	1545	945.0	2490
1a Nurse OPD				375	243.8	619	450	292.5	743
2 OPD assistant	216.7	137.5	354	216.7	137.5	354	260.0	165.0	425
3 OPD room (for orthopaedics)	687.5	431.3	1119	687.5	431.3	1119	825	517.5	1343
4 OT team	900	562.5	1463	900	562.5	1463	1080	675	1755
5 OT room	1050	637.5	1688	1050	637.5	1688	1260	765	2025
6 Radiographer	125	62.5	188	125	62.5	188	150	62.5	213
7 X-ray room	125	62.5	188	125	62.5	188	150	75	225
8 Anaesthetist	150	75	225	150	75	225	150	90	240
9 OPD room (for anaesthesiology)	150	75	225	150	75	225	150	90	240
10 Cardiologist	11.25	5.6	17	11.25	5.6	17	13.5	6.8	20
11 OPD room (for cardiologist)	11.25	5.6	17	11.25	5.6	17	13.5	6.8	20
12 Bed (days)	2250	1350	3600	2250	1350	3600	2700	1620	4320
13 Nurse (ward)	2250	1350	3600	2250	1350	3600	2700	1620	4320

We now can see from the results of the scenarios for process improvement of the hip surgery pathway that the throughput time of the diagnostic phase can be reduced by five days, that the substitution of the surgeon by an Outpatient Department (OPD) nurse for the follow-up visits frees up more than 600 hours annually for the orthopaedic surgeon, which could be used to treat an extra 135 patients annually.

13.4 Discussion

We have presented a simple approach in this chapter, using a pathway description to develop a process model that can be used to make calculations of the performance of the pathway, including an indication of the amounts of resources which are necessary to deliver an annual volume of services. We have also illustrated that this model can be used to project the expected performance of the pathway if suggestions to improve the pathway were to be implemented. Though the model support is very simple, we think that it is adequate for the purpose of improving the performance of a pathway.

A more sophisticated way to develop a model of the care pathway would be to analyse data from patients treated over one year and develop descriptions of pathway variants using data mining techniques. See, for instance, Perer et al. (2015) and Scheuerlein et al. (2012). Though this might result in more reliable descriptions, it would also require expert knowledge on datamining, which would make the exercise more complicated and less transparent for the healthcare professionals involved in the pathway. This is compared to using the familiar pathway, and expert knowledge of healthcare professionals involved in the pathway. In this case, the added value of a more complicated methodology will probably not outweigh the advantages of our simple model.

13.5 Questions and exercises

Build an operational model of a care process:

1. Analyse data per patient on all encounters with healthcare professionals over one year, within the context of a care process resulting from a (referral for a) particular healthcare condition
2. Make a flowchart of the care process, visualising the flow between activities, the decision points and the waiting times
3. Calculate average waiting times, percentages of patients following a specific trajectory, throughput times of diagnosis/treatment/follow-up phase, etc. and add this information to the flowchart
4. Use the flowchart and the results of the analyses to build an operational model of the care process in Excel, by modelling:
   a. Inflow of patients per year.
   b. Each step in the diagnostic phase, therapeutic phase and follow-up phase in terms of:

      i. Content of the activity.

     ii. Percentage of patients making use of the activity.

    iii. Duration of the activity.

    iv. Type and amounts of resources used for the activity.

  c. The different trajectories followed by patients, linking to the activities that are part of each trajectory.

5. Use the model to make performance calculations:

  a. Throughput times.

  b. Amount of waiting.

  c. Resource requirements.

6. Use the model to make a number of scenario analyses:

  a. Impact of increased demand.

  b. Impact of extra resources.

  c. Impact of a lean pathway, removing waste in terms of unnecessary steps and unnecessary waits.

References

Perer A, Wang F and Hu J (2015). Mining and exploring care pathways from electronic medical records with visual analytics. *Journal of Biomedical Informatics*, 56, 369–378.

Scheuerlein H, Rauchfuss F, Dittmar Y, Molle R, Lehmann T, Pienkos N and Settmacher U (2012). New methods for clinical pathways – business process modeling notation (BPMN) and tangible business process modeling (t.BPM). *Langenbeck's Archives of Surgery*, 397(5), 755–761.

14 Comparative OM analysis of stroke services in six EU countries

*Jan Vissers, Sylvia Elkhuizen
and Mahdi Mahdavi*[1]

Case positioning

This case was part of the EU–funded 'Managed Outcomes' project, in which service delivery for four different patient groups by a regional network of healthcare providers in each of six EU countries was investigated. The case presented describes the patient journey and care process for stroke patients in the six regions investigated and analyses them on their performance in terms of resource use, costs and patient experience. In Figure 14.1 we have positioned the case in the framework we use for case studies in this book.

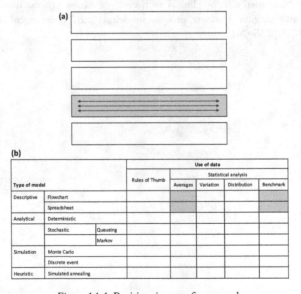

(a)

(b)

Type of model			Rules of Thumb	Use of data			
				Statistical analysis			
				Averages	Variation	Distribution	Benchmark
Descriptive	Flowchart						
	Spreadsheet						
Analytical	Deterministic						
	Stochastic	Queueing					
		Markov					
Simulation	Monte Carlo						
	Discrete event						
Heuristic	Simulated annealing						

Figure 14.1 Position in case framework.

1 We would like to thank colleagues from the partner organisations in Managed Outcomes with whom we have collaborated in the Stroke Study: Uwe Konerding (Universität Bamberg, Bamberg, Germany), Raquel Faubel (Universidad Politècnica de València, Valencia, Spain), Tom Bowen (Balance of Care Group, London, United Kingdom), Paulus Torkki (Aalto University, Helsinki, Finland) and Elpida Pavi (National School of Public Health, Athens, Greece).

DOI: 10.4324/9781003020011-17

In Figure 14.1(a) we have indicated the planning levels addressed in the case and whether the focus is on unit, chain or network operations management (OM), and in Figure 14.1(b) the type of model used in the case and the use of data.

We see that the case mainly addresses one of the tactical levels, i.e., the patient group level of planning. The combination with an Excel-based model of the process allows us to calculate the resources required for the patient group to deliver the services projected at an annual level. It is a chain OM approach as only one patient group is included. In the case, forms of descriptive modelling are used, i.e., a process flowchart and an Excel model of the process. Data wise, the case makes use of data, mainly based on averages of durations of operations, and average workloads on resources. As six different stroke services are analysed in the same way, the case allows for a comparative analysis, i.e., a benchmark of a small number of stroke services.

14.1 Introduction

Stroke is one of the leading causes of death and long-term disability of adults in the world. On average, 15 individuals per hour die of stroke globally. With a mortality rate of 25% within one month and 50% within one year, stroke is one of the most fatal diseases worldwide (Churilov and Donnan, 2012). The burden of stroke and its economic impact on families and health systems is increasing globally because of ageing populations and escalating trends of co-morbidity conditions (Mukherjee and Patil, 2011). It is estimated that 16.9 million people suffered from a first-occurrence stroke in 2010, while 33 million people were living with the consequences of a stroke. The mortality of stroke decreased by 42% in developed countries from 1970 to 2008. However, compared with this sharp drop in the mortality, the incidence of stroke decreased at a smaller rate. This in turn leads to an increase in the prevalence of stroke and thus increased demands on healthcare and social care systems (Mukherjee and Patil, 2011). In terms of costs, stroke accounts for 3–4% of total healthcare expenditure globally (Struijs and Baan, 2011).

Stroke is caused by disrupted supply of blood to the brain, which may lead to permanent brain damage. As an emergency condition, every second counts in diagnosis and treatment of stroke patients. All stroke patients should be admitted to a facility with a stroke care unit, or at least a multidisciplinary team of stroke professionals, preferably within six hours from the onset of symptoms (Aboderin and Venables, 2003). This limited time window indicates that fast-track emergency response and acute treatment, and therefore effective stroke service OM, could be a matter of life and death for stroke victims (Schminke, 2007). The importance of stroke management is represented in goals and aims set for the future by formal declarations. The 2006 Helsingborg Declaration on European Stroke Strategies for instance has set goals on five areas of 'organization of stroke services, management of acute stroke, prevention, rehabilitation, evaluation of stroke outcome and quality assessment' to be achieved by 2015 (Kjellström et al., 2007).

Stroke care encompasses a spectrum of services including community education, emergency dispatch, acute and sub-acute treatment and rehabilitation (Gropen et al., 2009). These stroke services are typically assigned to be delivered by healthcare providers (departments or institutions) in regions (Park and Schwamm, 2008). A collection of providers from a provider network by means of explicitly defined collaboration (Provan and Milward, 2006) or implicitly as collections of providers jointly visited by (a population of) stroke patients (Provan and Sebastian, 1998). Stroke provider networks have become increasingly popular during recent decades to improve stroke care in geographical regions (Provan et al., 2011). In such networks, the health and wellbeing of patients relies on the service operations of the provider network as a whole. By stroke service operations we mean a set of services that uses or consumes resources to improve stroke patient outcomes. Analysis (evaluation) of relationships between operations and outcomes of provider networks is crucial in developing an evidence base for effective provision of stroke services for a population by regional networks (Provan and Milward, 2001). Through such analysis, results of stroke networks in terms of outcomes will be linked to the performance of services and processes. Making links between results and operations, and then comparing both operations and outcome performance between provider networks, is a form of benchmarking (Zairi, 1998). Benchmarking generates a management evidence base for learning and imitating. Networks with poor performance can learn from best practice networks by comparing operations and outcomes.

The case study that we present in this chapter was made part of the EU-funded 'Managed Outcomes' project in 2010–2012 (Elkhuizen et al., 2010). The purpose of the Managed Outcomes (MO) project was to develop an OM and demand-based approach for delivery of health services for four patient groups that constitute important challenges to healthcare in Europe: type 2 diabetes, stroke, hip osteoarthritis and dementia. We developed a methodology for an OM and demand-based approach which enabled us to translate demand in a specific region into services and resource requirements, and to relate services to outcomes measured in clinical systems, the perceptions of patients using these services and the costs of these services. We also tested this approach in case studies in each of the countries participating in the MO project: Finland, Germany, Greece, Netherlands, Spain and the United Kingdom. For the purpose of this contribution to the book we will concentrate on the six[2] case studies for stroke.

---

2 Actually five, as the data of the Erlangen (Germany) stroke case are incomplete.

For the 'problem analysis' (Section 14.2) we provide more information on the six stroke cases considered, and then formulate some research questions that we would like to address. Next, we elaborate on the methodology developed for MO and for the case studies (Section 14.3). Then we present the results of the comparative analysis (Section 14.4). We end with a discussion and reflection on the stroke study (Section 14.5).

14.2 Problem analysis

14.2.1 Stroke services considered

The six case studies were arbitrarily selected, depending on the contacts of the researchers involved. The six stroke services showed considerable differences in setting, partners and volumes of patients (see Table 14.1, data are from 2010).

As one can see from Table 14.1, the six cases show considerable difference in geography and population, ranging from the Keski-Suomi case with a very low population density to the Valencia and Brighton cases with very high population densities.

If we look at the partners involved in the stroke service, we see that three hospitals have to refer haemorrhagic stroke patients to another hospital for a neurosurgical treatment and that there are small differences in the involvement of rehabilitation, homecare and nursing homes.

From the patient volumes we see that ischemic strokes are most frequent, and that in some cases not all ischemic stroke patients are admitted to a special stroke unit; in these hospitals a considerable number of patients are admitted directly to a ward.

14.2.2 Research questions

The initial data in Table 14.1 on patient numbers already indicate that there are differences in the way hospitals handle the flow of stroke patients. We concentrate in the remainder of this chapter on ischemic stroke patients.

We are interested to see whether there are material differences between the six cases in the patient journey of ischemic stroke patients, and where this leads to a better performance in service quality and outcomes. More specifically we have the following research questions:

1. What are differences in the process of stroke care delivery: differences in the type of services, differences in the amounts of services, differences in the routing along service pathways?
2. What are differences in the performance of the stroke services: speed of delivery, waiting times, throughput time, use of resources, costs, service quality?

Table 14.1 Overview of stroke services considered

Cases	Keski-Suomi (FI)	Erlangen (G)	Athens (GR)	Tilburg (NL)	Valencia (SP)	Brighton (UK)
Geography & population						
Total population in area	273,000	236,264	3,191,329	458,220	515,000	1,293,900
Catchment population stroke network	273,000	463,263	3,191,329	341,313	266,320	365,500
Area in sq. km	19,950	642	3,808	931	133	120
Population density (inhabitants per sq. km)	14	368	838	492	3872	3044
Stroke service partners						
Ambulance	x	x	x	x	x	x
Emergency department	x	x	x	x	x	x
Stroke unit/neurology ward	x	x	x	x	x	x
Internal medicine ward			x			
Neurosurgical ward	elsewhere	x	elsewhere	x	x	elsewhere
Rehabilitation	x	x		x	x	x
Homecare		x		x	x	x
Step down care						x
Nursing home	x			x	x	
PATIENT VOLUMES						
Ischemic cases	538	508	150	676	478	449
- via stroke unit	538	508	94	676	225	270
- direct to ward			56		253	179
Haemorrhagic cases	238	105	26	88	285	130
Ischemic incidence/100,000	197	110	107	198	179	123
Haemorrhagic incidence/100,000	87	23	19	26	107	36

3. What are differences in the outcomes of the stroke service: clinical outcomes, perceived health status and satisfaction?
4. To what extent can these differences in performance and outcomes be attributed to the differences in the way the patient journey is designed?

Therefore, we are investigating the process design of each stroke service and its performance. See Figure 14.2 for a visualisation.

We use this analysis approach for each case and then compare the cases on their performance. As we have only five complete cases, this will limit the possibilities of establishing statistical significance in our analyses. Therefore, we aim at a comparative analysis that enables us to learn from differences found.

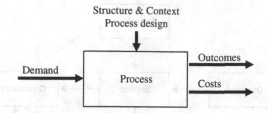

Figure 14.2 Research model for investigating process design and its performance.

14.3 Methods

14.3.1 *Managed Outcomes methodology*

For the comparative analysis for each of the four patient groups chosen for illustrating the MO approach (type 2 diabetes, stroke, osteoarthritis, dementia), it was very important to develop a common framework for describing the care processes and their performance. The methodology developed in MO has already been described in Chapter 7. We present the main components here and refer for more information to Section 7.2.

The main components of the MO approach are a generic framework to describe provider networks and their services, the operationalisation of the framework in a set of concepts with definitions that allow quantification, and an operational model that relates demand for services to outcomes and costs that helps us perform analyses of patient journeys.

This generic framework relating to operations of provider networks and their outcomes, as presented in Figure 14.3, is an extension of the well-known model from Donabedian (1966).

As Figure 14.3 shows, the demand from patients suffering from a health problem triggers the delivery of services by healthcare providers, which results in outcomes. These services are provided in a structure developed by healthcare providers, consisting of a constellation of resources (facilities, equipment and staff). As services are provided through co-creation with patients, the behaviour of patients influences services and also affects outcomes.

The generic conceptual framework is further elaborated by disaggregating the five main entities into subcomponents which can subsequently be defined to analyse the journeys of a set of patient subpopulations through a provider network (see Table 14.2).

Figure 14.4 illustrates how the elaboration of components and subcomponents can be used in an operational model to analyse the journeys of patients in different demand segments.

We see from Figure 14.4 that the demand from a population in a region can be disaggregated into demand locations and demand segments. A distinction

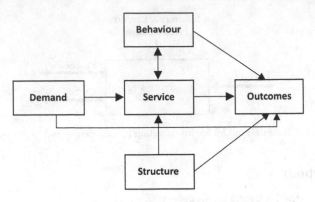

Figure 14.3 Generic Health Service Operations Framework.

in demand location might be, for instance, urban or rural – as patients living in a rural area typically have a longer distance to travel or might be living more healthily. A 'demand segment' refers to a group of patients who have the same disease but are also comparable in the amounts of resources required. For chronic diseases this often requires a distinction between stages of the disease, as advanced stages often require more – and different – resources than the early stages. For acute illnesses it might be necessary to differentiate between groups of patients that require conservative treatment versus surgical treatment, or patients who do not need follow-up treatment versus patients who require a lot of rehabilitation services. A well-considered distinction in demand segments helps to describe better the different types of patient journeys that otherwise would be unnoticed when all patients are considered as one group.

For each of the demand segments, services can be defined, consisting of service elements and a journey along the service elements. Demand segments and patient journey by segment result in expected patient flows, also taking into account patient behaviour impacts such as 'no-show' at a clinical appointment. As the resource requirements are defined at the level of service elements, we can calculate the amount of resource required for each demand segment. Furthermore, we can calculate the annual output of the system under study, expressing this as the number of services produced and the amount of resource required. We can then translate this into annual costs per patient in a demand segment (as the costs are defined at the level of service element).

The output of the system can be related to both health outcomes and service experience outcomes. When the same demand segments are used in all parts of the model, we can also differentiate outcomes between demand segments.

Table 14.2 Components and subcomponents of the generic health services network operations model

Component	Subcomponent	*Definition*
Demand	Health service user	Service user refers to the individual patient who demands health services. Service user is defined with regard to demographic characteristics, disease history, and disease – specific medical conditions requiring the health services.
	Demand segment	Segments refer to mutually exclusive subsets of the population of health service users with a common demand for health services (e.g., because of sharing a same health condition).
	Demand location	Locations define areas within the geographical areas which are meaningful to distinguish because of differences in demand and or geographical, socioeconomic and political characteristics.
Service	Service element	A service element is the atomic unit of service. For each service element the resource requirements specify the type of resources (see below) required to perform the service element, as well as the expected usage of each of these types (e.g., in hours). A service element can be described in terms of an operational performance (waiting times, frequency, length of stay, transitions to another service element) and a financial performance i.e., cost. The costs of a service element are defined as the sum of the costs of the required resource usages (see below).
	Service journey	A service journey consists of a partially ordered set of service elements, which are provided to health service users from a demand segment. Operational and financial performances of a service journey are aggregated from corresponding service elements performance. The costs of a service journey are defined as the sum of the costs of the service elements involved. Transition probability refers to the distribution of health service users from the demand segment corresponding to the service journey over possible succeeding demand segments (and corresponding service journeys).
	Service user journey	User journey refers to the sequence of services that a health service user follows (defined through the sequence of service journeys). The costs of a service user journey consist of the sum of the costs of the service journeys involved.

(Continued)

Table 14.2 Continued

Component	Subcomponent	Definition
Structure	Resource	A resource is a means to provide a service. Resources are described according to their type, availability, capacity and unit cost. With regard to type, resources are distinguished into devices, facilities and human resources. Resource availability refers to the amounts of resources which is available to deliver services per time period. Resource capacity refers to the amount of health service users that can be treated in a time period. Resource cost refers to the monetary cost of a resource per unit (e.g., per hour).
	Service provision point	Provision point refers to a location where resources required to provide a service are located. Access to provision point is measured by physical distance of and travel time from the demand location of the health service user to the provision point.
	Service provider	A health service provider is a person or a legal entity who/which delivers health services to patients.
Behaviour	General health related behaviour	General health behaviour refers to the lifestyle of the health service user, such as smoking, diet, and physical exercise behaviour
	Service-related behaviour	Service-related behaviour refers to behaviour which directly relates to the health services, e.g., treatment adherence or follow-up to advice by service provider.
Outcome	Health outcomes	Health outcomes are features of the health service user's health. A variety of quite different health outcomes can be considered ranging from perceived health related quality of life as reported by the health service user to specific clinical outcomes as reported by the healthcare provider.
	Service outcomes	Service outcomes regards both provider measures on service performance (such as waiting times) as well as health service users' perceptions of service provisioning, and the valuation of the service provisioning by health service users.

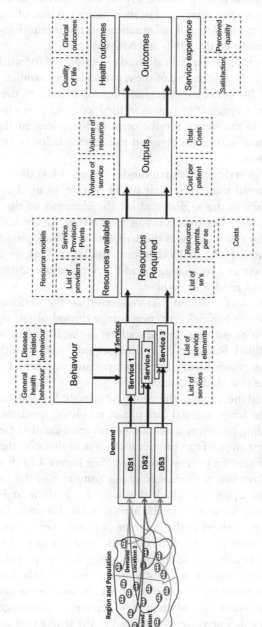

Figure 14.4 Generic operational model of patient journeys as used in Managed Outcomes.

14.3.2 Case study methodology

The operational models for diabetes, stroke, osteoarthritis and dementia were developed in case studies performed in six countries as part of the EU Managed Outcomes project. For detailed information on the methodology used in this project see Elkhuizen et al. (2010) and Mahdavi (2015).

As this chapter is based on the case studies performed for stroke, we provide more information on the content of these particular case studies. The case studies took place in 2010–2011 in a regional setting in each of the six countries.[3] For each case study a project team was formed, consisting of a manager or team leader in charge of the stroke service organisation (often in the hospital) and one healthcare professional involved in the service delivery process, and one or more researchers.

Based on the generic operational model (Figure 14.4) the teams developed a specific operational model for their stroke service, using data on population and stroke patients in the region and on the elements of the stroke services delivered by the different partners involved in the stroke service. For the stroke work, the Spanish case study was the template for developing the operational model. This template allowed other case studies to look at the operational model for Valencia and to change or add services and resources to allow for specific operational models elsewhere.

The case study also involved data collection on the performance of stroke services (such as speed of delivery, percentage thrombolysis, mortality), and a survey among stroke patients with questions on health status before and after treatment (Modified Ranking Scale), satisfaction with health (EQ5D) and experiences. The questionnaire for stroke patients was tested in Spain before being used in the case studies elsewhere.

We demarcated the scope of the stroke process studied for the purpose of the case studies to the acute hospital care phase, involving specialist stroke services – thereby excluding prevention and long-term rehabilitation (see Figure 14.5).

One of the first steps of the project team was to describe the stroke process in detail in the form of a process flowchart. See Figure 14.6 for an example of such a process flowchart for ischemic stroke from one of the case studies.

We see in the upper left block the activities performed in the timespan between the stroke incident and the arrival at the hospital. In the lower left block, activities performed in the emergency room, such as tests and interventions, are listed. Most patients with ischemic stroke then go to the stroke unit to stabilise their health condition, and during their stay at the stroke unit a number of activities is performed, listed in the middle of the lower right block. Patients with haemorrhagic stroke are brought to a neurosurgical ward for neurosurgical intervention and after their recovery from surgery they stay in the neurology ward. The patients admitted to the stroke unit are moved to the neurology ward after their stabilisation, and during their stay on the ward make

---

3 In the Erlangen case not all parts of the case study were performed.

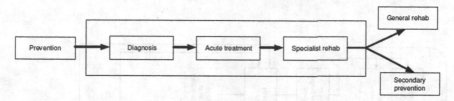

Figure 14.5 Demarcation of stroke process for case studies.

use of the activities listed in the upper right block. They leave the hospital for further rehabilitation after their discharge from the hospital.

The project team then collected further information on the process in different ways, making use of documents on the organisation of the stroke service and data on activities performed for stroke patients and the performance of the process such as speed of delivery, waiting times and length of stay – available in the hospital information system or in special registrations for the stroke service. To organise and analyse these data for comparison we used a format with the different elements of the stroke chain as presented in Figure 14.7.[4]

As can be seen from Figure 14.7 we used the operational model (Figure 14.4) as the backbone for the analysis of the stroke chain.

As we have previously shown, in the Greece, Spain and UK cases, some of the patients are not admitted to the stroke unit but directly admitted to a ward. This implies that in these cases we have to distinguish for the analysis of the patient journey between patients who are admitted to the stroke unit (a) and patients who are directly admitted to a ward (b). In terms of the generic operational model these patient groups are treated as different demand segments.

14.4 Results

We have clustered the results according to the following components of the operational model: demand, services, patient journey, resources, outcomes. For each of these clusters we have selected some results to illustrate the comparison.

14.4.1 Demand

To illustrate differences in demand between the cases we present information on the percentage of older patients and on the incidence of stroke.

Based on the data in Table 14.1 we have compared the six cases below on the percentage of the population aged 70 years or more (Figure 14.8).

---

4 The operational model for stroke is elaborated in an Excel format for each stroke service studied. The data of the operational models of the stroke study are available in the online material.

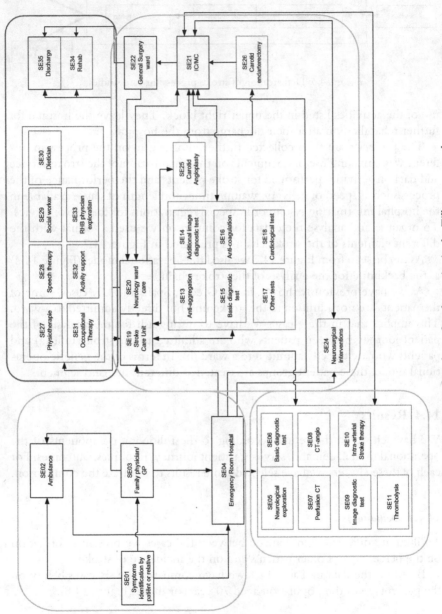

Figure 14.6 Process flowchart of stroke service in the Tilburg case study.

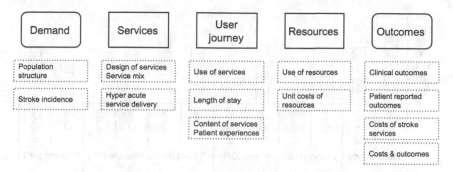

Figure 14.7 Format for data collection and analysis of the stroke service.

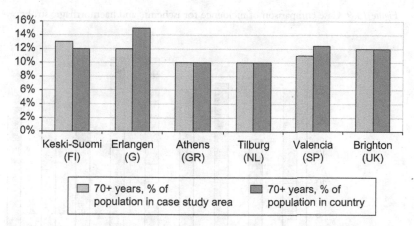

Figure 14.8 Case comparison for percentage of population 70+ (region/national).

As we can see from Figure 14.8 the percentage of population over 70 years or more is higher in the cases from Finland, Greece and the UK.

In Figure 14.9 we compare the cases on the incidence for ischemic and haemorrhagic stroke.

From Figure 14.9 we can see that the incidence of stroke is higher in the cases from Finland, the Netherlands and Spain.

14.4.2 Services

To illustrate differences in services provided in the cases, we present information on the service mix, on the performance of service delivery in the hyper-acute phase of the stroke when speed is most important, and on the percentage of patients with thrombolysis.

In Figure 14.10 the six cases are compared in terms of the (average number of) services received for the delivery of care to an ischemic stroke patient.

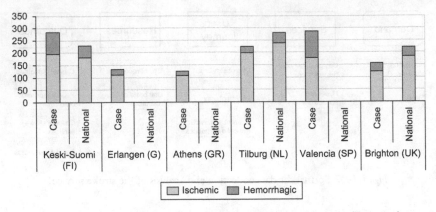

Figure 14.9 Case comparison of incidence for ischemic and haemorrhagic stroke.

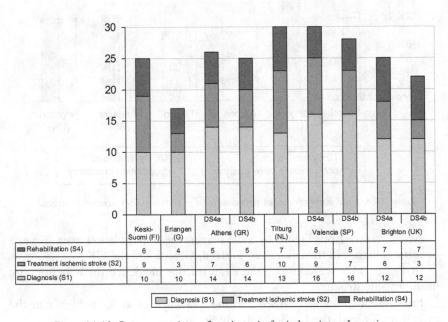

Figure 14.10 Case comparison of service mix for ischemic stroke patients.

From Figure 14.10 we see that Tilburg and Valencia provide the highest total number of services to stroke patients. Valencia is highest for the diagnosis, Tilburg is highest for the treatment, and Tilburg and Brighton are highest for the rehabilitation.

In Figure 14.11 the cases are compared in terms of their performance on speed of delivery of services in the initial phase of the stroke. Regrettably, not all data is complete.

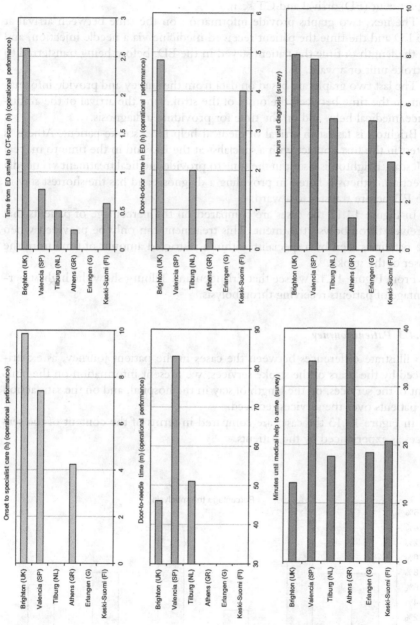

Figure 14.11 Case comparison of performance of speedy delivery in initial phase of stroke.

The first two graphs show data from the hospital information systems on the time between the onset of the stroke and the first contact with a healthcare professional who delivers specialised care, and on the time between emergency department (ED) arrival and CT scan.

The next two graphs provide information on the time between arrival at the ED and the time the patient received medicine via a needle injection, and on the length of time the patient stayed in the ED, before being transferred to a stroke unit or a ward.

The last two graphs are based on data from the survey and provide information on the time between the onset of the stroke and the arrival of the ambulance/medical help, and on the time for providing a diagnosis.

Brighton is fastest in arrival of medical help for a stroke patient, Athens is fastest in the first contact with a specialist at the ED and in the time to make a CT scan, Brighton is fastest in the time to provide medical treatment via needle injection. Athens is fastest in providing a diagnosis and has the shortest stay in the ED before transfer to a ward.

In Figure 14.12 the cases are compared on the percentage of patients that received thrombolysis treatment. This treatment can only be provided when the patient is seen by a specialist within a restricted amount of time from the onset of the stroke.

From Figure 14.12 we see that Erlangen and Tilburg show the highest percentage of patients receiving thrombolysis.

14.4.3 Patient journey

To illustrate differences between the cases in the patient journey, as experienced by the users of the stroke services, we present information on the content of the services, on the length of stay in the hospital, and on the satisfaction of patients over the services received.

In Figure 14.13 the cases are compared in terms of the content of the services as experienced by the patients.

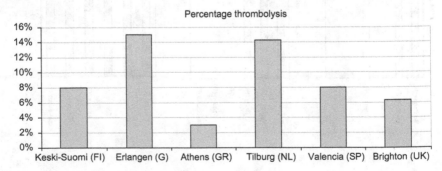

Figure 14.12 Case comparison in percentage of patients receiving thrombolysis.

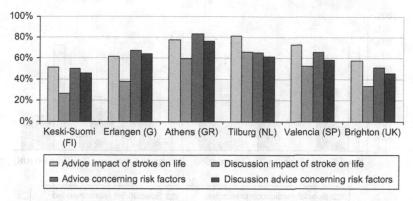

Figure 14.13 Case comparison on the content of services as experienced by patients.

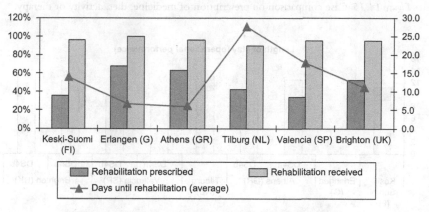

Figure 14.14 Case comparison on follow-up rehabilitation.

From Figure 14.13 we see that Tilburg shows the highest percentage of patients receiving advice and having a discussion on the impact of stroke on life. Athens shows the highest percentage of patients receiving advice and having a discussion concerning risk factors.

In Figure 14.14 the cases are compared in terms of the follow-up rehabilitation after the stay in the hospital.

From Figure 14.14 we see that almost all patients have received follow-up rehabilitation, much higher than the prescription level reported by the patient. The average time it took patients to start their follow-up rehabilitation was shortest in Athens and Erlangen (six days) and longest in Tilburg (28 days).

In Figure 14.15 the cases are compared in terms of prescribed medication, diet or activity or therapy.

From Figure 14.15 we see that Tilburg shows the highest percentage of patients with a special medication prescribed, Athens and Valencia have the

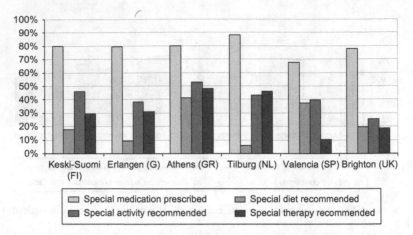

Figure 14.15 Case comparison on prescription of medicine, diet, activity or therapy.

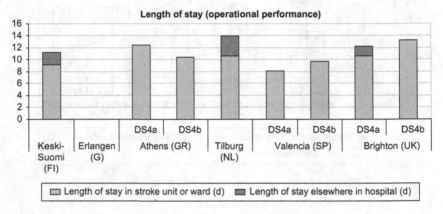

Figure 14.16 Case comparison on average length of stay.

highest percentage of patients with a special diet recommended (while the Finland, Greece and Netherlands cases show much lower percentages), and Athens and Tilburg show high percentages on activity and special therapy prescribed.

In Figure 14.16 the cases are compared in terms of their average length of stay in the hospital.

From Figure 14.16 we see that the total length of stay is longest in Tilburg (14 days, including three days on a transfer ward) and shortest in Valencia (at eight days).

In Figure 14.17 the cases are compared in terms of satisfaction of patients with the services received, based on the short form of SERVQUAL, compared with best and worst imaginable service, or the average satisfaction score.

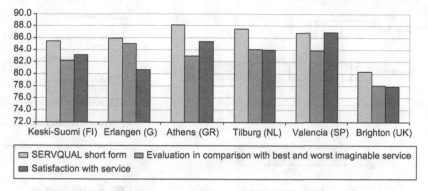

Figure 14.17 Case comparison on satisfaction with services.

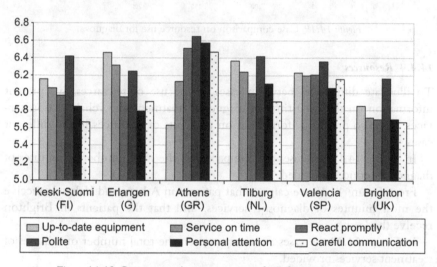

Figure 14.18 Case comparison on aspects of satisfaction over services.

From Figure 14.17 one can see that Athens, Tilburg and Valencia score highest on satisfaction with services and Brighton the lowest.

In Figure 14.18 the cases are compared in terms of satisfaction of patients on aspects of the service as experienced by patients.

From Figure 14.18 one can see that patients in Erlangen are most satisfied on up-to-date equipment, patients in Erlangen/Tilburg/Valencia are most satisfied on the timeliness of services and patients in Athens are most satisfied on the prompt reaction, the politeness, the personal attention and the careful communication of healthcare providers. Patients in Brighton are the least satisfied across the different aspects of the services received (with the exception of the politeness of healthcare staff).

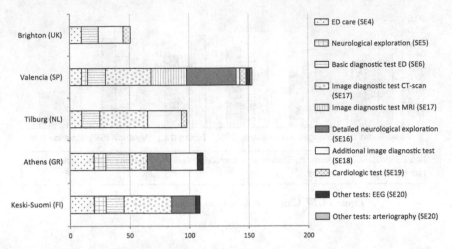

Figure 14.19 Case comparison on resource use for diagnosis.

14.4.4 Resources

To illustrate differences between cases in the use of resources, we present information on the total time of diagnosis, treatment and rehabilitation services. We also provide information on the costs of resources in the different cases.

In Figure 14.19 the cases are compared on the total number of minutes of diagnostic services provided.

From Figure 14.19 we can see that patients in Athens and Valencia receive the most minutes of diagnostic services, and that the patients in Brighton receive the least.

In Figure 14.20 the cases are compared on the total number of minutes of treatment services provided.

From Figure 14.20 one can see that patients in Brighton and Athens receive the most minutes of treatment services, and that the patients in Valencia and Keski-Suomi receive the least.

In Figure 14.21 the cases are compared on the total number of minutes of rehabilitation services provided.

From Figure 14.21 one can see that the patients in Keski-Suomi and Tilburg receive the most minutes of rehabilitation services, and that the patients in Valencia and Brighton receive the least.

In Table 14.3 the cases are compared on the unit costs of a number of services.

From Table 14.3 one can see that the unit costs can vary widely between cases. The explanation for these differences may be that it was not always clear how the unit costs were built up.

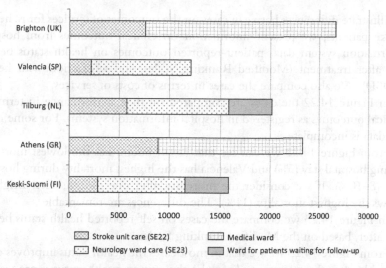

Figure 14.20 Case comparison of resource use for treatment.

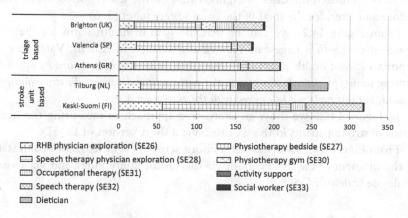

Figure 14.21 Case comparison on resource use for rehabilitation.

Table 14.3 Unit costs (in euros) per case

	Keski-Suomi (FI)	Erlangen (FG)	Athens (GR)	Tilburg (NL)	Valencia (SP)	Brighton (UK)
Ambulance	500		37,5	310	310	310
ED care	302	•	11	180	124	124
Stroke unit	1300		661	412	584	450
Neurology ward	500			299	320	
Medical ward			560			400
Physiotherapy	76		6	33	20	20
Discharge ward	150			150		
Shortstay ward					224	

14.4.5 Outcomes and costs

To illustrate differences between cases on the outcomes of services for ischemic stroke patients, we present information on clinical outcomes from hospital information system data, patient-reported outcomes on health status before and after treatment (Modified Ranking Scale), and satisfaction with health (EQ5D). We also compare the cases in terms of costs of services.

In Figure 14.22 the cases are compared on their performance in terms of clinical outcomes as registered in hospital information systems. For some cases the data is incomplete.

From Figure 14.22 we can see that Keski-Suomi has the lowest mortality during hospital stay (3%) and Valencia has the highest mortality during hospital stay (8–10%). If we consider the mortality after one month, then Brighton shows the highest mortality (11%). The differences are remarkable.

In Figure 14.23 we compare the cases on self-reported health status before and after, based on the Modified Ranking Scale.

From Figure 14.23 we see that in most cases the health status improves considerably after the treatment. To make the gain in health status more visible, we have compared the cases in Figure 14.24 on the self-reported health status before and after, for the total of the most severe states (3–6).

From Figure 14.24 we can see that the gain in health status for the most severe states (3–6) is largest in Tilburg and smallest in Athens; Valencia even reports a loss of health status after treatment (*which might be caused by differences between scoring by patients admitted to the stroke unit and patients directly admitted to a ward, but this could not be checked with the survey data*).

In Figure 14.25 we show an alternative approach to measuring the health status of stroke patients in the six cases, via a short version of EQ5D.

From Figure 14.25 we see that Tilburg scores best in terms of health status at the moment of the survey, both via the Dolan utility index and via a visual analogue scale of EQ5D.

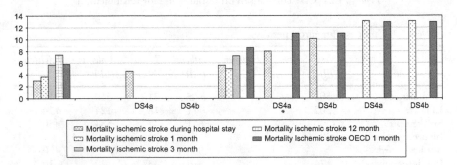

Figure 14.22 Case comparison on clinical outcomes of stroke services.

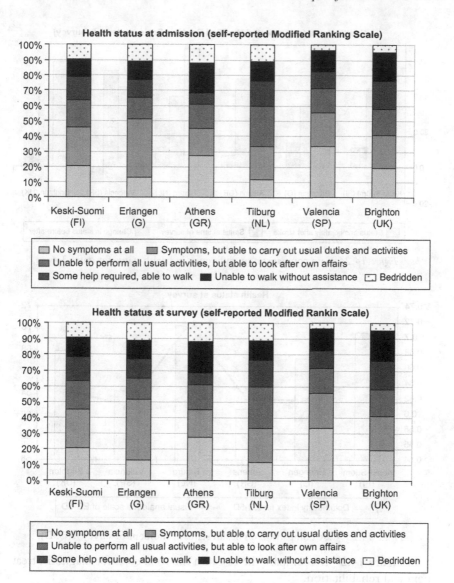

Figure 14.23 Case comparison on self-reported health status before and after (Modified Ranking Scale).

In Figure 14.26 we compare the cases on self-reported satisfaction with health and on the amount of adaptation of life to accommodate impairments caused by stroke.

From Figure 14.26 we see that patients in Keski-Suomi are most satisfied with their health, and that patients in Tilburg had to adapt their life the least to impairments caused by stroke.

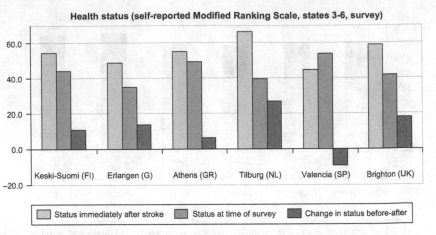

Figure 14.24 Case comparison on difference in health status for states 3–6.

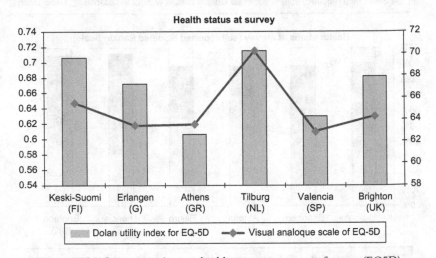

Figure 14.25 Case comparison on health status at moment of survey (EQ5D).

In Figure 14.27 we compare the cases on the total costs for diagnosis, treatment and rehabilitation.

As we can see from Figure 14.27 the costs of stroke services are lowest in Valencia (c. €4000) and highest in Keski-Suomi (more than €8000). The differences are remarkable.

After these different one-dimensional analyses of quality and costs, we have tried to relate performance and outcomes in a few two-dimensional analyses below.

We will first relate the speed of delivery to health outcomes, then time until medical help arrived versus percentage of thrombolysis treatment, and lastly costs to health outcomes.

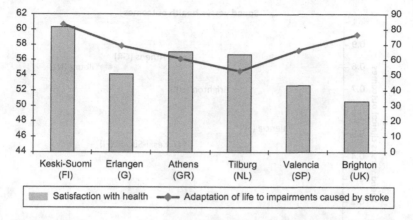

Figure 14.26 Case comparison on satisfaction with health and on adaptation of life to impairments.

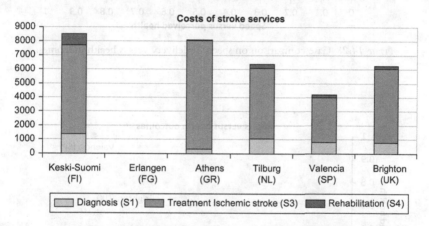

Figure 14.27 Case comparison on the costs of services.

In Figure 14.28 we compare the cases on the speed of delivery in the hyperacute phase versus health outcomes.

From Figure 14.28 we see that Tilburg, Athens and Brighton are most efficient in combining speed of delivery and clinical outcomes, and that Tilburg and Athens are most efficient in combining speed of delivery and perceived health.

In Figure 14.29 we compare the cases on their efficiency in producing clinical outcomes and perceived health outcomes.

As Figure 14.29 shows, Tilburg, Valencia and Brighton are most efficient in producing high clinical outcomes, and Valencia and Brighton are most efficient in producing high perceived health outcomes.

In Figure 14.30 we compare the cases for the time until medical help arrived versus the percentage of patients which received thrombolysis treatment.

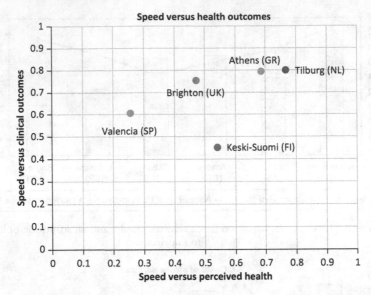

Figure 14.28 Case comparison on speed of delivery versus health outcomes.

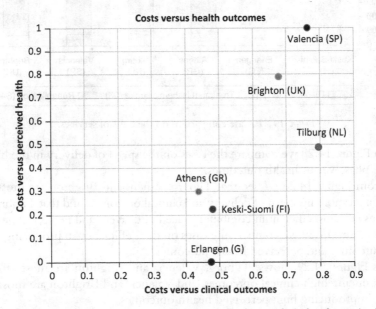

Figure 14.29 Case comparison on efficiency in producing clinical and perceived health outcomes.

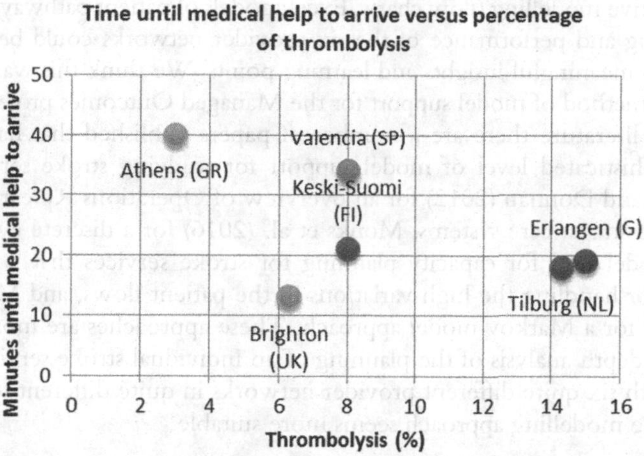

Time until medical help to arrive versus percentage of thrombolysis

Figure 14.30 Time until medical help and percentage thrombolysis.

From Figure 14.30 we can see that Erlangen and Tilburg both show a high level of thrombolysis treatment in combination with a short time for arrival of medical help.

14.5 Discussion and reflection

The case study presents the results of an approach to relate outcomes to operations of provider networks that deliver services to a specific patient group, i.e., patients with a stroke. This approach was applied in a regional setting in six countries that participated in the EU-funded Managed Outcomes project. As there were only five complete cases, it was only possible to perform a comparative analysis by showing the differences, see where the differences were remarkable, and try to find plausible explanations for the differences.

The case study shows that by carefully describing the setting of the case, the process of care delivery, the use of resources – making use of a common methodology and formats – it is possible to compare the six networks– despite the differences in setting, volume of patients and design of the process – and to develop interesting insights about their performance. By starting with simple one-dimensional analyses of demand, services, user journey, use of resources, outcomes and costs, we developed insight into the functioning and performance of the different stroke services. Then we were able to perform a few meta-level analyses, to identify, for instance, the most efficient cases in producing clinical outcomes and perceived health outcomes. This rather 'crude' analysis could only be justified after carefully studying the functioning and performance of the individual cases. The meta-level analysis helped to formulate learning points from the comparative analysis that could be beneficial for the different cases investigated and for other similar cases.

When reflecting on the modelling used in this case, we see that by using forms of descriptive modelling (flow charts, Excel models of patient pathways, etc.) the functioning and performance of the six provider networks could be analysed, leading to meaningful insights and learning points. We think this was the most adequate method of model support for the Managed Outcomes project.

In the literature there are a number of papers published that have used a more sophisticated level of model support for studying stroke services. See Churilov and Donnan (2012) for an overview of Operations Research contributions to stroke care systems, Monks et al. (2016) for a discrete event simulation model tool for capacity planning for stroke services that is especially suitable for handling the high variations in the patient flows, and McClean et al. (2015) for a Markov model approach. These approaches are more suitable for an in-depth analysis of the planning of an individual stroke service. In our case – with six quite different provider networks in quite different settings – a descriptive modelling approach seems more suitable.

14.6 Questions and exercises

Why is the approach followed here called a comparative analysis and not a benchmark?

Why is it not a network OM approach, even though we are studying a regional network of healthcare providers?

What other items of information are important to complete the description of the stroke process (Figure 14.7)?

What is the unit of analysis in Figure 14.7?

How could we have produced stronger statistical evidence for differences found?

14.7 Appendix: operational model for ischemic stroke

This appendix contains information on the operational models used in the six case studies on stroke. As the Erlangen case is incomplete, the description is often based on five cases. For the three cases that use two ways of treating ischemic stroke patients (Greece, Spain, UK), a distinction is made into a and b descriptions. For some parts of the description data can be incomplete.

14.7.1 Demand

According to the stroke model, three aspects of demand are important: demand location, demand segment and demand characteristics. We do not further distinguish demand location by urban or rural areas. On the demand for stroke care, we focus only on cerebral infarction (ischemic stroke) as the demand segment in this research, given its prevalence. We then split this segment into two subsegments with potentially different services and structure: patients with ischemic stroke admitted via a stroke unit (DS4a) and patients diagnosed with ischemic stroke not admitted via a stroke unit (DS4b). In Table 14.4 we list the demand segments and the number of patients in each.

14.7.2 Services

Service elements provided in three regions are shown in Table 14.5.

As defined in the stroke model, the services for a demand segment constitute a service journey. The service user journey for the ischemic demand segment consists of three services: diagnosis (S1), ischemic stroke treatment (S2) and rehabilitation (S3). Each of these services consists of a set of service elements (see Table 14.6).

The service journeys in Table 14.6 are derived from the comparative description of the stroke model. The percentage of patients using these service elements can vary by region. Not all regions use all service elements. Table 14.7 shows the percentage use of diagnosis service elements.

As shown in Table 14.7, up to basic diagnostic tests in the ED (SE6), regions provide roughly the same percentage of tests. Use of CT scan and MRI is different between regions. In three regions (Keski-Suomi, Tilburg and Brighton), use of MRI is not reported. Use of CT scan in Athens differs from other regions.

The percentage of patients who use each potential service element of ischemic stroke treatment is given in Table 14.8. Percentages of patients who use anti-aggregation, stroke care unit and neurological ward vary between regions, most obviously between Brighton and other regions.

In Table 14.9 percentages of patients who use rehabilitation service elements are given.

The proportion of patients using various service elements and their sequential relationships create service user journeys that can differ by region. We do not have data for the sequence of service elements for all networks, however the main flow is roughly the same (see also Figure 14.4) in the main text.

Table 14.4 Demand for stroke care

	Keski-Suomi (FI)	Erlangen (G)	Athens (GR)	Tilburg (NL)	Valencia (SP)	Brighton (UK)
Total stroke cases (incl. TIA)	776	771	176	1218	846	724
Cases (DS4, ischemic)	538	508	150	676	478	449
via stroke unit (DS4a)	538 (100%)	508 (100%)	94 (63%)	676 (100%)	225 (47%)	270 (60%)
direct to ward (DS4b)			56 (37%)		253 (53%)	179 (40%)
Cases (DS3, haemorrhagic)	238	105	26	88	285	130
Cases (DS2, TIA)		158	5	454	83	145

Table 14.5 Service elements in regions

Athens (GR)	Tilburg (NL)	Valencia (SP)
Symptoms identification	Symptoms identification	Symptoms identification
Ambulance	Ambulance	Ambulance
Primary care visit/family internist visit	Family Physician/GP	Primary care visit
Emergencies department care	Emergency room care	Emergencies department care
Neurologic exploration	Neurologic exploration	Neurologic exploration
Basic diagnostic test	Basic diagnostic test ED	Basic diagnostic test
Perfusion CT	Perfusion CT	Perfusion CT
Angio CT (CTA)	Angio CT	Angio CT
Anti-aggregation	Anti-aggregation	Anti-aggregation
Anti-coagulation	Anti-coagulation	Anti-coagulation
Thrombolysis	Thrombolysis	Thrombolysis
Referral for neurosurgery	Neurosurgery	Neurosurgery
Discharge	Hospital at homecare	Hospital at homecare
Basic diagnostic test	Discharge	Discharge
Detailed neurologic exploration	Basic diagnostic test ward	Basic diagnostic test
Image diagnostic test: MRI or CT-Scan	Detailed neurologic exploration	Detailed neurologic exploration
Additional image diagnostic test	Image diagnostic test: MRI or CT-Scan	Image diagnostic test: MRI or CT-Scan
Cardiologic test	Additional image diagnostic test	Additional image diagnostic test
Other tests: EEG and arteriography	Cardiologic test	Cardiologic test
Referral carotid angioplasty	Other tests: EEG and arteriography	Other tests: EEG and arteriography
Stroke unit care	Carotid angioplasty	Carotid angioplasty
Internal medicine ward care	Stroke unit care	Stroke unit care
Intensive care	Neurology ward care	Neurology ward care
RHB physician exploration	Neurosurgery ward care	Neurosurgery ward care
Physiotherapy bedside	Intensive care	Intensive care
Speech therapy physician exploration	RHB physician exploration	RHB physician exploration
Speech therapy	Physiotherapy bedside	Physiotherapy bedside
Social worker	Speech therapy physician exploration	Speech therapy physician exploration
First follow-up	RHB ward care	RHB ward care
	Physiotherapy gym	Physiotherapy gym
	Occupational therapy	Occupational therapy
	Speech therapy	Speech therapy
	Social worker	Social worker
	UMCE care	UMCE care
	Carotid endartectomy	Endartectomy
	Intra-arterial stroke therapy	
	Acceleration of blood coagulation	
	Surgery ward	
	Dietician	
	Activity support	
	Rehabilitation	

Table 14.6 Service elements per service journey

Diagnosis journey	Ischemic stroke treatment journey	Rehabilitation journey
• Symptom identification (SE1) • Ambulance (SE2) • Primary care visit (SE3) • ED care (SE4) • Neurological exploration (SE5) • Basic diagnostic test ED (SE6) • Perfusion CT (SE7) • Angio CT (SE8) • Image diagnostic test CT-scan (SE17) • Image diagnostic test MRI (SE17) • Basic diagnostic test ward (SE15) • Detailed neurological exploration (SE16) • Additional image diagnostic test (SE18) • Cardiologic test (SE19) • Other tests: EEG (S20) • Other tests: arteriography (S20)	• Anti-aggregation (SE9) • Anti-coagulation (SE10) • Thrombolysis (SE11) • Intra-arterial stroke therapy • Carotid angioplasty (SE21) • Endartectomy (SE35) • Stroke unit care (SE22) • Neurology ward care (SE23) • Internal medicine/medical ward • Ward for patients waiting for follow-up • UMCE care (SE34) • Intensive care (SE25)	• RHB physician exploration (SE26) • Physiotherapy bedside (SE27) • Speech therapy physician exploration (SE28) • Physiotherapy gym (SE30) • Occupational therapy (SE31) • Activity support • Speech therapy (SE32) • Social worker (SE33) • Dietician

14.7.3 Structure

The structure of stroke care considers the use of the stroke care unit and resources. Three regions (Keski-Suomi, Tilburg and Erlangen) admit all patients with stroke to a stroke care unit. Service elements for treatment of ischemic stroke are provided in such units by a multidisciplinary team of professionals. In contrast, Valencia, Athens and Brighton are triage-based systems, in which only up to 63% of patients are treated in a stroke care unit.

For a service element, a resource is defined which has a type and a unit of measurement (time or number). Duration or service time assigned to provide the service elements is the most common unit of resource for service elements in ischemic stroke. Another indicator for comparison makes use of 'usage ×number × duration' per service element to calculate the total amount of resource time used.

Service use (in minutes) per service element of stroke services is given in Tables 14.10–14.12

Table 14.7 Percentage of patients who use service elements for diagnosis (S1)

Service elements for diagnosis	Keski-Suomi	Athens		Tilburg	Valencia		Brighton	
		DS4a	DS4b		DS4a	DS4b	DS4a	DS4b
Symptom identification (SE1)	100	100	100	100	100	100	100	100
Ambulance (SE2)	100	100	100	85	80	80	80	80
Primary care visit (SE3)	10	10	10	10	10	10	10	10
ED care (SE4)	100	100	100	100	100	100	100	100
Neurological exploration (SE5)	100	100	100	100	100	100	100	100
Basic diagnostic test ED (SE6)	100	100	100	100	100	100	100	85
Perfusion CT (SE7)				1	1	1		
Angio CT (SE8)		3	2	1	0.5	0.3	1	1
Image diagnostic test CT scan (SE17 a)	100	56	41	100	95	95	95	95
Image diagnostic test MRI (SE17 b)		17	33		75	75		
Basic diagnostic test ward (SE15)	100	100	100	100	100	85	100	85
Detailed neurological exploration (SE16)	100	100	100		100	85	100	85
Additional image diagnostic test (SE18)		72	75	95	10	10	70	70
Cardiologic test (SE19)		36	30	15	20	15	20	20
Other tests: EEG (SE20)	3	3	5	5	3	3		
Other tests: arteriography (SE20)					5	5		

Table 14.8 Percentage of use ischemic stroke treatment service (S2)

Service elements for treatment	Keski-Suomi	Athens		Tilburg	Valencia		Brighton	
	DS4	DS4a	DS4b	DS4	DS4a	DS4b	DS4a	DS4b
Anti-aggregation (SE9)	100	100	100	95	85	70		
Anti-coagulation (SE10)	8	4	2	5	1	10	1	10
Thrombolysis (SE11)	8	3		8	8	0	8	
Intra-arterial stroke therapy				5				
Carotid angioplasty (SE21)	1	2	2	1	1	1	1	
Endartectomy (SE35)	5	5	5	5	1	1	1	1
Stroke unit care (SE22)	100	100		100	100		100	
Neurology ward care (SE23)	100			100	85	95		
Internal medicine/medical ward			100					100
Ward for patients waiting for follow-up	100			100				
UMCE care (SE34)					5	5		
Intensive care (SE25)	1	2	2	1	1		1	

Table 14.9 Percentage of service element use in rehabilitation service (S3)

Service elements for rehabilitation	Keski-Suomi	Athens		Tilburg	Valencia		Brighton	
		DS4a	DS4b		DS4a	DS4b	DS4a	DS4b
RHB physician exploration (SE26)	95	98	30	95	80	70	80	50
Physiotherapy bedside (SE27)	100	100	30	95	80	70	80	50
Speech therapy physician exploration (SE28)	50	49	20		32	20	32	20
Physiotherapy gym (SE30)							16	8
Occupational therapy (SE31)	10			5			15	8
Activity support				10				
Speech therapy (SE32)	50	49	20	40	32	20	40	25
Social worker (SE33)	5	2	4	5	5	3	5	3
Dietician				50				

Table 14.10 Average use of service elements in diagnosis service (S1)

	Keski-Suomi	Athens		Tilburg	Valencia		Brighton	
Diagnosis (S1)	DS4	DS4a	DS4b	DS4	DS4a	DS4b	DS4a	DS4b
Symptom identification (SE1)	1			1	1	1	1	1
Ambulance (SE2)	60	68	68					
Primary care visit (SE3)	1	2	2	1	1	1	1	1
ED care (SE4)	20	20	20	10	10	10	10	10
Neurological exploration (SE5)	10	10	10		10			
Basic diagnostic test ED (SE6)	15	20	20	15	15	15	15	13
Angio CT (SE8)		0		0.1	0.0		0.1	0.1
Image diagnostic test CT scan (SE17)	40	17	12	40	38	38		
Image diagnostic test MRI (SE17)					30	30		
Basic diagnostic test ward (SE15)	15	60	60	15	15	13	10	9
Detailed neurological exploration (SE16)	20	20	20		45	38		
Additional image diagnostic test (SE18)		22	23	29	3	3	21	21
Cardiologic test (SE19)				5	6	5	6	6
Other tests: EEG (SE20)	3.6	4	6		4	4		
Other tests: arteriography (SE20)					2	2		

Table 14.11 Average use of service elements in treatment of ischemic stroke (S2)

Treatment Ischemic stroke (S3)	Keski-Suomi	Athens		Tilburg	Valencia		Brighton	
	DS4	DS4a	DS4b	DS4	DS4a	DS4b	DS4a	DS4b
Anti-aggregation (SE9)				1				
Anti-coagulation (SE10)								
Thrombolysis (SE11)	4.8	4		5	5		5	
Intra-arterial stroke therapy				8				
Carotid angioplasty (SE21)	1.8	4	3	1	2	2	2	
Endartectomy (SE35)	4.23	5	5	5	1	1	1	1
Stroke unit care (SE22)	2880	17,856		5760	4320		15,264	
Neurology ward care (SE23)	8640			10,080	6120	13,680		
Internal medicine/ medical ward			14,400					19,008
Ward for patients waiting for follow-up	4320			4320				
UMCE care (SE34)					144	144		
Intensive care (SE25)	40	144	130	58	58		58	

Table 14.12 Average use of service elements in rehabilitation service (S3)

Rehabilitation	Keski-Suomi	Athens		Tilburg	Valencia		Brighton	
	DS4	DS4a	DS4b	DS4	DS4a	DS4b	DS4a	DS4b
RHB physician exploration (SE26)	57	29	9	29	24	21	24	15
Physiotherapy bedside (SE27)	150	210	64	114	96	147	96	60
Speech therapy physician exploration (SE28)	15	15	6		10	6	10	6
Physiotherapy gym (SE30)							24	12
Occupational therapy (SE31)	20			10			30	16
Activity support				18				
Speech therapy (SE32)	75	58	24	48	19	18	48	30
Social worker (SE33)	1.5	1	1	3	3	2	3	2
Dietician				50				
Total	319	313	104	272	152	194	235	141

Table 14.13 Average costs per patient in diagnosis service (S1)

Service elements Diagnosis	Keski-Suomi DS4	Athens DS4a	Athens DS4b	Tilburg DS4	Valencia DS4a	Valencia DS4b	Brighton DS4a	Brighton DS4b
Symptom identification (SE1)								
Ambulance (SE2)	500	38	38	264	248	248	248	248
Primary care visit (SE3)	9	4	4	10	10	10	10	10
ED care (SE4)	302	11	11	180	124	124	124	124
Neurological exploration (SE5)	0	40	40					
Basic diagnostic test ED (SE6)	250	84	84	190	209	209	209	178
Perfusion CT (SE7)				1	4			
Angio CT (SE8)		2	1		1		2	2
Image diagnostic test CT-scan (SE17)	175	36	26	142	124		124	124
Image diagnostic test MRI (SE17)								
Basic diagnostic test ward (SE15)	100	31	31	130	67	57	67	57
Detailed neurological exploration (SE16)	50	40	40					
Additional image diagnostic test (SE18)		47	19	135	13	13	91	91
Cardiologic test (SE19)		12	10	19	40	30	40	40
Other tests: EEG (SE20)	1.5	0.2	0.3		1.6	1.6		
Other tests: arteriography (SE20)					59.6	59.6		

Table 14.10 shows that Brighton provides less service time on average. In this region some diagnostic tests are not provided and for some others that are provided, the average use is lower than other regions.

As shown in Table 14.11, all regions provide stroke unit care. For patients not admitted via a stroke care unit (in triage-based regions), care is provided in either a neurological ward or an internal medicine/medical ward. Athens and Brighton do not provide neurological ward care. A higher average service use per patient in triage-based regions could be caused by the fact that only severe patients are admitted via a stroke care unit in these regions.

For calculation of the service time for rehabilitation we do not include the rehabilitation physician exploration as time used for rehabilitation but as time for planning. The totals in Table 14.12 therefore exclude this service element.

Cost per service and service journey (total costs of ischemic stroke) in a region are also calculated using 'usage × amount of resource per service

Table 14.14 Average costs per patient in treatment of ischemic stroke (S2)

Service elements Treatment	Keski-Suomi	Athens		Tilburg	Valencia		Brighton	
	DS4	DS4a	DS4b	DS4	DS4a	DS4b	DS4a	DS4b
Anti-aggregation (SE9)								
Anti-coagulation (SE10)								
Thrombolysis (SE11)								
Intra-arterial stroke therapy				455				
Carotid angioplasty (SE21)	5	7	6	3	6	6	6	
Endartectomy (SE35)	235	311	313	293	130		455	
Stroke unit care (SE22)	2600	8196	0	1647	1752		4770	
Neurology ward care (SE23)	3000			2096	1359	3037		
Internal medicine/medical ward			5596					5280
Ward for patients waiting for follow-up	450			450				
UMCE care (SE34)					22	22		
Intensive care (SE25)	48	176	158	69	48		48	

Table 14.15 Average costs per patient in rehabilitation service (S3)

Rehabilitation	Keski-Suomi	Athens		Tilburg	Valencia		Brighton	
	DS4	DS4a	DS4b	DS4	DS4a	DS4b	DS4a	DS4b
RHB physician exploration (SE26)	86	13	4		75	65	75	47
Physiotherapy bedside (SE27)	380	42	13	125	63	97	63	40
Speech therapy physician exploration (SE28)	45	6	3		30	19	30	19
Physiotherapy gym (SE30)	0						16	8
Occupational therapy (SE31)	45			8			10	5
Activity support								
Speech therapy (SE32)	223	12	5	74	·10	10	26	16
Social worker (SE33)	2			5	3	2	3	2
Dietician				92				

element × cost per resource unit'. Using this information facilitates producing average costs per patient at region level (Table 14.13). Usage, amount of resource per element and unit cost of resource are drivers of differences in service use and costs between regions and therefore a topic for analysis and comparison between regions. The cost data (euros per unit) presented in

Tables 14.13 to 14.15 is not adjusted by purchasing power parity of the different countries involved and therefore cannot be simply compared between regions.

References

Aboderin I and Venables G (2003). Stroke management in Europe. *Journal of Internal Medicine*, 240(4), 173–180.

Churilov L and Donnan GA (2012). Operations research for stroke care systems: an opportunity for the science of better to do much better. *Operations Research for Health Care*, 1(1), 6–15. https://doi.org/10.1016/j.orhc.2011.12.001.

Donabedian A (1966). Evaluating the quality of medical care. *The Milbank Memorial Fund Quarterly*, 44(3), 166–206.

Elkhuizen S, Bowen T, Forte P, van de Klundert J, Konerding U, Mahdavi M, Torkki P and Vissers J (2010). *Operations management and demand-based approaches to healthcare outcomes and cost-benefits research*. Erasmus University, Rotterdam.

Gropen T, Magdon-Ismail Z, Day D, Melluzzo S and Schwamm LH (2009). Regional Implementation of the stroke systems of care model: recommendations of the northeast cerebrovascular consortium. *Stroke*, 40(5), 1793–1802. https://doi.org/10.1161/STRO KEAHA.108.531053.

Kjellström T, Norrving B and Shatchkute A (2007). Helsingborg declaration 2006 on European stroke strategies. *Cerebrovascular Diseases (Basel, Switzerland)*, 23(2–3), 231–241. https://doi.org/10.1159/000097646.

Mahdavi M (2015). *Building the bridge between operations and outcomes. Modelling and evaluation of health service provider networks*. PhD Thesis, Erasmus University Rotterdam, Rotterdam. https://repub.eur.nl/pub/77858/Mahdavi_THESIS_Final.pdf.

McClean S, Qiao Y and Fullerton K (2015). STOPGAP: stroke patient management and capacity planning. *Operations Research for Health Care*, 6, 78–86. https://doi.org/10.1016 /j.orhc.2015.09.007.

Monks T, Worthington D, Allen M, Pitt M, Stein K and James MA (2016). A modelling tool for capacity planning in acute and community stroke services. *BMC Health Services Research*, 16, 530. https://doi.org/10.1186/s12913-016-1789-4.

Mukherjee D and Patil CG (2011). Epidemiology and the global burden of stroke. *World Neurosurgery*, 76(SUPPL 6), S85–90.

Park S and Schwamm LH (2008). Organizing regional stroke systems of care. *Current Opinion in Neurology*, 21(1), 43–55. https://doi.org/10.1097/WCO.0b013e3282f4304d.

Provan KG, Beagles JE and Leischow SJ (2011). Network formation, governance, and evolution in public health: the North American quitline consortium case. *Health Care Management Review*, 36(4), 315–326.

Provan KG and Milward HB (2001). Do networks really work? A framework for evaluating public-sector organizational networks. *Public Administration Review*, 61(4), 414–423.

Provan KG and Milward HB (2006). Health services delivery networks: what do we know and where should we be headed? *HealthcarePapers*, 7(2), 32–36 & 68–75.

Provan KG and Sebastian JG (1998). Networks within networks: service link overlap, organizational cliques, and network effectiveness. *Academy of Management Journal*, 41(4), 453–463.

Schminke U (2007). Acute stroke monitoring. European standards. *Udar Mozgu - Problemy Interdyscyplinarne*, 9(2), 52–57.

Struijs JN and Baan CA (2011). Integrating care through bundled payments - lessons from the Netherlands. *New England Journal of Medicine*, 364(11), 990–991. https://doi.org/10.1056/NEJMp1011849.

Zairi M (1998). *Benchmarking for best practice*. Butterworth-Heinemann, Abingdon, UK.

15 Analysing process and unit OM performance for general surgery

Sylvia Elkhuizen

Case positioning

The case is based on an assignment for students following a seven-week course on Health Services Operations Management, as part of a Master's in Healthcare Management. The assignment concerns the planning of patients who are admitted for general surgery in a hospital in the Netherlands. The objective of the assignment is that students are able to analyse patient data on problems in the management of patient flows and resources, from a process operations management (OM) perspective as well as from a unit OM perspective. In Figure 15.1 we have positioned the case in the framework we use for case studies in this book.

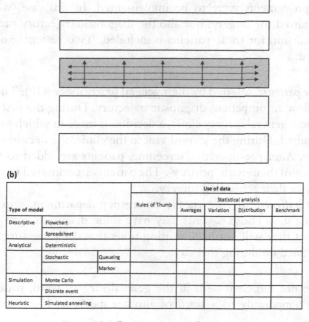

Figure 15.1 Position in case framework.

DOI: 10.4324/9781003020011-18

In Figure 15.1(a) we have indicated the planning level addressed in the case and whether the focus is on unit, chain or network OM, and in Figure 15.1(b) the type of model used in the case and the use of data. We see that the case addresses a tactical level of planning, i.e., the allocation of resources to units. It is a network OM problem as we include delivery processes for two (aggregate level) patient groups (elective and urgent patients), and use of resources in units. The emphasis is, equally, on process OM (throughput and waiting time) as well as unit OM (performance in use of resources). In the case a form of descriptive modelling is used, i.e., use of a spreadsheet model. Data wise, the case makes use of individual patient data, and calculations are based on averages and standard deviations of throughput and waiting times and use of beds.

15.1 Introduction

The general surgery specialty in a mid-size hospital experiences challenges in organising patient services and managing resources. To develop more insight into the problems faced, and possible mechanisms that could explain the problems, the board of directors of the hospital asks for a thorough quantitative analysis and advice how to handle the problems and develop improvements. This analysis should, first of all, underpin the areas where improvements are necessary. Subsequently, you analyse the expected consequences of potential improvements, by making well-motivated adjustments in patient processes and in the planning of processes, and by quantifying the expected performance if these improvements were to be implemented. In this case, we focus on patients admitted for surgery, but also the diagnostic trajectory preceding the hospital admission for those patients is included. Two patient groups can be distinguished:

- *Elective patients*, referred by their general practitioner (GP). These patients first follow an outpatient diagnostic trajectory. During the first visit to the outpatient general surgery clinic, a decision is made in which examinations are required. During the second visit to the clinic, the decision for surgery is made. After pre-operative screening, patients are added to the waiting list, some of them with 'priority'. The patients are admitted to the ward on the day of their scheduled surgery.
- *Urgent patients*, arriving via the emergency department, require surgery the same day. Those patients may have some diagnostic tests before surgery, but they will not have waiting times that delay the surgery and can be operated on during that day.

If there are not sufficient beds in the general surgery ward, patients can be transferred temporarily to a ward of another specialty. However, from the viewpoint of quality of care, this is not an optimal situation. Patients will be transferred back to the general surgery ward as soon as a bed becomes available.

The board of directors wants to have insight in the performance of the care process for patients (in terms of throughput time and waiting time), and in the performance of the ward (in terms of use of beds). Data is made available of all patients who had surgery in 2019. To allow for a complete analysis, some data of patients that were admitted in 2018, but discharged in 2019, is also available. The ward has 56 beds.

In Section 15.2 we describe what patient data are used for the analysis, and what type of analyses are performed. In Section 15.3 we present the elaboration and results of the process OM performance analysis, and in Section 15.4 we present the elaboration and results of the unit OM performance analysis. In Section 15.5 we analyse a few scenarios for improvement.

15.2 Methods

In this methods section we first present the data that is available for the analysis (Subsection 15.2.1) and then describe the types of analysis we perform (Subsection 15.2.2).

15.2.1 Data

For each patient, the hospital made data available for the assignment (characteristics of the patient, date of referral by the GP, dates of visits to the clinic, date of entry to the emergency department (if visited), dates of tests and examinations, date of joining the waiting list, category of urgency, date of pre-operative screening, date of admission, date of surgical procedure, date ready for discharge, discharge destination and date of discharge (see Table 15.1).

The data is made available in an Excel file, see Figure 15.2 for an illustration of the available data.

15.2.2 Types of analysis

With this data, several analyses can be performed. The assignment was to provide insight into the performance of the care process, and in the performance of the ward. The first part concerns the OM of the process chain, and the second part the OM of a unit. Chapter 5 provides suggestions for the types of analysis for process OM performance. Chapter 4 does the same for unit OM performance.

Based on these suggestions, the following analyses were performed for the case study hospital, see Table 15.2.

Table 15.1 Data available for the assignment

Item no	Item	Description
1	Patient number	Number used for identification of the patient
2	Age	Age of the patient in years
3	Gender	Gender of the patient (male/female)
4	Referral GP	Date that the patient was referred by the GP to general surgery
5	First visit clinic	Date of the first visit to the outpatient clinic of general surgery
6	Attendance at emergency department	Date of attendance at emergency department
7	Blood sample taking	Date that blood sample was taken
8	X-Ray	Date that X-ray examination was performed
9	CAT scan	Date that CAT scan was performed
10	MRI	Date that MRI was performed
11	Second visit clinic	Date of the second visit to the general surgery clinic
12	Pre-operative screening	Date that the pre-operative screening was performed
13	Patient on waiting list for surgery	Date that the patient was put on the waiting list
14	Urgency category	Category of urgency of the patient (standard, priority, urgent)
15	Admission date	Date that the patient was admitted for surgery
16	Surgery date	Date that the surgery procedure took place
17	Patient ready for discharge	Date that the patient was ready for discharge
18	Discharge destination	Destination of the patient after discharge (home, home with homecare, rehabilitation)
19	Discharge date	Date that the patient was discharged

15.3 Process OM performance analysis

As the first step of the analysis, we suggest developing a process flow model of the diagnostic trajectory for non-urgent patients referred by the GP. It is important to have a view on the patient process before using the data. The view on the process helps to understand the data and offers a background for interpreting the results of analyses of the data. Figure 15.3 provides a flow model of the diagnostic trajectory.

We see from Figure 15.3 that the diagnostic trajectory starts – after referral by the GP and waiting for the first visit – with a first visit to the general surgeon in the outpatient clinic. Then a blood sample can be taken, and an X-ray performed. In case extra diagnostics are required, a CAT or an MRI scan can be performed – after a wait for an available slot at the radiology department. The diagnostic trajectory ends with a second visit to the general surgeon, in which decisions are made on the treatment or follow-up.

patient number	age	gender	referral GP first visit	first visit ambulatory care	entrance Emergency Department	blood sample taking	X-Ray	CAT scan	MRI	second visit ambulatory care	Pre-operative screening	Patient on waiting list for surgery	urgency category	admission date	Surgery date	Patient ready for discharge	Discharge destination	Discharge date
6023204	58	male	1-okt-18	29-okt-18		29-okt-18	29-okt-18			9-nov-18	23-nov-18	23-nov-18	standard	2-jan-19	2-jan-19	5-jan-19	home with home care	7-jan-19
8139265	56	female	9-okt-18	5-nov-18		5-nov-18	5-nov-18			19-nov-18	30-nov-18	30-nov-18	standard	2-jan-19	2-jan-19	5-jan-19	home with home care	8-jan-19
5486134	66	male	11-okt-18	8-nov-18		8-nov-18	8-nov-18			20-nov-18	30-nov-18	30-nov-18	standard	2-jan-19	2-jan-19	5-jan-19	rehabilitation	7-jan-19
9772240	48	male	28-sep-18	23-okt-18		23-okt-18	23-okt-18		13-nov-18	27-nov-18	3-dec-18	3-dec-18	standard	2-jan-19	2-jan-19	8-jan-19	home with home care	11-jan-19
3112130	72	female	5-okt-18	29-okt-18		29-okt-18	29-okt-18			9-nov-18	21-nov-18	21-nov-18	standard	2-jan-19	2-jan-19	6-jan-19	home with home care	11-jan-19
4817886	43	female	16-okt-18	8-nov-18		8-nov-18	8-nov-18			20-nov-18	29-nov-18	29-nov-18	standard	2-jan-19	2-jan-19	6-jan-19	home	6-jan-19
7474911	49	female	31-aug-18	28-sep-18		28-sep-18	28-sep-18			8-nov-18	16-nov-18	16-nov-18	standard	2-jan-19	2-jan-19	5-jan-19	home	5-jan-19
9770212	63	female	11-sep-18	4-okt-18		4-okt-18	4-okt-18		25-okt-18	19-nov-18	24-dec-18	24-dec-18	priority	2-jan-19	2-jan-19	6-jan-19	home with home care	8-jan-19
7950851	58	female	26-okt-18	20-nov-18		20-nov-18	20-nov-18	30-nov-18	1-nov-18	14-dec-18	24-dec-18	24-dec-18	priority	2-jan-19	2-jan-19	6-jan-19	home with home care	7-jan-19
9074258	52	female	22-okt-18	15-nov-18		15-nov-18	15-nov-18	29-nov-18		10-dec-18	24-dec-18	24-dec-18	priority	2-jan-19	2-jan-19	5-jan-19	home with home care	7-jan-19
6529863	44	female	24-sep-18	22-okt-18		22-okt-18	22-okt-18	31-okt-18		12-nov-18	26-nov-18	26-nov-18	standard	2-jan-19	2-jan-19	4-jan-19	home	4-jan-19
5590429	48	female			3-jan-19	3-jan-19							urgent	3-jan-19	3-jan-19	13-jan-19	home with home care	15-jan-19
4294617	49	female	8-nov-18	4-dec-18		4-dec-18	4-dec-18			14-dec-18	24-dec-18	24-dec-18	priority	3-jan-19	3-jan-19	6-jan-19	home with home care	8-jan-19
4585169	48	female	18-okt-18	13-nov-18		13-nov-18	13-nov-18			25-nov-18	3-dec-19	3-dec-19	standard	31-dec-19	31-dec-19	6-jan-20	home with home care	8-jan-20

Figure 15.2 Snapshot of the available data in Excel file.

Table 15.2 Overview of analyses

No	Analysis	Description	Remarks
Process OM performance			
1	Process flow model	Process flow model of diagnostic trajectory of non-urgent patients	Always a good start for analysis
2	Descriptive statistics on waiting times	Descriptive statistics on percentage of patients that follow each step in the trajectory, and on waiting time for each step	Gives insight into the patient flow
3	Distribution of waiting time	Frequency chart of the distribution of waiting time for CAT scan, MRI and surgery	More detailed insight, to see how many patients have waited too long
4	Throughput time	Throughput times for diagnostic trajectory and treatment trajectory	To see where gain is possible in throughput time
Unit OM performance			
1	Patterns in resource use	Weekly patterns for outpatient units, weekly and seasonal patterns for inpatient units	Can the patterns be explained for?
2	Use of beds	A histogram of the number of beds in use during the year	Shows how often beds need to be borrowed
3	Discharge delay	A table with frequencies of delay in discharge for the different discharge destinations	Clarifies which destination may cause unproductive use of beds

As a next step of the analysis, Table 15.3 provides descriptive statistics on the percentage of patients who follow the different steps in the diagnostic trajectory, and on the length of the waiting time at each step.

The descriptive statistics in Table 15.3 give a first insight. We see that all patients have a blood sample taken and an X-ray (which can be performed directly), and that 40% of the patients have a CAT scan (with a wait of about 10 days), and that 21% have an MRI (with a wait of about 22 days). Then after about 13 days the second visit to the outpatient clinic takes place.

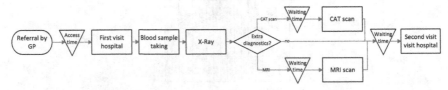

Figure 15.3 Process flow model of the diagnostic trajectory of non-urgent patients.

Table 15.3 Descriptive statistics on waiting times (in days) in the diagnostic process of non-urgent patients

All numbers in days	First visit to outpatient clinic	Blood sample taking	X-ray	CAT scan	MRI	Second visit outpatient clinic
Percentage of patients	100%	100%	100%	40%	21%	100%
Average	25.0	0	0	9.6	21.8	13.1
Median	25	0	0	9	21	13
Modus	28	0	0	8	21	14
Stdev	2.6	0	0	2.4	4.3	1.7
Min	21	0	0	3	5	7
Max	32	0	0	16	40	19

We can also look at frequencies in a frequency chart, as shown for the waiting time of a CAT scan in Figures 15.4 and 15.5 (cumulative).

We can conclude from Figures 15.4 and 15.5 that it takes a little more than two weeks to have all patients seen for a CAT scan.

Then after the second visit, patients are put on a waiting list and have to wait for surgery. The waiting time for surgery is shown in Figure 15.6.

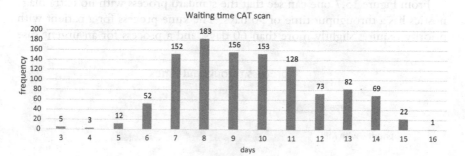

Figure 15.4 Frequency chart of the waiting time for a CAT scan.

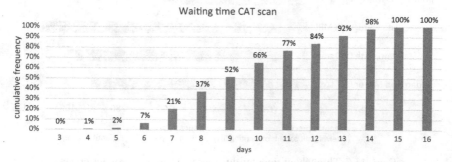

Figure 15.5 Cumulative frequency chart of the waiting time for a CAT scan.

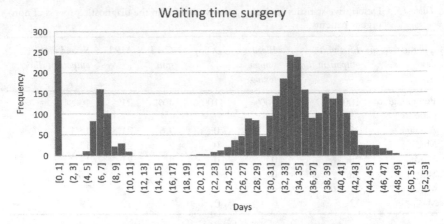

Figure 15.6 Histogram waiting time for surgery.

We see from Figure 15.6 that we can clearly distinguish the three urgency groups (urgent, priority and standard) in the distribution of the waiting time for treatment.

In Figure 15.7 the throughput times of the patient process are provided for different urgency categories and variants in the process.

From Figure 15.7 one can see that the standard process with no extra diagnostics has a throughput time of 90 days. The same process for a patient with priority requires slightly more than 60 days, and a process for an urgent case

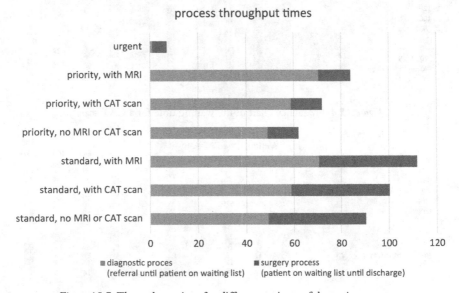

Figure 15.7 Throughput time for different variants of the patient process.

Table 15.4 Performance related to Treeknormen

	First visit outpatient clinic	*CAT scan*	*MRI*
percentage of patients within 21 days	12%	100%	51%
percentage of patients within 28 days	96%	100%	94%

less than 10 days. Extra diagnostics increase the throughput time with about 10 days (CAT scan) or more than 20 days (MRI).

In Table 15.4 we relate the waiting times for first visit and diagnostic test with a standard for waiting time that is used in the Netherlands, i.e., the so-called 'Treeknormen': 80% of the patients should be seen within three weeks with a maximum of four weeks (Nederlandse Zorgautoriteit, 2017).

From Table 15.4 we can see that the access time for first visits and the waiting time for MRI do not perform according to the Treeknormen. This should be a reason for an improvement effort.

15.4 Unit OM performance analysis

We can first look at patterns in the resource use of units. For outpatient units, insight into weekly patterns provides much insight in how the units are used. Figure 15.8 gives an example for the first visits to ambulatory care.

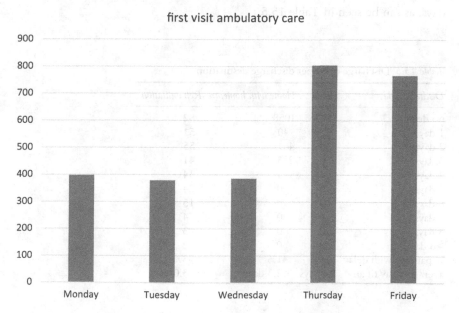

Figure 15.8 Weekly patterns in scheduling first visits.

From Figure 15.8 we can see that, apparently, the clinic schedules about twice the number of appointments on Thursdays and Fridays, compared with the other days of the week. This has also consequences for the walk–in X–ray and blood sample taking facilities.

For the ward, we can analyse the utilisation of the beds. Given that we have 56 beds in the ward, we can create a run chart for the utilisation (see Figure 15.9).

The run chart in Figure 15.9 gives a good impression of the development of the use of beds over time. The utilisation varies in most weeks between 70% and 100% but shows a dip in some weeks (which often can be explained, e.g., holidays), and there are also many weeks that the utilisation is more than 100%. Notice that we count the beds used on another ward as 'utilised capacity', and therefore, the utilisation can become more than 100%. If we don't include this, the utilisation will have a maximum of 100% for each day, but this gives less insight in the problem of bed shortages.

Then we can make a frequency diagram of the bed occupancy during the year, see Figure 15.10.

From Figure 15.10 we can see that on 38 days of the year (10.4%) one or more beds were borrowed from other wards for patients treated by general surgery. In total, 105 patients' days on other wards are used.

Part of the bed shortage may be related to patients with discharge delay. Patients can be discharged to different destination, as shown in Figure 15.11.

We see that not all patients are discharged at their 'ready for discharge' date. The delay differs per discharge destination, in occurrence and in number of days, as can be seen in Table 15.5.

Table 15.5 Discharge delay per discharge destination

Discharge delay	Home	Home with homecare	Rehabilitation
no delay	774	1058	82
1 day	55	40	51
2 days	36	461	55
3 days	0	233	41
4 days	0	4	34
5 days	0	0	24
6 days	0	0	15
7 days	0	0	4
8 days	0	0	3
>8 days	0	0	2
% patients with delay	11%	41%	73%
average delay (if any)	1.4 days	2.3 days	3.0 days

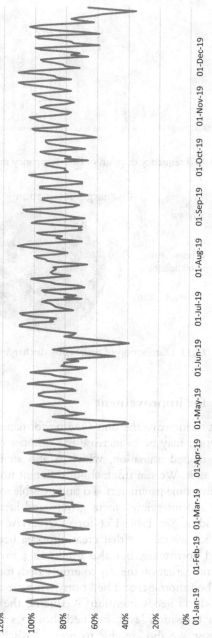

Figure 15.9 Run chart for the bed utilisation in the ward.

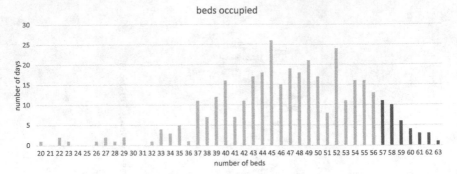

Figure 15.10 Frequency diagram of bed occupancy during the year.

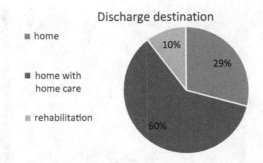

Figure 15.11 Distribution of patients by discharge destination.

15.5 Scenarios for improvement

Suppose we want to improve the unit OM performance to reduce bed shortages. The first option may be to increase the number of beds, but this comes with a reduction in bed utilisation, which is also an important performance parameter for the unit. We can think about different improvement possibilities and compare the outcome parameters. To find possible solutions, we can use our data analyses, but also interviews, focus groups and literature may be a source for improvement ideas. See Table 15.6 for an overview of scenarios and results.

From Table 15.6 we can see that creating extra beds helps to reduce bed shortages and bed borrowing, but also results in a lower utilisation of beds. Discharging patients earlier on the day to empty beds for new patients can have much impact, as bed shortages and bed borrowing are almost gone; however, the low bed utilisation needs attention. Reducing the number of beds to 52 results in a better utilisation level, but bed shortages and bed borrowing are back again. Suppose we also are able to prevent discharge delay by arrangements with discharge destinations. The impact is great again, as bed shortages and bed borrowing are almost gone. As a last step we can reduce the number

Table 15.6 Scenarios for improvement of bed utilisation

Scenarios Outcome parameters	Current situation (56 beds)	Extra beds (60 beds)	Early discharge (56 beds)	Early discharge and reduction of beds (52 beds)	No discharge delays (56 beds)	No discharge delays and reduction of beds (52 beds)
Utilisation (including extra beds)	84.3%	78.6%	69.9%	75.3 %	72.1%	77.7%
Number of days with bed shortages	38	7	1	10	1	17
Number of patient days on another ward	105	12	1	22	1	38

of beds to 52 again and accept the amount of bed shortages and bed borrowing and are happy with the resulting bed utilisation. These scenario analyses do not give one optimal option, but it gives an overview of options and their effect on the performance parameters. It is a management decision to weight these outcomes and make a balanced decision.

15.6 Discussion

The case illustrates that a relatively modest set of data that is easily available in most hospitals, can be used to develop a good insight into problems faced by hospital management.

Performing straightforward analyses of process and unit OM performance, provides a basis for developing scenarios for improvement.

The level of model support in this case is relatively modest, i.e., spreadsheet modelling, but adequate. Of course, there are many possibilities to use more sophisticated models for this case, but why would you do this if the simple model is adequate to help make the right decisions?

15.7 Questions and exercises

Think about other process- and unit-related analyses you can perform with this data. You can use the online material for the analyses.

The scenarios for improvement are focused on the unit. Can you think about improvement options for the patient process?

Reference

Nederlandse Zorgautoriteit (2017). Beleidsregel TH/BR-025, Beleidsregel toezichtkader zorgplicht zorgverzekeraars Zvw. https://puc.overheid.nl/nza/doc/PUC_21832_22/1/.

16 Master scheduling of medical specialists

Jan Vissers[1]

Case positioning

The case investigates how the planning of a group of medical specialists – belonging to the same specialty – can be improved. In a master schedule they define what type of activity they are performing during the different days of the week and parts of the day. This master schedule is then used to organise sessions in outpatient clinics or operating theatres. In Figure 16.1 we have positioned the case in the framework we use for case studies in this book.

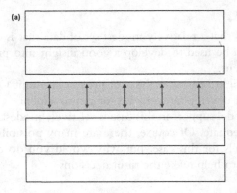

Figure 16.1 Position in case framework.

1 The case is based on a case study in the previous version of the book, authored by Erik Winands, Anne de Kreuk and Jan Vissers.

DOI: 10.4324/9781003020011-19

In Figure 16.1(a) we have indicated the planning levels addressed in the case and whether the focus is on unit, chain or network operations management (OM), and in Figure 16.1(b), the type of model used in the case and the use of data.

We see that the case addresses the tactical level of planning, where resources are allocated to specialties or departments. In this case the resources of the unit 'medical specialists of specialty X' are allocated to outpatient and inpatient departments where sessions are organised that make use of a medical specialist. The focus is on the tactical level of planning. It is a unit OM approach as it concerns the efficient allocation of medical specialists as a resource. In the case, a form of heuristic is used, i.e., simulated annealing, belonging to the group of local search techniques. Data wise, the case makes use of average durations of sessions and activities.

16.1 Introduction

Medical specialists are the key operators in hospital processes. Patients will see a medical specialist in different phases of their journey through the hospital: during a visit to the outpatient department to discuss the complaint, the diagnosis, the therapy or the follow-up after an admission; during a diagnostic procedure in a diagnostic department or a surgical procedure in the operating theatre department; during a ward round in cases where the patient is admitted. These activities of medical specialists are organised in sessions: a clinic session in the outpatient department, in which the specialist sees a number of outpatients; an operating theatre session in the operating theatre department; a ward round, visiting all patients admitted to a nursing ward.

From the perspective of the OM of hospitals, medical specialists represent a very important hospital resource. However, the topic of planning of medical specialists is often not covered in hospital planning. Frequently, the availability of specialists is a bottleneck for the efficient use of other resources. Therefore, the planning of capacity of specialists, in terms of their availability for performing operations, is an important area for improvement. This is a challenge as specialists do not like to be scheduled or regarded as a resource. One area and opportunity for working together with specialists on improving the performance of specialist planning, is to develop a schedule for the different activities of specialists in a hospital, for instance outpatient clinic sessions, operating theatre sessions, ward rounds, etc.

BOX 16.1 THE CASE STUDY HOSPITAL

The case study hospital – that acted as a pilot setting for the development of the model – is a 400-bed hospital in the Netherlands, operating on two sites separated by a distance of 20 km. The pilot concerned the orthopaedics speciality. This speciality struggled with its schedule as it had to operate on the two sites of the hospital, with only five orthopaedic surgeons available. The questions requiring answers were:

- What is the performance of the current schedule of activities?
- What would be the gain in performance if activities were concentrated on one site per day instead of time being lost changing sites during the day?
- Could a schedule be developed that took better account of the preferences of individual specialists in terms of the order of activities within the day, but which did not compromise the overall performance of the specialty?

We use data of this specialty to illustrate the planning problem and the model.

The rest of the paper is organised as follows. Section 16.2 gives a more detailed description of the planning problem, together with the positioning of the case study in the reference framework of this book and a short review of the relevant literature. In Section 16.3 we elaborate on the planning problem of master scheduling of medical specialists and discuss the components of a model that would allow the evaluation and optimisation of master schedules. Section 16.4 describes the model developed for the problem, including the solution approach implemented in MediPlan. In Section 16.5 we show how the developed model can be applied in practice. Section 16.6 gives a reflection on the strength and the weakness of the study and some recommendations for further research.

16.2 Planning problem

Consider the following: a group of specialists wanted to develop a new schedule for their activities in a two-location hospital setting. Based upon interviews about their current schedule and their objectives and ideas for a revised schedule, a proposal was developed that was thought to meet their objectives. The proposal was discussed with the group of specialists and received much criticism. Some of the objectives were not properly understood and formulated, new objectives were added, and many arguments, that were not very concrete, were used to propose further changes. The project team – consisting of one of the specialists, a manager and the external management consultant – developed a new schedule, taking into account the comments of the group of specialists. The process described here went on for about four months during which time eight different proposals were put forward, before a final proposal was accepted and implemented (Vissers, 1994).

In the evaluation of the process the project team concluded that the process could have been speeded up considerably if they had possessed a tool that was able to handle the different performance criteria and capacity restrictions related to the planning problem and was able to generate a number of alternatives. In this chapter we concentrate on the planning problem for a single specialty within a hospital. More specifically, this case study deals with the evaluation and optimisation of the basic schedules for a specialty, the so-called *master schedules*. Each specialty has its own master schedule. These schedules may vary a little from week to week due to an absence of specialists, but in principle each weekly schedule is derived from this master schedule. A complicating factor in the development of a master schedule is the fact that not all activities have to be carried out every week. A small fraction of the activities follows a bi-weekly, or even a four-weekly, pattern.

In the case study hospital, we wanted to avoid the pitfalls described above by developing a tool that enabled the generation of master schedules for specialist activities in hospitals. In this chapter we aim to answer the following research question: *how to construct master schedules for the activities of specialists which deliver good performance, in a reasonable amount of time, while satisfying given capacity restrictions?*

There are a number of criteria that need to be taken into account to develop a good master schedule. First of all, a master schedule needs to meet the output targets for the hospital at an annual level. From the issue of the efficient use of resources, it is also important to have activities of one type (for instance operating theatre sessions) well spread throughout the week. Then, preferences of individual specialists also have to be taken into account, for instance, the order of activities within one day or the avoidance of a transfer within one day between different sites of a hospital.

The level we consider in this case study is concerned with the issue of how to organise these sessions in order to provide the service levels agreed upon, while maintaining an efficient organisation of activities. Efficiency is a key issue at this level, because the way sessions in outpatient departments and the operating theatre department are allocated determines whether or not peaks and troughs are introduced in the workload of diagnostic departments and wards. See also the distinction between 'leading' and 'following' resources in Chapter 4 on unit logistics.

16.2.1 *Literature review*

The issue addressed in this chapter, i.e., specialist capacity planning, has received little attention in the past. Most literature on the scheduling of hospital resources concerns beds (Wright, 1987; Bagust et al., 1999; Ridge et al., 1998), operating theatres (Blake, 2002; Guinet et al., 2003; Sier et al., 1997), outpatient departments (Brahimi and Worthington, 1991; Lehaney and Paul, 1994; Rising et al., 1973; Cayirli & Veral, 2003). These all refer to departments where interaction takes place between the resources of a specific department and specialist capacity. However, the above illustrations only focus on a part of the capacity of the specialist. Literature references to papers that take into account the total capacity of a specialist and concentrate on scheduling all the activities of specialists are scarce and hard to find, see, for instance, Gunawan and Lau (2013).

16.3 Elaboration

This section elaborates on the planning problem of master scheduling for medical specialists. In particular, we discuss the data of an orthopaedics speciality in a two-site hospital. We start with presenting the current master schedule used by the orthopaedic surgeons, and then reflect on the different components that should be taken into account when modelling the planning problem. We emphasise here that the presented schedule is a stylised reflection of the original schedule used by the orthopaedics speciality. Several minor and major adjustments have been made to the data of the pilot hospital in order to facilitate the problem description, the model formulation and the presentation of the results. Nevertheless, the case study still clearly demonstrates the problematic nature of master scheduling for medical specialists as well as the virtues of the developed model in a practical setting.

Suppose we deal with a group of five orthopaedic surgeons working on two locations, A and B. Table 16.1 provides information on the activities of each of the surgeons per day of the week.

Based on this schedule, and also some interviews with surgeons and managers from operating theatres and outpatient departments, one can make the following observations that play a role in a proper description of the planning problem:

- The surgeons perform a number of different types of activity.
- Most of these activities are organised on a weekly basis, a few on a bi-weekly basis.
- Each day of the week is divided into two parts: AM and PM.
- The number of activities that need to be scheduled each week should be sufficient to meet the annual output targets.
- The way sessions of one type (for instance: operating theatre sessions) are distributed over the days of the week is bounded by a restriction on the availability of this type of resource (for instance: only one operating theatre available for orthopaedics per day of the week).

Table 16.1 Current master schedule orthopaedic surgeons

	Monday		Tuesday		Wednesday		Thursday		Friday	
	AM	PM	AM	PM	AM	PM	AM	PM	AM	PM
Surgeon 1	OT A	Other A	Other A	OPD A	OT A	Ward A	OPD A	Ward A	OPD A	
Surgeon 2	OPD A	Ward A	DIAG A^2	Ward B	OPD B	OT B	OT A	OT A^2	OPD B	DIAG B
Surgeon 3	OPD B	Ward B	OT A	Ward A	OT B	OPD B	OPD A		OT A	
Surgeon 4	OT B	OT B	Ward A	Ward B	OPD A	OT A	OPD B	OPD A	OPD A	OT A
Surgeon 5	OPD A	OT A	OPD A	OT A^2		Ward A	OPD B	OPD B	OT B	OPD B

(OT: operating theatre, OPD: outpatient department, DIAG: diagnostic procedures, Ward: scheduled ward round, A: location A, B: location B, Other: other activities, OT A^2: bi-weekly operating theatre session at location B, etc.)

- Preferences in order of activities within a day exist at the level of individual specialists.
- In evaluating the performance of a schedule different criteria play a role.

We discuss these components of the planning problem below.

16.3.1 Frequency of activities

Each day of the week is divided into a fixed number of blocks, so-called *day parts*. The specialty of orthopaedics uses two day parts for planning during a day. Tables 16.2 and 16.3 provide information on the weekly and bi-weekly activities that have to be carried out by the individual specialists. The majority of the activities follows a normal weekly pattern. Notice that the orthopaedic surgeons do not have to carry out activities on a four-weekly pattern.

16.3.2 Capacity restrictions

The coordination between the specialties under consideration and the rest of the hospital (for instance, other specialities and departments) takes place via so-called *capacity restrictions*. These restrictions may under no circumstances be

Table 16.2 Weekly activities for the specialists

	Operating		Outpatient		Wards		Diagnostic		Other	
	A	*B*	*A*	*B*	*A*	*B*	*A*	*B*	*A*	*B*
Surgeon 1	2	0	3	0	1	0	0	0	2	0
Surgeon 2	1	1	1	2	1	1	0	1	0	0
Surgeon 3	2	1	2	2	1	1	0	0	0	0
Surgeon 4	2	1	2	2	1	1	0	0	0	0
Surgeon 5	1	1	2	2	1	0	0	0	0	0

Table 16.3 Bi-weekly activities for the specialists

	Operating		Outpatient		Wards		Diagnostic		Other	
	A	*B*	*A*	*B*	*A*	*B*	*A*	*B*	*A*	*B*
Surgeon 1	0	0	0	0	0	0	0	0	0	0
Surgeon 2	1	0	0	0	0	0	1	0	0	0
Surgeon 3	0	0	0	0	0	0	0	0	0	0
Surgeon 4	0	0	0	0	0	0	0	0	0	0
Surgeon 5	1	0	0	0	0	0	0	0	0	0

Table 16.4 Capacity restrictions for operating theatres

	Monday		Tuesday		Wednesday		Thursday		Friday	
	AM	PM	AM	PM	AM	PM	AM	PM	AM	PM
Location A	1	1	1	1	1	1	1	1	1	0
Location B	0	1	0	0	1	1	0	0	1	0

violated by the master schedule. The following capacity restrictions are to be included in the model:

- All activities of an individual specialist have to be scheduled in the master schedule in order to meet the production targets of the speciality.
- The number of operating theatres and outpatient units available for the specialty in each day part and at each location is limited.

The capacity restrictions for the number of operating theatres are listed in Table 16.4, in which the number of available operating theatres is given for each day part on both locations. Furthermore, there are always two, and one outpatient unit available for orthopaedics at Location A and Location B, respectively. Notice that the capacity restrictions for the number of operating theatres at Location B are tight, i.e., the specialty needs at least four operating theatre sessions a week at this location to perform all the operations and this is exactly the number of sessions available each week.

16.3.3 *Evaluation criteria*

To be able to evaluate the performance of a master schedule, different *criteria* should be included in the model. These criteria may be violated, if necessary, but each violation reduces the performance of the master schedule. The criteria address the following issues:

1. The need to sequence activities in any day such that a transfer between locations for an individual specialist is avoided.
2. The need to accommodate the wishes of individual specialists in terms of their preferred day part for a specific activity or preferred sequencing of activities.
3. The need to spread activities (operating theatre sessions and outpatient clinic sessions) over the day parts of the week per group of specialists and per location.
4. The need to spread activities (operating theatre sessions and outpatient clinic sessions) over the day parts of the week per individual specialist.

We held interviews to investigate the preferences of the orthopaedic surgeons with respect to day parts for activities or sequences of activities:

- Surgeon 1 preferred to have the activities indicated by *other* at Location A on Monday afternoon and Tuesday morning.
- Surgeon 2 preferred to perform the *diagnostic sessions* at Location B on Thursday afternoon.
- Surgeon 3 wanted the *half day off* to be preceded by a *ward round* at Location B.
- Surgeon 4 wanted to do the *ward rounds* at Location A on Tuesday morning.
- Surgeon 5 had no specific preferences.

Moreover, we used these interviews to discuss the importance of the above evaluation criteria according to the orthopaedic surgeons. Table 16.5 shows the weighting factors, which reflect the relative importance of the criteria. This means that the preferred sequences of activities are very important, whereas transfer between locations within one day and preferred day parts for specific activities are considered only of medium importance. Finally, the spreading of activities for both the individual specialists and within the speciality is of (almost) no importance to the orthopaedic surgeons.

16.4 Model

In this section we translate the presented scheduling problem into a mathematical model in the form of an integer quadratic programming (IQP) problem. In the following subsection (16.4.1) we first describe the solution approach. In Subsection 16.4.2, the mathematical model is formulated. Subsection 16.4.3 describes the implementation of the solution approach in a software tool, called MediPlan. For more detailed information, see De Kreuk and Winands (2001).

16.4.1 Solution approach

To find optimal master schedules for medical specialists in which the bi-weekly and four-weekly activities are integrated, three steps have to be followed:

1. Construction and optimisation of a schedule with the *weekly activities*.
2. Addition of the *bi-weekly activities* to the weekly schedule and optimisation of this bi-weekly schedule.

Table 16.5 Weighting factors for relative importance of criteria

Criteria	Weight
Location transfer	5
Preferred day-part	7
Preferred sequence	10
Spreading of activities for specialists	0
Spreading of activities within the specialty	2

3. Addition of the *four-weekly activities* to the bi-weekly schedule and optimisation of this four-weekly schedule.

IQP is used to formulate a mathematical model that finds the optimal schedules. In the optimal schedules the capacity restrictions mentioned in the previous section have to hold, while the number of criteria that are violated is minimised.

16.4.2 Mathematical model

In this section the optimisation model is described mathematically. For ease of presentation, we only show the mathematical model for the weekly activities. Let t denote the day parts in one week ($t \in \{1,\ldots,10\}$), and let S denote the total number of specialists. All possible activities get a number, which is shown in Table 16.6.

To describe the capacity restrictions, the following parameters are introduced:

- $F_{a,s}$ is the number of day parts for which specialist s ($s \in \{1,\ldots,S\}$) has to perform activity a ($a \in \{1,\ldots,11\}$). So $\sum_{a=1}^{11} f_{a,s} = 10$.

- $g_{a,t}$ is the maximum number of specialists that can perform activity a on day-part t ($t \in \{1,\ldots,10\}$).

To describe the criteria, for which the violations have to be minimised, the following parameters are introduced:

- c_i is the weight of a violation of criterion i ($i \in \{1,\ldots,5\}$).
- $w_{s,t}$ is equal to the number corresponding to the activity that specialist s *wants* to perform on day part t ($w_{s,t} \in \{1,\ldots,11\}$). $w_{s,t}$ equals zero if specialist s has no preference on the corresponding day part.

For every day part an activity has to be assigned to every specialist. This gives the following decision variable:

Table 16.6 Activities

Number	Activity	Number	Activity
1	Operating theatre, location 1	6	Operating theatre, location 2
2	Outpatient clinic, location 1	7	Outpatient clinic, location 2
3	Ward rounds, location 1	8	Ward rounds, location 2
4	Diagnostics sessions, location 1	9	Diagnostics sessions, location 2
5	Other, location 1	10	Other, location 2
		11	Day part off, no location

- $x_{s,t}$ is equal to the number corresponding to the activity that specialist s *has* to perform on day part t ($x_{s,t} \in \{1,\ldots,11\}$).

The capacity restrictions form the constraints of the optimisation model. The first capacity restriction is that all activities of an individual specialist have to be scheduled in the master schedule in order to meet the production targets of the specialty, i.e.:

$$\sum_{t=1}^{10} 1\left[x_{s,t} = a\right] = f_{a,s} \text{ for all } a \in \{1,\ldots,11\}, s \in \{1,\ldots,S\}.$$

($1[x]$ is the indicator function, which becomes 1 if x occurs). The second type of capacity restrictions is that the number of operating theatres and outpatient units available for the specialty at each day part and at each location is limited. This is given by:

$$\sum_{s=1}^{S} 1\left[x_{s,t} = a\right] \leq g_{a,t} \text{ for all } a \in \{1,6\}, t \in \{1,\ldots,10\},$$

$$\sum_{s=1}^{S} 1\left[x_{s,t} = a\right] \leq g_{a,t} \text{ for all } a \in \{2,7\}, t \in \{1,\ldots,10\}.$$

The criteria that have to be minimised form the objective of the optimisation problem.

The first criterion is that it is preferable that no sequence of activities is scheduled in one day that requires a transfer between locations for an individual specialist. This criterion is described by:

$$\sum_{s=1}^{S}\sum_{t=1}^{5} 1\left[x_{s,2t-1} \leq 5 \wedge 6 \leq x_{s,2t} \leq 10\right] + \sum_{s=1}^{S}\sum_{t=1}^{5} 1\left[6 \leq x_{s,2t-1} \leq 10 \wedge x_{s,2t} \leq 5\right]$$

A second criterion is that a violation should be given if the preferred day part for a specific activity for an individual specialist is not assigned, i.e.:

$$\sum_{s=1}^{S}\sum_{t=1}^{10} 1\left[w_{s,t} \neq 0 \wedge x_{s,t} \neq w_{s,t}\right].$$

There are also (not)–preferred sequences of activities for individual specialists. Here, only the mathematical formulation is given to violate if preferred sequences of activities do not occur, but the formulation for the non-preferred sequences is almost identical. That is,

$$\sum_{s=1}^{S}\sum_{t=1}^{10}1\Big[x_{s,t}=a\wedge x_{s,t+1}\neq b\Big],$$

where a and b represent the first and second activity in the preferred sequence, respectively. The other criteria have to do with the spreading of the activities over the day parts per week per group of specialists and per location and also the spreading per individual specialist. These criteria are included in the model by calculating the spreading of the activities in the usual way. The mathematical formulations are not given here, since it would make the model look unnecessary complex. For more information on these formulations, see De Kreuk and Winands (2001).

Summarising, the problem of the master scheduling of medical specialists can be formulated by the following IQP:

Minimise $c_1\left(\begin{array}{c}\displaystyle\sum_{s=1}^{S}\sum_{t=1}^{5}1\Big[x_{s,2t-1}\leq5\wedge6\leq x_{x,2t}\leq10\Big]\\[2mm]+\displaystyle\sum_{s=1}^{S}\sum_{t=1}^{5}1\Big[6\leq x_{s,2t-1}\leq10\wedge x_{x,2t}\leq5\Big]\end{array}\right)$

$\qquad\qquad +c_2\left(\displaystyle\sum_{s=1}^{S}\sum_{t=1}^{10}1\Big[w_{s,t}\neq0\wedge x_{s,t}\neq w_{s,t}\Big]\right)$

$\qquad\qquad +c_3\left(\displaystyle\sum_{s=1}^{S}\sum_{t=1}^{10}1\Big[x_{s,t}=a\wedge x_{s,t+1}\neq b\Big]\right)$

Subject to

$$\sum_{t=1}^{10}1\Big[x_{s,t}=a\Big]=f_{a,s}\quad\text{for all }a\in\{1,\dots,11\},s\in\{1,\dots,S\}$$

$$\sum_{s=1}^{S}1\Big[x_{s,t}=a\Big]\leq g_{a,t}\quad\text{for all }a\in\{1,6\},t\in\{1,\dots,10\}$$

$$\sum_{s=1}^{S}1\Big[x_{s,t}=a\Big]\leq g_{a,t}\quad\text{for all }a\in\{2,7\},t\in\{1,\dots,10\}$$

$$x_{s,t}\in\{1,\dots,11\}$$

16.4.3 Implementation

The model described in the previous section is implemented in a software tool called MediPlan.[2] MediPlan uses the solution approach consisting of three steps, i.e., constructing and optimising a schedule with weekly activities, addition of the bi-weekly activities and addition of the four-weekly activities. Each of the steps in the solution procedure consists of two parts: *the construction of an initial schedule* and *the development of alternative schedules* with a higher performance. The development of alternative schedules in each step is continued until the decision maker is satisfied with the schedule and wants to proceed to the next step.

The following two steps are followed to construct the initial weekly schedule:

1. Schedule the weekly activities for which capacity restrictions are imposed (i.e., operating theatre sessions and outpatient clinic sessions) in such a way that these capacity restrictions are satisfied.
2. Schedule the rest of the weekly activities (i.e., diagnostics sessions, ward rounds and other activities) randomly over the idle day parts of the schedule.

It is important that the number of activities that have to be scheduled does not exceed the number of day parts that are available for the different activities. The initial bi-weekly schedule is made in the same way. This means that we firstly schedule the bi-weekly activities with capacity restrictions in the doubled weekly schedule without violating these capacity restrictions. Secondly, the remaining bi-weekly activities are randomly added to the schedule. The initial four-weekly schedule is constructed by applying the exact same procedure to the bi-weekly schedule.

To generate an alternative schedule, two different activities of a specialist in the schedule are selected and exchanged. When generating alternative weekly schedules all activities may be chosen and exchanged. However, in the optimisation of the bi-weekly schedule the weekly activities are fixed, which means that they cannot be selected for exchange. When optimising the four-weekly schedule, the weekly and bi-weekly activities are fixed. In the exchanging process capacity restrictions are constantly checked. In this way a variant of the current schedule is made that is feasible given the capacity restrictions.

After the exchange of the activities, the score of this schedule variant is computed. In order to decide whether the variant will be accepted or not, we make use of a technique called *simulated annealing*, belonging to the *local search* family (see e.g., Aarts and Korst, 1989). Local search methods have the goal to

---

2 The Mediplan model is available as part of the online material.

find a solution in a large solution-set in a smart and fast way and concentrate on problems that can be formulated unambiguously in terms of mathematical terminology and notation. Furthermore, it is assumed that the quality of a solution is quantifiable and that it can be compared to that of any other solution. Finally, it is assumed that the set of solutions is finite.

Simulated annealing comes down to the following steps:

1. Generate a variant of the current schedule as explained above.
2. Calculate the score of the variant.
3. If the variant has a higher performance than the current schedule, accept the variant as a new schedule; if not, the variant is accepted as the new schedule with a predetermined probability (the probability of acceptance of lower performing variants gradually decreases).
4. Continue with Step 1.

The probability of acceptance of a variant with a lower performance helps to overcome local optima. Local optima are schedules that have a better score than all the schedules that can be obtained by exchanging activities but are not the best possible schedule (global optimum). By gradually reducing the probability of accepting lower performance variants, the algorithm is able to find an optimal (global) solution by only using a limited number of runs.

16.5 Results

In this section we show the output of MediPlan for this case study, i.e., the optimal schedule together with its score, and present a discussion of the output.

The master schedule for the specialty of orthopaedics generated by MediPlan is shown in Table 16.7. For ease of presentation, we only depict and discuss the weekly schedule. This master schedule was constructed in only a couple of

Table 16.7 Final weekly master schedule for the specialty of orthopaedics

	Monday		Tuesday		Wednesday		Thursday		Friday	
	AM	PM	AM	PM	AM	PM	AM	PM	AM	PM
Surgeon 1	OPD	Other	Other	OPD	Free	OT	Ward	Free	OT	OPD
	A	A	A	A		A	A		A	A
Surgeon 2	OT	Free	Free	OPD	OT	OPD	Ward	DIAG	OPD	Ward
	A			B	B	B	B	B	A	A
Surgeon 3	Ward	OT	OPD	OPD	OPD	OT	OPD	OT	Ward	Free
	A	A	A	A	B	B	B	A	B	
Surgeon 4	Ward	OT	Ward	OT	OT	OPD	OPD	Free	OPD	OPD
	B	B	A	A	A	A	A		B	B
Surgeon 5	OPD	OPD	Free	Ward	OPD	Free	OT	OPD	OT	Free
	B	B		A	A		A	A	B	

minutes, which is a significant reduction in process time compared to the old situation, as sketched in the Section 16.2.

Table 16.7 summarises the performance of the above master schedule on the different criteria included in MediPlan. This master schedule satisfies the imposed capacity restrictions with respect to the limited number of operating theatres and outpatient units. It is immediately apparent that the generated schedule violates no criteria concerning preferred sequences and day parts of activities. Furthermore, in the entire week only one orthopaedic surgeon has to transfer between locations within one day. The bottom line of Table 16.8 shows the total score of the master schedule.

If we compare this with the performance of the original schedule (Table 16.1), we can make the following observations:

- The original schedule also showed one transfer on Tuesday (Surgeon 4) between locations, contributing 5 points to the score.
- In the original schedule, one wish for a preferred day part (Surgeon 2 on Thursday afternoon) was violated, contributing 7 points to the score.
- Also, the sequence order of activities for Surgeon 3 (half day off preceded by ward round at location B) was violated, contributing 10 more points to the score of the original schedule.
- The spreading of activities was not considered in the original schedule and will certainly produce a higher contribution to the score for the original schedule than the revised schedule.

Summarising, the score of the original schedule is much higher than that of the revised schedule. The new schedule shows fewer violations and a better spreading of activities.

16.6 Reflection and further development

We want to start this section with a discussion of the quality of the model on both the performance of the generated master schedules and the speed of the process involved. After all, the aim of this research was the development of a method or a tool that could both *improve* and *speed up* the process of constructing master schedules. Besides the case study presented, MediPlan has been

Table 16.8 Score for the master schedule

Criteria	# Violations	Score
Location transfer	1	5
Preferred day art	0	0
Preferred sequence	0	0
Spreading of activities for specialists	–	0
Spreading of activities within the specialty	–	3.8
TOTAL		8.8

tested on various theoretical examples and on the speciality of gynaecology within the same hospital (see De Kreuk and Winands (2001), for more details). Based on these implementations of MediPlan we may conclude that the model worked successfully with respect to the performance of the generated master schedules. Furthermore, MediPlan also reduced the process time of developing master schedules significantly in the practical implementations. Once the decision maker had been able to define relevant performance criteria and capacity restrictions, the generating of a schedule with maximal performance took only a couple of minutes. Although further testing is needed, the first (positive) applications of the model encourage further use for other specialties and other hospitals.

We would like to end with a possible extension of MediPlan that can support hospitals in the coordination of schedules for specialties and departments such as operating theatres and outpatient departments. After all, most of the work of the specialist is regulated by these department schedules. Between these department schedules high degrees of dependency exist, i.e., a delay in one department may cause delays in successive departments. For example, if an operating session takes more time than scheduled, the specialist might not be able to start a clinic session in the outpatient department at the correct time. This dependence is often a bottleneck when one wants to redesign a schedule for a specific department. If, for instance, some shifts are to be made in the clinic schedule, what will be the consequences for the other activities of the specialist? A further complication is that the workload of the medical service departments is, to a large extent, dependent on the outpatient clinic schedule. At times of a fracture clinic, for example, many patients will visit the X-ray department. Therefore, a direct relationship exists between the clinic schedule of the outpatient department and the workload of some medical service departments. When looking at changes in the working day of a specialist these *second-order effects* also have to be taken into account. Therefore, an interesting topic for further research would be to analyse the match between the master schedules for individual specialties generated by MediPlan and the department schedules. Undoubtedly, there is great demand from hospitals for a decision support tool visualising and optimising the coordination between and within the individual specialty schedules and the department schedules.

16.7 Questions and exercises

Based on the data of Tables 16.2 and 16.3, what is the minimum number of operating theatres and outpatient units needed by the orthopaedics specialty in a week at Location A?

What is the relationship between the master schedule of a specialty on the one hand and the production targets and waiting lists of the specialty on the other?

Define one or more capacity restrictions for a master schedule in addition to the ones presented in Subsection 16.3.2. By whom are these restrictions imposed (e.g., another specialty, another department or the hospital board)?

Define one or more performance criteria for a master schedule in addition to the ones presented in Subsection 16.3.3.

References

Aarts E and Korst J (1989). *Simulated annealing and Boltzmann machines.* John Wiley & Sons, New York.

Bagust A, Place M and Posnett JW (1999). Dynamics of bed use in accommodating emergency admissions; stochastic simulation model. *British Medical Journal*, 319, 155–158.

Blake JT (2002). Using integer programming to allocate operating room time at Mount Sinai hospital. *Interfaces*, 32, 63–73.

Brahimi M and Worthington DJ (1991). Queuing models for out-patient appointment systems – a case study. *Journal of the Operational Research Society*, 42(9), 733–746.

Cayirli T and Veral E (2003). Outpatient scheduling in health care: a review of literature. *Production and Operations Management*, 12(4), 519–549.

De Kreuk ACC and Winands EMM (2001). *MediPlan: het optimaliseren van meer-wekelijkse roosters van specialisten in een ziekenhuis.* Project report, Faculty of Mathematics and Computer Science, Eindhoven University of Technology (in Dutch).

Guanwan A and Lau HC (2013). Master physician scheduling problem. *The Journal of the Operational Research Society*, 64(3), 410–425.

Guinet A and Chaabane S (2003). Operating theatre planning. *International Journal of Production Economics*, 85, 69–81.

Klaasen SAM (1996). *Beslissingsondersteuning bij roosteroptimalisering in ziekenhuizen.* MSc thesis, Eindhoven University of Technology (in Dutch).

Lehaney B and Paul RJ (1994). Using SSM to develop a simulation of outpatient services. *Journal of the Royal Society of Health*, 114, 248–251.

Ridge JC, Jones SK, Nielsen MS and Shahani AK (1998). Capacity planning for intensive care units. *European Journal of Operational Research*, 105(2), 346–355.

Rising E, Baron R and Averill B (1973). A system analysis of a university health service outpatient clinic. *Operations Research*, 21(5), 1030–1047.

Sier D, Tobin P and McGurk C (1997). Scheduling surgical procedures. *Journal of the Operational Research Society*, 48, 884–891.

Vissers JMH (1994). *Patient flow based allocation of hospital resources.* Doctoral thesis, Eindhoven University of Technology.

Wright MB (1987). The application of a surgical bed simulation model. *European Journal of Operational Research*, 32, 26–32.

17 Cardio care simulation

Modelling the interaction between resources

Jan Vissers[1]

Case positioning

The case is based on a project in a hospital that experienced difficulties in managing cardiology patient flows. The limited capacity of the cardio care unit (CCU) led to much pressure on patient flows in the cardiology subsystem. If new patients arrive from the emergency department (ED), and all beds are full, decisions have to be made to transfer patients from the CCU to a regular ward. A simulation model was built to enable investigating different options to make the problem more manageable. The model made clear what the effects of, for instance, telemetric beds at a ward are for use of resources and pressure on early discharge. In Figure 17.1 we have positioned the case in the framework we use for case studies in this book.

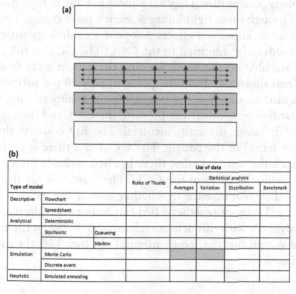

Figure 17.1 Position in case framework.

1 The case is based on a case study in (Vissers et al., 1999), authored by Jan Vissers and Gijs Croonen.

DOI: 10.4324/9781003020011-20

In Figure 17.1(a) we have indicated the planning levels addressed in the case and whether the focus is on unit, chain or network OM, and in Figure 17.1(b), the type of model used in the case and the use of data.

We see that the case addresses two levels of tactical planning. The focus is on the allocation of resources to units. However, also the more detailed tactical level of allocation to patient groups is covered as trajectories of patient groups are used for describing the patient flows between units. It concerns a network operations management (OM) approach, as it combines unit and process perspectives, however, the emphasis is on unit because of the manipulation of the available capacity of the resources involved. In the case, a form of Monte Carlo simulation is used, as emergency patient flows are generated by using random numbers. Data wise, the case makes use of data, mainly based on averages and standard deviations of durations of operations, and average percentage of patient flows between units.

17.1 Introduction

The cardiology inpatient flow is characterised by a high percentage of patients that are non-scheduled. These patients often arrive by ambulance at the ED and need to be admitted immediately to the CCU. When they have recovered sufficiently, they are transferred to a regular ward which specialises in the care of cardiology patients. After full recovery, patients are discharged and seen at the outpatient department for follow up.

Though physically separated, the units (ED, CCU, ward) are tightly linked by the cardiology patient flow. They act almost as a 'cardiology hospital' within the hospital. Through these tight linkages, even a small change can cause a disturbance and many knock-on effects. Suppose a cardiology patient arrives at the ED and needs to be admitted to the CCU. The CCU is full and there are also no beds available on the ward. Sending the patient away to another hospital is not a real alternative from the point of view of the patient (increase in anxiety, extra time required) or the hospital (poor quality of care, lost income). Within the 'cardiology hospital' the pressure increases, and there is much contact by phone between the units involved. The ED contacts the CCU and announces the arrival of the patient. The CCU says there is no bed available, but they will ask the ward whether there is a bed available for a patient that is 'most' ready for discharge from the CCU. The ward will say that all beds are occupied, but they will investigate whether one of the patients on the ward can be discharged early or whether a bed can be borrowed from another ward. This case study deals with this delicate relationship between the ED, the CCU and the ward within the 'cardiology hospital'. In Box 17.1 the case study setting is introduced.

BOX 17.1 THE CASE STUDY HOSPITAL

The cardiology speciality in the case study hospital struggled with limited inpatient resources such as ward beds, cardio care beds and nursing staff. Over a number of years staff involved at the hospital (medical, nursing, management) have developed a number of ad hoc measures to tackle a range of problems. Examples are: to create temporary overcapacity by placing beds in an examination room, and to discharge or transfer patients whenever there is no bed available. These measures were not satisfactory as they tended to trigger negative side effects such as: unacceptable workloads for departments and transfer of patients during the night.

The hospital wanted to get more of a grip on this planning problem and not to have to constantly resort to ad hoc solutions. The request was to analyse the current practice and to give advice on how to improve the logistic management of cardiology patients.

Section 17.2 describes the planning problem, including the most important difficulties in handling the cardiology patient flow and the different variables that play a role in the problem and the research questions. Next, in Section 17.3 the planning problem is elaborated, and the approach followed to tackle the problem is described. Section 17.4 describes the model that has been developed: its background, outline and assumptions. In Section 17.5 the results of the simulation-experiments that were carried out with CardioSim are discussed; this enables an assessment of the effects of different scenarios for improvement. Finally, Section 17.6 gives the conclusions of this project and the recommendations for the further application and development of the model.

17.2 Planning problem

Admissions, transfers and discharges of cardiology patients cause constant logistical problems. The different actors in cardiology differ in their interpretation of the problem. The CCU says that the inflow of patients stagnates; due to insufficient screening at the ED non-cardiology patients are admitted to the CCU and cardiology patients are incorrectly placed in the CCU. This leads to excess demand for the CCU, causing patients to be transferred at inconvenient hours (evening and night-time). The emergency department says its throughput of patients stagnates, because they cannot get 'rid' of their cardiology patients. The wards complain over the untimely transfers and discharges and the inconveniences for patients. The cardiologists had accepted the inevitability of this situation and had learnt to cope with it; in the beginning they did not have much confidence in the project and in finding a structural solution to the problem. Summarising, to cope with the patient flow enormous flexibility was developed in creating an extra bed, in an examination room, in the day-unit or – when necessary – in the corridor. This led to an ad hoc work approach and no insight into the consequences of measures taken.

Box 17.2 provides some background information on cardiology patient flows and the resources available to handle the flow.

BOX 17.2 CARDIOLOGY PATIENT FLOWS AND RESOURCES

The hospital had three cardiologists, who admitted about 1400 patients in 1997; 1000 of these were emergency admissions while 400 were admitted as electives. In the CCU, nine care beds were available for the treatment of cardiology patients and 28 beds on nursing ward F1. This nursing ward had three more beds that were in principle assigned to other specialties. This allocation of beds was not used in a strict sense; sometimes cardiology occupied more than 28 beds and sometimes the other specialties occupied more than three beds. There were no limitations for emergency admissions – due to the large distance to other hospitals. Regarding elective treatment, coronary angiographies (CAGs) and percutaneous transluminal coronary angiographies (PTCAs) were performed at a neighbouring hospital. These patients stayed before and after treatment in the hospital. Due to government planning regulations the hospital had to reduce its number of beds by 40 in a few years' time; therefore, extra beds for cardiology were unlikely to become available.

17.2.1 Literature review

The planning problem of cardiology patient flows has not been studied often before. However, analogies can be drawn with intensive care units (ICUs) and EDs. A CCU can be considered as a dedicated ICU for cardiology patients. In both cases patients – once stabilised – are to be transferred as soon as possible to regular nursing wards. Patients stay only on these specialised wards as long as it is necessary for their condition. The temporary stay and short duration of stay is also a common feature with the ED. To be able to model the flow of patients, one needs to look at the state of the system in a more detailed manner, for instance at each hour of the day and night. To model regular wards, often a period of a day or half a day is sufficient detail for representing the flow. Queueing approaches as well as simulation is used for representing the behaviour of these units.

The modelling of ICUs has been studied by Macfarlane (1996) and Ridge et al. (1998). Riley (1996) has developed a simulation model of an ED. Most of these studies focus only on the ICU or the ED and do not include the flows from these units to the regular wards. Vissers et al. (1999) have looked at the interaction between the CCU and the regular cardiology ward. This study is used for this case study.

While the previous studies focus on the internal flow of patients within the unit or between units, other studies focus on the inflow of new patients and dealing with long waiting lists for cardiology patients who need to undergo a surgical procedure, for instance Akkerman and Knip (2004).

17.3 Elaboration

The problems mentioned before had existed for a long time. The staff involved had discussed these matters frequently – but without result. It became necessary to develop a new perspective to the problem. By defining the problem primarily as a logistic issue it became possible to reopen the debate. The logistic approach followed is illustrated in Figure 17.2.

The uppermost box contains the inflow of cardiology patients, with a distinction between emergency and elective admissions. Within each type of admission different categories of patients can be distinguished.

The next box refers to the care processes for cardiology patients. The most important variables describing the care process of a patient category are the routing, the treatment protocols used, the resources that are available and the available equipment.

The arrow from this box refers to the resource requirements resulting from these processes, expressed in the number of nursing days required at the CCU and the ward. The resource requirements combined with the available resources lead to the occupancy of resources for each type of resource involved.

Whenever occupancy rates rise above certain levels it produces logistic problems (lower box). The most important logistic problems are logistic transfers (early transfers of patients from the CCU to empty a bed for a new patient) and logistic discharges (early discharge of patients from a nursing ward to empty a bed for other patients). It needs to be said that in practice logistic problems are disguised by the flexibility to create temporarily extra capacity. Moreover, the right moment for transfer or discharge is not a fact that can be easily determined in an objective way.

The most important arrow in Figure 17.2 is the connection between logistic problems and the box 'organisation of care processes'. This feedback signal can lead to a change in the way processes are currently organised. The added

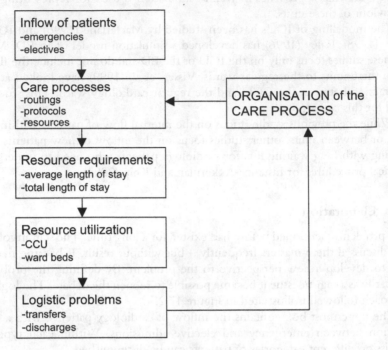

Figure 17.2 Logistic approach followed in case study.

value of using a model such as CardioSim is that possible consequences of these changes can be assessed in advance.

Table 17.1 contains the characteristics of inflow, care process and resource requirements per patient category.

For each of the patient categories identified the table shows whether they are labelled as emergency or elective, what the annual number of patients is, what proportion is treated without prior admission, what the routing of the care process is, and what the average length of stay is in the CCU and the ward. Most elective categories do not use the CCU; some categories do use the CCU for half a day according to the protocol.

17.4 Model

To improve the insight into the development process of the CardioSim[2] model we first present the modelling problem (Subsection 17.4.1); then we present

---

2 The CardioSim model is available via the online material.

Table 17.1 Characteristics per patient flow

| Inflow | | | | | Length of stay CCU (days) | | length of stay F1 (days) | |
No.	Description	Emergency/elective	Annual number	% external	Routing	avg	std	avg	std
1	Unstable angina pectoris	Emergency	227	–	CCU-F1-discharge	1.8	2.2	5.3	4.5
2	Myocardial infarction	Emergency	193	–	CCU-F1-discharge	2.6	1.9	8.2	4.6
3	Arrhythmias	Emergency	159	–	CCU-F1-discharge	1.1	1.9	5.7	4.2
4	Heart failure	Emergency	174	–	CCU-F1-discharge	2.1	1.7	10.8	5.3
5	Others emergency	Emergency	183	–	CCU-F1-discharge	1.2	1.1	6.4	4.9
6	Non-cardiac problems	Emergency	84	–	CCU-discharge	0.5[1]	0	0	0
7	PTCA	Elective	60	67%	external-CCU-F1	0.5[1]	0	4.0	0
8	Heart catheterisation	Elective	228	88%	external-F1	0	0	1.0	0
9	Cardioversion	Elective	108	100%	CCU-discharge	0.5[1]	0	0	0
10	Pacemaker implantation	Elective	48	100%	F1-discharge	0	0	4.0	0
11	Observation arrhythmias	Elective	48	100%	F1-discharge	0	0	6.0	0
12	Observation heart failure	Elective	25	100%	F1-discharge	0	0	8.0	0

[1] length of stay according to protocol

the outline of the model (Subsection 17.4.2) and the assumptions made during the process of developing the model (Subsection 17.4.3).

17.4.1 Modelling of the planning problem

The CCU and the cardiology nursing ward (F1) together constitute the inpatient cardiology system in the case study hospital. We did not include the ED in the model, as we were focussing on the functioning of the CCU and the ward. However, we did include the emergency patient flow from the ED to the CCU. The cardiology patient flow is the outcome of a complicated logistic process. The patients enter the system via CCU or F1 and can follow different routings through the system. As both cardiology departments have limited capacity the flow and throughput of patients is restricted. In practice a department can be fully loaded, causing an increased workload for medical and nursing staff. Moreover, sometimes patients need to be transferred or discharged at an early stage and not planned, as new emergency patients arrive and need to be admitted.

The properties of this process are difficult to analyse without the support of a model. As the process is very complex, we have chosen a simulation model. In comparison to an analytical model (for instance a queueing model or a mathematical model) as a simulation model offers more possibilities to experiment with different scenarios and to compare their results. A simulation model also imitates the reality of cardiology more realistically. First, a representative flow of patients (in terms of arrival times, length of stay, etc.) is generated by using the data collected on cardiology patients. Next, the generated flow of patients is processed by the system, and we can determine some performance measures, such as the average occupancy and peak occupancies, the number of transfers that were forced by the arrival of new patients, etc. The advantage of such a quantitative model is that the consequences of a wide range of policy decisions can be envisaged almost instantly. Moreover, the model allows for an objective assessment of different options; personal judgment is often not very reliable when it comes to the size of an impact of a change made. Before we give a description of the model's structure it should be emphasised that a quantitative model also has its limitations. The model will strictly follow the rules that are implemented in the model's structure. In the reality of a hospital, it can sometimes be better to deviate from the rules if a situation requires it.

17.4.2 Model description

The model presupposes the CCU and F1 departments and an inflow of emergency and elective patients. Figure 17.3 illustrates the structure of the model.

Contrary to an elective admission an emergency patient can arrive at any moment of the day. Table 17.2 contains information regarding the arrivals of emergency patients for the different periods of the day.

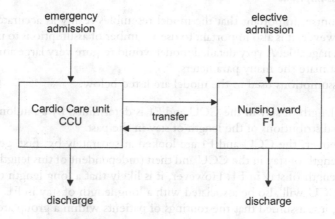

Figure 17.3 Structure of the model.

Table 17.2 Arrival of emergency patients per time period

Time period	Percentage of all emergency patients	
	daytime (8.00–18.00)	night-time (18.00–8.00)
Monday–Friday	56.4%	20.4%
Saturday–Sunday	10.6%	12.6%

For each patient a length of stay is generated for CCU and F1 (one of either is allowed to be zero). When the stay of a patient in the CCU is completed, the patient is transferred to a nursing ward. When the length of stay at F1 is also completed the patient is discharged. If a patient arrives at a fully occupied department, the patient with the shortest remaining length of stay is transferred or discharged. The model developed is in fact a network of a number of stations linked by patient flows and limited due to the resources that are available.

The model is next defined by answering the following questions. How can the arrival pattern of emergency cardiology patient be described? How are the lengths of stay of a patient in the CCU and the ward determined? What happens when there is no capacity left in the CCU or F1? These questions were answered using data that were collected for the purpose of this project (sample data and standard statistics of the hospital). When answering these questions, a distinction is made between different groups of patients based on their lengths of stay (see Table 17.1). Also, a distinction is made between daytime and night-time arrivals to be able to handle different levels of inflow during these hours (see Table 17.2). It is important to notice that the model uses stochastic routines to generate arrivals and lengths of stay. This implies that the current more-or-less random patterns in arrivals and lengths of stay are taken into consideration.

17.4.3 Assumptions

It is, of course, important that the model resembles reality as accurate as possible. However, it is also important to use a number of assumptions to make the model manageable. A very detailed model would require very large amounts of data to estimate the many parameters.

The assumptions used in the model are listed below.

- The length of stay in the CCU and F1 is determined by a random sample from distributions of the length of stay in the past.
- Moreover, the CCU and F1 are looked at separately by, first, generating the length of stay in the CCU and then (independent of this length of stay) the length of stay in F1. However, it is likely that a long length of stay in the CCU will also be associated with a long length of stay in F1.
- Also, it is assumed that the routings of patients within a group are similar. Apart from the normal routing admission–CCU–F1–discharge, also the routings admission–CCU–discharge or admission–F1–discharge are possible. However, both options cannot be followed at the same time.
- A patient who returns to the CCU from F1 has travelled the route twice and is treated in the model as two separate patients. Moreover, it is assumed that the number of readmissions at the CCU is equally distributed over the different patient categories.
- The lengths of stay for CCU and F1 are supposed to be independent of the status of the system. In this way the degree of flexibility in transfer and discharge is limited. Also, it is assumed that the planning of elective admissions is independent of the workload status at the CCU and F1.
- Finally, it is assumed that the hospital cannot decide to use some spare beds. When all beds in a ward are occupied, any new admission inevitably leads to a forced transfer or discharge. In practice, nursing staff in such a circumstance can place a patient temporarily in a spare bed, while looking for a better solution. This, however, disguises the logistic problem, and was thought not to be acceptable; attention should be focussed on the structural dimensions of the planning problem.

These assumptions sometimes act as a limitation of the model. However, we do not see it as a failing of the model that it does not incorporate crisis measures (e.g., shortening lengths of stay when beds are full). This is because we want the model to support developing strategies which reduce the need for crisis measures.

17.5 Results

In using the model, the following approach has been followed. First, ideas for changing the organisation of care processes to solve the problems have been generated by brainstorming. A number of these ideas were then elaborated as a scenario to be tested by the model. The parameters of the scenario were fed into the model. The simulation model was then run to give the results produced by the scenario. The model's results concern the occupancies of the CCU and the nursing wards, the number of logistic problems per day of the week (daytime and night-time) and the percentage of admissions that need to be transferred or discharged early for logistic reasons.

17.5.1 Simulated scenarios

The following example scenarios are presented to illustrate the use and possibilities of CardioSim:

- The current situation.
  This scenario will act as a reference point for the other scenarios.
- An increase in the number of beds on the nursing ward.
  Suppose the number of available beds at F1 is increased by four beds.
- Extension of the possibilities for monitoring (telemetrics) the wards.
  This allows for an earlier transfer of patients from the CCU.
- Shortening of the treatment programmes of patients with an acute myocardial infarct.
- Setting up a separate emergency heart unit.
  This includes. amongst others: better triage (more precise selection of patients), better distribution of patients over the CCU and F1, prevention of very short admissions (less than six hours).

17.5.2 Simulation results

The results of the simulation can be summarised in two tables. First, however, the output of the model is illustrated in Figure 17.4; for the scenario 'current situation' the occupancies of CCU and ward are shown, and the logistic problems (transfers and discharges for logistic reasons). Table 17.3 summarises the occupancy of the CCU and in F1 for the different scenarios, Table 17.4 gives the logistic problems. The results are averages over 400 simulated days (about one year); this produces accurate results for the average: the deviation is less than 0.1% at day level. The start-up period for the simulation is 28 days (about one month); after this period the cardiology system is filled with patients and the occupancy levels are stabilised.

In the current situation the CCU has an occupancy rate of almost 65% and the nursing ward of almost 90%; for the CCU 10% of the transfers have a logistic reason and in the ward 16% of the discharges are for logistic reasons.

Increasing the bed capacity in F1 by four beds results in a lower bed occupancy in F1 (82%) and a decrease of the logistic discharges at F1 (6%).

The use of telemetrics for F1 decreases the workload for the CCU (lower occupancy: 58%; less logistic transfers: 6%) but increases the workload for F1 (higher occupancy: 91%, more logistic discharges: 20%).

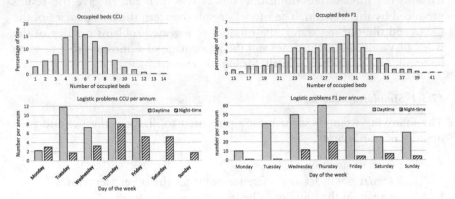

Figure 17.4 Occupancies and logistic problems for 'current situation'.

Table 17.3 Bed occupancy of CCU and F1

Scenario	CCU (9 beds)		F1 (31 beds)	
	Occupied beds	Occupancy rate	Occupied beds	Occupancy rate
Current situation	5.8	64.3	27.8	89.5
F1: plus 4 beds	5.8	64.3	28.6	81.8
Telemetrics at F1	5.2	57.8	28.2	91.1
Shorter treatment	5.8	64.3	26.0	84.0
Emergency heart unit	5.0	55.5	27.2	87.8

The occupancy figures for the CCU are to be interpreted with a margin of 4% (standard deviation of 0.22); the F1 figures have a margin of 2 % (standard deviation of 0.54).

Shorter treatment in F1 relieves the workload for F1 (lower occupancy: 84%, less logistic discharges: 9%).

A separate emergency heart unit relieves the workload for both CCU and F1. The occupancy of the CCU goes down considerably, from 64% to 56%, and the occupancy of F1 decreases slightly (from 90% to 88%). The logistic transfers at the CCU decrease considerably (from 10% to 5%), and the logistic discharges at F1 decrease also considerably (from 16% to 12%).

To summarise: the intervention helps for that part that is aimed for. Some scenarios produce better results for one department and worse results for other departments or vice versa. The last scenario produces better results for both departments, but this is probably also the most expensive solution.

Table 17.4 Logistic problems (per week)

Scenario	Logistic transfers CCU (per week)			Logistic discharges F1 (per week)		
	daytime	night-time	perc.	daytime	night-time	perc.
Current situation	1.15	0.79	10%	4.03	0.92	16%
F1: plus 4 beds	1.15	0.79	10%	1.49	0.45	6%
Telemetrics at F1	0.73	0.45	6%	4.78	1.34	20%
Shorter treatment	1.15	0.79	10%	1.92	0.62	9%
Emergency heart unit	0.47	0.32	5%	3.09	0.70	12%

The logistic problems have margins for CCU/daytime of 22% (standard deviation 0.29), CCU/night-time margin 24% (standard deviation 0.22), and F1/daytime margin 25% (standard deviation 1.13), F1/night-time margin 20% (standard deviation 0.24).

17.6 Reflection and further development

The following conclusions can be drawn from the project. The problem is not solved yet but has become manageable. There is no straightforward solution presented, but instead a tool that supports the exploration of possible solutions.

The main learning point for the staff involved during the CardioSim development process is to think in terms of (the organisation of) care processes, enabling one to rise above the level of ad hoc solutions for the short term and investigating lasting solutions for the future. The thinking in terms of processes also creates the awareness that it is not only concern with improvements that is sought but also the thinking through of consequences. In this, CardioSim proved to be a powerful tool. CardioSim did also contribute to a better understanding of the current situation. For example, non-cardiology patients in the CCU only caused minor stagnations in the system – a finding that was in contrast to the original perception of the problem.

The most important application of the model is to compare the results of different options to improve the logistics of cardiology patients. It is not so difficult to predict the direction of the impact, but the size of the impact is much more difficult to estimate correctly. Moreover, the simulation offers the possibility of combining different scenarios in the assessment.

To summarise: CardioSim helps the staff involved to analyse the current situation and to explore possible solutions, with an objective assessment of the consequences of alternatives.

We propose to increase our experience with further application of CardioSim in the hospital considered and, if the occasion arises, in other hospitals. It will be important to involve cardiologists in these applications. To formulate scenarios requires input from cardiologists; the consequences of, for instance, more telemetric facilities on the length of stay for the different categories of patients considered can only be taken into consideration by medical expert input. Based on this experience the model can then be further improved.

17.7 Questions and exercises

What arguments can be used to justify the boundaries drawn in this study for focussing the study on the CCU and the ward? What arguments can be used for a wider system modelling approach?

Formulate one or more other scenarios that could be tested with the current simulation model.

Formulate one or more other relevant scenarios for improving the patient flow of cardiology that would require an adaptation of the model. What would need to be adapted in the model to produce results for these scenarios?

Calculate the number of beds required in the CCU and the ward, using the data in Table 17.1, and average occupancy levels of 70% for the CCU and 90% for the ward.

Why are the target occupancy levels for the CCU and the ward different? What average occupancy levels would you suggest as targets for the CCU and the ward?

References

Akkerman R and Knip M (2004). Reallocation of beds to reduce waiting times for cardiac surgery. *Health Care Management Science*, 7(2), 119–126.

Macfarlane JD (1996). Some problems in modelling intensive therapy units. In Kastelein A, Vissers J, Van Merode F and Delesie L (eds), *Managing health care under resource constraints, Proceedings of the 21st meeting of the European working group on operational research applied to health services*, Eindhoven University Press, Eindhoven, 99–104.

Ridge JC, Jones SK, Nielsen MS and Shahani AK (1998). Capacity planning for intensive care units. *European Journal of Operational Research*, 105(2), 346–355.

Riley J (1996). Visual interactive simulation of accident and emergency departments. In Kastelein A, Vissers J, Van Merode F and Delesie L (eds), *Managing health care under resource constraints, Proceedings of the 21st meeting of the European working group on operational research applied to health services*, Eindhoven University Press, Eindhoven, 135–141.

Vissers J, Croonen G, Siersma V and Tiemessen H (1999). Simulation of the cardiology patients flow in a hospital setting. In De Angelis V, Ricciardi N and Storchi G (eds), *Monitoring, evaluating, planning health services*. World Scientific, Singapore, New Jersey, London, and Hong Kong, 162–173.

Index